D0992405

HITLER'S ARMY

HITLER'S ARMY

The Evolution and Structure of German Forces

By the Editors of Command Magazine

COMBINED BOOKS
Pennsylvania

PUBLISHER'S NOTE

Combined Books, Inc., is dedicated to publishing books of distinction in history and military history. We are proud of the quality of writing and the quantity of information found in our books. Our books are manufactured with style and durability and are printed on acid-free paper. Our logo reflects our commitment to the modern and yet historic art of bookmaking.

We call ourselves Combined Books because we view the publishing enterprise as a "combined" effort of authors, publishers and readers. And we promise to bridge the gap between us—a gap which is all too seldom closed in contemporary publishing.

We would like to hear from our readers and invite you to write to us at our offices in Pennsylvania with your reactions, queries, comments, even complaints. All of our correspondence will be answered directly by a member of the Editorial Board or by the author.

We encourage all of our readers to purchase our books from their local booksellers, and we hope that you let us know of booksellers in your area that might be interested in carrying our books. If you are unable to find a book in your area, please write us.

For information, address:
Combined Books, Inc.
151 East 10th Avenue
Conshohocken, PA 19428

The chapters in this book have appeared previously in Command magazine.
This edition copyright © 1996 by Command magazine.

All rights reserved. No part of this publication may be reproduced, stored in a retrieval system or transmitted in any form or by any means, electrical, mechanical or otherwise without first seeking the written permission of the publisher.

Library of Congress Cataloging-in-Publication Data
Hitler's army: the evolution and structure of German forces, 1933-1945 / by the editors of Command magazine.
         p.   cm.
    Includes index.
    ISBN 0-938289-55-1
  1. Germany. Heer—History. 2. Germany. Heer—Organization. 3. World War, 1938-1945—Campaigns. 4. Germany—Politics and government—1933-1945.
I. Command magazine (San Luis Obispo, Calif.)
UA712.H52   1995
940.54'1343—dc20   95-45509
                                    CIP

Printed in the United States of America.

Contents

Chapter I

Introduction

Every book needs a framework around which it can be organized, and for that we've selected four major themes that, we feel, taken together will give the reader a thorough understanding of Hitler's army. Those themes are: 1) weaponry, tactics and organization; 2) politics; 3) strategy; and 4) operational studies.

Weaponry, Tactics and Organization

"Building the Beast" begins this section by describing the role and workings of the Germans' training and replacement army.

"Infantry on the Eastern Front" analyzes the organization of the German infantry divisions, the changes wrought in them by the expansion of the army for Barbarossa, and the deterioration caused by the huge losses suffered in the east.

"Corps Organization" provides a brief but detailed analysis of this flexible higher-level command structure, using the *46th Motorized Corps* as its model.

"Battlegroup Friebe" gives insight into the kind of units the Germans put together (literally) in order to fight the war at the operational level. The description of the organization of this brigade-sized formation illustrates the German penchant for, and mastery of, the ad hoc battle group.

"Volksgrenadier Divisions" discusses the critical role of these emergency units raised late in the war, telling how the Germans increasingly had to try to substitute firepower for manpower.

The two articles, "General Principles: The Offense and Defense in German Doctrine," and "East Front Tactics: 1945," show how all of the above came together to form theory and provide for practice.

Four short pieces on the Mark I Panzer, assault guns, tank destroyers and rocket artillery round out the section by giving insight into the advantages and shortcomings of those classic German weapons systems.

the advantages and shortcomings of those classic German weapons systems.

The first section of the book ends by comparing and contrasting the German army at its height in 1940-41 with the United States' World War II army at its peak in 1944-45.

Politics

These next two articles cover the weakening and dispersion of the German war effort due to internal Nazi politics. "Luftwaffe Field Divisions" tells the incredible story of how hundreds of thousands of German air force personnel were wasted by being sent into ground combat in those ill-prepared organizations. "Leibstandarte" describes the rise of that unit in particular, and the SS in general, into a virtual state-within-a-state.

Strategy

"Proud Monster: The Barbarossa Campaign," and "Death and Destruction" analyze the wishful thinking that characterized the Germans' planning for the campaigns that more than any others shaped the final course of the entire war.

"Blitz Army, Siege Führer" presents the radical but revelatory theory that Hitler's personal view of strategy was at complete variance with the type of army he built and the doctrine its panzer generals espoused.

Operational Studies

These articles give insight into critical campaigns and battles that are more often overlooked in typical English-language histories.

"What if They'd Fought: Czechoslovakia 1938," "Poland '39," and "Arras: 1940" describe the German army while it was still on its way up. In so doing, much light is shed on the reasons for the Allies' early inabilities to halt the Blitzkrieg.

"Smolensk-Yelnia" describes the first time the Soviets (and anyone else for that matter) stopped the Germans, managing to launch a coherent counterattack during Barbarossa.

"Krim: Von Manstein in the Crimea," tells the story of that famous German Field Marshal's masterful campaign to capture Sevastopol, while simultaneously having to fend off two major Soviet offensives.

Introduction

This campaign clearly illustrates the ability of the Germans to use mobility to offset enemy numeric superiority.

"Demyansk" was the first significant use of aircraft to provide supply to encircled German forces. The operation was a seeming success, yet the overconfidence it bred later helped bring on the disaster at Stalingrad.

At "Narva" in 1944 the Soviets finally began to overturn the German position in the Baltic countries—but it wasn't easy.

At "Aachen" the Germans again demonstrated their ability to raise new units and create new successes from earlier wreckages. When the battle began the Allies were still saying "Home by Christmas;" when it was over, everyone knew another hard campaign still lay ahead.

At "Budapest" and "Berlin" during the spring of 1945, fighting on for what can only be called "spite's sake," the Germans once more illustrated it ain't over 'til it's over.

—The Editors

Chapter II

Building the Beast
The World War II Training and Replacement Systems of the German Army
by Dirk Blennemann

Prior to the start of World War II the organization and administration of the German army were based on the division of the country into 15 command areas, or *Wehrkreis*. Each contained the headquarters and component divisions of a corps. At the same time, the command areas provided the territorial basis for conscription, administration of army property, local defense, and virtually all other military matters. The commander of each command area was also the commander of its corps, which he would lead into the field on the outbreak of war.

The command areas and their corps were numbered with Roman numerals from I to XIII, plus XVII and XVIII when Austria was annexed. Thus *I Corps* was located in command area I, and so on. The missing numerals, XIV, XV and XVI, were used for three non-territorial corps set up to control the motorized infantry, light, and armored divisions, respectively. In 1938 another non-territorial corps (XIX) was created to control Austrian light and armored divisions. After the Polish campaign in 1939, two new command areas (XX and XXI) were put in place in the newly annexed areas there.

Field Army & Replacement Army

In August 1939 the German army was split into two parts that were each to perform different functions for the remainder of the war. The field army conducted active military operations. Accordingly its corps were immediately organized into armies, an administrative unit that had not existed during peacetime. Those armies, in turn, were placed under the control of army groups, which were directly responsible to the army high command for the conduct of operations.

The replacement army was devoted to training, procurement and administration in the zone of the interior (basically the national territory of Germany). It was put under the deputy commander-in-chief, and was responsible for maintaining the field army at authorized strength by the dispatch of replacements, the formation of new units, and the supply of material, as well as continuing to perform normal military administrative functions at home.

Mobilization

The German mobilization for the Second World War was a gradual process lasting several months. The armed forces high command was determined to avoid the mistakes of 1914, when millions of men were drawn into the army almost overnight, where they hurriedly formed mostly second-rate reserve and national guard (*Landwehr*) divisions. So many men pulled so quickly from the economic life of the country also brought on great disruption in that sphere of life. For World War II, the reservists were called up individually, and upon induction were mixed into regular divisions already containing experienced personnel. Thus most of the units formed during 1939 quickly became as efficient and well organized as the original ones.

Replacement & Training System

The German replacement and training system was based on two factors: 1) the soldiers in each division should be drawn from the same command area; and 2) there should be direct affiliation between the units of the field army and those of the replacement army.

At the outbreak of the war, each German division had one field replacement battalion with three companies of riflemen. Those units were pools of trained soldiers standing by to replace casualties. After the Polish campaign most field replacement battalions were used to form new divisions, and by the time of the invasion of the west in May 1940 there were only a few such units still holding men. But by the time of the invasion of the USSR in 1941, all divisions had reformed their field replacement battalions. Over the course of the war many of these battalions were used in critical situations as combat units, and so were lost, but through V-E Day all German divisions maintained them as part of their structures.

The field replacement battalions' ranks were filled by drawing from the divisional replacement unit (see below), and from stragglers, veterans of dissolved formations, and soldiers returned from field hospitals. The field replacement battalions of new divisions would first be termed field recruit battalions, and were completely filled out with new men. Such units would have their titles changed after three months of training.

In addition to the divisional replacement battalion, which accompanied the divsion into the field, every German unit in 1939 left behind in its home command area a battalion cadre designated as its replacement unit. An infantry regiment, for example, left behind an infantry replacement battalion, bearing the same number, which inducted and trained recruits, dispatched them to its field regiment as needed, and received personnel back from the field when they were to be discharged, and back from the hospital after recuperating.

Field units were authorized to request replacements when there was a manpower deficiency of more than 10 percent in its authorized strength. Replacements for specialist troops, such as communications personnel or technicians, were to be requested as soon as their absence began to hamper the efficiency of the unit.

After the Polish campaign nearly two thirds of the replacement battalions were used to form new divisions, and a basic change occurred in the affiliation system for the infantry regiments. Single replacement battalions became the replacement unit for all the infantry regiments of one infantry division or two static or security divisions. The other components of a combat division—the artillery regiment, the reconnaissance, anti-tank, engineer, and signals battalions—were similarly affiliated with replacement battalions of their types back in the command area. This modified system was used until the end of the war.

It was also common practice in the command areas to collect groups of trained replacements of various combat arms and organize them into transfer battalions, for the purpose of overseeing their move to the combat zone. Transfer battalions would usually be attached to the rear echelons of a fighting division on the front, and from there the personnel were sent forward into the various divisional components as needed. Normally all cadre personnel left the transfer battalions as soon as they reached their destination division, moving back to the replacement battalion headquarters in the home command area. But in emergency situations so-called combat-transfer battalions were formed and put into the line as fighting units.

To make control of the system more efficient, up to six replacement battalions might be organized into replacement regiments. At the beginning of the campaign in the west in May 1940 the available replacement regiments were even organized to form six replacement divisions designated A through F. Those divisions were made part of the field army and stood ready to replace the expected heavy casualties. The following August all the field replacement divisions were dissolved, but the same procedure was again repeated in the east during 1941 and 1942. In May 1941, replacement battalions were used to form an occupation division in the Balkans, but that summer the unit was converted into a regular light infantry division and given to the field army.

The growing shortage of manpower and the need to garrison conquered territories necessitated the split, in August 1942, of all replacement battalions into two elements. One element of each was assigned to continue handling induction and replacement, and retained the replacement battalion designation. The other element was designated a training battalion. They were to receive new soldiers from the replacement battalions, give them the necessary training, then send them back to the replacement battalion. About 80 percent of the original strength of the old, unified replacement battalions was moved into the new training battalions. While the diminished replacement battalions remained in their home command areas, the new training battalions were sent to occupied territories.

The purpose of this change was to use the training soldiers as occupation forces—thus freeing more field army units for the active fronts—while not seriously disrupting those recruits' induction and training. During 1944, as occupied areas were lost, most replacement and training battalions were again brought together in their home command areas and given the combined designation of replacement and training battalion.

While used as occupation units, the training battalions were put under the control of training regiments and training divisions, but still remained as part of the replacement army. In the east, some of these units were also assigned line of communications and anti-partisan duties, and a few were even redesignated "security divisions."

Also starting in 1942, the training battalions located outside Greater

GERMAN CORPS AREAS

GG = General Government
B & M = Bohemia & Moravia

Germany were organized into a new type of unit designated as reserve divisions (but again remaining part of the replacement army). Unlike the training divisions, these reserve divisions were organized as regular field army infantry or armored divisions and were controlled by reserve corps. They proved excellent units for occupation and defensive missions, as well as for conducting training exercises. Due to the high losses suffered in the east, in 1943 some of the reserve divisions were redesignated as regular divisions of the field army. In February 1944, five reserve divisions were redesignated as static divisions and sent to man the Channel coast in anticipation of the Allied invasion.

Divisions destroyed at the front still left a core of affiliated survivors in the replacement army—mainly staff and rear echelon personnel and specialists—bringing about the establishment of yet another new kind of division during 1944 and 1945. So called "shadow divisions," were built up from such surviving training and replacement units, along with whatever survivors of the destroyed parent division might be returned from hospitals. After a few weeks of retraining, the shadow divisions took the number of their destroyed parent and were sent to the field army for combat service. Given the desperate circumstances, this expedient of mixing veterans with green troops to form new divisions—but ones that also came with instant traditions—proved highly successful.

During the summer and autumn of 1944, more than half of the existing reserve divisions were converted into regular divisions of the field army. That resulted in the shrinking of the replacement army from 2 million soldiers at the end of 1943 to about 1 million late in 1944. Then, in January 1945, Hitler prohibited the further use of the terms reserve, replacement and training in reference to divisions.

Conclusion

At first glance the replacement and training system of the German army appears complex and cumbersome, but it worked well. For example, during 1944 the Germans lost a total of 75 infantry-type divisions totaling 229 regiments (47 divisions/160 regiments in the east; 28 divisions/69 regiments in the west and Italy). During that same period, however, this system allowed for the creation of 66 new divisions totaling 200 regiments. If the resulting units could not be favorably compared in quality to the ones destroyed, such numbers still remain amazing given that it was the fifth year of a world war. In addition to its original training and replacement function, the replacement army was also successful at conducting occupation, anti-partisan and line of communications duties.

The successes of this system came from strong organizational and historical foundations. Systematic universal military training of all the manpower of a country was first introduced in Germany, and was developed there to the highest degree of refinement. At the same time, the traditional affiliations between the regular units of the field army and those of the replacement army, combined with its mixing of recruits and veterans, formed great cohesion among the men in each unit. Of course, by 1945 even such an outstanding system could no longer overcome the high casualties and materiel shortages brought on the German army by a series of high level strategic, political and economic blunders unmatched over the entire course of world history.

Sources

Klebe, R. *Das deutsche Ersatzheer*. Rotterdam: Lekturama-Verlag, 1978.

Mueller-Hillerbrand, B. *Das Heer 1933-1945*. Frankfurt: Mittler & Sohn, 1969.

Riedel, H.; *Die deutschen Ersatz- und Ausbildungseinheiten 1939-1945*. Stuttgart: Desch Verlag, 1972.

U.S. War Dept. *Handbook on German Military Forces*. Baton Rouge: Louisiana State Univ., 1990 (reprint of 1945 U.S. Army documents).

Chapter III

German Infantry on the Eastern Front in 1941

by Chris Perello

Of the 141 divisions taking part in Operation Barbarossa, 108 of them (76%) were non-motorized infantry. These divisions, plodding along at the speed of a marching man, were incapable of the rapid concentration and deep exploitation that made the blitzkrieg possible. The Germans were aware of their infantry's shortcomings, but their economy was incapable of producing the motor vehicles needed to motorize them, and even less capable of supplying the fuel to run all those vehicles.

After the successful conclusion of the 1940 campaign, the German General Staff had drawn up plans to motorize the entire army, but that would have meant reducing its size to no more than 70 divisions. The invasion of Russia required greater numbers than that, so the marching divisions were retained. In fact, to help equip the 18 new panzer and motorized divisions formed after the fall of France, the infantry divisions lost many of the motor vehicles they had, their place being taken by more horsedrawn vehicles. Thus the infantry of 1941 was less mobile than it had been in France the year before.

The tactics chosen by the Germans for the invasion, the *Kesselschlacht* or cauldron (pocket) battle, were based on the division of the army into mobile and non-mobile portions. The infantry divisions simply couldn't keep up with the mobile formations on the deep and fast drives called for by the Blitz theorists, but there were too few mobile divisions to defeat the Soviets alone.

Not only could the German economy not motorize the entire army, it could not really support an army of the size fielded in 1941. Few divisions outside the eastern front could be maintained at their full authorized strength. There were only 130 replacement battalions available, representing less than 10 percent of the invading army's strength. In 1942, thousands of skilled workers were scheduled to be returned to the civilian economy—they had been "borrowed" from industry to maximize the number of divisions available.

The shortage of trained officers and NCOs was even worse. The limitations of the Versailles Treaty meant a whole generation of Germans had never received military training. The tiny peacetime army of 100,000, though trained to a high standard, was insufficient to lead the mass army of 1941. Only by calling up World War One veterans, Austrian officers, and policemen, could the shortage be made up. Even so, the rapid expansion came at the cost of quality leadership, especially in the infantry divisions, which were at the bottom of the priority list for officers, as they were for manpower, motor vehicles and equipment.

Starting in the mid-1930s, new divisions had been added to the army in "waves." Each wave was organized and equipped in a similar fashion to ease administrative burdens, but the army as a whole had a wide variety of organizations and equipment lists. Only the 42 divisions of the first two waves (plus the mobile divisions, some of which were formed by converting first-wave divisions) had anything like a full complement of leaders and technical specialists. Many officers thought the new divisions compared unfavorably with those of 1914 in marksmanship, night- and close-combat training and fieldcraft.

Organization

The basic German infantry fighting unit was the squad of 10 men, armed with a light machinegun (LMG), a submachinegun and eight rifles. Nearly every major combatant power in WWII used a similar organization, but there was one critical difference: in every other army, the LMG (or automatic rifle) was used to supplement the rifle fire of the squad; in the German army, the LMG was the squad.

On defense, the LMG provided the firepower to stop enemy attacks; the riflemen protected the LMG and helped carry ammunition for it. On the attack, the LMG would pin enemy defenders while the riflemen worked their way forward to assault enemy positions with grenade and bayonet. Built around the concepts of the WWI *Stosstruppen* (Shocktroops), the squad was expected to operate independently, calling for help only when absolutely necessary.

German Infantry on the Eastern Front in 1941

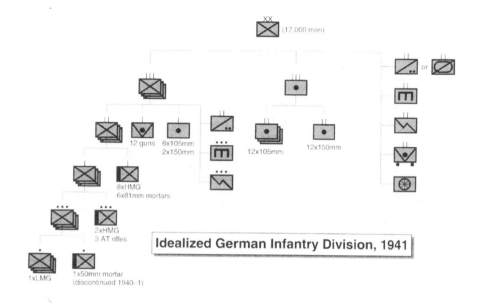

Idealized German Infantry Division, 1941

Each commander above squad level was expected to accomplish much the same. That is, at each command level, the commander was given three or four maneuver units and one or two support units with progressively heavier weapons. Those weapons could be employed en masse or detached to reinforce a subordinate unit for a particular mission. German doctrine emphasized the formation of *ad hoc* battle groups at every level, which made German units more flexible than comparably-sized units in other armies.

The infantry regiment was the smallest permanent infantry organization. Companies were formed and disbanded at the discretion of the regimental headquarters, and were often transferred from battalion to battalion as the situation demanded. Platoons and squads were consolidated within the company as needed. After mid-1941, battalions also were disbanded and reformed.

The machinegun (or heavy weapons) companies could be deployed as whole units, or could be broken up to provide direct and indirect fire support to the line companies. The machineguns used were identical to the LMGs in the infantry squads, but were mounted on tripods for greater stability and accuracy. They also had larger crews to carry more ammunition and more spare barrels to enable constant firing. (Squad MGs had to fire a series of short bursts or risk overheating). Early in the war, some of these companies were even capable of conducting indirect machinegun fire to create dead zones.

This was an old and honored World War I tactic that disappeared as training standards fell.

The regimental artillery company was equipped with light artillery pieces that were used for direct fire. The purpose of the company was to give the regimental commander heavy fire support for assaults, not as a supplement to divisional indirect fire.

The regimental anti-tank companies were equipped mostly with inadequate 37mm guns or captured French 47mm pieces. The new 50mm guns were still in short supply, so were being parceled out to all units in ones and twos as they became available. After encountering the Soviets' T-34 and KV-1 tanks, these companies were often supplemented by field pieces from the divisional artillery, again in ones and twos.

The remaining support platoons of the regiment were not found in all units. The engineers were actually "pioneers," specialists in the use of explosives and mines rather than construction or bridging. The reconnaissance unit was likely to be bicycle-mounted rather than motorized.

The artillery regiment formed the core of the division's firepower on both attack and defense. In fact, some officers felt the infantry had become too dependent on artillery support, sacrificing speed and wasting ammunition. The artillery's effectiveness was hampered by the fact the guns were horsedrawn, and because the shortage of trained personnel, radios and vehicles prevented formation of observation battalions in most divisions. It was therefore difficult to achieve rapid and flexible concentrations of artillery fire.

Nearly every division had the authorized battalion of truck-towed anti-tank guns, mostly 50mm plus some of the new 75mm pieces. Again, captured French and Czech equipment was used to fill some gaps. The remaining support battalions were found in the 42 first-class divisions, but were weaker or non-existent in the others.

Though the infantry divisions moved no faster than their predecessors in the Kaiser's army, they were trained using the same concepts as the mobile units. The emphasis was on infiltration of enemy lines and exploitation of opportunities. Mission orders were given in broad terms, with subordinate commanders *expected* to use their initiative in carrying them out, and with the assumption the larger formations would follow and support a successful subordinate unit. The purpose of combat was as much to shock the enemy into submission as to kill him outright.

Ebb

The underlying weaknesses of the German war machine were brought home by the heavy losses during Barbarossa. By September, the average infantry division in *Army Group Center* was about 1,600 men under-strength. This represented only 10 percent of total personnel strength, but more than half the riflemen, who incurred most of the casualties. Administrative and support troops were drafted into the squads, but they were inadequately trained and insufficient in number to maintain combat strength for long.

By early December, the average infantry company could field no more than 60 men: platoons, companies, and even battalions were consolidated to maintain company strength. Those under-strength units proved adequate for defense, since the firepower of the LMG was undiminished. In one example from early 1942, a German company of only sixteen men occupied a front of nearly a mile, with each man armed with his own LMG. This company stopped several attacks by a full Soviet regiment.

But attacking was a different story. The machineguns could only pin defenders; they could not take ground. That required assault parties of riflemen. The failure of the final German offensive around Moscow was as much due to a lack of riflemen as anything else.

The German infantry never recovered from the losses of 1941. For the 1942 offensive, only those divisions in the spearhead were brought to anything near full strength. For the rest, official strength was reduced to nine men per squad, 90 per company and two battalions per regiment: a total rifle strength less than half the original. Even that existed only on paper. Many regiments could keep only one battalion on the line, leaving the other in the rear as a depot unit. Companies increasingly became small combat groups formed around a few LMGs and one or two mortars or anti-tank guns, with the regiments constantly forming new companies to maintain a fresh reserve, however small.

From 1942 on, the infantry divisions formed a thin and brittle line, and the brunt of the battle fell to the mobile divisions. The German infantry bled to death in Russia.

Running Total of German Casualties During
Operation Barbarossa 6/22/41 - 1/1/42

These figures include killed, wounded and missing. The numbers in parenthesis represent the percentage of the total German armed forces fighting in the east.

13 July	92,120	(3.6%)
13 August	389,924	(10.0%)
26 August	441,100	(11.6%)
30 September	551,039	(16.2%)
13 November	699,726	(20.6%)
31 December 1941	930,903	(26.00%)

Soviet Infantry

Like the Germans, the Soviets fielded an army formed largely of foot-mobile infantry divisions. On paper, the Soviet division was similar to the German, using the 3-plus-1 fractal organization with supporting arms at each level. But there were important differences on the ground.

Soviet doctrine, though paying lip service to the idea of initiative at all levels, was wedded to operations by massed formations on a large front. Command was exercised from the top down; subordinate units were tied to the movements of their parent formations.

This tendency was exacerbated by Stalin's purges. In raw numbers, the Soviet officer corps had been severely reduced. Worse, those remaining were less willing to take the initiative, preferring the safer route of obeying orders explicitly. Soviet tactics became cumbersome and predictable, reducing effectiveness and increasing losses. The problem only got worse after the severe losses during Barbarossa. It was not until 1943 that Soviet leadership became generally competent, and even then it could not match that of the Germans.

The Soviets also did not have enough technical specialists and equipment to properly man so sophisticated an organization. In particular, radios, radiomen and trained artillery observers were in short supply. Before, and especially after, the start of Barbarossa, the Soviets began stripping their infantry divisions of specialist formations, consolidating them at higher headquarters. The division became a mass of rifle and submachinegun armed infantrymen. They were supported by a mass of mortars and light field pieces, but these were used primarily for direct fire. This not only limited the flexibility

German Infantry on the Eastern Front in 1941

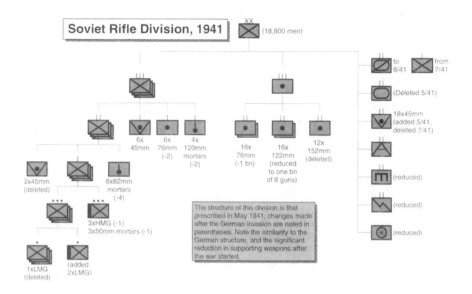

Soviet Rifle Division, 1941 — (18,800 men)

The structure of this division is that prescribed in May 1941; changes made after the German invasion are noted in parentheses. Note the similarity to the German structure, and the significant reduction in supporting weapons after the war started.

of the division's firepower, but increased losses, as the artillery had to be placed in the forward battle zone to be used in that way.

Still, the Russian infantry could fight effectively. The individual Soviet infantryman was physically hardy, fatalistic, and needed less material support than his German opponent. He was especially effective in the many forests of northern and central Russia. The sheer volume of firepower generated by the rifle divisions exacted a heavy toll on the Germans.

More importantly, the Soviets had a military age male population twice as large as Germany's. They could go on feeding full-strength units into the fight long after the Germans were exhausted.

Chapter IV

German Corps Organization in World War II

by Dirk Blennemann

In assessing the strength, combat value or tactical and operational flexibility of a German corps, army, or army group during the Second World War, many writers have made the mistake of simply counting the divisions and attached heavy units, such as tank, anti-tank and artillery battalions. Especially at corps level, simple calculations can be misleading, since there were usually a wide variety of support and supply units assigned to such headquarters. As one example, consider the *46th Motorized Corps* as it was on 22 June 1941, the start of Operation Barbarossa, the invasion of the Soviet Union.

The corps' support and supply units were intended to be able to supply, maintain and coordinate the predominant form of heavy equipment (tanks) within the corps. But even within such a "motorized" corps, not all the support units were fully equipped with their own vehicles.

The presence of the senior supply, artillery and engineer commanders and staffs was critical to the success of the corps. They gave the corps commander the flexibility to reorganize not only corps units, but those from the major combat formations, for special tasks and missions. For example, if an assault was planned in the sector of the *10th Panzer Division*, while both *Das Reich* and the *268th Infantry Divisions* were relegated to quiet sectors, the corps commander could augment the panzer division's artillery by withdrawing two artillery battalions from each of the other two divisions and committing the corps artillery under the control of the *ArKo* and the two regimental artillery staffs. That would give the *10th Panzer Division* the support of six additional regular artillery battalions (about 72 guns, twice the panzer division's organic artillery), plus one rocket launcher battalion

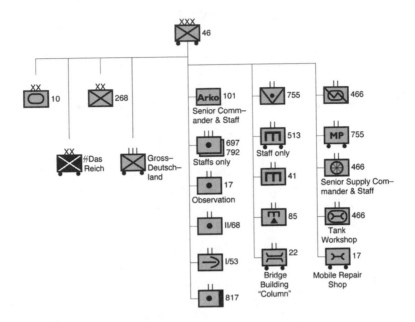

(a dozen rocket projectors, each with five or six tubes), all under a coordinating command structure and without disrupting the formal chain of command of any of the corps' main formations.

Artillery "switched" in such situations using this system was often able to remain in place and even continue to use the same communications net. Such flexibility made it difficult for the enemy to determine the main effort (*Schwerpunkt*) of German attacks, and also provided German corps with defensive options when dealing with enemy counterattacks.

As the war progressed, the extra staffs within the corps began to serve other critical purposes: the collection of stragglers, the formation of small emergency (*Alarm*) units, and the mobilization of full blown battlegroups (*Kampfgruppen*). Since each of the senior commanders and staffs possessed at least rudimentary communications assets, they could quickly be converted into headquarters controlling the various fragments of combat units that were often all that were left in the wake of an Allied advance.

Besides the many examples of this provided by the experience on the eastern front, the stabilization of the western front along the Siegfried Line in September 1944, after the Allied breakout and pursuit across France and Belgium, also underlined the value of this technique. To a large extent it was the existence of such staffs, already organized and in place, that accounted for the amazing resiliency and cohesion of the German army during the last two years of the war.

In examining any German order of battle from World War II, it is critical to distinguish among the several types of corps headquarters that showed up on the army lists. The regular infantry corps headquarters were designated as "corps commands" (*Korpskommando*), whereas prior to 1942 panzer and motorized corps had the prefix "panzer," or the suffix "motorized," added. All three types were fully capable combat headquarters, with the main difference between the infantry and the latter two types being the degree of motorization and mechanization within their support and supply elements.

Static commands, initially created to control rear areas, were more and more often committed to active sectors after 1943. Such headquarters were designated "higher commands" (*Höhere Kommandos*). Such organizations might have support units assigned to them, but they lacked the flexibility of the regular corps because the critical senior staffs and commanders were usually missing. In addition, such headquarters had few if any mobile signals troops, and were often hard pressed to effectively control two or three combat formations in fluid combat situations.

It was also almost always true that the personnel assigned to such higher commands were either green, old, or physically impaired, and their equipment usually consisted of captured or obsolete items. But army commanders to whom such corps were assigned would often try to compensate by redistributing their assets from other corps as quickly as possible. Thus, within a month or so after arriving at the front, a higher command might well have been made functionally indistinguishable from a regular corps.

Finally, none of these organizational types should be confused with the corps detachment (*Korpsabteilung*) or corps group (*Korpsgruppe*), both of which were completely impromptu creations. The corps detachments were created late in 1943 and early 1944 from fragments of decimated divisions and independent units. In reality they were nothing more than makeshift divisions given a misleading designation in hope of throwing off Allied intelligence analysts and bolstering the fighting spirit of the German soldiers in them. Corps groups were corps headquarters temporarily augmented with extra staffs, support units and senior commanders to better carry out special missions or act as a temporary replacement for an army headquarters.

Chapter V

Armored Battle Group Friebe

by Dirk Blennemann

During World War II, the German armed forces, like most others, maintained standard tables of organization and equipment for their units. Companies, troops and batteries were combined in standardized combinations to form battalions, regiments, brigades and divisions. In practice, though, all types of units in the Germany army, navy, air force and SS came to be considered as groups or pools. Sub-units would be withdrawn from those organizations to form *Kampfgruppen* (battle groups), which functioned as teams designed for specific missions, offensive and defensive. Battle groups varied in size from a company or two with attached close support weapons, to regiment and brigade sized units made up of several battalions reinforced with tanks, artillery, anti-tank, anti-aircraft, engineer and reconnaissance elements.

Since missions and circumstances varied, each battle group was likely to have a unique structure. In the final sense, though, the composition of a battle group was dictated less by theory of what elements should be put together for an ideal arrangement than by the demands of emergency situations that often had to be met with whatever insufficient and dissociated units were at hand.

Battle groups could be put together for short, long or evolving missions. In all cases, an effort was made to place a maximum number of combat elements in a battle group to make it as self-sufficient as possible in action. That approach was taken because every battle group assigned to a mission was a self-contained organization for battle and administration. They were not supposed to depend on other units to carry out their missions, and any required coordination with other units would be arranged in advance whenever possible.

One of the outstanding characteristics of the German military

Panzerkampfgruppe Friebe
26 March 1944

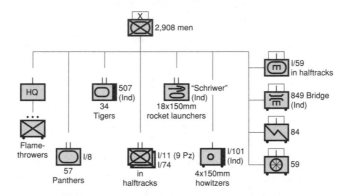

during World War II was its adherence to the principle of unity of command. At the battle group level that manifested itself in a practice that put all units engaged in a single mission under one commander, who was in turn tasked by one higher command authority with responsibility for the success of the mission. This principle was so deeply ingrained in practice that battle groups were usually identified by the name of their commander.

Even elements drawn from different service branches serving together in one battle group would do so under one commander chosen from among all the involved services. Likewise, as early as basic training, great emphasis was placed on cooperation among the services and among different arms and branches within services.

Thus the German battle group system was at once rigid, flexible, economical and deceptive. It was rigid in the sense all units from any single pool of unit types were kept as nearly alike as possible. It was flexible because the principle of combining units from the various pools was utilized to obtain any kind of combat organization required for a specific purpose. It was economical in that it enabled combat commanders to concentrate combat power at the most critical points without changing overall dispositions. It was deceptive in the sense it prevented the enemy from making an easy estimate of German strength available in any particular situation.

One typical example of a German armored battle group was *Panzerkampfgruppe Friebe*. Named after its commander, Col. Friebe, this unit was organized within *Army Group South* during the second half of March 1944 to serve as a kind of fire brigade within its area of operations. Friebe, commander of the *74th Panzergrenadier Regiment, 8th Panzer Division*, brought with him his regimental HQ and *I Battalion* (German battalions were identified by Roman numerals). To this was added a number of other combat, support and service units from *8th Panzer*, along with a battalion from *9th Panzer Division* and several independent units from corps and army headquarters.

The unit first saw action on 20 March 1944 at Brody, and thereafter in the area of Tarnopol. It was used mainly for delaying actions and counterattacks against Soviet mechanized spearheads. Between 15 and 17 April, the battle group destroyed 74 tanks, 108 guns and a dozen mortars of the Red Army. In May, the battle group was disbanded and its surviving elements used to reinforce other depleted mobile formations.

Chapter VI

The German Volksgrenadier Division, 1944-45

by Dirk Blennemann

From the outbreak of World War II through 1942, only comparatively minor changes were made in the organization of German infantry divisions. The official divisional strength for that period was about 15,000 to 17,000; but starting in 1942, several new tables of organization and equipment were issued for the infantry divisions that brought about huge changes in their strength and makeup. In all these reorganizations the trend was toward economizing manpower while increasing firepower.

The earlier, gradual changes had resulted in lowering the official strength of the infantry division to approximately 11,000 to 13,000 by the start of 1945. But the most revolutionary change came with the introduction of the *Volksgrenadier* (People's Grenadier) division in August 1944. The creation of this new type of unit stemmed from growing German manpower shortages and the changed political situation within the Reich after the failed attempt to assassinate Hitler on 20 July.

After the destruction of *Army Group Center* and the Allied advance across France and the Low Countries (July/August), the German manpower problem reached crisis levels. It became necessary to collect all available reserve, replacement and training units around the regimental and divisional staffs that had survived those Grand Alliance offensives. These hastily organized new divisions were at first given a variety of names, such as *Sperr* (Blocking), *Kampf* (combat), and *Grenadier*. But by September, all surviving new divisions were renamed *Volksgrenadier* and given standardized organizational and equipment tables.

On the political and administrative side, as a result of the command shake up that followed the failed July bomb plot against Hitler, *Reichsführer-SS* Heinrich Himmler was given charge of the replacement army. His administration put a number of new bureaucratic reforms in place. Army paperwork was simplified and administrative economy was emphasized. Navy, air force and labor service personnel were shifted into the army, and the *Volkssturm* (People's Force) militia was created.

All these efforts culminated in the standardization of the *Volksgrenadier* division. The very title, *Volks* (People's), stresses the political significance of their creation as something resulting from an extreme national crisis. To further increase such awareness and foster *esprit de corps* among their members, subordinate and supporting units within the divisions were also redesignated: artillery became *Volksartillerie*, rocket launchers became *Volkswerfer*, combat engineers became *Volkspionier*. Officer appointments to the various *Volks* units were controlled directly by Himmler.

Another aspect of all this was the fact that with Himmler overseeing the process, the creation of the *Volks* units increased SS influence over the regular army. It would be wrong to say, however, the members of *Volks* units became interchangeable with those of the SS. It should also be noted the *Volkssturm* had nothing directly to do with *Volks* army units, though the two were often confused in Allied field reports during the last half-year of the war.

From an organizational point of view, the significance of the *Volksgrenadier* divisions lay in the decreased personnel (average total strength of about 10,072), coupled with an increase in light automatic weapons, particularly submachineguns and assault rifles. A quarter of each division's personnel consisted of army veterans, a second quarter was made up of green troops, the third quarter was drawn from convalescents, and the last 25 percent were former air force and navy personnel. At first the *Volksgrenadier* divisions lacked experienced officers, NCOs and specialists for signal, service and maintenance units; but that problem was ameliorated by the transfer of some of the needed types from the older divisions of the army. In general, then, the troop quality within the *Volksgrenadier* divisions was comparable to that of the other divisions in the German army at that time.

One advantage the *Volksgrenadier* divisions had over the older types lay in the fact their infantry equipage—especially individual infantry weapons—were almost all brand new and therefore of the most modern types available. The same couldn't be said for their artillery

The German Volksgrenadier Division, 1944-45

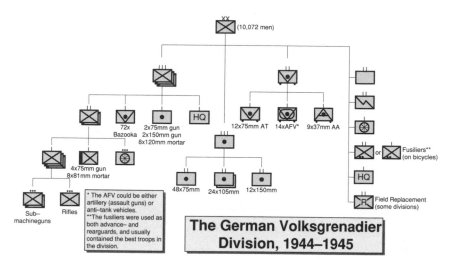

The German Volksgrenadier Division, 1944–1945

establishments, however, most of which were formed by simply amalgamating previously independent army units. The divisions were also lacking in both motorized and animal transport (426 vehicles, 119 motorcycles and 3,002 horses). The 1,522 bicycles added proved insufficient to fill the need.

During the final stages of the war, German defensive operations became increasingly passive. Whereas the army formerly placed great stress on immediate and strong counterattacks as the most effective means of thwarting an attacking enemy, by 1944 the tactical mobility and reserves required by that doctrine were increasingly missing. Accordingly, emphasis was switched to the construction of strong defensive positions, and defensive counterattacks were reduced to strictly local affairs. In sum, late war German military operations can be seen to have degenerated into nothing more than large-scale holding and delaying actions involving no more strategy than keeping Grand Alliance forces away from the person of Adolf Hitler for as long as possible.

The creation of *Volksgrenadier* divisions was a logical result of that strategic degeneration. As the fronts began to reach German soil, service, supply and administrative units were reduced to the absolute functional minimum, thereby freeing manpower, equipment and commanders from all duties other than combat.

When committed to a static defense based on strong prepared positions, the *Volksgrenadier* divisions were generally as effective as the earlier German infantry divisions and had the advantage of using less manpower, equipment and supply to achieve that effectiveness. However, in any situation calling for mobile combat, the *Volksgrenadiers* quickly became overmatched and could not hold up.

During early 1945, virtually all remaining German infantry divisions were reorganized along lines almost identical to those of the *Volksgrenadiers*. We can therefore conclude that when compared to Germany's overall efforts in 1944-45, the *Volksgrenadiers* must be ranked among their few success stories.

Chapter VII

General Principles
Attack and Defense in the German Army During World War II
by Dirk Blennemann

The outstanding characteristic of German military thinking during World War II was centered around the belief that only the offensive can achieve success in battle, particularly when combined with the element of surprise. German military education and training therefore always emphasized the need for aggressiveness and boldness in all operations.

The fundamental goal within German offensive doctrine was to encircle and destroy the enemy using fire and movement. Toward that end the various combat arms were to be brought together against the enemy in such a way as to cause surprise while also generating superiority in force and firepower. The Germans were, in fact, the first to realize (based on their experiences from the First World War) that even the most formidable force is never sufficient to gain decisive superiority across an entire front. Therefore a point of main effort (*Schwerpunkt*) was to be selected for the breakthrough, and only narrow sectors were assigned to the attacking units.

In selecting the *Schwerpunkt*, the Germans considered the weaknesses in the enemy's defensive position as well as the suitability of the natural terrain, the approach routes, and the possibilities for supporting fire. Once the attack was launched, the *Schwerpunkt* forces were to get to their objective as fast as possible, regardless of the opposition or developments elsewhere. Ideally, sufficient reserves were to be available to the attacking commander to be able to widen the penetration, maintain the overall impetus, and protect his flanks.

While the bulk of the heavy weapons, air support and reserves were massed at the *Schwerpunkt*, other sectors of the front would also be engaged by diversionary forces. Though the Germans always selected a *Schwerpunkt*, they usually also planned for shifting that main effort if they met unexpected success elsewhere. Allowing for such diversions and unplanned, opportunistic shifts required sufficient reserves be organized and concentrated beforehand.

Another critical and outstanding characteristic of the German military system was unity of command. All units engaged in an attack were put under one commander, who in turn reported to only one authority with overall responsibility for the success of the mission. Even units of different service branches would serve together under one commander chosen from among the involved forces. Great emphasis was always placed on cooperation among the services and the different branches within them, even down to the basic training level.

Vocabulary of the Offensive

The Germans have long devoted a large measure of their national energies to both the study and application of the science of war. As a result, their language—similar to the Eskimos' many words for "snow"—contains a rich vocabulary describing different forms of the attack.

The frontal attack strikes the defender at what is usually his strongest point, and therefore requires absolute superiority in men and materiel. In theory, frontal attacks should only be made across terrain that allows the attacking force to break through and quickly get into the depths of the enemy position. To tie down the enemy on the flanks of the breakthrough, the frontage of the attack is usually set wider than the actual *Schwerpunkt* within it. Adequate reserves were considered necessary to counter the certain employment of the enemy's reserves. Not surprisingly, this form of attack was viewed the most difficult to execute.

An attack directed at one or both of the defending "wings" was considered to have a better chance of success than a frontal attack. Only a portion of the defenders' weapons would be faced, and only one flank of the advancing force was exposed to enemy fire during the approach. Often the forcing back of one wing would provide opportunities to develop a wing attack into a flank or envelopment attack.

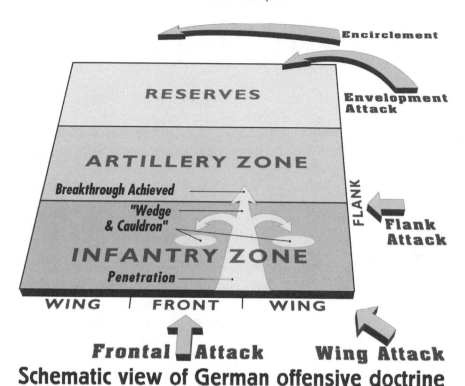

Schematic view of German offensive doctrine

The flank attack was considered the most effective attack. Such attacks were developed from either the approach march, via a turning movement prior to actual engagement, or from deliberately planned, longer flanking marches. Executing such maneuvers close to the enemy would usually only be done in favorable terrain and at night. The flank attack attempts to surprise the enemy, hitting him in such a way he has no time to mount effective countermeasures. Attacks would be launched simultaneously against both flanks only when the Germans considered their forces to be clearly superior to the enemy's.

The enveloping attack was actually a combination of the frontal and flank techniques, and was especially favored by the Germans. The enveloping forces would be directed against either or both the defenders' flanks, and was accompanied by a simultaneous frontal attack aimed at fixing in place their main forces. The success of an envelopment depended on the extent to which the enemy was able to redeploy his units in the threatened direction(s). Of course, the deeper that enveloping forces drove into the enemy's flanks, the greater became the danger they would themselves be counter-enveloped. The Germans therefore emphasized the necessity of strong, experienced reserves, coupled with the organization of the enveloping forces in depth.

In an encirclement the enemy was not attacked at all along his front (or perhaps only by light diversionary forces), while the main attacking force passed entirely around him with the objective of completely maneuvering him out of position. This was a particularly decisive form of attack, but at the same time one usually more difficult to execute than a flanking or enveloping attack, and one requiring extreme mobility and deception.

Penetration & Breakthrough

Penetrations and breakthroughs were not actually separate forms of attack by themselves, but rather were terms used to describe the exploitation of a successful frontal, wing or flank effort.

A penetration was said to have occurred when the continuity of the enemy front was first broken. The broader that initial penetration, the deeper the wedge that could be driven. It was considered important to have strong reserves available to block enemy attempts to counterattack (usually on the flanks) the penetration.

German units were trained to exploit penetrations to the maximum, leading to a full breakthrough before effective enemy countermeasures could be taken. The deeper and more swiftly the attacking force penetrated, the more effectively frustrated would be the defenders' attempts to close their front again by withdrawal toward the rear. The Germans didn't consider a penetration successfully and entirely evolved into a breakthrough until the attack had reached and overcome the defenders' artillery positions. Once that was done, reserve units would be committed to turn and roll up the remainder of the enemy's line from the newly created flanks of the penetration/breakthrough. This maneuver was referred to as "wedge and cauldron."

Pursuit

Pursuit was considered to have begun when the defender was no longer able to maintain his position and abandoned the combat area with the bulk of his force. The objective of the pursuit was nothing less than the complete annihilation of the retreating and routed enemy. Accordingly, it was conducted across as broad a front as possible by means of both fire and movement. Every effort was made to get around and in front of the now moving enemy to effect a surprise entry into his rear areas.

Effective pursuit efforts required great initiative from the commanders at all levels of the operation. To be successful pursuits usually had to be started the instant the enemy retreat was seen to be under way, even though the attacking troops might already be exhausted from their initial effort. The idea was to deny the enemy any quiet time to pause and reconstitute his defense. Naturally, then, the fastest moving, most mobile, forces were the ones selected for pursuits, usually tank and armored infantry units well supported by aircraft.

Meeting Engagements

In meeting engagements the advantage lay with the side that first succeeded in completing effective preparations for an attack, thereby depriving the enemy of his freedom of action. The advance guard of any advancing German force was always tasked with quickly using fire and maneuver in such a way as to secure that freedom of action for their side. When both sides attacked immediately from march columns, the decisive factors were then the initiative of the junior officers and the overall efficiency of the troops they led.

Attacking in General

Most of the successes the Germans gained during World War II were achieved in offensive actions conducted by motorized (wheeled) and mechanized (tracked) formations. Their original Blitzkrieg tactics were in fact based on their belief in the irresistible power and speed of such units operating independently while well supported by ground attack aircraft. During the final stage of the war, though the offensive tactics of the Germans became considerably less bold and aggressive than they had been during 1939-42, the fundamental theory behind them changed remarkably little. Specifically, they came to stress much more tank-infantry-artillery coordination since unlimited air support was no longer available to them, and man-held anti-tank weapons had gained greatly in lethality.

Still, the main weight of all German attacks during the war was borne by their panzer (armor) divisions. Where infantry divisions were employed offensively they were limited to local attacks conducted on comparatively small scales, or to mop up operations in the wake of the mobile formations. At the doctrinal level (if not always in practice), the Germans in fact never advocated the use of infantry in full-scale attacks against fixed defenses.

German offensive tactics always aimed at outflanking or encircling the main area of the enemy defense with motorized and mechanized formations. The straight-leg infantry was intended for use in rolling up the enemy defenses in the rear, or participating in the penetration/breakthrough with the tanks to develop the wedge and cauldron.

A well trained officer corps and a thoroughly disciplined rank and file were the necessary ingredients for implementing such an aggressive philosophy. Before faulty national strategy set them fighting a multi-front war wherein attrition gradually denied them those two elements, the Germans met with great success. Prior to that erosion, the only weakness in their execution of the doctrine lay in their tendency to repeat the same pattern of maneuver and attack (a fault that was exploited by the better Allied commanders throughout the war).

The Defense

The German belief in the primacy of the offensive was so strong it even shaped their view of the defensive. They favored an elastic defense wherein great importance was placed on the idea of immediate and violent counterattacks as the best way of defeating an attacking enemy. Of course, such a defensive technique required great mobility and large reserves—things the *Wehrmacht* increasingly lacked as the war went on.

As the Germans were forced more and more into an all around defensive stance, which really amounted to nothing more than a huge delaying action, in practice their defensive doctrine underwent a devolution, with linear defense increasingly substituted for the more desirable elastic offensive-defense. Ever greater emphasis was placed on the construction of defensive positions, and counterattacks were usually reduced to just small-scale, local affairs. This late-war, passive type of defense was an expedient the Germans adopted in response to total Allied air supremacy and their own growing shortages in manpower and materiel. At the theoretical level, however, they never discarded their belief that offensive action forms the best defense.

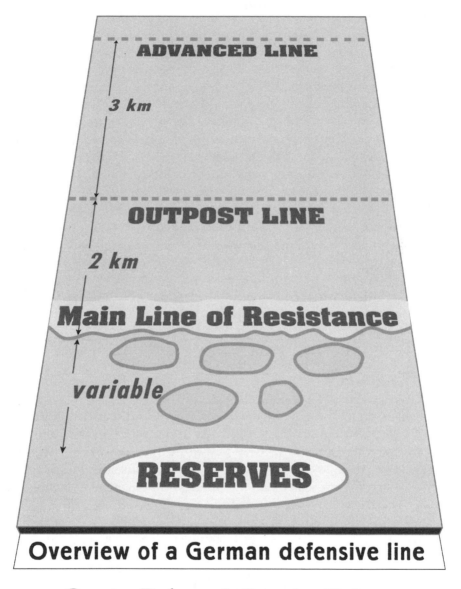

ADVANCED LINE

3 km

OUTPOST LINE

2 km

Main Line of Resistance

variable

RESERVES

Overview of a German defensive line

Counter-Defense & Covering Defense

The Germans made a distinction between a covering-defense and a counter-defense. It was the aim of the covering-defense to merely hold an area and thereby force the enemy to abandon his attack. The counter-defense was aimed at not only retaining ground, but also destroying the attacking enemy force through counterattacks. The kind of defense adopted in any given situation depended primarily on the amount and combat power of the German forces available to carry it out.

During the first half of the war, at those relatively few times and places they were on the defensive, German commanders were usually still able to determine the field of battle and thereby fix the main line of resistance on the ground. No matter what the terrain, the greatest emphasis was always placed on ensuring the unbroken continuity of the defensive line. In general, the width of a defensive sector assigned to a unit was approximately twice the width of the sector that would be assigned to the same unit when attacking.

The German defense of a position, whether hastily prepared or given time to be completely planned in all details, was conducted on the same offensively oriented principles. Unless constrained by manpower or materiel shortages to passively rely on the strength of manmade features and natural terrain, they preferred to achieve victory through the use of heavy concentrations of firepower backed by counterattacks from mobile reserves. They even applied the *Schwerpunkt* principle to the defense, but in mirror-fashion. That is, they would identify the attacking enemy's main point of concentration as quickly as possible, then set the German defensive *Schwerpunkt* opposite it.

Retreats were only ordered when all possibilities for success on the present battleline were exhausted. The objective of a retreat was to place enough distance between friendly and hostile forces to enable the former to conduct an orderly withdrawal, occupying new positions to the rear. Toward that end they would usually organize a covering force from the troops in closest contact with the enemy at the time of the retreat's start. Either whole units could be selected, or battlegroups made up of elements from several units.

A covering force's first task was to make the enemy go on believing the German line was still fully occupied. As the distance between the enemy and the retiring units increased, the Germans would form march columns while the freshest troops still available were organized into a rear guard. Armored reconnaissance battalions, because they combined both fire power and mobility, were considered particularly suitable for that job.

Kilometer Frontages Usually Allotted to Defending German & Soviet Units

	German	Soviet	
Infantry Battalion	0.8 to 2.0	1.2	Rifle Battalion
Infantry Regiment	1.6 to 4.0	3.0	Rifle Regiment
Infantry Division	8 to 10	6 to 10	Rifle Division
Panzer Division	3.6 to 6	6 to 9.6	Tank Corps

Defensive Positions

The Germans divided their defensive battlefields into four positions: the advanced position, the outpost position, the main line of resistance, and the reserve position.

The advanced position was closest to the enemy line and was usually set up five kilometers in front of the German main line of resistance, thus staying within range of their own medium artillery. Advanced positions were selected on the basis of good defensive terrain that provided observation points for friendly artillery and, if possible, also worked to deceive the enemy as to the location of the main line farther back. The troops manning the advanced position operated so as to make an attacking enemy deploy his troops from march prematurely and in the wrong directions.

German troops in the advanced position were not expected to hold at all costs. In the face of superior enemy numbers or firepower they were to retreat along predetermined routes under the cover of friendly artillery. The forces selected for the advanced position were therefore usually mobile reconnaissance detachments, made up mostly of armored cars, armored infantry, self-propelled anti-tank guns, assault guns and tanks: units that had both the firepower and mobility to make them suitable for such deployment.

The outpost position was usually established two kilometers in front of the main line of resistance. Its location would therefore always be in range of both medium and light friendly artillery. As long as the troops manning the advanced position remained in front of it, the outpost position would be only lightly occupied. Ordinarily, individual strongpoints within the overall outpost position would be manned by no more than an infantry platoon supported primarily by the fire of close-support weapons such as mortars and infantry guns. Anti-tank guns were often also assigned to the outpost position to repel hostile armored reconnaissance units. The main defensive weapon of

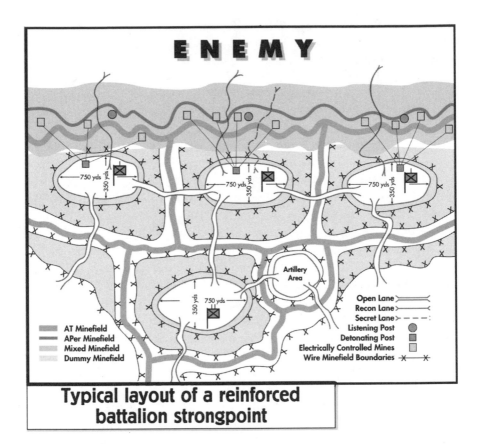

ENEMY

AT Minefield
APer Minefield
Mixed Minefield
Dummy Minefield

Open Lane
Recon Lane
Secret Lane
Listening Post
Detonating Post
Electrically Controlled Mines
Wire Minefield Boundaries

Typical layout of a reinforced battalion strongpoint

this area, however, was the heavy machinegun, which could fire out to a range of about one kilometer.

Good fields of fire were considered mandatory for all positions within the outpost area. Firing positions were usually selected at the forward edges of woods, villages, hedgerows and hills. Numerous decoy positions would also be constructed. Guards were posted, particularly at dusk and dawn, to provide warnings of enemy advances. Small, prepared counterattacks with limited objectives were often launched from outpost positions, with the aim of disrupting enemy preparations and gaining information.

Firing positions within the outpost area were also selected on the basis of facilitating unobserved withdrawal of those defenders to the main line of resistance once enemy pressure grew too strong. Several alternate positions would be prepared for each weapon, and shifts were made day and night to make it more difficult for the opposition to detect and dislodge the defenders. When an outpost position was abandoned, the withdrawal was likely to be covered by carefully registered fire from heavy weapons intended to discourage the enemy from immediately advancing.

The Germans organized their main battle line in depth, with individual strongpoints connected to form uninterrupted belts. These strongpoints, constructed to allow for all around defense, and surrounded by barbed wire obstacles and minefields, contained one or more heavy weapons, including machineguns, mortars, infantry guns, and riflemen. The smallest strongpoints constructed were intended to be occupied by reinforced squads. Such squad positions were normally incorporated into platoon strongpoints, company strongpoints, and so on up the organizational scale.

The Germans always attempted to make maximum use of reverse slopes in their defensive positions. Forward-slope positions were avoided whenever possible, since they could be detected early on by an approaching enemy, and were likely to be attacked by mass fire.

Since organizing a position in forests required great amounts of time and labor, and strong occupation was then needed to compensate for the poor observation, the Germans tried to avoid using such positions when time was short and labor scarce. On the other hand, towns and villages were considered excellent strongpoints, particularly if the buildings were of masonry. In defending such places, the Germans would locate their main battle line well within the most built up portion because the edges of urban areas, which always made easy targets for enemy artillery fire, were considered too vulnerable.

Wherever they defended the Germans adhered to the principle of "effect over protection." For example, though cutting and removing underbrush might increase the enemy's ability to spot defending troops, the enhancing effect such removal had on those same defenders' firing lanes was considered worth the increased risk. Of course, dugouts for riflemen and machinegun nests were still constructed with the idea of providing protection against enemy small arms, artillery and mortar fire. Whenever possible, three layers of logs and earth were used as cover. Trenches and wire barriers were placed along natural terrain lines such as hedgerows and the edges of fields to deny enemy infantry their most likely avenues of approach.

The Germans also endeavored to provide all parts of their defensive position with strong artillery and heavy weapons fire support. A detailed fire plan was prepared in advance by the infantry officers and then coordinated with the artillery. The mass of the available artillery would be used to lay concentrated fire both close to and well in front of the main battle line, and was sited to cover the spaces between the effective fire zones of the frontline units.

The supply of artillery ammunition was also carefully organized. When shells were scarce, the command specified, down to sections at times, the exact quantity to be used at each position. Every commander always sought to maintain his own emergency supply of ammunition.

The Germans soon learned that, by themselves, dense minefields in front of defensive positions were inadequate obstacles because the enemy could usually neutralize them with massed artillery fire or concentrated aerial bombardment before launching a large-scale ground attack. Beginning in 1942, German minefields were normally laid within the main battle line, with only a few dispersed at wide intervals in front of it. Particular stress was placed on the mining of roads, and often real mines were mixed with dummies. Aware that minefields and obstacles of all kinds were really only effective when covered by fire from various positions, they usually dug trenches and other fighting positions nearby. Machineguns and anti-tank weapons would then be sited to cover the entire area of minefields and obstacles.

During the last years of the war the Germans put increasing emphasis on the construction of obstacles and anti-tank defenses within their defensive positions. Whenever possible, they selected tank-proof terrain and natural tank barriers, such as steep slopes, to incorporate into their positions. Towns and villages were also regarded as excellent anti-tank positions because of the considerable infantry and artillery support armored units usually require to fight through such locales.

At first the Germans tended to construct anti-tank ditches well forward of their main battle line. But experience showed that such construction merely served to offer good jump-off positions for the enemy's infantry while also revealing the location of the main battle line. Increasingly, then, during the last two years of the war they more often dug anti-tank ditches in the area between the main battle line and their artillery positions. They were built in an uninterrupted line to avoid leaving any complete passage, no matter how circuitous, which might be exploited by the enemy.

German anti-tank guns were always dispersed in depth, with some

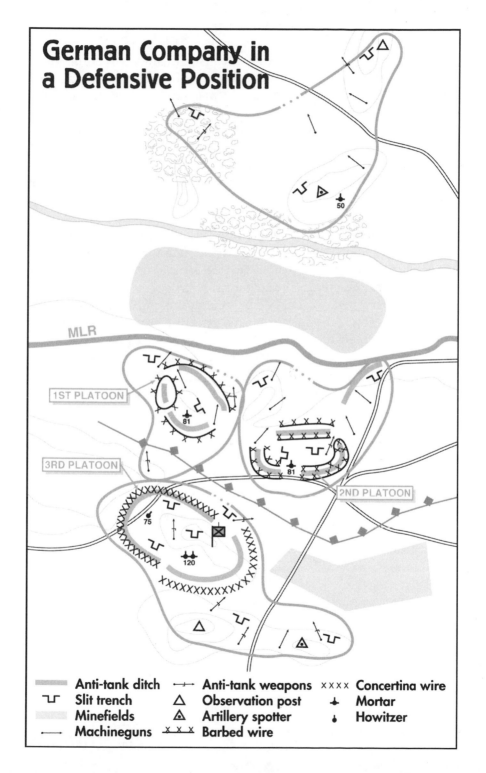

German Company in a Defensive Position

MLR

1ST PLATOON

3RD PLATOON

2ND PLATOON

▬▬ Anti-tank ditch	⊢→ Anti-tank weapons	×××× Concertina wire
⊐⊏ Slit trench	△ Observation post	⬥ Mortar
▬ Minefields	⚠ Artillery spotter	⬩ Howitzer
— Machineguns	××× Barbed wire	

49

well forward. In placing them they preferred positions in enfilade, or even on reverse slopes. Normally two to four anti-tank guns were deployed in each position, with light machineguns located around them to protect against enemy infantry assault. Considerable effort was often made to conceal anti-tank guns to prevent the enemy from discovering the location and strength of the anti-tank defense prior to his attack. Though single anti-tank guns sometimes engaged enemy armor at ranges up to one kilometer, they usually opened fire at about 250 meters.

German defense of their main battle line was based on stubborn resistance at individual strongpoints, local counterattacks against areas of immediate enemy penetration, and larger-scale counter attacks carried out by mobile reserves. Defenders in strongpoints were taught to continue their resistance even after they were surrounded, since their perseverance impeded the attackers' advance and facilitated counterattacks. German doctrine therefore prescribed that intact portions of a breached main battle line continue to fight, regardless of the immediate situation, until the appropriate higher command ordered a readjustment of the line.

Immediate local counter thrusts by the infantry at hand and whatever support elements happened to be near the enemy penetration endeavored to hurl back the enemy before he had a chance to establish himself. These small counterattacks were directed at the flanks of the enemy penetration whenever possible.

The reserve position was constructed far enough to the rear of the main battle line to compel the enemy artillery to move forward to bring it under fire. Mobile reserve units were also normally kept there. Troops in the main battle line would retire to the reserve position only under the heaviest pressure.

Sources

Clifford, M. Elizabeth, James F. Dunnigan, Virginia M. Mulholland, et. al., eds. *Strategy & Tactics Staff Study Nr. 1: The War in the East.* New York: SPI, Inc., 1977.

Freiherr von Boenninghausen, C. *Gefechtsbeispiele.* Koblenz, Germany: Verlag Wehr und Wissen, 1980.

Neugebauer, K.V. *Fuehrung und Gefecht der verbundenen Waffen.* Osnabrueck, Germany: Biblio Verlag, 1994 (reprint; original published 1921).

Steiger, R.; *Panzertaktik im Spiegel deutscher Kriegstagebuecher, 1939-1944.* Freiburg, Germany: Rombach Verlag, 1973.

U.S. War Dept. *Handbook on German Military Forces.* Baton Rouge: Louisiana State Univ., 1990 (reprint of U.S. Gov't. document originally published 1945).

Chapter VIII

Tactics on the Eastern Front, 1944-45
by John Desch

The Germans

When the Germans launched their offensive to relieve the defenders of Budapest at the start of 1945, they spearheaded their
effort, as usual, with several panzer divisions. Unfortunately for them,
due to severe shortages in every element of combat equipment and
manpower, there wasn't enough force available to duplicate the
massive armored offensives of 1939-43. The appearance of great
numbers of anti-tank weapons on the battlefield during the second
half of the war had also relegated the panzer arm to an equal—but
no longer automatically dominant—partnership with the other combat arms of infantry and artillery. More than ever, by late 1944,
balanced groupings of all-arms teams could be found in the front lines
of every army: the result of lessons learned in the previous years of
hard combat.

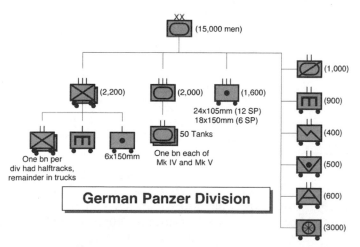

German Panzer Division

Given the state of the German economy and the overall situation in January 1945, it seems surprising the *Wehrmacht* was still capable of inflicting tactical defeats on their opponents. But there were several good reasons why the German army was able to preserve such long lasting effectiveness.

Foremost among those reasons was tank crew quality. There remained in most panzer units a core of veteran tank men; every battalion had its resident tank ace. It was usually found that one or two of the most experienced tank crews would rack up the lion's share of kills in every engagement, while many of the green crews never got off a shot. Unlike the infantry, which suffered terribly and experienced a steady decline as the war progressed, the tank units were able to maintain a reasonable level of combat proficiency. Instructors were regularly rotated out of the line and sent back to train recruits in the latest battle tactics. German to Soviet kill ratios of 5:1 were not uncommon.

There was also a better chance for a crew to survive a "brew up" than there was for infantrymen to survive a similar engagement. There were far lower casualty rates in the armor units than there were in the infantry. Most crews could get out of all but the most catastrophic hits on their tanks. Even the British, fighting in their box-like Cromwells and gasoline powered Shermans ("Like a Ronson [cigarette lighter]—lights first time, every time," went one saying of the time) suffered a casualty rate of only 1.5 crewmen per destroyed tank during Operation Goodwood in July 1944.

Still another reason for the continued German success with tanks was the excellent overall quality of those machines. Though the later models were lacking in engine power, they were unmatched in armor protection and fire power. The Tigers and King Tigers were ungainly on the battlefield, especially on the sodden, sometimes rice-paddy-like, central Hungarian plain, where they were often forced to stay on roads like so many ducks in a row. Yet when those same vehicles occupied good defensive positions, there was simply no way to pry them out without heavy casualties. The Soviets learned time and again the folly of charging Tigers and Panthers in set positions.

But the decline in overall battlefield agility meant the German heavy tanks were mediocre, if not poor, offensive weapons. The Panthers were faster, but were weak in side armor; even an old model T-34 with a 76mm gun could kill a Panther from the flank. Tigers, with their thicker hides, were like slow moving barns. Used *en masse*

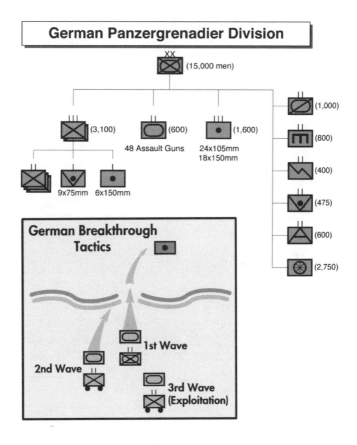

German Panzergrenadier Division

XX (15,000 men)

(1,000)

(800)

(3,100)

(600)
48 Assault Guns

(1,600)
24x105mm
18x150mm

(400)

(475)

9x75mm   6x150mm

(600)

(2,750)

German Breakthrough Tactics

1st Wave

2nd Wave

3rd Wave
(Exploitation)

in open terrain against an opponent weak in anti-tank weaponry, the Tigers and Panthers proved they could punch through when needed.

Though approaching obsolescence by 1944 in terms of its armor protection and gun power, Mark IVs still made up over half the panzer arm. It was cheap, easier to produce, maneuverable on the battlefield, and—most importantly—mechanically reliable. For many panzer commanders the Mark IV was always the offensive weapon of choice and deployed to the first wave of any attack.

German attacks came in waves. Depending on the situation, the heavy tanks might be used up front or—more often as the war continued—as an overwatch element for the lighter Mark IVs. The first wave's mission was usually to break through the fortified crust of the enemy line and get into his artillery positions with as much speed as possible. Panzergrenadiers riding in the fine *Hanomag* three-quarter tracked armored personnel carriers always accompanied the first wave to help take out enemy guns. Many Soviet guns had anti-tank capabilities, but were often caught poorly deployed in linear barrage formations by sudden panzer attacks and annihilated, thereby making the Germans' second wave task—that of mop up—much easier.

Of course, whoever coined the term "mop up" has been roundly cursed by generations of infantrymen. The task is far less easy than the term implies, because the remaining defenders are fighting from their primary defensive positions. For that reason, the Germans allocated most of their less mobile truckborne ("motorized") infantry to the second wave. Riding in trucks or on tanks until forced to dismount by enemy fire, these troops suffered proportionately heavier casualties than their armored comrades in the *Hanomags*.

The third wave exploited the success of the first two by driving into the enemy's administrative area. It was important for this force to remain intact prior to a breakthrough, because it was after that that most of the damage to the enemy was actually inflicted. Once the third wave of an assault was loose, only the timely arrival of reserves would permit the enemy force under attack to survive.

A key technical innovation in all of this was the *Hanomag*. It was one of the great mechanical success stories of World War II. This vehicle allowed the panzer grenadiers to keep up with the tanks in most situations, thereby preventing the number one cause of failed attacks: the separation of tanks and infantry at the objective. The *Hanomag*, unlike the American M3 halftrack, provided excellent protection against small arms and machinegun fire. With its three-quarter track system, it was far more mobile than a truck and significantly better than most armored cars.

Though the *Hanomags* couldn't always keep up with the panzers, the latter often moved at their own speed toward the objective, then waited under cover just short of it for the panzer grenadiers to catch up. Anyone who to this day has witnessed the Germans maneuver their tanks immediately realizes that for them there is only one speed—full ahead. In any case, cohesive groupings of tanks and infantry were usually at hand, and German mechanized forces— though often outnumbered—were thereby able to give a better account of themselves than mere numbers engaged would otherwise have indicated.

The Germans did not officially consider tanks to be the most effective anti- weapon, even though they invariably turned out be that in practice. Anti-tank guns were always found among their infantry. Tanks, rarely deployed along their defenses' main line of resistance, were kept in reserve for counterattacks. It therefore devolved upon the anti-tank guns to keep the infantry protected from enemy armor. A well placed anti-tank gun could often knock out five or 10 enemy tanks before its location was revealed to that attacking force. The preferred method of engagement was from the flank, where the forward looking tankers had less of a chance to detect the gun.

The problem with anti-tank guns was they generally couldn't be made mobile enough to survive for long in fluid fighting. The tanks' best advantages—mobility and surprise—were the best antidotes to the anti-tank gun threat. But frontal attacks against known nests of anti-tank guns were avoided like the plague by experienced tankers of all countries by the last year of the war.

The Soviets

The Soviets evolved a different philosophy concerning the employment of tanks. Unlike the Germans, their superbly organized tank and mechanized corps were rarely used to effect the tactical breakthrough of a main line of resistance. Rather, independent tank brigades and regiments were assigned to the assaulting rifle divisions after being specifically trained for that infantry support mission. Such units, which rarely performed well in tank versus tank combat, were deliberately leashed to the infantry and left behind by the exploitation units.

Once through the German main line or resistance, Soviet tank and mechanized corps did well in the pursuit role, though they tended to be considerably more flank conscious than their German and Western Allied counterparts. By 1944, the Soviets had mastered multi-corps mobile operations, and their successes reflected their painfully acquired skill.

At the tactical level, Red Army tankers never quite equaled the combat proficiency of their enemy. That occurred for several reasons, the first being that from mid-1943 until practically the end of the war, the Soviets lagged in tank technology. The T-34/85, the mainstay of the line units, was a good tank in many ways, but its gun power was markedly inferior to the Tigers and Panthers they faced. That, coupled with a crippling shortage of radios (usually only one per tank platoon,

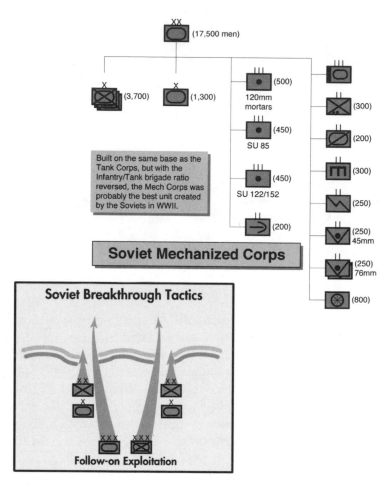

Soviet Mechanized Corps

Built on the same base as the Tank Corps, but with the Infantry/Tank brigade ratio reversed, the Mech Corps was probably the best unit created by the Soviets in WWII.

Soviet Breakthrough Tactics

Follow-on Exploitation

even in 1945), meant they often engaged the Germans at a distinct disadvantage.

The scarcity of radios was, in fact, much more a handicap than it might first seem. It is difficult to get the attention of a tank crew even when they have a radio and are monitoring it. Other signaling devices, such as flags, may appear sufficient in training, but once the bullets start flying and the tankers "button up" (close all hatches), such methods are useless. As long as the situation allowed the Soviets to use their well rehearsed approach tactics, the tankers without radios could follow the example of their unit leaders. But once something unforeseen occurred on the battlefield, such as a flank attack, the radio deficiency manifested itself in sluggish performance.

In technological quality, the "Stalin" series of Soviet tanks certainly rivaled the Tigers and Panthers, but those new "heavies" were kept in separate battalions, one per corps. That made sense because they couldn't keep up with the T-34s anyway, and when grouped together were easier to maintain. But as the corps commander's special reserve, the Stalin tanks were often committed to battle too late to decisively influence the outcome—by then too many T-34s would already have been wrecked. (Much the same arrangement worked better for the Germans with their Tigers because of superior radio communications and reaction times.)

Late war Soviet tank crew training, though much improved over what it had been in 1941-42, was still less sophisticated than that conducted by the Germans. Because losses to their attacking forces tended to be high (for the reasons described above), Soviet tank crews did not often survive long enough to improve their skills. That steady wastage prevented many units from improving their overall combat proficiency level.

In sum, despite the German panzers' tactical superiority, they were only able to delay—not prevent—their nation's defeat. That was because by 1944 they were constantly being outperformed by the Western Allies and Soviets at the higher levels.

Chapter IX

The First Panzer of World War II
by Michael S. Burrier

Even before the Nazis gained a chokehold on German politics in 1932, Heinz Guderian's ideas for a "war of movement" were being heard by receptive ears in Berlin's high places. Guderian's plan, of course, called for massed formations of armor as one of its main ingredients. Guderian, anxious to turn his strategic theory into a reality, had already conducted some training exercises during the summer of 1929, using cars mocked up to represent tanks. That display had been enough to convince even the lingering skeptics the time had come to ignore the Versailles Treaty ban on German armor and begin building the real thing.

The first mass-produced German tank began appearing in February 1934. Designed to be inexpensive and simple for fast production, it was to serve as a training vehicle while more powerful vehicles were being developed. Industry competitors— Krupp, MAN, Daimler-Benz, and Rheinmetall—had received secret invitations to build prototypes, but Krupp was the first to respond with a two-man vehicle designated the L.K.A.I.

Based closely on the British-built Carden-Lloyd Mark I of the 1920s, the L.K.A.I. I was armed with two 7.9mm machineguns in a small turret positioned to the right of the hull. The suspension consisted of four large road wheels on each side, with a rear idler that touched the ground. Armor thickness ranged from only eight to 13 milimeters, and was capable of resisting little more than small arms fire.

Since complete secrecy was of the utmost importance, the machine was given the designation *Landwirtschaftlicher Schlepper (LaS)*, or "Agricultural tractor."

Though the other invited manufacturers submitted ideas, the Krupp model prevailed. Full-scale production got underway in mid-

PzKpfw I Aus. B (Photo: Michael S. Burrier)

1934 on a vehicle modified only slightly from Krupp's original prototype. The production model was similar to the L.K.A.I. except the wheels were now smaller and leaf-sprung instead of coil-sprung as before. The most obvious change was the addition of an external beam covering the centers of the rear three wheels and idler.

When the troop-trial stage was reached later in the year, it was discovered that the feeble 57hp engine was inadequate to power the six-ton vehicle over difficult terrain. An upgraded 100hp engine was fitted. This necessitated the addition of another 43cm (1'5") to the superstructure and a fifth road wheel.

The need for the disguising name disappeared when rearmament went into the open in 1935. The machines now became known as *Panzerkampfenwagen Is* (armored fighting vehicle), or PzKpfw I. The approximately 300 machines with the old 57hp type became the Ausf. A. (production model A), and the 100hp models Ausf. B. About 1,500 of the Bs were eventually built.

With the heavier PzKpfw III and IV models still in short supply, over 800 PzKpfw I light tanks filled out the panzer divisions in the 1939 invasion of Poland. Some 523 were still in front line service during the 1940 Belgian, Dutch and French campaigns. A combination of poor Allied anti-tank doctrine and superior German blitzkreig tactics allowed the weak PzKpfw Is to perform beyond their objective capabilities.

Remarkably, even as late as the invasion of the USSR in 1941, some

PzKpfw I Ausf. A and B were still in front line service, though relegated to minor tasks. Production was finally phased out during that year.

The little known PzKpfw I Ausf. C, built by Krauss-Maffei and Daimler-Benz in 1939-40, was designed to provide mobile 20mm firepower support to reconnaissance and airborne units. The prototype was the first German tank with the interleaved wheels that the Panther and Tiger series later utilized. An order for 40 of the vehicles was never filled and the project was abandoned in 1941, giving way to a variant of the PzKpfw II called the Luchs (Lynx), which was in recon service by 1943 and looked remarkably similar to the Ausf. C.

Several other upgrades and variations were also tried over the course of the war. The *PzKpfw I Neuer Art verstärk* (new reinforced armor model), for instance, was developed for infantry support in December 1939 as a heavily armored (30-80mm) panzer with interleaved wheels. A prototype was built in June 1940, but the idea was later dropped.

Other PzKpfw I chassis were converted to engineer vehicles for use in placing explosives on the battlefield. A few of the Ausf. A models were turned into flamethrowers (*Flammpanzer I*) and were used by the Afrikakorps.

In general, though, since the PzKpfw I remained vulnerable no matter how much it was tinkered with, most of the remaining tanks were either up-armored and refitted with larger weapons, equipped with radios to serve as command vehicles, or were simply sent back to Germany to perform their original intended purpose, training.

Chapter X

World War II German Assault Guns
by Dirk Blennemann

In general, the assault gun (*Sturmgeschutz*) was a gun/chassis combination of already existing components. The carriage of the assault gun was a standard tank chassis with a modified hull. The vehicle's main weapon was not fitted in a turret, but carried in a fixed, armored superstructure with heavy frontal armor. This arrangement limited the traverse, but allowed the mounting of heavier guns on standard tank chassis than would otherwise have been possible, and also reduced the vehicle silhouette. Further protection was granted the assault guns by virtue of their well sloped superstructure and all around armoring.

About 90 percent of all German assault guns manufactured during World War II were equipped with various types of 75mm cannon, but 105mm (including howitzers), and even 150mm pieces were also mounted. In addition to the main armament, most assault guns also had one or two machineguns.

When compared to the other types of armored fighting vehicles fielded during the war, assault guns most closely resembled self-propelled artillery pieces. But the critical difference between the two types of weapon lay in the fact that the superstructure of self-propelled artillery was open at the top, and they carried only enough armor to protect their crews from small arms fire and shrapnel. In contrast, assault guns had closed tops and their armor was comparable to at least that of medium tanks. That gave assault guns the ability to duel with tanks on the battlefield.

Assault Gun Production, 1940-1945

	1940	1941	1942	1943	1944	1945	Total
Model III (short 75mm)	162	540	-	-	-	-	702
Model III (long 75mm)	-	-	702	3011	3840	836	8389
Model IV (long 75mm)	-	-	-	30	1006	105	1141
Model III (105mm Infantry Gun	30	-	-	-	-	-	30
Model III (150mm Infantry Gun)	-	-	24	-	-	-	24
Assault Howitzer (105mm)	-	-	9	204	903	192	1308

Grand Total: 11,594

Development

The title of "Father of the Assault Gun" must go to the famous German Field Marshal Erich von Manstein. In 1935 he composed a memorandum calling for the adoption of "assault artillery" within the infantry divisions. More particularly, he wanted the non-motorized infantry divisions—which throughout the entire period of the Third Reich constituted the bulk of the army's divisions—to gain some offensive breakthrough capability. Since all of the newly arriving tanks were being formed into armored or light mechanized divisions, some kind of mobile artillery was really the infantry's only practical alternative.

Manstein called for each infantry division to be reinforced with three batteries (six guns per battery) of assault artillery. After considerable discussion, the German army general staff agreed, and in 1936 the mission of the newly formed assault artillery units was laid down as follows: 1) provide close, heavy weapons support for infantry attacks, especially against machineguns and strongpoints; 2) supplement the divisions' other artillery in the indirect fire role; and 3) support the divisions in an anti-tank role.

The official birthday of the new weapon type was 15 June 1936. The *Artillery Demonstration Regiment* was established in Jüterbog and given the initial task of working out general orders and tactical specifics for the assault artillery.

It was quickly found the assault guns had to be equipped with at least a 75mm gun to be effective at their assigned tasks. In December it was decided to mount the 75s on standard Panzer III tank chassis. But since the armor, motorized infantry, and light mechanized divisions were still being given top priority for acquiring all vehicles, only five of the new assault guns were completed by the time the war started in September 1939. The *Artillery Demonstration Regiment*, in conjunction with the *Infantry Demonstration Regiment*, used the five available machines, along with some wooden mock ups, to train the crews necessary to at least form a cadre of assault artillerymen. The first actual batteries were raised early in 1940, and in March those units were given the official designation "assault gun."

In 1942 the role of the assault guns underwent decisive evolution with the adoption of the long-barreled 75mm gun. The old, short-barreled, low velocity guns were primarily suited for close support, and had been unable to perform well against state-of-the-art main battle tanks like the Soviet T-34. By rearming with the new piece, the assault guns were able to fully take on the role of active anti-tank weapon. In addition, their armor was thickened from 50 to 80mm.

Further improvements took place during 1943, with the addition of a top-mounted machinegun and side plates to better protect the tracks and hull flanks. By that point it had become clear the Panzer III was no longer able to perform as a first line tank, all production capacity for those machines was given over to assault guns. At the same time, some Panzer IV production was switched to assault guns, with those new machines designated *Sturmgeschutz IV*. The sloping of the superstructure was increased and a coaxial machinegun was integrated into the main gun shield.

In addition to those models, in 1942 two dozen modified *Sturmgeschutz III* vehicles were produced mounting 150mm infantry guns. These were intended solely for close support of infantry fighting in urban environments. Almost all were committed at Stalingrad and lost there. During the next year, 10 model III's were converted to carrying flamethrowers, but none of them saw action that way, and all were reconverted in 1944.

Organization & Employment

By 1938 it had become clear Germany's limited production capacity in armored vehicles would not soon allow equipping all infantry divisions with assault guns. The general staff therefore formed independent assault gun batteries of three platoons, each with two assault guns, for a total of six. In addition, each battery was given about a dozen halftracks for ammunition transport and fire control functions.

Gradually increasing production numbers made it possible to assign each battery seven assault guns (the extra gun went to the

The classic World War II assault gun, the Sturmgeschutz III, mounting a long-barreled 75mm gun.

battery commander) early in 1941. Prior to the start of the invasion of the Soviet Union, the independent batteries were organized into battalions, with three batteries in each, for a total of 22 (one additional for the battalion commander).

With the introduction of assault howitzers in 1943, the organization of the batteries was changed again that March. Now each battery consisted of seven assault guns and three assault howitzers, for a total of 10 vehicles per battery and 31 per battalion. The halftracks, however, were taken away.

In February 1944 a fourth platoon, with four vehicles, was added to each battery. The number of assault guns in one battalion was increased to 45 (three extras for the commander and his staff officers). A month later the independent assault gun battalions were redesignated assault gun brigades to avoid confusion with those units that had become organic parts of divisions.

During 1944 a few of the assault artillery battalions were reinforced with a company of motorized infantry and another of Panzer II light tanks. These new components were intended to improve the close-combat and reconnaissance ability of the brigades. They were redesignated assault artillery (*sturmartillerie*) brigades to distinguish them from the regular assault gun brigades.

The majority of the German assault guns committed to fighting during the war were organized into one or another of those independent units. During a battle they were assigned to the command of an army headquarters, which would in turn attach them among its divisions as needed. During 1940 and 1941 most assault guns were attached in pairs (by platoon) to non-motorized infantry regiments or battalions. The introduction of the long-barreled 75mm gun brought on a change in tactics; it then became common practice to attach entire battalions to a division or corps. About 80 percent of all the independent assault gun units saw action against the Soviets; another 15 percent fought in the west, with the rest appearing in the Balkans, North Africa and Italy.

Throughout the war the independent assault gun units were maintained as part of the artillery arm, retaining the basic organizational term "battery." The commander of an assault gun was referred to as the "gun captain," while the other crewmen were the "loader," the "layer," and the "driver." The crews wore a uniform similar to those of German tankers, but the color was gray rather than panzer black.

Between 1940 and 1944, nearly all mechanized *Waffen SS* divisions were given organic assault gun units. At first these were mostly companies, but parallel with the increasing importance and size of the overall *Waffen SS*, they gradually grew into full battalions of three companies each. During 1944 these organic assault units in the SS were redesignated as tank destroyers. Aside from the *Waffen SS*, only the crack formations within the air force's ground combat arm (like the *Hermann Göring Panzer Division*), and the army (like the *Grossdeutschland Panzer Division*) rated organic assault gun units. The basic units of these organic formations were referred to as companies rather than batteries.

At the war progressed, with ever rising losses in the east and the growing effects of Allied strategic bombing, the German armament industry was increasingly unable to equip all panzer divisions with tanks beginning early in 1943. To overcome that bottleneck, those divisions were supplemented with assault guns. Officially, the second battalion of a panzer division's tank regiment was to be equipped with Panzer IVs. In practice, however, assault guns were often mixed in there and throughout the regiment to overcome vehicle shortfalls.

By the last months of the war, even the tank units of the elite *Waffen SS* panzer divisions were being maintained in this manner.

By the end of the war it had also become common practice to completely substitute assault guns for the erstwhile panzer components of armored infantry divisions. These battalions held 42 assault guns organized into three companies. Each company in turn had 14 assault guns (two extra for the company commander and his deputy).

Conclusions

Without doubt, assault guns fulfilled a critical roll in the German armed forces during World War II. But an overall evaluation reveals the weapons had both strengths and weaknesses.

From the beginning, they were really nothing more than a stopgap measure to make up for a shortage of tanks. In that initial memorandum, Manstein wrote it would be best to supplement the infantry divisions with tanks, but he knew production limitations made that impossible. In contrast, the U.S. Army, which generally operated without any such material shortcomings, was able to attach whole tank battalions to most of its combat infantry divisions. In fact, the missions of those attached U.S. tank battalions and the German assault guns were almost identical.

The assault guns' main disadvantage lay in their turretless weapon's limited traverse compared to tanks. When attacked from the flank or rear, the whole vehicle had to be turned to meet the threat. That made it difficult to use assault guns in mobile battles, especially when used on the attack in place of tanks.

The assault guns proved most successful when used defensively as anti-tank platforms, and the refinements of 1943 and 1944 tended in that direction. Of course, since Germany had lost the overall initiative in the war by mid-1943, such a contribution is not to be minimized.

In his memoirs, the famous panzer leader Heinz Guderian claimed it would have been better for Germany to have concentrated all armored fighting vehicle production on tanks. That may well have been the best solution from a purely tactical point of view, but when economics is considered another desirable characteristic of the assault gun becomes clear. The production of an assault gun required only 70 percent of the time, material and skilled labor needed to produce a tank. In addition, the turretless configuration of the assault guns made it possible to mount heavier, more state-of-the-art, guns on what would have otherwise been obsolete tank chassis.

Taking these factors into account, it becomes clear it would have been impossible for Germany to carry on any kind of large-scale mechanized operations during the last year of the war without the use of assault guns.

Sources

Spielberger, W.J. *Sturmgeschuetze*. Stuttgart: Motorbuchverlag, 1991.

_____, *Von der Zugmaschine zum Leopard 2*. Muenchen: Bernhard & Graefe Verlag, 1979.

von Senger und Etterlin, F.M. "Deutsche Jadgpanzer1939-1945." *Wehrtechnische Monatshefte*, January 1957. Munich.

Chapter XI

German Tank Destroyers in World War II

by Michael S. Burrier

Prior to 1941, Nazi Germany had little need for mobile tank destroyers. Their standard Mk. III and IV tanks held their own against the French and British opponents they encountered in the West. After the *Wehrmacht* stormed into the USSR that summer, however, the situation changed dramatically.

The much acclaimed Soviet T-34 presented the first serious obstacle to the previously unstoppable panzers. Direct blasts from the T-34's long-barreled armament stopped the best the Germans had to offer.

One of the German vehicles then already in service and also well-suited for tank destroying was the *Sturmgeschutz III* (StuG III). The StuG III was an "assault gun" that had been developed for the artillery. It featured the Mk.III chassis and a turretless superstructure with 50mm armor plating. The most widely produced versions of the StuG III carried the 75mm armament of the Mk.IV panzers.

Until late-1943, StuG IIIs remained under the control of the artillery arm; after that, the panzer force was given control. Assault artillery brigades were soon formed, and each held 45 StuG IIIs, along with a small infantry detachment. This put the assault guns in the direct path of enemy tank formations, where the tank destroyers' true destructive capabilities could be fully utilized. By early 1944, nearly 20,000 enemy tanks had fallen prey to the fire of the StuG IIIs.

It was also during 1943 that the first German armored fighting vehicles appeared mounting the dreaded 88mm anti-tank gun—the Panzerjäger III/IV Hornisse (Hornet). At Hitler's insistence, that name was changed to Nashorn (Rhinoceros), to make it sound more aggressive to both the German public and the enemy.

The Nashorn, though, hardly lived up to its thick-skinned name-

Two examples of German attempts to develop a tank destroyer in World War II. The first, the Nashorn (top), was a failure; the second, the Jagdpanther, was a complete success. Both of these vehicles are on display at the U.S. Army Ordnance Museum at the Aberdeen Proving Grounds in Maryland. (Photos courtesy of the author.)

sake, since its armor plating was a woefully inadequate 10mm to 30mm. Its high superstructure also made the Nashorn a conspicuous target. Only 473 were built, as it quickly became apparent this first-generation 88mm gun carrier was not the answer Germany was looking for.

The next tank destroyer, the Panzerjäger Elefant (Elephant), was designed to correct the Nashorn's glaring faults. With a weight of 66.9

tons, an even more powerful version of the 88mm gun for its armament, and armor up to 200mm in critical areas, the Elefant was destined to be the ultimate tank destroyer—at least that is how the German high command envisioned it.

The Elefant's first major action was at Kursk in July 1943. Because of its massive armor protection and firepower (it could knock out a T-34 from three miles off), it was thought to be the perfect vehicle to lead the assault against the Soviet defenses there. With German infantry swarming around them, the Elefants crashed head-on into the blistering fire of the Soviets. Nothing could pierce their armor— which in essence proved to be their downfall.

Because they could not stop the Elefants, the Soviets allowed them to go by while concentrating on annihilating the accompanying infantry. Eventually, the Elefants were alone and were then destroyed by the simple expedient of torching flamethrowers into their ventilation shafts. In another incredible oversight, the Elefants had been designed without a single machinegun to ward off enemy infantry.

The failure of the Kursk operation left the German panzer forces a shambles. The high command now worked in earnest to at last develop a sensible mount for the 88mm gun. Using what was already available in the way of materials and designs, they finally developed a tank destroyer with the best of everything.

The chassis of the Mk.V Panther tank, with its interleaved wheel design and smooth ride, was chosen as the base. To that strong foundation, a low, sloped, sleek superstructure was attached. The armor was up to 120mm in places. A powerful 88mm L/71 anti-tank gun was the main armament, along with a machinegun to avoid a repetition of the Elefant debacle. The weight was a moderate but suitable 44.8 tons.

Preliminary manufacture began in December 1943 on the Panzerjäger Panther (as it was first known), and by May 1944, after undergoing a name change to Jagdpanther (Hunting Panther), the vehicle was put into full production.

The Hunting Panthers were deployed in heavy tank-destroyer battalions of 30 machines each. Usually controlled by corps or higher headquarters, they could be moved to the places where the enemy armor threat was greatest.

The Hunting Panthers were a complete success. For example, on 30 July 1944, in no more than a minute's time, three Jagdpanthers from the *654th Heavy Anti-Tank Battalion* knocked out eight British

Churchill tanks. Germany had at last found its ultimate tank destroyer.

Unfortunately for Berlin, only 382 of these remarkable weapons were ever constructed. Heavy Allied strategic bombing of German industry dashed hopes for the 150-per-month production schedule that had originally been planned.

Chapter XII

German Rocket Artillery
by Dirk Blennemann

Experimentation with rocket artillery began in the German army several years before the outbreak of World War II, but by 1939 there were still only a few launchers available for operational use. Quite simply, few high ranking German officers had any confidence in that kind of weapon. The launchers were in fact given to chemical warfare units (*Nebeltruppe*) in the belief their rocket-propelled rounds could best be used to disperse decontamination agents for the defense, or poison gas for the offense. As a result, German rocket artillery came to be called *Nebelwerfer* (smoke projectors), or *Werfer*, and later *Wurfgerät* (projector).

During the war's early years German rocket artillery saw virtually no action because the chemical units were held in reserve to wage gas warfare if that kind of fighting were to break out. But the picture changed after the invasion of the Soviet Union. The Red Army almost immediately began to commit large numbers of truck-mounted rocket launchers to action. The fierce reputation quickly gained by those weapons changed the German high command's view of rocket artillery, and late in the summer of 1941 all the available *Nebelwerfer* were released from reserve status. At the same time, production of the weapons was increased significantly, while development was pushed ahead to improve range and accuracy. (Much of that research was conducted under the direction of famed rocket scientist Werner von Braun.)

During the remainder of the war after 1941 the Germans introduced a dozen standard launchers in addition to a number of non-standard models (specialized designs that never went into large-scale production). The more commonly used types included the following: six-barreled 150mm; 10-barreled, 150mm self-propelled; five-barreled 210mm; along with four- and six-barreled 280mm and 320mm models.

The 150mm and 210mm projectors consisted of the original tube-type design mounted on a simple two-wheeled carriage. They were provided with elevating and traversing gears and were fired electrically. To prevent the weapon from being overturned by the rockets' blast, the barrels were fired separately in fixed order, with all rounds discharged in 12 seconds. To escape the blast, the crew would lie in a slit trench dug about 10 meters off to the side. A practiced crew could reload a launcher in about two minutes. The maximum range for the 150mm was about 7.5 kilometers, and about 8.5 for the 210mm. (The 210s were also equipped with tube adaptors that permitted firing 150mm rockets.)

The 150mm self-propelled launcher was mounted on the rear of a halftrack. Two horizontal rows of five barrels each were mounted on a turntable with a 360 traverse. It was also fired electrically, but the gunners could remain inside the vehicle. This model took only about a minute to reload. Most of these powerful weapons were given to the elite mechanized formations of the *Waffen SS*.

The 280mm and 320mm were by far the most feared by the Allies. These weapons were also often mounted on halftracks, and armored infantry (*Panzergrenadier*) companies sometimes had up to four of them for heavy support. Fixed launchers of these types were also regularly employed for stationary defense duties. In fact, many such launchers were built in the workshops of field units and so could often be adapted to the needs of particular tactical situations.

German rocket artillery grew into a formidable weapon type, capable of quickly laying great concentrations of smoke, or laying massed fire across target areas. Besides the enormous blast and destruction resulting in such target areas, the screaming sound of the rounds' rocket engines put additional psychological pressure on the shelled enemy troops.

During 1941 and 1942, the Germans treated their newly released rocket artillery units as adjuncts to the more orthodox gun artillery. The launchers were organized into independent battalions and used as shock weapons at the center of an attack (*Schwerpunkt*), or at the most critical part of a defense. That scheme changed in 1943, however, for both tactical and economic reasons.

As a result of steadily increasing Allied air superiority and their ground units' growing ability to conduct counterbattery fire, it became more and more important for the Germans to camouflage their artillery pieces, while also changing firing positions swiftly and often. Because the rocket projectors were relatively light and small in size, they were far more mobile than cannon and howitzers firing similar weights of shell. At the same time, the production of regular field guns required much more time, material and skilled labor than did rocket projectors. Thus, from 1943 on, rocket projectors came to represent an ever growing portion of overall German artillery assets.

But the projectors did suffer from some disadvantages. They lacked the accuracy and range of the field guns, while the noise and smoke generated by the flight of their rounds generally made it easy for the enemy to locate a firing unit's position. Rocket artillery therefore came to be considered inefficient for fire missions calling for hitting point (rather than area) targets, and for conducting counterbattery or harassing missions.

Sources

Buchner, A. *The Mission of the Chemical Troops*. Sonthofen, Germany: Arbeitsgeme-inschaft Werdertruppen, 1986 (in German).

Hahn, W. *Rocket Projectors*. Freiburg, Germany: Herder Verlag,1985 (in German).

Roepnack, A. *The History of German Rocket Artillery*. Bad Aibing, Germany: Steinmeier Verlag, 1960 (in German).

Chapter XIII

The 1941 German Army / The 1944-45 U.S. Army
A Comparative Analysis of Two Forces in Their Primes.

by John Desch

The world has not witnessed more powerful armies than those fielded by Hitler's Reich in 1941 and by the United States in 1944-45. Of course, in the absolute sense, it is impossible to determine which was better, since the time separating them kept them from fighting each other. Still, it is interesting to review the strengths and weaknesses of each, to highlight their similarities and differences, and to discuss why they were both so good.

German Soldiers and Units

It is axiomatic that a soldier fights better if he is well trained, confident in the effectiveness of his weaponry, and sees himself as a valued member of a cohesive unit. Though both armies under discussion here acknowledged this, it was the Germans who pursued the ideal of fielding maximally effective small units to a far greater degree than any other nation in World War II. That factor, more than any other, explains how they were able to perform so well for so long with such slender material resources against such unfavorable odds.

Everything in the German training and logistical systems—from divisional replacement battalions to returning indivdual convalescent soldiers to their former units—was geared toward the maintenance of cohesion down to the lowest organizational levels. In the military sense, "cohesion" embodies the idea that when everybody in a unit knows well everybody else in that unit, that unit will operate more

German Army Divisional Order of Battle
as of 3 September 1941

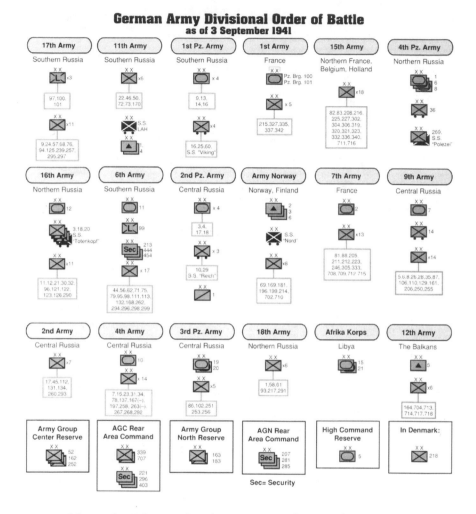

smoothly and stick together better in combat. Only in times of crisis (which occurred, of course, more and more frequently for the Germans toward the end of the war), when men and units of different services and different levels of training and experience were thrown together, did this system break down.

In 1941, with the victorious Polish and French campaigns behind them, the German army stood at the pinnacle of troop/unit quality. Veterans from both those campaigns filled the ranks. But reaching that pinnacle had not been an easy process. The uneven performance of the army in the Polish campaign had spurred a lengthy review and retraining program. Serious shortcomings had been noted in such matters as coordination between infantry and artillery, the aggressiveness of infantrymen under fire, and the relative ineffectiveness of the light divisions. These issues were only partly resolved by 10 May 1940, when the offensive in the west started. The organizational fixes dictated by the combat experiences of both the 1939 and 1940 campaigns were almost fully implemented before the onset of Barbarossa.

There were a number of factors that contributed to German unit cohesion. Since the reign of Frederick the Great, the German infantryman (or *Landser*) has been characterized by an unparalleled devotion to duty. The fact that politics was considered a matter of little consequence by the individual German combat soldiers of World War II actually helps explain why they fought so hard for so dubious a cause. They did not question the political motivations for invading Poland, Denmark, Norway, Belgium, Holland, France, Yugoslavia, Greece, etc., and they would not begin to do so even with the USSR. One's duty was to perform the task at hand to the utmost and leave the formulation of policy to others.

Contrary to popular belief, though, the small units of the German army were remarkably democratic in spirit—certainly much more so than in the American army. Emphasis was placed on collectively accomplishing missions, and communicating with one another laterally rather than hierarchically. With their immediate commander's intent thus disseminated directly to the soldiers' level, the troops were better able to see their missions through, even when losses were heavy among the junior leaders.

German divisions usually recruited all their personnel, including replacements, from within a single geographic area; so many of their soldiers entered service already having known each other for years. During the early part of the war at least, each division was responsible for training its own soldiers. This sacrificed army-wide standardization in training in order to fully integrate recruits into the divisions as quickly, directly and fully as possible.

When the division was on active duty, which was most of the time after 1939, a training battalion at its home station was responsible for training and forwarding replacements to the division. Noncommissioned officers from the division—virtually all of whom were battlewise after the French campaign—were rotated back from the line for assignments in the training battalion. This procedure worked in two ways: 1) the trainees quickly gained a sense of unit *esprit*; and 2) the most current battle tactics were given directly to the trainees by combat soldiers, rather than being filtered through a rear-echelon, conservative-minded, training bureaucracy. This procedure also yielded an unplanned benefit in that it allowed completely shattered divisions—like those lost at Stalingrad and in Tunisia—to be built anew, using the training cadre as a core of experience around which to form a reborn division.

The high level of cohesion all the above factors tended to instill in German units allowed them to continue functioning even after incurring losses that would have been completely destructive in other armies.

Unlike the U.S. Army, which had vast areas in which to train its divisons, the German army at first had to adopt a series of half-measures. Since German units were based on geographical areas and housed in *Kaserne* (barracks concentrations) of battalion size, there were never enough large training areas for division-sized and larger formations to operate together. Small local training areas were used extensively to perfect platoon- and company-level skills, but battalions and regiments had to travel to the few major training areas, such as Grafenwöhr and Jüterborg. Even at those large installations, space was extremely limited. Units were restricted to firing into small impact areas, which was good enough to train in the basics, but hardly realistic in terms of simulating battlefield conditions. Large-scale, multi-division, cross-country maneuvers were prohibited until after each year's harvest had been gathered in the fall.

Fortunately for the Germans, they acquired a good chunk of terrain when they conquered France and Poland. Officer and NCO schools were set up quickly at former French installations, like the one at Metz (which, incidentally, proved a serious obstacle to the American advance in 1944). At higher command levels, countless command post and map exercises were used to fill the void, but only during actual combat operations did those personnel receive the invaluable practical experience they needed. The campaigns of 1939-40 were critical in honing German army staff and headquarters officers to top-notch skill levels—skill levels which allowed them to maintain operational superiority over their enemies until 1944.

The American Situation

The United States Army had two important advantages over the other combatants of World War II. First, the lack of any direct overland threat allowed the Americans to mobilize an army at their (relative) leisure. Second, the late entry of the United States into the war provided time for its army's experts to study German doctrine before experiencing it directly.

At first it was thought about 200 divisions would have to be mobilized to fight the war, but that figure was later cut to 100. As it actually turned out, only 89 were established, and they proved to be enough. Without doubt, though, a major disaster on land would have caught the United States short of ready combat divisions to make it up.

The American watchword during the war was standardization. Everything done—in training, production, logistics, operations, and organization—reflected this business-like approach.

After bad experiences in the Civil War and World War I with geographically organized regiments, the Army had gone to a national system for both the regular and newly organizing divisons. Only National Guard divisions continued to be organized by state.

Individual recruits were shipped to large centers for their basic training, and were only assigned to specific units after graduation. The time lost by not putting the men into permanent small units from the very start was often compensated for by the great length of time most divisions spent training, from 12 to 18 months. The remarkable thing about the process was that it proved able to mold so many soldiers from diverse backgrounds into functional combat units.

The American soldier received good training. Though the German system was superior in terms of inculcating even the newest recruits with the most current combat tactics, the American standardized system still managed to produce soldiers who entered combat with the skills needed to survive and accomplish their mission.

One unfortunate aspect of the U.S. Army's methods lay in the fact that its infantry tended to receive a disproportionate share of lower quality troops. Soldiers in rear echelon units often labored under the very real threat that if they "screwed up" at their jobs there, they could and would be sent to the infantry. The notion seemed to be that anyone could stop a bullet, therefore many of the best recruits were shunted to technical and administrative jobs.

One important advantage in the American training system was the vast amount of real estate available for organizing and training divisions and corps. Large tracts of farmland in Kentucky and Tennessee were opened for maneuvers, in addition to the huge Army

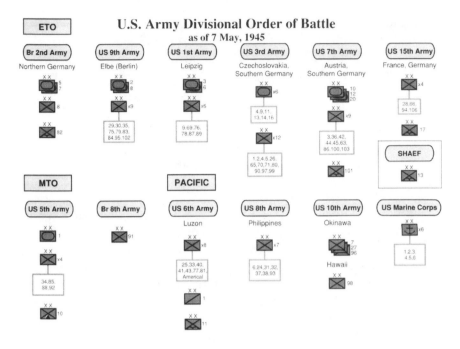

U.S. Army Divisional Order of Battle
as of 7 May, 1945

posts established in the west, at places like Camp Irwin in the Mojave Desert, and the Yakima Training Ground in the Pacific Northwest. All divisions participated in at least one corps-level maneuver before being shipped overseas. The result was most American divisions performed well after only a few weeks of shakedown in actual combat.

By 1945 the combination of standardized unit organizations and veteran soldiers to fill them had made the U.S. Army, division for divison, the most capable on the continent, and its performance reflected that. From 1 January to 1 May 1945, the Americans defeated the last major German offensive of the war, rebounded through some of the toughest terrain in Europe, in the nastiest weather the continent had seen in years, and played the leading role in completing the defeat of the *Wehrmacht* in the west.

Leadership

It is widely accepted by most military scholars that German junior- (lieutenants and captains) and middle-grade officers (majors and colonels) functioned superbly in their jobs. Excellent schools trained the most qualified candidates, who were then evaluated and assigned based chiefly on aptitude and potential.

A great deal of instruction was spent on combat tactics. In 1941 the junior leadership of the German army was at its peak. Losses in France had not been heavy, and most divisions carried a respectable complement of platoon and company commanders. After six months of Barbarossa, the attrition suffered among those same officers drastically reduced unit effectiveness. This became especially apparent among the first wave assault infantry divisions, which experienced a perceptible decline in combat power starting after 22 June. The problem was partially, but not fully, rectified by reducing the size of the infantry companies to account for less-experienced officers.

At higher levels of command, German leaders during World War II were almost universally competent, often inspired, and occasionally brilliant. This was partly due to the aftermath of World War I. Forced into massive reductions by the Treaty of Versailles, the German army retained only the finest officers, men who had demonstrated their prowess in and behind the trenches.

While it is difficult to cite examples of German incompetence at this level on the scale suffered by the other major combatants, it is also true many German generals were staunchly conservative. The doctrines and desires of the panzer experts were at first so poorly received that operations were often hampered by inter-clique rivalries. When it happened in Poland and France, the situation was saved because the Allies were themselves so befuddled it really didn't matter. When it happened in Russia, however, such squabbling contributed significantly to the defeat suffered in front of Moscow.

The United States' late entry into the war did not help the development of its junior leaders. New divisions were formed rapidly, forcing the army to strip regular and trained divisions of officers and NCOs to form cadres for new units. Several divisions were hit so often they never became battle-worthy, and all divisions suffered from the turbulence. Battle tactics never received proper attention in training; officers and NCOs had to sharpen their skills in combat, where high casualty rates among new units were often the price for the belated education.

Over time, however, the Americans showed an amazing capacity to learn. As overall combat proficiency increased among the soldiers, the junior leaders were more and more able to concentrate on mastering complex tasks. By the end of the war, virtually all the divisons in the European Theater of Operations (ETO) enjoyed roughly the same level of combat effectiveness—and that level was a high one.

German Doctrine

It is a popularly held notion the "Blitzkrieg" was a German invention patented at the start of World War II. In reality, that doctrine was actually a modification of an earlier one developed late in the First World War by a few progressive military thinkers from several countries. Without doubt, though, it was in Germany where a political apparatus first developed willing to give its military leaders the go-ahead and wherewithal needed to refine and implement the new techniques.

At its most general and basic, the primary objective of the Blitzkrieg was to resolve a campaign through decisive offensive action, rather than by the cumulative effect of attrition. German operations at all levels were organized toward the accomplishment of that goal.

Though armor is the flashy and potentially decisive combat arm, it was and is infantry that forms the bedrock on which every army must be built and centered. Infantry was the main offensive force in German World War II theory and practice. The infantry opened the breakthroughs and held the ground. Without those capabilities, no army can be victorious. Accordingly, the Germans divided their infantry divisons into "waves," with the first being the most capable offensively, and the second and third each relatively less so. Nearly all of the regular divisions raised before 1938 received a classification of "first wave."

The idea developed that each corps should consist of one or two first wave divisions along with one from the second wave. After the best units achieved a breakthrough, the follow-on units would exploit and consolidate the success. By the end of 1940, though, as even the newer units gained in experience and capability, the wave designation tended to mean less and less in practice. (It is of interest to note here that the German army continued to rate its divisions based on their *offensive* capabilities until the very end of the war, despite the overall defensive situation they were forced into during its entire second half.)

The German army was at its peak in 1941 because nearly all of its 120 line infantry divisions possessed their full offensive power. But it then suffered a sharp decline in offensive potential due to the massive losses on the eastern front.

By 1942, only one-third of the infantry divisions enjoyed anything resembling the effectiveness of pre-Barbarossa units, and that was achieved by stripping the rest of the divisions to dangerous levels. The defeat at Stalingrad therefore actually represented a far greater disaster than the mere number of divisions destroyed would seem to indicate. Those were all units that had been reinforced to full offensive potential. By mid-1943, only a dozen or so infantry divisions were left that had more than limited offensive potential. The burden of the attack fell increasingly and solely on the panzer divisions.

Those panzer divisions, though they were never a perfected organization, still served as the example the enemies of Germany emulated when building their own mechanized forces. Mobile divisions were designed to pass through the infantry-made breach in the enemy frontline and quickly press on into his rear echelons. The synergy of mobility and speed, firepower and combined-arms action was supposed to inflict psychological, more than physical, defeat on opponents. The Polish and French campaigns served as convincing demonstrations to the world that the tank and airplane employed together on the offensive could achieve decisive strategic results.

In 1941, though saddled with many technically inferior tanks and obsolete support aircraft, the panzer arm still reached the highest degree of relative superiority over its opponents it would ever attain. The most important element of the panzer divisions—the panzer grenadiers (mechanized infantry)—proved superbly proficient at clearing the way for the tanks.

New tank and gun models eventually would give individual German tank crews a technical edge, but Allied competence also improved steadily, until their average crew quality level surpassed that of the Germans in 1944. The overall battlefield advantage enjoyed by the Germans would never again be as pronounced as that enjoyed during their first months in the USSR.

In some ways, the German army's artillery arm turned out to be its organizational stepchild. With most mechanization devoted to the panzer units, little could be spared for the artillery; it remained mostly horse-drawn throughout the war. A shortage of radios, spotter planes, and ammunition also hampered the artillery. Throughout most of 1941, though, the *Luftwaffe* was strong enough to offset the weaknesses of the artillery arm. But German artillery pieces were adequate, the crews were well trained and the fire-control techniques were good. As the chronic shortage of infantry set in and the *Luftwaffe*'s capabilities declined, German defenses relied increasingly on artillery.

No discussion of the German army of World War II can exclude the

Luftwaffe, since the fortunes of the two were linked. When the *Luftwaffe* reigned supreme, the German army was victorious. When the *Luftwaffe* stumbled, the army found its tasks much more difficult to accomplish.

Lavish resources were provided to the air arm, yet it still proved to be the weak sister among the services. Its command failed to maintain a steady flow of new pilots, there was a consistent lack of in-theater maintenance, and the need to deploy an ever greater amount of resources to defend the heartland against Allied strategic bombers, all contributed to the *Luftwaffe's* steady decline. But in 1941 the Allies were still playing catch-up. The edge in pilot and aircraft quality still favored the Germans, despite their recent debacle over Britain. As events in Russia showed, the German army could still count on the kind of support they had enjoyed during the Polish and French campaigns.

Doctrine mandated close cooperation between the *Luftwaffe* and the army. Staff officers were often exchanged between the two services, and depending on how well the intermediate commanders got along with each other, the working relationship between ground and air was usually good.

U.S. Doctrine

U.S. doctrine in 1944-45 had grown to be very similar to that practiced by the Germans in 1941, though it was by no means a carbon copy.

The U.S. Army has often been accused of favoring attrition strategies, rather than decisive offensive action, to defeat its enemies. Though a case can be made that American advances tended to be more flank-conscious than the Blitzkrieg operations conducted by the Germans in their hey-day, the history of its late-war operations really overturn that charge. Every combat order was oriented toward the accomplishment of a decisive result. Often, though, the staunch nature of some defense, such as the one conducted by the Germans in Normandy, reduced American operations to slugfests. In such cases the Americans employed their wealth of fire support to help defeat the enemy through attrition. That was rarely the desired method of operations.

The nature of combat in the war was changed significantly by the advent of infantry-held anti-tank weapons. No longer could masses of tanks rule the battlefield alone. Tactical requirements increasingly called for balanced groupings of infantry, armor, artillery and supporting services. These trends were highlighted time and again during the 1944 campaign in France. The infantry experienced difficulties in pushing forward without tank support, and the armor couldn't get anywhere without riflemen. Being good students, the Americans absorbed what the Germans had to teach about combined-arms methodology, then improved on it. Air and logistical support operations, in particular, were bettered.

An important aspect of American tactical organization was generally known as the "pool" concept. The idea was that units of all types would be organized with standard Tables of Organization and Equipment (T.O.&E.s) throughout the army. In theory, such standardization would allow support battalions of tanks, artillery, combat engineers, etc., to be attached and reattached to divisions as operational conditions (the enemy, the weather and the terrain) dictated.

Unfortunately, the pool concept worked better on paper than it did in practice. Units unaccustomed to working with one another faced difficult problems of coordination when first thrown together. For example, infantry divisions often had no opportunity to work with attached tank battalions until they were actually in their area of operations. Once there, it was universally found that a great deal of training or experience (or both) were needed to cement tank-infantry teams.

Sadly, the U.S. Army got a crash course in such operations in the Normandy bocage country, where smooth and effective tank-infantry cooperation was essential for success. The basic problem proved to be one of communication. Buttoned up inside their machines, tank commanders and gunners experienced difficulty in acquiring targets. Because armor and infantry radios operated on different wave lengths, the tanks were often equipped with handheld wireless sets. They, however, proved difficult to monitor over the noise of battle. Telephone sets installed by signals troops proved vulnerable to artillery and small arms fire. Occasionally communications were reduced to having some brave infantryman jump up and down in front of a tank to get its crew's attention. Other expedients included having several men in each tank-supported squad load nothing but tracer ammunition in their weapons and all fire at a a prime target until the tankers saw it and followed up with high explosive shells.

The U.S. Army learned the lessons of combined-arms cooperation in Normandy, and by the time its divisions reached the Rhine most of its combat leaders had quietly discarded the "pool" concept, allowing units to develop habitual relationships.

The pool idea was not a complete failure, though. Artillery units continued to follow a modified form of the doctrine throughout the war (one which is still present, though in further modified form, in the present U.S. Army). Specially trained forward artillery observers (FAOs), attached to infantry units down to platoon level, were able to call in fire support from any available artillery battalion within communications range. Those observers often came to identify more with the infantry units they were assigned to than with their parent artillery battalions.

It was the corps- and army-level artillery battalions that were retained in pools and loaned to divisions according to the parameters of specific missions. It became common, therefore, for a division faced with a particularly tough mission to be supported by up to a dozen artillery battalions.

The standard U.S. infantry division was admirably organized for the war they had to fight in 1944-45. With an attached tank battalion and enough wheeled vehicles (either immediately on-hand or on-call from higher echelons) to motorize all of its infantry, and at least four battalions of supremely efficient field artillery to provide strong and flexible fire support, they were, for all practical purposes, powerful "panzer grenadier" divisions.

As in the 1941 German army, the U.S. infantry division of 1944-45 was primarily responsible for seizing and holding terrain. During the last months of the war, they became so proficient they were able to operate over wider frontages than had earlier been believed possible, and were readily capable of forming tailored mechanized task forces for pursuit operations if the armored divisions were otherwise occupied.

On the battlefield, by 1944, the American rifleman had developed a reliance on effective artillery support. Good communications with the artillery and proper fire control were always top priority with veteran infantry commanders.

Indeed, the success of German counterattacks could be foretold by how responsive U.S. fire support was in that engagement. German daylight counterattacks—with tanks or without—against emplaced veteran American infantrymen with a functioning communications net were defeated in virtually every case. If the Germans chose to counterattack at night, or in limited visibility, or in a fluid situation, or if the American artillery was for some reason in disarray (as it was for much of the Battle of the Bulge), then they stood a fair chance of success.

Rarely did the threat of tanks buckle an American line effectively supported by artillery. Normally the German infantry would be stripped away from their tanks by concentrated small arms fire, then the tanks themselves would be shot up with bazookas. Often it was enough just to drop artillery on a German attack to break it up.

One tactic—Time on Target—was reserved for particularly tough situations. As many as 20 artillery battalions would time their fire in such a way as to have all the shells impact on the target at the same moment. This technique, when followed up quickly by infantry and tanks, enjoyed an amazing 82 percent success rate.

American infantrymen did not prove particularly adept at fighting in woods or other conditions in which the effectiveness of artillery was significantly hampered. If a particular patch of woods could be bypassed, it was. U.S. positions in such areas often proved vulnerable to infiltrating German units, who had learned much from the Soviets in the ways of forest fighting.

On the other hand, American infantry became proficient at fighting in urban terrain. There were several reasons for that. First, much more firepower—some of it from direct-fire artillery—could be brought to bear more easily against nests of resistance in towns and cities. Also, small groupings of tanks and infantry (which the U.S. Army had become highly adept at forming by this time) were the ideal ground force to smash urban defenders. In urban situations, the American army almost always gave better than it got.

Weapons and Logistics

With the exception of the MG34 light machinegun, which added so much to their infantry squads' firepower, and the Sdkfz 251 halftrack, which gave their panzer grenadiers excellent protection while allowing them to keep up with the tanks, the German army's weapons were only equivalent, and were often inferior, to those of their enemies. Their medium tanks (the Mark III and Mark IV) held their own in North Africa against British tanks, but were inadequate against the heavier Soviet models just then beginning to be issued in large numbers. German rifles, mortars, aircraft and artillery pieces were all adequate, but not superior to those possessed by the Allies. Of course, weapons themselves do not make for victory; it's how they are handled and deployed that matters.

In logistics, the German army of 1941 left a great deal to be desired. The German industrial base was still on a quasi-peacetime footing, and simply could not provide the mechanization needed to fully support forces operating at great distances from railheads. The confiscation of French vehicles helped for a while, but in the end they mostly served to complicate maintenance problems that were already severe. Even had there been enough vehicles and replacement parts to go around, there still remained the issue of providing the lifeblood for such a force—fuel.

The German army operated throughout the first half of the war and achieved all its greatest victories on a logistical shoestring. It then had to continue to operate that way when its enemies began pushing toward the borders of Germany and reconquering resource areas during the second half.

The U. S. Army fielded several excellent weapons by 1944-45. The M1 Garand semi-automatic rifle provided American infantrymen with the ability to throw relatively massive amounts of firepower against their adversaries. Together with the Browning Automatic Rifle (BAR), the M1 went a long way toward redressing the serious American deficiency in machineguns.

The bazooka was considered a suicide weapon by some, and it was bulky to carry, but it proved to be so effective against German tanks that those forces simply did not venture into towns and woods without their own infantry support. Many seesaw engagements were decided by a brave bazookaman popping off at some tanks at the last instant. There is no doubt American resiliency was greatly enhanced by this weapon.

No other single item of equipment—weapon or otherwise—influenced the course of World War II more than American trucks. The entire family of American motor vehicles, from Jeeps to 10-ton trucks, enjoyed unsurpassed reputations for mechanical reliability, maneuverability and cargo capacity. Before rail and inland water networks were fully operational late in 1944, almost the entire Allied offensive effort on the western front was truckborne. By the time of the final offensive in March-April 1945, every American division was able to fully motorize its infantry.

It is staggering to imagine what could have happened in 1941 had the German army been anywhere near so lavishly equipped with trucks. Even just a few thousand 2.5-ton trucks could have been decisive in the drive on Moscow.

In terms relative to its enemies, the U.S. Army was logistically supported on a scale of which its opponents could only dream. Of decisive importance were the vast quantities of shells constantly available to the field artillery battalions. The heavy fighting in Normandy, and later during a brief period in the Siegfried Line Campaign, forced temporary conservation measures. But even at those times, American shell expenditures far outweighed the German effort. By 1944-45, a large part of the American Army's combat capabilities were only made possible by its logistical prowess. In fact, during the final campaign in Germany, the Americans suffered virtually no logistical constraints. Commanders did not have to modify their operational planning because of supply limits—certainly a first in warfare.

Conclusions

Given all this, then, had they somehow been able to meet and fight at the same place and time, which force would have won—the German army of 1941, or the American of 1944-45? Most likely the Americans. The Germans would have had an edge in junior leadership, professional elan and small unit cohesion, but that would probably have been matched and overturned by the immense U.S. advantages in firepower and logistics. Undoubtedly, though, it would have been one hell of a fight.

Chapter XIV

The Luftwaffe's Field Divisions
A Study in Failure
by Steven H. Sandman

Most readers are probably familiar with the German word *Luft-waffe*, knowing it translates into English as "air force," and that it is most often used to define the Nazis' air war efforts during the Second World War. Fewer, however, are aware that as the war progressed so too did the *Luftwaffe*'s responsibilities on the ground. In fact, by mid-1944 the German "air force" had fielded approximately 400,000 ground troops in four armed components: 1) some 21,000 anti-aircraft ("Flak") guns and crews; 2) eight parachute divisions (actually elite light infantry by that late date in the war, with two more still to come before V-E Day); 3) the *Hermann Göring Parachute-Panzer Corps*; and 4) 22 field divisions.

All of those formations were significant in one way or another to the overall development of the war in Europe, but it was the last category, the *Luftwaffe*'s field divisions, which marked that service's full entry into the arena of large-scale ground combat. In fact, no other air force before or since has ever been tasked to develop such a huge group of infantry divisions intended to fight shoulder to shoulder with those of a regular army. That the *Luftwaffe* was drawn in such a direction represents perhaps the sorriest chapter in its ill-fated history.

The First Steps

The *Luftwaffe* was forced to form its first non-parachute infantry units out of sheer, desperate self-preservation. In December 1941, as the Red Army launched its first massive counteroffensive on the eastern front, the German air force was in desperate shape. It was overextended along a fighting front that stretched from the Arctic to the Black Sea. Its air formations had been seriously depleted by the losses suffered during the previous six months of intense offensive action, and was further weakened by the transfer to the Mediterranean of *Luftflotte 2* just days prior to the start of the Soviet counterattacks.

As the Soviet effort gained momentum, the *Luftwaffe* command found itself in a new situation: advances by Red Army spearhead units and partisan bands were for the first time endangering its airfields and command and control facilities. But the regular army and *Waffen SS*, the other two service components of Hitler's ground forces, were of course also fighting for their survival and had no units to spare to support the suddenly exposed *Luftwaffe*. The air force was told it would have to "draw upon its own resources" to save itself.

Accordingly, all personnel not absolutely critical to the maintenance of their units were drawn from the anti-aircraft, signals, supply, command staff, security and ground crew echelons. They were formed into ad hoc companies and battalions and immediately thrown into action. Of course, the officers, NCOs and men who were thus sent into the trauma that is modern ground combat for the first time had only the usual *Luftwaffe* basic training. Their combat capabilities were therefore largely limited to static, point-defense.

The First Actions

The first battalion-sized commitment of the *Luftwaffe*'s new infantry component took place in the *Army Group Center* sector of the eastern front during January 1942, at Rzhev. That was followed in March by the airlifting of several *Luftwaffe* infantry battalions into the Demyansk pocket, where they were used to defend the critical resupply airfields. Those same battalions were organized into *Brigade Schlemm* (after its commander, Maj. Gen. Alfred Schlemm), which fought as part of *2nd Panzer Army* and then *4th Army* before being disbanded in June. Another *Army Group Center* air force unit during the same period was *Luftwaffe Battalion Moscow*, which was for a time expanded into *Luftwaffe Regiment Moscow* before being disbanded.

In the *Army Group North* sector, *Group Meindl* (also named after its commander, Maj. Gen. Eugen Meindl), a regimental-size unit, was formed during the spring of 1942. It was disbanded in December, but was perhaps the best of all the early *Luftwaffe* infantry units in that it had the distinction of being mentioned twice in armed forces high command reports during its existence.

In the far north in Finland, where no serious Soviet threat to *Luftwaffe* ground installations ever really took place, *Luftflotte 5* still jumped on the infantry bandwagon by mobilizing *Luftwaffe Battalion 1* to guard its airfields.

Only in the Ukraine, behind *Army Group South*, did the *Luftwaffe* fail to form any infantry unit that winter. It seems since that was the first area of the front across which the Germans had been forced onto the defensive, it also became the first sector to stabilize. The crisis levels reached by *Army Groups North* and *Center* were never duplicated in the south that winter, so the emergency formation of *Luftwaffe* ground units was skipped.

These first *Luftwaffe* infantry improvisations can be considered successful within their limited scope. Unfortunately for Germany's later war efforts, however, those first successes became magnified in the mind of the *Luftwaffe*'s commander-in-chief, Reichsmarshal Hermann Göring, into something rivaling the performance of the army's best units. Göring's new mindset would cost his service much blood later on.

Dispositions of the Luftwaffe Field Divisions Winter 1942-43

USSR, Army Group North: 1, 9, 10, 12, 13, 21
USSR, Army Group Center: 2, 3, 4, 6
USSR, Army Group South: 5, 7, 8, 15
France: 16, 17, 18, 19 (to Italy, 6/44)
Italy: 20
Balkans: 11, 12
Norway: 14

The Creation of the Field Divisions

A second manpower crisis hit the overextended Germans late in the summer of 1942. This time Field Marshal Wilhelm Keitel, chief of staff of the armed forces high command, proposed to help solve it by transferring 20,000 surplus personnel from the navy and 50,000 from the air force into the army's replacement system.

Göring, who viewed the *Luftwaffe* as his personal fiefdom of men and materiel, immediately and bitterly opposed the suggestion. Maintaining his personal power and prestige, which were already declining below what they had once been, was his main concern. But he also objected to seeing his airmen, who had a reputation for being more dedicated National Socialists than most in the regular army, given over to the older service. (After all, the *Luftwaffe* had been entirely a Nazi-era creation and its doctrines reflected that.) The Reichsmarshal therefore made a counter proposal to his *Führer*. He said he would provide 200,000 new infantrymen if he was allowed to form them into entirely new divisions that would remain in the *Luftwaffe*.

Hitler, for several reasons, immediately accepted Göring's offer. First, by that point in the war, having been disappointed by its failure to conquer the Soviet Union, and having sacked several of its senior officers, the *Führer* was already describing the army as "reactionary," "Wilhelmine," and not entirely prepared for the all-out struggle for survival then beginning in the east. Second, given his obsession with numbers, the more divisions Germany had in the field the better it seemed to Hitler—no matter what the actual combat power of those units might be. Third, and perhaps most important, the creation of the field divisions allowed him to extend his political policy of divide and rule. That is, he ran Germany by creating competing and over-lapping power centers, among which only he had the authority to be final arbiter. Thus the *Waffen SS*, along with the expanding *Luftwaffe* ground forces, could serve as counterweight to any future attempts by the army to end the Nazi regime.

On 17 September 1942, Göring called upon *Luftwaffe* officers of all ranks to volunteer for positions in the new field divisions; two days later the same invitation was issued to the rank and file.

The authorization of the field divisions caused an immediate and severe strain in the army's supply system. It was the army that had to provide the new units with all their needed weapons (except for anti-aircraft guns, which the *Luftwaffe* provided from its own stocks), munitions, vehicles, horses, etc. Given the critical situations then developing in North Africa and the USSR, the timing of the new demands could not have been much worse.

To the Front

Between 15 October 1942 and 15 May 1943 the *Luftwaffe* formed 22 field divisions. They were consecutively numbered, with the last being disbanded before its formation was completed. In addition to the field divisions, four field corps headquarters (1st through 4th) were also established in November 1942. One of them, the 1st, was made responsible for overseeing the raising of the field divisions.

The original intention was to use the field divisions on relatively quiet fronts, such as in Norway and the pre-Overlord western front, and in static warfare positions such as the Leningrad area in the east. The idea was that the army divisions thus released from the line could then be used for offensive action. But that initial deployment scheme largely had to be abandoned after the difficult winter battles of 1942-43. Two-thirds of the field divisions went to the eastern front, and for the most part they were not used there to man narrow, quiet sectors. On the contrary, desperate circumstances dictated the new units be immediately thrown into the worst crisis areas of the front.

Structural Problems

Without doubt, the poorest performing components of the field divisions were their light infantry regiments. Though relatively well equipped, their efficiency was greatly reduced because of their having to perform various engineering and support missions. This problem was especially acute in the first eight divisions, which were really only large brigades in strength. The overburdening of the infantry regiments had dire consequences. The diversion of their manpower for non-infantry tasks caused the divisions' front lines to be even thinner than what was already passing for normal in the army. Reserves within the divisions, when any were available at all, tended to be weak.

The field divisions' artillery regiments could not be said to be well equipped. Not only was it smaller than its army counterpart, it was equipped largely from foreign-made guns captured from Czechoslovakia, France and the USSR. Those guns ranged in various sizes from 75mm to 155mm, so providing ammunition and replacement parts quickly became a logistical nightmare. The artillery component is the backbone of every infantry division, so the deficiencies here created only more problems for the infantry in the line.

The high command also failed to provide sufficient reconnaissance and engineer assets for the field divisions. The company sized units of those types that were all that was included in most of the field divisions could not possibly perform their specialized tasks at divisional scales. Had those critical combat support units been of proper

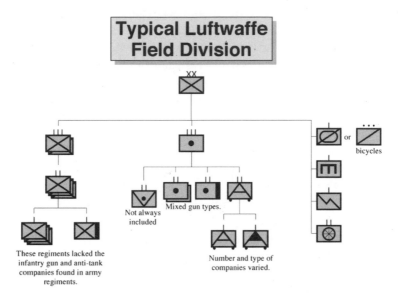

Typical Luftwaffe Field Division

These regiments lacked the infantry gun and anti-tank companies found in army regiments.

Not always included

Mixed gun types.

Number and type of companies varied.

or bicycles

A Comparison of Luftwaffe Field & 1944 Army Infantry Divisions

	Field Divisions'44	Infantry Divisions
Machineguns	552	656
Mortars	32	76
Anti-Tank Guns	12	21
Infantry Guns*	10	24
Self-Propelled Assault Guns	0	14
Field Artillery	24	48
Light Anti-Aircraft	44	12
Heavy Anti-Aircraft**	12	0
Total Manpower	12,500	12,300
Infantry	4,900	4,900
Moter Vehicles	600	615

Notes

*75mm and 150mm guns

**88mm guns

battalion size, they could have lifted some of the burdens off the infantry while also serving as reserves in a pinch.

Since radio communications played a critical role in *Luftwaffe* air operations, it is perhaps most surprising that the field divisions were each authorized only one signals company, rather than the army's standard battalion. This fact alone goes a long way toward explaining these divisions' ineffectiveness in fluid situations.

Personnel Problems

Göring wanted his new forces to be staffed entirely with *Luftwaffe* personnel, from the commanding generals down to the private soldiers. The problem with that lay in the fact that at the time the *Luftwaffe* had only two other fighting ground combat divisions: the *7th Flieger* and the *Hermann Göring*. That was a completely insufficient base from which to draw cadres for 22 infantry divisions, especially in terms of filling the senior slots. The decision to keep the army from providing the field divisions with any significant number of instructors and command personnel more than any other factor condemned the new units to mediocrity and worse.

The commanders of the field corps and divisions were drawn mostly from the flying formations, the anti-aircraft artillery and general staff. The large majority of those officers had, at best, only company-level experience commanding infantry combat operations. Leading infantry corps and divisions in modern combat is not a skill that can be learned in a brief time or mastered through courses of instruction. The priceless factor of direct experience at all levels of ground command, along with knowledge of logistics, tactics and the orchestration of different combat arms, was almost totally lacking in these men. That same deficiency also extended into the field divisions' NCO corps, most of whom were simply promoted from the ranks and likewise lacked the tactical skills necessary for infantry fighting.

Yet another problem for the field divisions was caused by the decision to have them retain *Luftwaffe* uniforms, with their blue color and distinctive markings, as battle dress. That allowed the Soviets to quickly identify them in the line, while at the same time clearly delineating their sector of the front between adjacent army units. Thus these inexperienced and weak units often drew the brunt of Soviet attacks onto themselves.

Fate of the Field Divisions

1st Destroyed near Leningrad, January 1944.
2nd Disbanded 1/44; sub-units destroyed in Bagration offensive, 7/44.
3rd Disbanded 1/44; sub-units destroyed in Bagration offensive, 7/44.
4th Surrounded and destroyed in Vitebsk, Belorussia, 7/44.

5th	Destroyed in southern Russia early in 1943.
6th	Surrounded and destroyed in Vitebsk, Belorussia, 7/44.
7th	Mauled on the Chir River defense line; dispanded 5/43; survivors transferred to the 15th Field Division.
8th	Mauled on the Chir River defense line; dispanded 5/43; survivors transferred to the 15th Field Division.
9th	Mauled in Soviet offensive near Leningrad 2/44, disbanded.
10th	Mauled in Soviet offensive near Leningrad 1/44, disbanded.
11th	Still active on V-E Day on the southern sector of the eastern front.
12th	Trapped in the Courland pocket in Latvia, it ended the war there.
13th	Mauled in Soviet offensive near Leningrad 2/44, disbanded.
14th	Stationed in Norway and Denmark, this unit never saw combat.
15th	Mauled at Taganrog in the autumn of 1943, disbanded
16th	Mauled at Caen, 7/44; reformed, it fought until V-E Day in the west.
17th	Destroyed in France, 8/44
18th	Destroyed in the Mons pocket, 8/44
19th	Mauled in Italy, 6/44; it was reformed into a Volksgrenadier division, finishing the war on the western front.
20th	Mauled in Italy, 6/44; it was disbanded 1/45.
21st	Trapped in the Courland pocket in Latvia, it ended the war there.
22nd	Disbanded before being committed to action.

Given all these problems, it is not surprising that the *Luftwaffe* field divisions were allowed to remain under their parent service's control only until 1 November 1943. At that time they were transferred into the regular army (less their anti-aircraft guns, which were kept by the air force), and redesignated as "field divisions (light)." Out of the approximately 250,000 original members of the units, some 90,000 had already become casualties by that point. Unfortunately for those soldiers serving in them, their units' continued existence in the army led to few improvements in performance. By the end of the war, only three field divisions were still in existence.

Sources

Jagolski, Georg. *Die Luftwaffe Felddivisionen*, 1942-45. Self-published, 1987.

Keilig, Wolf. *Das Deutsche Heer*, 1939-1945, 3 vols. Bad Neuheim, Germany: Podzun Verlag, 1956.

Madeja, Victor. "The *Luftwaffe* Land Army," *Strategy & Tactics* magazine, no. 20, Jan/Feb 1970, pp. 3-10.

Mitcham, Jr., Samuel W. *Hitler's Legions: The German Army Order of Battle, World War II*. New York: Stein & Day, 1985.

Müller-Hillebrand, Burkhart. *Das Heer, 1933-1945*, 3 vols. Frankfurt a. M., Germany: E.S. Mittler & Sohn, 1969.

Warlimont, Walter. *Inside Hitler's Headquarters*, 1939-45. New York: Praeger, 1964.

Chapter XV

A Combat History of 1st SS Panzer Division

by Blaine Taylor

In 1945, the Nazi regime was overthrown by foreign armies invading Germany, and not by an internal revolt of the Reich's people, as had happened in 1918, when the Kaiser was forced to abdicate in the midst of wide civil unrest. The Nazis remembered well that unrest, and they feared its recurrence as World War II drew to a close.

Hitler had been determined from the start that he would not suffer a fate similar to the Kaiser's. On 17 March 1933, less than two months after being named Reich Chancellor, he ordered Josef "Sepp" Dietrich to establish a private guard for him in Berlin. The *Führer* feared a *putsch* from both his own increasingly radical and unruly Stormtroopers (the SA or "Brownshirts"), and from the conservative army command, some of whom wanted to strangle the Nazi political movement in its infancy.

In that way the *Stabwach* (or Staff Guard) came into being. It was upgraded and expanded on 9 September, when it became the *Adolf Hitler Standarte*. On 9 November its name was changed again to the *SS Leibstandarte Adolf Hitler*—or LAH in acronymic form.

Unlike the SA chief, Ernst Röhm, who had sought to replace the "gray rock" of the national army with his stormtroopers, Sepp Dietrich sought to make his men part of its traditions. The regular army men appreciated the nuance, and following the "Blood Purge," when the radical SA men were liquidated, no less a figure than the Minister of War, Gen. Werner von Blomberg, presented the infant LAH with rifles and machineguns of its own. At the same time, Hitler, already grateful for the personal loyalty shown to him by the SS, promoted his favorite "Old Fighter," Dietrich, to the rank of SS Lieutenant General. (Dietrich's name is also the German word for

Gen. Josef "Sepp" Dietrich at the Führer's home overlooking the village of Berchtesgaden. He wears the collar tabs of a Waffen SS Obergruppenführer (Lt. Gen.) and the Knight's Cross of the Iron Cross at the throat. On his right breast pocket he wears a ribbon of the Beer Hall Putsch Commemorative Badge and in his button hole the 1939 Iron Cross eagle pin. Over his left breast pocket are medal ribbons, while below (top to bottom) are the Nazi Party Golden Membership Badge, a WWI armored assault badge (left) and the 1939 Iron Cross pin over the actual 1914 Iron Cross (right). On his left sleeve is the cuff band "Adolf Hitler" for the SS LAH. The German armed forces were near-unique at that time in that their officers and men wore all their orders, medals and decorations into combat. (Eva Braun Hitler Albums)

"Skeleton Key," and that emblem was later emblazoned on LAH vehicles in World War II.)

At first the primary duty of the SS was to guard Hitler and other top members of the Nazi leadership, in their homes, offices, and while moving between the two. The secondary role of the LAH was to serve as showcase parade troops—or, in the vernacular of the amused regular army generals who at first looked down their noses at them: "asphalt soldiers."

Every January 30th, to mark Hitler's ascension to power, the black-uniformed troops goosestepped down the Wilhelmstrasse in Berlin. They marched again each April 20th to celebrate his birthday, and yet again on *Reichsparteitag* in Nuremburg to open the Nazi youth rallies.

Able to recruit from all over Germany (the only SS unit so privileged), the LAH soon became the elite of the elite, drawing the cream of the Nazi crop coming up from the ranks of the Hitler Youth Organization. All *Leibstandarte* men were volunteers, aged 17-22, with a minimum height of 5'11" (later raised to 6'1/2"), and in top physical shape. Heinrich Himmler, the SS chief, demanded they also be "pure Aryans," and able to prove their ancestry back to the year 1800 for enlisted personnel and 1750 for officers. Indeed, Himmler boasted, "Until 1936, we did not accept a man in the *Leibstandarte*... if he had one filled tooth."

In April 1934, the LAH expanded to 1,500 men, and with the entry into its ranks of professional soldiers like Paul Hausser, Wilhelm Bittner and Felix Steiner, the troops began taking on a decidedly more martial bearing—even when not parading.

After the LAH spearheaded the reoccupation of the Saarland for Hitler in 1935, the unit was given—alone among all other SS formations—the privilege of wearing white belts, crossbelts and ammunition pouches, as part of a uniform designed personally by their commander Dietrich.

By 1938, anti-Hitler conspirators in the regular army had to take Dietrich's guard force into account in their planning for a coup. But after Hitler triumphed at München, getting all he demanded without war, the conspirators remained quiet, and the LAH troops were again among the first German soldiers into the new territories. (Earlier, they had accompanied Hitler into Vienna at the time of the *Anschluss*.)

As the notoriety of the LAH grew, so did its independence from the rest of the SS organization. In March 1938, a sullen and bristling Himmler wrote to Dietrich complaining:

> Your officers are so gracious as to honor me, personally, but otherwise the Leibstandarte SS Adolf Hitler is an undertaking for itself which does what it wants and which doesn't need to trouble itself about superior orders, and which thinks about the SS leadership only when some debt or other, which one of its gentlemen has incurred, has to be paid, or when someone who has fallen in the mud has to be pulled out of the mess. Please do not forget that what you do as first commander of the Leibstandarte SS Adolf Hitler will naturally be taken as right by the next 20 commanders. I do not believe that you have adequately considered that this would be the beginning of the end of the SS in future years.

But Dietrich continued to mold the LAH to his own desires, with Hitler's backing. After its May 1939 field maneuvers impressed Hitler, he added artillery to the unit's infantry components.

When the war began and the LAH took part in the invasion of Poland, it suffered its first casualties: seven killed and 20 wounded. Hitler, of course, followed that campaign closely, and marked his Reich Chancellery battle maps with the name "Sepp" whenever the LAH moved forward. From that point on, the *Führer* always gave "his" unit the toughest assignments, and also those most likely to render it the chance to acquire glory, as well as add lustre to Hitler's own name.

The LAH's next combat deployment came in Holland, in May 1940; after which the unit pushed on into France, helping to corner the BEF at Dunkirk, where they took 750 prisoners. Next, the LAH struck across the Marne River, soon thereafter ending its 1940 combat operations engaging units of the French Alpine Army near the Italian border. The LAH's losses in the west were 111 killed and 390 wounded.

Immediately after that greatest-of-all Nazi victories, Dietrich was awarded the Knight's Cross of the Iron Cross, while Hitler declared to the unit: "It will be an honor for you, who bear my name, to lead every German attack."

Though the LAH trained for Operation Sealion, the projected cross-Channel invasion of England, its men were spared either a watery grave or a triumphal march down London's avenues when

The original standard of the LAH from 1933-40, seen here in a parade in Berlin in about 1935. (Heinrich Hoffmann Albums in the U.S. National Archives)

Hitler scrubbed that mission altogether. At Metz on 12 August 1940, Himmler brought the news the unit was to not only receive Hitler's personal standard to henceforth carry into battle, but that it would do so in the future as an expanded, "strong brigade." Early the next spring, the LAH was again expanded, this time to full divisional status.

From Metz, the LAH was transferred to Axis Bulgaria to prepare for the coming invasion of the Soviet Union. When Hitler decided he first had to secure his invading armies' deep right flank by securing the Balkans, the LAH again led the way, taking over 600 Yugoslav POWs during the fight, while losing only two of its men killed and

*Standard presented by Adolf Hitler to the LAH for
its exemplary combat record in Poland in 1939 and
the West in 1940. (National Capital Historic Sales)*

another five wounded. The LAH also performed well during the
conquest of Greece, though the fighting there was fiercer.

The invasion of the Soviet Union began a new kind of war for the
LAH, a bitter political struggle between the "asphalt soldiers" of
Hitler and the Red Army soldiers ruled by Josef Stalin. Far from being
the "subhumans" portrayed in Nazi propaganda, the Soviets instead
proved to be formidable fighters.

In the first 19 days of fighting in the Soviet Union, the LAH lost

100 vehicles, but nevertheless helped crack the Stalin Line and take the town of Zhitomir. After the Uman operation, the unit was credited with taking 2,200 prisoners and destroying 64 enemy tanks. Having crossed the Dniepr River in October, the LAH took part in another pincer operation that trapped seven Red Army divisions.

Despite those successes, the Germans were already beginning to be awed by the vast size of the land they had come to conquer. One LAH soldier wrote home from somewhere on the endless Steppe: "This is true desert country. Movement is visible for miles. Clouds of smoking, red-brown dust hang over our moving columns and pinpoint our exact positions....The only signs of life are the dead tree trunks of telegraph poles. Without them, it would be difficult to orient oneself."

It was during this period the Soviets claimed, after the war, that Dietrich ordered the execution of 4,000 prisoners in retaliation for the discovery of two lost SS companies. Their 103 officers and men had been hanged in an orchard. (Whether Dietrich personally ordered the reprisal killings has been debated in several biographies and SS histories published in the years since.)

In October, Dietrich's men found themselves using their artillery against Soviet gunboats along the Black Sea coast, then advancing to capture the port of Mauriopol, where they sank one ship and captured others. Next they took Taganrog, but the November rains and mud brought the general advance to a halt. Winter was looming; on 13 November a sharp drop in temperature neutralized the anti-freeze in the LAH's vehicles, but it also re-solidified the roads.

For the first time, morale in the LAH began to slacken. The Soviet state seemed uncaring as to the number of soldiers and the amount of real estate it lost to the Germans. There were ever more Soviets to fight, and they fought ever harder.

The LAH managed to occupy Rostov on the 22nd, but proved unable to hold it. Army Group South's withdrawal on the 28th came as a rude shock to Hitler, since it was the first strategic German pull back of the war. Field Marshal von Rundstedt was relieved, in favor of a more politically correct (in Nazi terms) commander, Field Marshal Walther von Reichenau.

Such a fate, however, did not befall Sepp Dietrich. On 13 December he was awarded the Oak Leaves to his Knight's Cross; an article in the official SS newspaper, *The Black Corps*, lionized him, and Hermann Göring called him "The pillar of the Eastern Front."

The *1st SS Panzer Division*
at its organizational peak,
1942–43

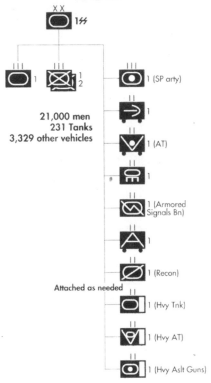

21,000 men
231 Tanks
3,329 other vehicles

1 (SP arty)

1 (AT)

1 (Armored Signals Bn)

1 (Recon)

Attached as needed

1 (Hvy Tnk)

1 (Hvy AT)

1 (Hvy Aslt Guns)

All this praise from high ranking Nazis led many in the regular army to believe Dietrich had a hand in the sackings that took place among the ranks of the *Wehrmacht*'s senior officers at that time. Actually, records show that at least in Rundstedt's case, Dietrich attempted to defend the old commander to Hitler. Meanwhile, party circles spread rumors Rostov had been lost only because the army had left the LAH in the lurch there.

At any event, while Dietrich was being feted in Berlin (and nursed frostbitten toes), his men went into winter quarters outside Taganrog, on the Sea of Azov coast. During this period, the LAH was reinforced with more tanks and the transfer from Berlin of a fifth infantry battalion Hitler had previously held back to fulfill the LAH's original guard role.

Early in July 1942, Hitler's fear the Western Allies would attempt an invasion along the Channel coast led him to transfer his praetorians back to France. On 29 July the division marched through the French capital in a triumphal parade down the Champs Elysees. Rundstedt was there to take the honor as the new Commander-in-Chief West, having been reinstated to command by Hitler, at least in part because of Dietrich's testimony on his behalf. With the repulse of the Allied raid at Dieppe on 19 August, the specter of a second front, for that year at least, receded.

Dietrich turned 50 on 28 May. With his new 22-year-old bride, he moved into a sumptuous Berlin home presented to him by Hitler.

During this second tour in France, the LAH took part in the occupation of Vichy France, entering Toulon on 26 November. A less properly military accomplishment is revealed in the division's medical records for this period, which indicate 7,000 of Dietrich's men contracted venereal diseases while in France. This number was bad enough to draw an angry letter of reprimand from Himmler, but it doesn't seem to have had any effect.

In December 1942, the LAH was sent back to the Soviet Union again, this time as part (with the *Das Reich* and *Totenkopf SS Divisons*) of the newly formed *SS Panzerkorps*. The new corps' first mission was to recapture Kharkhov, which they did handily in March 1943, not knowing that drive would mark the last clearcut German victory in the east. Some 11,000 SS men died in those early 1943 winter battles—a far greater total than those of the early war's casualty lists.

For his part in the Kharkhov victory, Dietrich was again decorated, this time with the Swords to his Oak Leaves of the Knight's Cross, and once more the Nazi propagandists waxed lyrical. Göbbels lauded him as "the Nazi Blücher" (after the famous Prussian marshal of the Napoleonic Wars). But for the first time there were desertions from the LAH (which now numbered some 21,000 men on its roster).

Mussolini's overthrow curtailed the division's participation in the abortive German Kursk offensive in July 1943. Shortly after the LAH was moved to Italy, the Soviets again took Kharkhov, this time for good.

The Soviets convened a warcrimes tribunal in liberated Kharkhov on 15 December 1943. There they charged some captured SS men (and Dietrich *in absentia*) with the earlier massacre of Soviet wounded in a hospital that had been overrun. Six months later, the British also listed Dietrich as a war criminal for the first time, indicting him as "the most prominent figure" of the military SS.

Surprisingly, Dietrich never stood trial at Nuremburg, as he very well might have, nor did the Western Allies hand him over to the Soviets, as they did several lesser figures.

While it certainly appears the Soviet charges against Dietrich more than met the inter-Allied war crime standards of the time, it should be remembered conditions on the Eastern Front were brutal on both sides. Millions of Soviets and hundreds of thousands of Germans simply disappeared without a trace. One prominent example, the Katyn Forest massacre of Polish officers captured in 1939, caused controversy for five decades before Moscow admitted they, and not the SS, had done that dirty deed.

This ambiguity and mutual guilt may be one answer to the mystery of why the Western Allies never handed Dietrich (or any other military SS member, for that matter) over to the Reds. Another factor may have been the military and political climate that prevailed in divided and occupied Germany in 1945, as the Cold War was beginning. At least one top American general—George S. Patton—wanted to provoke a war with the Soviets and use the captured SS to help fight it. That same rationale led the OSS/CIA to employ other Nazis, such as Reinhard Gehlen and Klaus Barbie, after the war's end.

At any rate, when the LAH was moved to Italy in mid-summer 1943, Dietrich, after ten years at its head and increasingly disenchanted with the course of the war in the east, turned over command to Theodor Wisch (another original SS member). During the changeover, Dietrich became somewhat too vocal with his unease, thus earning himself another letter of reprimand from Himmler: "I know better than anyone what you think about the war in Russia...[Yet] it is clear to us that the Russians can and will be beaten in the foreseeable future."

From July through October 1943, the LAH was used to occupy various parts of northern Italy, disarm units of the formerly allied Italian Fascist armed forces, and guard the Brenner Pass through the Alps.

Meanwhile, though he had relinquished command of the division, Dietrich retained that of the *SS Panzer Corps* (now termed *1st SS Panzer Corps*). He therefore spent time planning for the corps' role in the hard fighting sure to result when the Allies finally landed in France—an event everyone knew could no longer be far off.

On 22 October that planning was interrupted when the LAH was again shunted eastward to help shore up what was becoming a crumbling front in Russia. Dietrich was ordered to resume his divi-

April, 1943—Dietrich with his LAH SS Division staff pose for a formal picture on the Russian Front. Dietrich stands at center with clasped hands, with Kurt Meyer on his right. Dietrich's successor as commander of the Division, Theodor Wisch, is second from left in the second row, while his Chief of Staff, Rudolf Lehmann (later a chronicler of the Waffen SS in several postwar books) is just behind Dietrich's left shoulder. (U.S. National Archives)

sional command. A benchmark of decline was reached for the LAH during this tour in the east when, on 20 November 1943, its units for the first time failed to reach their ordered combat goal.

In the spring of 1944, as the thawing mud once more slowed the tempo in the east, Dietrich was again moved west, without his division, to resume counter-invasion planning. This time Dietrich found himself under the command of Field Marshal Erwin Rommel, a man he had last encountered during the Polish Campaign in 1939. Then Rommel had merely been the commander of Hitler's guard battalion; now he was the commander of an army group. (After the war, Dietrich showed himself indisposed toward Rommel, declaring to Canadian army interrogators: "What did he [Rommel] know of war...? All he could do was stand on a tank, baton in hand, and shout 'I am the King of Africa!'")

Like both Rommel and Hitler, Dietrich was surprised at the location of the Allied landings when they finally came—Normandy. Indeed, on 6 June 1944, Dietrich was in Brussels, attending to the refitting of the LAH, which had once again been brought west, this time to serve as the core of the mechanized reserve.

As Rommel had predicted, the overwhelming Allied air superiority effectively prevented German armored reserves from moving up quickly to the invasion front. Because of continued uncertainty on Hitler's part as to the genuineness of the Allied effort, the LAH itself was only ordered into action on 13 June, a full week after the landings.

On 17 July, Rommel and Dietrich met and he allegedly agreed (this is still controversial today) to the Field Marshal's opening of secret negotiations with the Western Allies if the straining front once cracked open. Later that same day, however, Rommel's car was strafed by an Allied fighter, and his severe wounds required his hospitalization. Three days after that, the generals' bomb plot against Hitler failed, and Rommel was eventually implicated, along with dozens of others. Dietrich, however, was not among the accused, and his exact role in the affair remains murky.

On 1 August, in fact, Hitler awarded Dietrich the Diamonds to his Swords of the Knight's Cross. At the ceremony, when Dietrich tried to discuss the desperate situation in Normandy, Hitler terminated the conversation by forbidding any mention of the topic. From that point on, Dietrich appears to have become more and more alienated from the war, referring to Hitler privately as a "madman" who had irretrievably lost the war for Germany.

After the success of the Americans' Operation Cobra, Dietrich and his command, along with the rest of the German forces in France, began a hectic retreat to the east and across the Seine River. On 11 September, Hitler relieved Dietrich of command, which immediately caused rumors to fly through the armed forces the SS man had been implicated in the plot. As it turned out, however, the "sacking" was really only a transfer to a new command; the just-forming *6th SS Panzer Army*.

Like the German armed forces in general, the LAH saw the quality of its replacements deteriorate as the war dragged on. Particularly during the last year of the war, the once all-volunteer, all-Aryan division began accepting ethnic Germans from outside Germany proper, and some men in their forties and fifties.

On the eve of the final battles of the war, the Belgian fascist and SS veteran of the war in Russia, Leon Degrelle, wrote of Dietrich: "[With] his legs wide apart, his face as red as a turnip, Sepp expatiated at length on the strength of the Anglo-American air force and on the ravages of the strafing planes, but he wasn't especially worried. He gave everyone great thumps on the back, drank cognac with every breath, and went back to his room at five o'clock in the morning vigorously supported by four giants of the guard."

That was Dietrich's state when the *Führer* selected him to spearhead the German counterattack in the Ardennes, what would be the greatest single battle for the U.S. Army in World War II. Indeed, his command became the very centerpiece in the attack Hitler hoped would again turn the tide of war in Germany's favor.

Dietrich himself had little confidence in Hitler's final grand design, as he told a Canadian interrogator after the war:

> I had merely to cross a river, capture Brussels and take the port of Antwerp, and all this in the worst months of the year...through countryside where snow was waist deep and there wasn't room to deploy four tanks abreast, let alone six armored divisions, with divisions that had just been reformed and contained chiefly raw, untried recruits, when it didn't get light until eight in the morning and was dark again at four in the afternoon, and at Christmas time!

Despite his misgivings, it was to Dietrich and the SS that Hitler gave this last chance for victory. The *Führer*, by now almost completely alienated from his regular army commanders, wanted to make certain any victories achieved would be perceived by the German people as won by the SS, the Party, and himself. Of course, there was to be no German victory, and the offensive began to founder in places as early as the third day of the drive.

But it was not the eventual loss of the battle that mattered most to Dietrich. Rather, it was the massacre of American POWs that took place during it that would dog him for the rest of his days. A total of 155 surrendered U.S. soldiers were machine-gunned at Bullingen and Malmedy by SS Col. Joachim Peiper's spearhead unit—an offense for which Dietrich and 73 other LAH men were brought to trial in occupied Dachau after the war.

Dietrich's foreknowledge of those events is still the subject of debate in military history circles. When asked what to do with the prisoners, he is said to have replied, "Prisoners? You know what to do with them!" Which, of course, is a statement that can be interpreted several ways. It is probable that Dietrich was deliberately vague, wanting on the one hand to prosecute the desperate offensive as ruthlessly as possible, while also knowing in the back of his mind the war was lost no matter how far he got in the Ardennes, and that he might afterward be tried and hanged as a war criminal.

As it turned out, Peiper and 43 other members of his Ardennes battlegroup were at first sentenced to death for their crimes; Dietrich and 22 more were condemned to life terms, and another 18 SS men received 10, 15, or 20 year sentences. The initial U.S. Army prosecution was poorly carried out, though, using such tactics as fake execution threats, false witnesses, and mock trials to gain some confessions. That set off a flurry of reinvestigations, which eventually got caught up in the issue of the Cold War, involved the notorious Senator Joseph McCarthy, and even reached to the U.S. Supreme Court at one point.

In the end, no one was executed for the crimes at Malmedy; Dietrich was paroled in 1955, and Peiper and all the others convicted walked out of jail within a year after that. (Peiper was eventually killed in a fire bombing of his Alsace home in 1976, allegedly carried out by some vengeful French radicals.)

Following the failed offensive, despite criticism of his command performance, Dietrich still had friends in high places in Berlin, such as Hitler's powerful personal secretary Martin Bormann, who continued to refer to the SS general as "dear old Sepp," and "our greatest asset in the west."

In January 1945, Dietrich and his men were given their last assignment. They were transferred back to the Eastern Front, this time to Hungary, near Lake Balaton. They were to drive on Budapest and link up with the surrounded German garrison still resisting there. But that offensive, too, turned out to be a failure. In a rage, Hitler shouted, "If we lose the war, it will be Dietrich's fault!" He also demanded the men of the LAH return their uniform cuff bands bearing his name, and ordered Himmler to go to the front and collect them personally (an order the SS chief silently declined.)

When the staff of the LAH heard of the episode they threw their decorations into a chamber pot and had it, along with a severed, uniformed arm bearing a cuff band, sent to Hitler in Berlin. (There is no record of it actually reaching its addressee). As for Dietrich, he only told his staff: "This is the thanks [we get] for everything."

After Budapest fell, Vienna soon followed. Hitler was dead on 30

April, and the war ended on 8 May. Dietrich and his wife surrendered to Master Sgt. Herbert Kraus, of the U.S. Army's 36th Infantry Division. That NCO remarked that Dietrich seemed "not anything like an army commander, but more like a village grocer." It was an anti-climactic end to so controversial a military career. The LAH managed at the last minute to disengage from the Soviets and surrender to the Americans—another anti-climax.

Dietrich spent the remaining 21 years of his life as an apologist for the military SS, and those veterans in turn revered him as "their commander" until his death in 1966.

Today, virtually every study of elite military forces and shock troops includes the military SS in general and LAH in particular. Despite the horror—perhaps because of it—military historians' fascination with the *Leibstandarte Adolf Hitler* likely will never fade.

Chapter XVI

Proud Monster
The Barbarossa Campaign Considered
by Ty Bomba

A German veteran of the Barbarossa campaign once told me the three factors he believed brought about his nation's defeat in the USSR: 1) the Soviet Union was too big to be campaigned across in one year; 2) the winter climate there was too harsh to allow for continued offensive operations; and 3) the Red Army was too huge to be destroyed before that winter came.

As soon as he'd finished with his explanation, I realized I'd been given the kind of succinct "I was there" look at the bottom line truth about something so big it continues to elude scholars who spend whole careers on it. So I will warn you here, the rest of this chapter does no better than explain some of the details and telling points that lay behind the veteran's summation.

The Soviet Union Was Too Big

This was probably the single greatest factor contributing to the German failure. In all their campaigning prior to Barbarossa, the Germans had taken on opponents whose countries were of a size small enough to allow their geographic vitals to be gobbled in one giant clap-shut of the armored pincers' jaws. Poland, the low countries, France and the Balkans were each geographic areas small enough to be taken by the invaders in one mechanized lunge. That is, after the Germans' panzers broke into those places, and after their mechanized spearheads met, they had always managed to cut off the defenders' heartlands from the rest of their territories.

The western and central Europeans had literally no room in which to get a breathing space, no time to learn how to defeat a Blitzkrieg

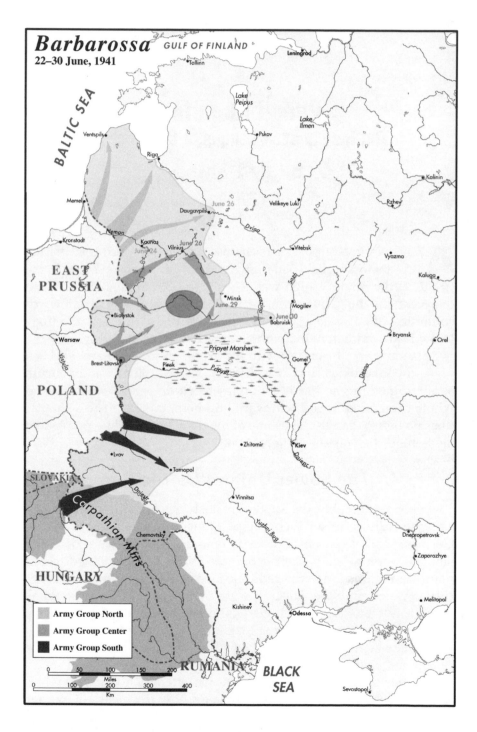

Barbarossa
22–30 June, 1941

GULF OF FINLAND

BALTIC SEA

EAST PRUSSIA

POLAND

SLOVAKIA

HUNGARY

Carpathian Mtns

Pripyet Marshes

RUMANIA

BLACK SEA

Leningrod
Tallinn
Lake Peipus
Lake Ilmen
Pskov
Ventspils
Riga
Kalinin
Memel
Velikeye Luki
Rzhev
Daugavpils
June 26
Dvina
Neman
Kronstadt
Kaunas
June 26
Vilnius
June 24
Vitebsk
Vyazma
Kaluga
Minsk
June 29
Mogilev
June 30
Bobruisk
Bialystok
Bryansk
Orel
Warsaw
Brest-Litovsk
Pinsk
Pripyet
Gomel
Bug
Zhitomir
Kiev
Lvov
Tarnopol
Dniestr
Vinnitsa
Chernovtsky
Dnepropetrovsk
Zaporazhye
Yuzhni Bug
Kishinev
Odessa
Melitopol
Sevastopol

Army Group North
Army Group Center
Army Group South

0   50   100   150   200
Miles
0   100   200   300   400
Km

before it was already over. Likewise, working in theaters of those limited sizes, the panzers were able to complete their job before attrition—both human and mechanical—got to be too debilitating a problem.

That phase of the war came to an end for the Germans as soon as the Barbarossa project was put on the drawing boards. The area of the European portion of the Soviet Union alone was greater than the sum total of all acreage previously conquered by the Nazis. The changed perspective, and the Germans' perplexity over it, is made apparent by examining the various plans Hitler's staffs came up with after he set them to work.

Gen. Erich Marcks' plan called for the reconcentration of the central and southern army groups, once the operational barrier of the Pripyet Marshes had been bypassed, for a grand drive on Moscow. Walter Warlimont's Operations Department of the Armed Forces High Command (OKW) prepared another plan (the "Lossberg Study"), which took cognizance of the potential Soviet threat to the Reich's vital oil resources in Romania. That document stipulated the southern army group be strong enough to ensure its ability to initiate and complete large pincer operations in the western Ukraine, before it too joined the other groups for the climax around Moscow. Gen. Franz Halder, at the Army High Command (OKH), first wanted a huge, 1914 Schlieffen-style "wheel" across northern Russia to the Black Sea. But when confronted with the sheer logistical impossibility of that he changed his mind, and called instead for a direct, concentrated push straight through Belorussia to Moscow, with secondary and tertiary efforts to the north and south, primarily for flank protection.

Hitler himself came up with a plan calling for strong drives along the Baltic coast to Leningrad and through the Ukraine to Kiev and the Crimea. With the flanks thus secured, the best way to finally dispose of Moscow (and, one assumes, the final destiny of the entire USSR), could be decided at the time of execution.

The one thing all the plans agreed on was the necessity of carrying out the decisive battles of annihilation west of the Dvina and Dniepr River lines. From the German point of view that was vital because to the east of those rivers the geography opened, fan like, to such an extent that when the invaders spread out to overrun and occupy it they would have to sacrifice the concentration of force needed to maintain momentum in any further pitched battles. The Red Army would obligingly stand west of the rivers and be annihilated, the plans explained, because for it to retreat farther east would be to risk the loss of the vitally productive industrial and Russian-ethnic heartlands.

The exact pathways the advances took after crossing the Dvina and Dniepr lines were seen as less important than that their essential characteristic would be more like a pursuit and mop-up than serious combat. The Soviets' cohesion was already to have been smashed—what followed east of the two rivers was really hoped to be post-climactic, with its exact details variable and flexible even during execution, because there would be no more serious opposition.

The German planning process for Barbarossa shows how even the most professional organization can fall prey to wishful thinking when forced to carry out tasks beyond its means. The various studies and wargames held during Barbarossa's planning phase clearly showed geography and logistics would begin to work against the invaders once the Dvina/Dniepr line was crossed. But Hitler demanded a plan and a victory; therefore—obviously and inescapably—the basic assumption taken up had to be that the Soviets would fight where the Germans needed them to if the big win were to be gained.

Their organizational drift toward wishful thinking was compounded by the fact the Germans were forced to conduct their planning with incomplete data. Even today we're far from having all the documentation we'd like on the Soviet situation in 1941. That was, of course, even more true for the Germans then. Stalin's regime was the archetype of what political scientists call a "closed society" (even compared to the Nazis). The Germans had no real idea about the actual size of the Red Army, and the most recent detailed maps of Russia they had available were those made by the Kaiser's army during the First World War.

Thus the plan finally adopted was really an awkward compromise that tried to combine the best features of the preliminary outlines. The southern-most forces would at first stand on the defensive in Romania to ensure the safety of the oil fields there. *Army Group South*, springing from southern Poland, was strengthened enough to give it the ability to drive alone into the rear areas of any forces the Soviets might throw into such an oil offensive, yet it was not reinforced enough to become the primary driver of the whole invasion. (Also unknown to the Germans, the Soviet high command had recently wargamed an oil invasion scenario, and even the most zealous proponents among them for the offensive had to admit the results

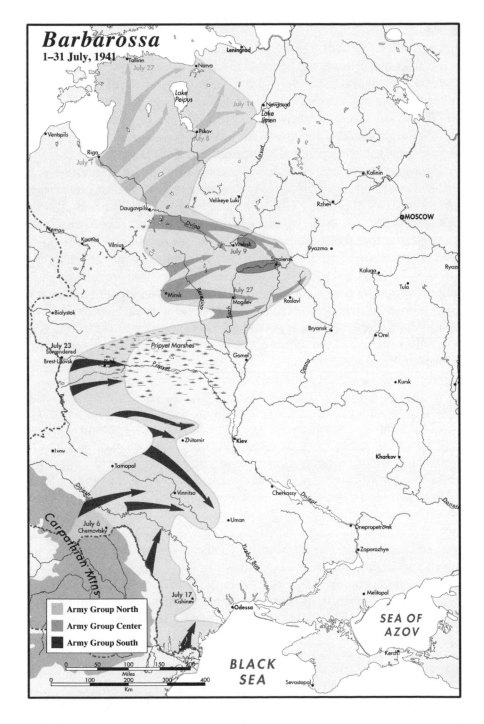

Barbarossa
1–31 July, 1941

Army Group North
Army Group Center
Army Group South

showed the inability of the Red Army to carry out such cross-border moves in 1941.)

Army Group North was given enough strength so it too—it was hoped—could operate without needing reinforcement from its neighbor in the center. That left *Army Group Center* with insufficient resources to smash directly to Moscow on its own. So allowance was made for its later reinforcement from the north and south once Smolensk was taken, provided circumstances indicated such a move would guarantee success in a quick blitz to the Kremlin.

If all that seems muddled, it was. The Germans knew there was a good chance they were finally over-reaching their armed forces' grasp. However, or so the countering rationalizations went, that had always seemed to be the case in the earlier campaigns. Those previous victories, though looking like acts of clockwork precision in retrospect, had actually been carried out in improvised, chaotic and unsure fashion. In the end, victory had gone to the bold—not to the over-cautious. In sum, as the invasion's launch date approached, the German high command was confident it had come up with enough of a plan; the rest was detail, really, and could be dealt with as it came up. The overall excellence of the *Wehrmacht* was to be depended on to generate a big win one more time.

The Winter Was Too Harsh

One of the often repeated misconceptions about this campaign goes that because the Germans planned and counted on the war in the east being a short one, they didn't take steps soon enough to begin the manufacture of needed winter uniforms and gear. Yet anyone who's spent a winter anywhere in Europe north of the Alps knows an army doesn't have to go to Russia to experience a need for seasonal equipment and clothing. That equipment and clothing in fact existed, and in the needed amounts, but they existed in the wrong places—at depots in Germany far from the front.

The transportation infrastructure east of the Soviet-German border was less developed than that west of it, and the destruction caused by the invasion did nothing to improve capacity. One official of the German Railway Authority noted gloomily in a report to Berlin in August that, no matter how often commanders made the point to combat troops about the desirability of capturing Soviet rolling stock intact, there seemed nothing the soldiers enjoyed more than shooting up trains.

At first the decrease in carrying capacity eastward could be made up by directly trucking (and hauling in horsedrawn wagons) the materiel from the depots to the front. The *Luftwaffe* could also be counted on to keep key spearhead units in supply via air drops. But as the distance from the border to the front increased beyond the 300-400 kilometer mark, the efficiency of those stopgaps rapidly fell.

The situation can be likened to an individual's blood flow on a cold winter day. In the abdomen, close to the heart itself, the blood-carrying arteries are many and thick; but the farther one goes toward the extremities, the scarcer and finer the transport arteries become. The result is the fingertips and toes get cold.

On a vastly larger scale, that was what was happening to the German army in the east by late October, as they got ready to carry out their final offensives around Leningrad, Moscow and Rostov. By then they were far enough from the Reich's logistical heart to be down to mere capillary carrying capacity. In terms of movable tonnages, the Germans were faced with the choice of shunting forward enough of all kinds of supply to sustain their forces for less demanding defensive operations, or bringing up enough ammunition and POL (petroleum, oil, lubricants) supplies, at the cost of everything else, to allow for continuation of the attack. The decision, made in the well heated rooms of high command headquarters, seemed obvious.

Even under such constraints, though, one of the radio-telephone conversations between Hitler and Gen. Heinz Guderian in late December is instructive in showing how a good army can make one kind of supply serve another purpose. Guderian was complaining to Hitler about having trouble stopping the Soviets' T-34-led breakthroughs. The *Führer* asked why he didn't use the 88mm Flak guns to destroy them as in previous encounters. The general explained the ground was now frozen so hard he needed to save his artillery rounds to blast holes for the infantry to sleep in at night. Experience had already shown if he didn't get his *Landser* below ground level they'd freeze to death.

The panzer men also proved masters of innovation during the winter crisis. They got by the necessity of painfully starting each tanks' cold engine from scratch by designing a "cold water exchanger," which pumped warmed coolant from one engine to another. They also devised track extenders, called "east chains," which in-

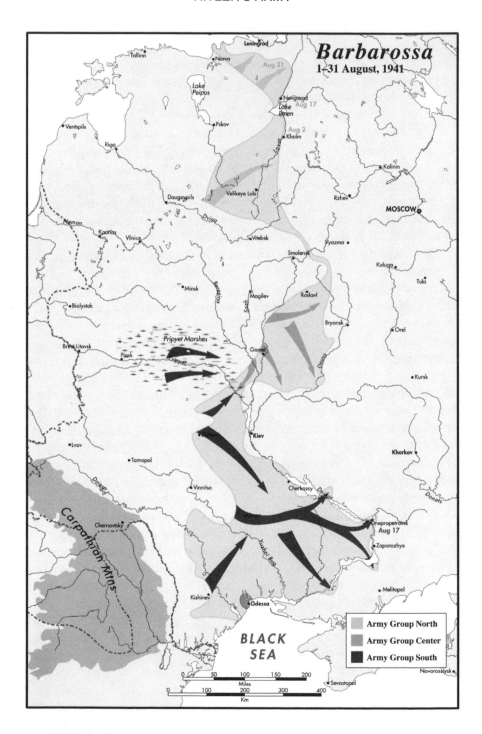

Barbarossa
1–31 August, 1941

Army Group North
Army Group Center
Army Group South

BLACK SEA

creased their narrow-treaded machines' mobility across snow and ice (though even the best east chains failed to bring the panzers up to the T-34's fabled cross-country mobility standards).

Taken on its own, then, the Russian climate was important, but probably not decisive, in bringing about the German failure.

The Red Army Was Too Huge

If one were to sum up Operation Barbarossa in one sentence, the best thing that could probably be said is it was what happened when the best army in the world attacked the biggest army in the world.

By the summer of 1941, the German army stood unrivaled as wizards of mechanized warfare. They were thoroughly practiced in the most advanced tactical doctrine in the world, and that, coupled with bold (if incomplete) strategic planning at the top, had honed those soldiers into a so far unstoppable instrument for the carrying out of their government's policies anywhere in Europe, from the Arctic to the Mediterranean, that tank treads and hobnail boots could reach.

Beyond the day-to-day motivation for fighting well so as not to let down his buddies (*Waffenbrudern*), the German soldiers were also steeped in—what seemed to them—the great historic justice of their cause. That is, English language sources often make the point Hitler used the unfairness of the Versailles Treaty as a propaganda standard around which he could rally his countrymen, obtaining their support for all kinds of aggression. That is true as far as it goes, but it does not really go far enough.

To the Germans of the post-World War I era, Versailles, loathsome as it was to them, was really no more than the tip of a great historic iceberg of injustices, indignities and horrors that the accident of geography had placed upon them. Located in the center of the continent in such a way that any European nations making war would virtually have to go through Germany to do it, the *Vaterland* had for over 500 years served as the cockpit of western civilization. That era—or so the founding of the Third Reich seemed to promise—was finally at an end, and the German soldiers were well aware and proud of their role in that ending. They knew the job of conquering the Soviet Union was to be a big one—indeed, the biggest one—but if they couldn't do it no one could.

In 1941, even the Soviet high command knew their forces were no real match for the Germans in any kind of even fight. In January, after a general staff wargame was held in Moscow pitting the German Army against the Red on the sand table, with the latter getting clobbered, a silence fell over the room. Then the chief of staff at the time, Gen. K. A. Mertskov, attempted to break the gloomy spell by claiming no wargame could reflect the true "qualitative superiorities" of the Soviet rifle divisions over the enemy. Stalin instantly shut him up by countering that such "bragging" was "the stuff for agitators, not realists."

Of course, the Soviets didn't have to fight on anything like even terms. They used the advantages given them by their country's size and climate, coupled with their numeric superiority, to first outlast and then repel the invaders. What they lacked in tactical sophistication they more than made up in firepower and grim tenacity. In essence, the Red Army—or at least that part of it the Germans knew to exist when they attacked—did stand and was destroyed west of the Dvina/Dniepr line. The trouble for the Germans lay in the fact that destruction amounted to only about a third of the actual Red Army.

The typical Red Army soldier also had his own sources of deep motivation. Though it seems hard to believe now, from the vantage point of a time when Communism has been repudiated in its national birthplace, in 1941 there were still many who believed the USSR was germinating the world's glorious socialist future within its borders. When revolutionary romanticism flagged, there was still old fashioned Russian patriotism and the tradition of stoic heroism to draw on. Most important of all, when even those things failed, there still remained the bald fact the Soviet armed forces and populace lacked any practical alternative to resistance, much as they might have liked to find one.

A few months into the invasion, German Field Marshal Gerd von Rundstedt, commander of *Army Group South*, remarked to Hitler that his intelligence staffers estimated about 2.5 million Ukrainians would come forward to bear arms for the Greater Reich if they were treated decently. The *Führer* curtly dismissed the idea by stating he had "not invaded the east to give rifles to the Slavs." He had, in fact, invaded it to kill them—if not all of them right away, at least enough (30 million by Göring's estimate) to make for rapid clearing of the place for German colonization.

At the time, the infamous "final solution" death camp system that

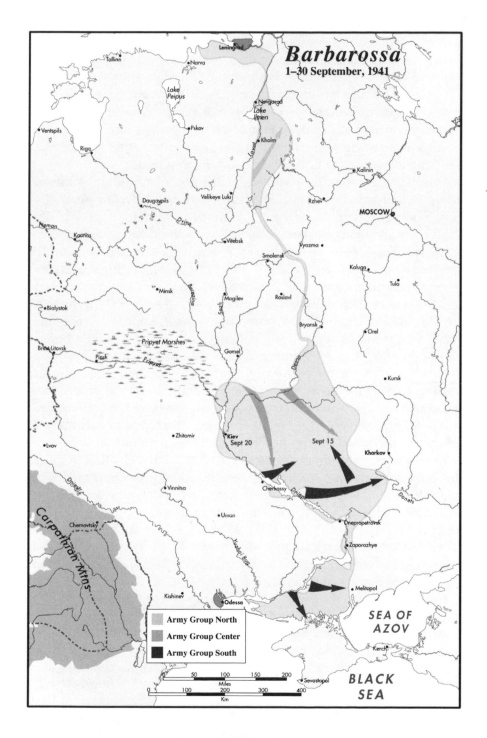

would blossom and expand after 1942 was not yet in place. But their earlier campaigns in central Europe and the Balkans had already shown the Nazis to be masters at improvisation when it came to race war, and they outdid themselves in the USSR. Four motorized "Special Action Groups" (*Einsatzgruppen*), each of about battalion size followed the combat troops into the east. Their assignment was to eliminate any and all "undesirables": Jews, Gypsies, Communists, the intelligentsia, along with anyone else who even remotely looked like they might pose some threat to the coming new order.

The Special Action Groups unleashed a frenzied ethnic and political slaughter behind the advancing front. Their zeal often inspired the local populations to join in with their own spirited pogroms. By winter, the Germans expanded the killing beyond racial, ethnic and political boundaries, setting in motion policies aimed at simply depopulating entire areas, such as intercepting all food shipments into selected occupied cities. The madness reached, and was maintained at, a level that eventually led one non-Jewish Ukrainian survivor of the war to calculate he'd had to commit some 40 capital offenses (as defined by the Germans: curfew violations, owning winter boots, harboring anti-German sentiments, etc., etc.) just to survive.

Soon even the most politically apathetic and unpatriotic Soviet soldiers had an excellent reason to go on fighting to the bitterest of ends: revenge. Revenge for massacred and starved family and destroyed homes; revenge for executed friends and raped sweethearts—revenge, finally, just for the hell of it, the satisfaction of it.

Even a cursory study of the idiotic, evil and self-defeating policies the Germans put into practice in the east leaves a modern reader in total disbelief. The Germans later came to call what happened to them and their country in 1945 the *Niederschlagen*—literally, the "beating down." Taken in perspective, though, the fact there are any Germans at all left alive today can probably serve as an indicator that the Russians are at heart a basically compassionate people. (Cynics would say they are merely pragmatic.)

Of all the factors the Germans had the power to manipulate during the invasion, it was undoubtedly their Nazi racism that doomed them. They gave their eastern opponents no real alternative to death or, at best, slavery. Of course, the amazing fact some quarter-million "easterners" still volunteered to fight for the Germans between 1941 and 1945 bears stark testimony to the brutality and bankruptcy of Stalinism too.

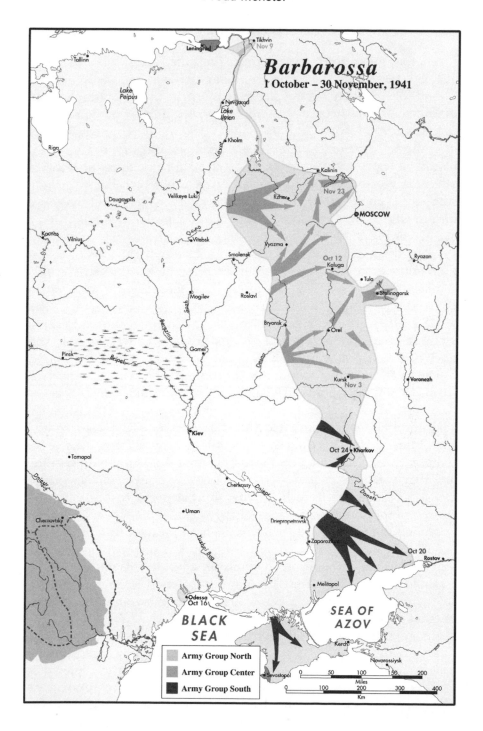

Barbarossa
1 October – 30 November, 1941

Army Group North
Army Group Center
Army Group South

Stand Fast

Another misconception sometimes presented in the literature dealing with the end of the Barbarossa campaign has to do with Hitler's "stand fast" order to his troops that winter. The line of argument goes that the German dictator was indeed correct to insist on a no-retreat policy before Moscow once the Soviets began their counteroffensive in earnest. To have given in to the generals and ordered a retreat would have proven disastrous, this argument runs, since the hitherto offensively oriented *Wehrmacht* would have been unable to make a smooth psychological switch to retreat mode. The idea is that once told to withdraw, the German army would simply have fallen apart and never been able to reform.

Not only does that line of reasoning lack any logic of its own, but numerous examples belie it from later in the war when German armies—and ones far more wasted than those before Moscow in 1941—did survive strategic retreats.

Had Hitler ordered a general retreat late in 1941, and had even a worst case collapse of the front resulted from it, his Reich would still have had its overall survivability enhanced by the experience. As the Germans fell back westward, the same logistical constraints that had tripped them up would have begun operating against the Soviets.

Again, taking performances from later in the war as a measure, the very best line the Soviets could have expected to reach by spring was Riga-Minsk-Odessa. When 1942's summer campaigning season arrived with the chastened Germans hunkered down on that line—the line they were not beaten back to historically until mid-1944—there could not have been much serious thought given to resuming the strategic offensive. Hitler—just as he shut down the nascent Sea Lion operation when the *Luftwaffe* disappointed him over Britain—would probably have looked for an out. After such a reversal he could no longer have kidded himself an offensive solution was even remotely possible against the USSR. He might have tried for a compromise treaty, or at least set up a rationalized and reserve-backed eastern defense policy.

Imagine, then, the task before the Western Allies when all those hundreds of thousands of troops, and thousands of tanks, lost in the east from 1942 through 1944 were instead available for the defense of Fortress Europe, or even for Mediterranean expeditions. As late as November 1943, Gen. Eisenhower feared the Germans might go over to such a strategy in the east and thereby create for themselves an unbeatable reserve.

Conclusions

As explained early in this article, the old German veteran had gained through personal experience a succinct understanding of the broad historical factors at work in the USSR during the campaign of 1941. But it was probably British Field Marshal Bernard Montgomery who capsulized the whole thing best when, at a press conference shortly after V-E Day, he was asked what new additions to the science of warfare had been generated by World War II. He answered there were at least two new axioms given certification: "One—never invade China; and two—never invade Russia."

Soviet Railways in 1941

For decades, perception of the big problem the Germans had with Soviet railroads when they invaded in 1941 was seen to have been converting their non-standard gauge (track width) to that of the central European norm. But that perception has been wrong, at least according to one recently declassified report. The document was written for the U.S. Army shortly after the war by Hans Klein, who served as the German army high command's "Technical Officer for Operational Railway Transportation" during 1941-42.

Since the gauge conversion required going from the wider Soviet track to the narrower German, Klein explains, that change posed what was really the simplest of engineering problems for the invaders to solve. Along stretches where the retreating Soviets hadn't had time to thoroughly destroy the rail beds (which was most of the time during the blitzkrieg Barbarossa campaign), all the Germans had to do was pull up the spikes, move the rails toward each other a bit, and spike them down again. No surveying, blueprints, or new construction was needed.

The real trouble was the Soviets built and ran wider (and longer and heavier) locomotives. Those locomotives, being so much bigger than their German counterparts, were therefore able to carry more fuel and water—and thus could go much farther between service stops. For example, the average distance between Soviet service installations on the Brest-Litovsk to Moscow line was 138 kilometers. When the *Wehrmacht* moved in, their railway troops had to build from scratch one major service installation between each pair the Soviets already had in place. Those stations had to include locomotive sheds, repair shops, slag pits, turntables, sidings, water towers, etc., and needed skilled labor and scarce heavy equipment to complete them. (In comparison, track gauge conversion could usually be accomplished employing only primitively equipped conscript labor.) Almost none of this had been planned for, Klein says, and the resultant confusion and delay was the real drag on German railway utilization in the east in 1941.

In a similar and also just recently declassified report, this one written by another German supply officer named Werner Bodenstein, we learn two more facts about the invaders' railroad supply system in 1941.

First, except for a few railroad engineering troops provided by the army, all the German railway personnel who went east in 1941—locomotive engineers, train crews, station managers, skilled workers, etc.—were civilian employees of the Reich Railroad Authority, and thus didn't come under military discipline. That meant they tended to work normal civilian hours and—incredible as it may seem—most took their authorized two week Christmas break in mid-December and went home for the holidays. So just as the German army was plunging into its greatest crisis to date—the first Soviet winter counteroffensive—most of the cadre of its rail supply system was home in Germany, no doubt hoisting a few in honor of the brave troops at the front.

Bodenstein offers another reason the high command found it so difficult to get food and winter clothing to the fighting troops that winter. At the big supply depots in Greater Germany, trains were put together with specific unit-destinations in mind. That is, if a supply train were being prepared for the *14th Panzer Corps*, the various cars would be loaded according to a certain formula for supplying a panzer corps: so much food, so much clothing, so much POL (petroleum, oil, lubricants), so much ammunition.

As each car was loaded and sealed, its lock had a color-coded tag placed on it, identifying its contents as belonging to one of those four major supply categories. The trouble occurred as the trains plowed their way toward the front. Each time they stopped for service along the route, the local troops (often with their command's connivance) would examine the tags and "liberate" some food, clothing and POL for themselves. Invariably, by the time a mixed-supply train reached the unloading stop for its destination combat unit, all that was left aboard was ammo. The rear area personnel had no need for that stuff, and were only too glad to see the frontliners had as much of it as they could use.

Two expedients were employed in an attempt to overcome this problem. First, a few of the most outrageous pilferers were hanged at easily seen places near the stations. That worked wonders to instill "National Socialist Ardor" among their cohorts. Second, though the mixed-train loading practices were continued, the packing authorities began labeling all cars as ammunition carriers. The ruse didn't always work, but it did result in a good many trains being shunted directly to the front without cargo loss.

Chapter XVII

Death & Destruction
1942-1944 on the Russian Front
by Ty Bomba

I t can in no way get worse [for Germany on the eastern front], only better. There can be no doubt we will have classical successes in the forthcoming operations . . .." That was how Adolf Hitler consigned the failure of his 1941 campaign in the Soviet Union to the past, and held forth the prospect of ultimate success in the new year to his ally and fellow dictator Benito Mussolini, early in the spring of 1942.

Not only Hitler, but virtually all of those in his command structure—or at least those in it not actually living day-to-day at the front—had convinced themselves in getting through the first Soviet strategic counteroffensive they had weathered the worst that could possibly be thrown at them. In April 1942 the army high command intelligence branch concluded in its summary report on the situation in the east: "The enemy can no longer withstand losses such as he took in the battles from Bialystok to Vyazma-Bryansk. He also cannot for a second time throw reserves into the scales the way he did in the winter of 1941/42."

Indeed, when Stalin took the premature decision to turn the Moscow counterattack into a strategic offensive all along the front, he needlessly added another 60 to 80 division equivalents to the tremendous wastage already suffered by the Red Army—almost 6.8 million soldiers killed or captured since the German invasion began— without getting much in return. Even as the futile spring fighting wore on, a report from the intelligence service of the People's Commissariat of Defense warned the "correlation of forces" between the two sides was again changing to the point where it would be "inexcusably shortsighted" not to expect a renewed German attack in the coming summer campaigning season.

That's not to say the Soviets were outnumbered—far from it. There were about 3.5 million German and Axis satellite troops in the USSR on 28 June 1942, the day the renewed Nazi drive kicked off. Of that number there were about 330,000 Romanians, 300,000 Finns, 70,000 Hungarians, 68,000 Italians, 28,000 Slovakians and 14,000 Spaniards, along with numbers of other ethnic groups and nationalities. That compares to a Soviet army of about 5.5 million at the front, with roughly another 1.5 million in uncommitted reserve formations.

The Soviets on that day fielded 6,000 tanks, the Germans only about 3,300. The Soviets had 2,600 combat aircraft, the Germans 2,770. The Soviets had 55,000 artillery pieces; the Germans had only a fraction of that number, maybe 8,000. Further, the Germans were lacking about 35,000 trucks and other motor vehicles called for in their tables of organization and equipment—motor transport wastage during Barbarossa had been about 75,000 vehicles. Even stripping all the trucks from the infantry and replacing them with horses didn't come anywhere near solving the mobility problem. Many more thousands of horses had also died than had been replaced during Barbarossa.

Of course, numbers alone seldom tell the whole of any story—and that's true in spades when considering the history of the eastern front. Col. Trevor N. Dupuy, who during the past couple decades became a central figure in the quantitative analysis approach to military history, estimated that during this period the combat effectiveness of each German asset, when compared to its Soviet counterpart, varied somewhere between 3.10 and 2.34 to 1. The 1942 Soviet high command's appreciation of the situation lacked Dupuy's decimal point precision, but they clearly understood qualitative factors were still tipping the scales against them.

Hitler never voiced any doubts. Shortly before New Year's Day, Gen. Friedrich Fromm, then chief of the German army's manpower and armament replacement apparatus, argued to the *Führer* that the Reich should forego all major offensive operations that year and use it as a time of large-scale rebuilding. That was nonsense, Hitler assured him; the plan for 1942 was to once and for all "clear the table" in the east.

Thus as the spring mud season ended and the last of the hurried German replacements and new equipment moved toward the front, the question being pondered was not "if," but "where?"

Economies of Scale

Stalin's Soviet Union contained within it four major industrial areas: the Moscow region, the Donets Basin, the Urals, and the Kuznets Basin in western Siberia. Operation Barbarossa had succeeded only in disrupting production in the first region, while also capturing some of the second. The other two areas were virtually unknown to the Germans and would remain even out of effective range of the *Luftwaffe*'s bombers for the whole war.

Still, in just getting as far as they had, the invaders succeeded in greatly disrupting many critical aspects of Soviet production. Comparing the first six months of 1941 with the first half of the following year shows electricity generation in the USSR fell by about 45 percent; coal production was off by 61 percent; oil pumping and refining went down by 32 percent; pig iron tonnages dropped 74 percent, and steel fell 64 percent.

But despite that (again comparing those two periods), tank production doubled to 11,200—four times the German 1942 first-half figure— including 3,000 state-of-the-art T-34s. Artillery manufacture rose by 43 percent, for a total of 53,000 pieces; mortar production tripled; ammunition went up five percent, while combat aircraft turn-out held steady and handguns, rifles and machineguns nudged up somewhat.

The secret behind the Reds' ability to keep turning out the weapons of war even as their basic industries were captured, destroyed or forced to shut down while relocating eastward, resided in two factors. First, though exact figures are not yet available, it appears the amount of pre-war stockpiling of strategic materials in the USSR was immense, well planned and efficiently carried out. Simply, the Soviet economy was able to draw down on huge stocks of supplies to keep going, even while the original resource areas were themselves lost to production.

Second, the Soviets were operating from an all-around larger economic base than the Germans. Stalin's confidence in the socialist discipline of the Russian masses gave him the freedom to devote large parts of that economy, in both the absolute and relative senses, to war production. For example, by 1942 metalworking made up almost 57 percent of Soviet industry, and virtually all of it was committed to winning the war. In contrast, only about 43 percent of the Reich's economy was taken up with metalworking, and (incredibly) only

about 30 percent of that much smaller figure was engaged in war production.

Even after the Stalingrad debacle, when Reich Propaganda Minister Josef Göbbels, speaking in Hitler's name, declared that battle to have been "the great tocsin of German destiny," demanding Germany go to a "total war" economy, little was actually accomplished. That same month (January 1943), a decree was issued ordering "all" non-war industries and businesses to be closed so their resources could be more productively used elsewhere. In reality, however, the closings came to include only such businesses as night clubs, luxury bars and restaurants, jewelry stores, custom clothing manufacture, and hobby supply shops. Hitler never had a faith in the German people corresponding to the kind Stalin had in the Russians—which has to be one of history's greatest ironies, considering the *Volk* stayed true to their leader through the most bitter of ends.

Selecting the Target

The debate in the German high command on just where exactly to strike to "clear the table" in the east had actually begun shortly after the massive encirclement of Red Army units around Kiev late the previous summer. Geographic reality dictated there were really only two choices: Moscow or the Donets/Caucasus. The army staff was quick and clear in its recommendation: "Moscow is the central point of all Russian life. It is also the western terminus of the land bridge between European and Asiatic Russia and has decisive operational import for Soviet offensive plans."

Hitler allowed himself (against his better judgment, he would later claim) to be swayed into making the Moscow decision then; but that operation's failure only served to confirm in him ever after the idea that the south was the truly critical area. In describing the debate that went on between Hitler and his generals about the target for 1942's offensive, English language writers tend to concentrate on what damage the *Führer* thought he would be doing to the Soviets by seizing the south. Actually, it's as likely he was driven in his thinking more by what he knew getting the Caucasus oil would do for Germany. A German naval intelligence report, of which Hitler was aware, reckoned the Soviets had at least a five month stock of oil on hand with which to maintain the tempo of their operations even after the Caucasus fell.

According to the economic plan with which Germany had begun the war in 1939, production of all petroleum/oil/lubricant (POL) supplies in 1941 fell 25 percent below what had been called for. That shortfall immediately had effects on Axis strategy. For example, the German invasion of the west in 1940 began when it did, rather than sooner, not because of the weather, but because sufficient hydrogenation plants had not yet come on line before that time to allow full mobility for the gas- and oil-guzzling panzers. Likewise, German and Italian fleet actions during 1939-42 were not as desultory and small as they were because Hitler had no understanding of the sea war's significance. He was no Adm. Mahan, but he knew what he'd had to pay for those ships, and he certainly wanted to get his money's worth from them operationally. The practical choice, though, came down to giving the army enough POL to roll or the fleets enough to sortie.

On the Soviet side, the mere acknowledgment that a renewed German effort had to be expected that summer was not enough to end the debate on where it would be launched. Both the State Defense Committee and the General Staff Intelligence Branch concluded the weight of the new onslaught would fall, at least at first, in the south toward the oil. But Stalin was convinced the primary target would be Moscow.

As early as 1918, during the Russian Civil War, Stalin had put forth a theory on the "Stability of the Rear." In it, he stated that as long as the "vital rear area" was held intact the Communist regime could survive any invasion. He defined the "vital rear" as the Russian ethnic heartland lying generally between and east of the line Moscow-Leningrad. Soviet dispositions to meet the 1942 attack clearly reflected the dictator's continued commitment to that view. On 1 July, with *Army Group South*'s tanks already beginning to advance, the southern half of the Soviet position (roughly on the line Orel-Rostov) had only about 30 percent of the available manpower.

Plans, Plans, Plans

Stalin was wrong in the obvious sense Moscow was not to be target number one for the Germans in 1942. He was right, though, in as much as that city surely was on the target list, and pretty high on it. That is, after Hitler codified his southern strategy in *Führer Directive No. 41* on 5 April, he did not rest easy. There followed a blizzard of other operations orders, which—had they all been launched and carried to a successful end—no doubt would've given the eastern "table" a good clearing that year. Those supplemental operations were as follows.

Operation Beggar's Staff was to have been an attack aimed at eliminating the Oranienbaum Bridgehead on the Baltic coast west of Leningrad. It was never carried out due to a lack of the necessary assault troops and air support.

Operation Blücher was a proposed five-division combat assault from the Crimean peninsula across the Kerch Straits into the Taman peninsula, originally planned for August. It was carried out on 2 September, in a much reduced fashion, after the quick collapse of Soviet resistance in front of the main German assault did away with its raison d'etre.

Operation Derfflinger was a July/August plan calling for *9th Army* to drive northwest from Rzhev to cut off the Soviet Toropets salient extending out of the western Valdai Hills. It was also canceled for lack of assault troops.

Operation Hobgoblin was a combined German navy and air force operation put into effect from July to November. It aimed at interdicting Soviet boat traffic and pipelines across Lake Ladoga to besieged Leningrad. German and Italian navy E-boats were transported to Finland, then taken overland to bases on the northwest lake shore. During its execution the operation suffered from lack of a unified command to run it and simply not enough hulls in the water to maintain a thorough blockade. The effort finally had to be scrubbed in late November, when the lake began to freeze.

Operation Kremlin was the plan for a renewed offensive against Moscow by *Army Group Center*. It was first put out only as a deception, but was then worked up to the point of actually distributing operations maps to the local commanders when the initial Soviet reactions to the Germans' southern drive seemed to presage a quick Red collapse. Kremlin was put off to await developments, and of course was never revived.

Operation Salmon Catch was a proposed German-Finnish project, planned for August-November, aimed at severing the Murmansk railroad where it ran along the White Sea coast. The ever skeptical Finnish high command, however, set the fall of Leningrad and the advance of *Army Group North* to the Svir River as preconditions for Salmon Catch's launch—hence the plan's still birth.

Operation Sturgeon Catch was the code name for Gen. Erich von Manstein's assault on and capture of the fortress city of Sevastopol, carried out from 7 June to 4 July. Manstein's toughest assignment to that time, it almost had to be called off half way through when it seemed casualties were mounting too fast. But a surprise German amphibious assault across the narrow bay north of the city succeeded in turning the Soviets' strongest forts on Sapun Heights, thus moving things forward again. Organized Soviet resistance ended on 30 June, but isolated pockets held out through the 4th.

Things got so tough at one point Manstein asked for the just-captured British commandant of the North African fortress of Tobruk to be paradropped into Sevastopol. Tobruk had earlier become such a pan-Allied propaganda symbol of resistance, he felt this kind of direct proof of its fall to the Germans might serve to weaken the Reds' resolve. The request was turned down, though, and *11th Army* had to go ahead and take Sevastopol the old fashioned way.

When it was finally over, Gen. von Manstein became Field Marshal von Manstein, about 90,000 Soviet POWs were taken, and the Germans had suffered close to 150,000 killed or wounded themselves.

Operation Northern Lights was to have seen Manstein and his proven fortress busters in *11th Army* capture Leningrad during September and October. The move was first preempted, then eventually canceled outright, by repeated Soviet attacks to break into the beleaguered city. Manstein was thus forced to turn his attention to the defense of the siege ring, which he did with his usual thoroughness, but taking too much time and suffering too many casualties in the process. By the time *11th Army* was set to go against the city proper again, the Soviets had jumped off with their own grand offensive down at Stalingrad, putting out the northern lights for good.

Operation Dovecoat was to have been another Manstein operation for October/November. He was to have overseen another attempt to destroy the Soviet Toropets salient, or at least the northwestern part of it. The attack had to be called off once every spare soldier was sent south to resist the Soviet counteroffensive around Stalingrad.

Operations Hurricane and Whirlwind were twin *4th* and *2nd Panzer Army* operations intended to pinch off the Sukhinichi salient south of Moscow in August. The *2nd Panzer Army* actually got a force of three panzer divisions together and jumped off with what was to have formed the southern pincer (Whirlwind) on 11 August. But Soviet fortifications, fanatic resistance and counterattacks held the gains to about 20 miles. (They had to make 70 to score a pinch off.) Hurricane, the projected northern arm, was never launched due to a lack of assault troops.

Vine and Winkelreid were twin operations aimed at widening— Vine in the north, Winkelreid on the south—German access to the Demyansk salient in October. Vine was canceled due to lack of sufficient air support and a belated realization widening the corridor into the salient from the north wouldn't provide a good all-weather road. Winkelreid (the name of a character from German mythology who specialized in rescuing trapped damsels) was carried out in early October and succeeded in broadening the two-mile-wide corridor to about 10 miles.

Operation Seydlitz was an attack carried out between 2 and 12 July aimed at stabilizing and shortening the western flank of the Rzhev salient. A classic pincer operation, it netted 37,000 Soviet prisoners, 220 destroyed Red tanks and 500 wrecked artillery pieces. On almost

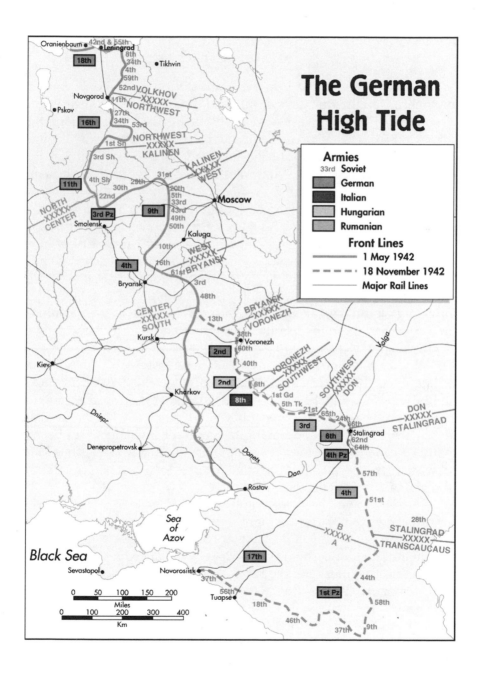

The German High Tide

Armies
33rd Soviet
German
Italian
Hungarian
Rumanian

Front Lines
1 May 1942
18 November 1942
Major Rail Lines

any other front in almost any other war those numbers would've been impressive enough to mean something—but not on the eastern front in 1942.

To Stalingrad

When the German attack in the south started in late June, gaining momentum in the first days of July, the onslaught was so irresistible even Stalin recognized it would have been futile to resist along the original front. The "vital rear" was not directly threatened by the loss of terrain down there, so for the first and only time in the war the Soviet high command not only authorized, it ordered, a strategic withdrawal.

This is where in guessing wrong about the Germans' priority target, Stalin inadvertently saved his forces from another summer fiasco. Had he earlier thought more about the south and reinforced it accordingly, given his previously demonstrated tendencies of command, it seems doubtful he'd have been as quick to let those units retreat eastward. His determination to make an all-out fight of it probably would have increased in direct proportion to the amount of troops he had there to meet the German attack.

In the open steppe country in the dry season it is doubtful even a Soviet force concentration like the one before Moscow, where it was strengthened by extensive fortifications and terrain far more favorable to the defense, could have held against the panzers. In such a scenario, Stalin would have, in fact, probably given Hitler just what the German dictator was looking and hoping for: giant encirclement and pocket battles close to the *Wehrmacht*'s supply bases. That was the same kind of warfare the Germans had enjoyed the previous year before crossing the Dvina and Dniepr River lines.

There is yet another interesting twist to this episode of the war. The retreat order from the Soviet high command was sent out on the night of 6 July, to go into effect the next morning. But as early as 3 July the commander of the German attack, Field Marshal Fedor von Bock, was explaining to Hitler over the radio that the Soviets "were gradually getting smart." That is, they were learning to evade encirclement by going over to a mobile defense and timely retreats. Further, the *6th Army*'s war diary noted a general Soviet retreat was already underway on the morning of 6 June. As early as 2 July a captured officer from the Soviet 21st Army's headquarters told those questioning him control of Red Army subordinate units in the south had already slipped from army headquarters.

It may well have been, then, that the Soviet high command's order did not indicate an instance of flexibility and strategic insight on Stalin's part. Strong evidence indicates the order may actually have been just an after-the-fact certification and cover up for what had already been initiated by the battlewise frontline troops on the spot.

At any rate, by late July, one month into the new German offensive, only 70,000 Soviet prisoners had been bagged by the attacking *Army Group South*. They had expected to do five to 10 times that amount of business by then. Hitler sacked von Bock and, in a futile attempt to find success in other ways and in new directions, committed the strategic error of splitting his forces in front of an unbeaten enemy.

The Iron Dream

From the point when Hitler split *Army Group South* into *Army Groups A* and *B*, sending the first off toward the Caucasus and the latter into Stalingrad, the strategic situation could really only have one outcome: eventual German defeat. With neither of the two new mini-army groups having sufficient strength to carry out its own task, while simultaneously diverging to pursue their assignments, it only remained to work out the details of the coming debacle.

The forces sent south to the mountains—Operation Edelweiss—first experienced a repeat of the just finished kick off battle; the Soviets ran before them. This was clearly not a Moscow-authorized retreat: at the end of July the Germans intercepted an army level radio message sent to the Kremlin. "We are going back," it stated tersely; reprisals against retreating troops no longer had any slowing effect.

For a time, then, *Army Group A*'s advance averaged 30 miles a day, but that was still not enough to be decisive. The distance from Rostov to Baku is about 750 miles, which is about the same distance between Warsaw and Moscow. The Red Army would need another two years to get back to Poland; the Germans were to have reached the shores of the southern Caspian Sea before winter came to the high mountain passes about 15 September. By the end of August, Field Marshal Wilhelm List's forces had reached the northern edge of the Caucasus, but more and more his army group was stalled by lack of supply and weakened by transfers of forces. Both the supplies and manpower were being sent north to the all-consuming city fight in Stalingrad.

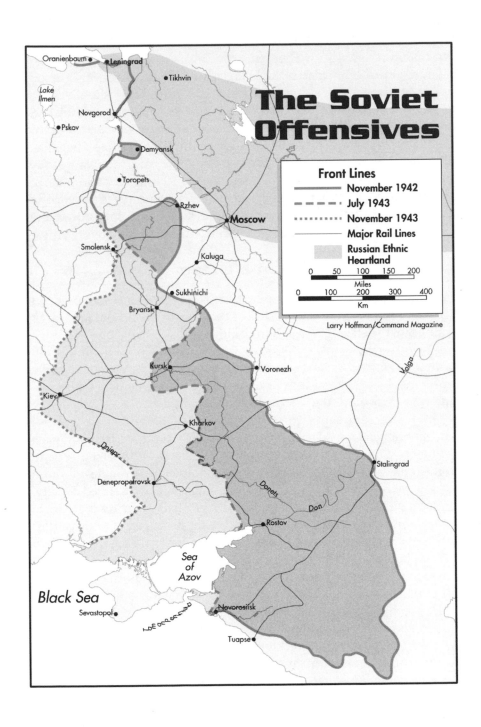

The Soviet Offensives

Front Lines
November 1942
July 1943
November 1943
Major Rail Lines
Russian Ethnic Heartland

Miles
0 50 100 150 200

Km
0 100 200 300 400

Larry Hoffman/Command Magazine

Oranienbaum
Leningrad
Tikhvin
Lake Ilmen
Novgorod
Pskov
Demyansk
Toropets
Rzhev
Moscow
Smolensk
Kaluga
Sukhinichi
Bryansk
Kursk
Voronezh
Kiev
Kharkov
Dniepr
Volga
Stalingrad
Denepropetrovsk
Donets
Don
Rostov
Sea of Azov
Black Sea
Sevastopol
Novorosiisk
Tuapse

Outside that city, the Germans had to forego a relatively easy chance to take the place when, during the first week of September, Marshal Georgi Zhukov launched three Soviet armies into a counter-attack against *6th Army's 14th Panzer Corps*. Those units had raced ahead of the marching infantry to reach the Volga north of Stalingrad.

The Soviet counterattacks forced Gen. Friedrich Paulus, *6th Army's* commander, to decide between rescuing the swamped panzers or taking the city proper while it was still only lightly defended. He chose the first course not out of any sense of duty to the desperate tankmen, but simply because the two fights were not really separate. The Soviets smashing into *14th Panzer Corps* had no intention of stopping once that force had been liquidated. To have failed to stabilize his northern flank first would really only have put *6th Army* into the situation it actually did find itself in later in the year—surrounded.

The rest of the Stalingrad story is too well known to require telling again, but a quick examination of some numbers highlights the depth and awfulness of the cauldron the Germans had thrown themselves into when they accepted battle in the city's streets. During the first days of their offensive, German casualties had averaged one or two men killed per division per day—about the same as they had been during Operation Barbarossa's happy time the summer before. Upon reaching the city, though, the tempo changed. Daily losses of over 250 in killed, wounded and missing *per regiment* became common.

By 6 October, *6th Army's* war diary noted the average battalion strength (about 850 authorized) of the assault formations were down to about 75 men, NCOs and officers combined. Two weeks later the army had lost a total of over 40,000 men. As one war diary entry dryly concluded: "The occupation of the entire city is not to be accomplished in such a fashion."

Envelopments, Cleaving Blows and Strategy's End

Hitler's determination to push the city fight to a successful end forced him to put all available assault formations into Stalingrad. That left nothing more than under-equipped and poorly motivated Romanians, Italians and Hungarians to hold the flanks. When the Soviets smashed through those weak sectors and pocketed *6th Army* that winter, they carried off one of war's most difficult maneuvers, the double envelopment.

The double envelopment is difficult to perform not only because it requires near perfect timing between the two pincer arms but, as Zhukov himself noted after the war, the defeat of an entire double pincers operation actually requires only the defeat of one of its arms. That the Soviets were so successful at Stalingrad was due in no small part to Hitler's nearly complete cooperation with and adherence to their script by keeping his trapped army sitting passively, awaiting a rescue from the outside that never came.

The Soviets for a brief time fell in love with the maneuver, attempting no less than 10 more envelopments before the return of the spring mud forced a halt. True, some of those were not full *double* envelopments, since they attempted to substitute geography (that is, a handy coastline) for the second arm. Still, of them all only two were successful (against the Hungarians and their immediate German neighbors); the rest ended in high Soviet losses and complete or near complete failures.

The reason for the Soviet reversal of fortune was that von Manstein, temporarily given a free hand by his rightfully abashed Führer, gave maneuver the same precedence in the German defense it had previously only held in the offensive *blitzkriegs*. Being free to concentrate strength against weakness again created a situation where the German army could once more perform as it had been trained.

By the next summer, after defeating Hitler's desperate Kursk offensive, Stalin announced to his staff as they prepared to put their own new attack plans into operation, he'd "had enough" of envelopments. Instead, the far simpler doctrine of the "cleaving blow" was usually substituted for pincer operations. Plainly put, "cleaving blow" is really only a high flown name for a head on, combined arms, smash-in attack aimed at nothing more complicated than piercing the enemy line, followed by as deep an exploitation as supply and reinforcements permitted.

Von Manstein's mobile defense could have parried that Soviet approach, first by sidestepping the blow itself, then counterattacking its exposed flanks or base. By then, though, Hitler was firmly back in the command saddle, and again mandated the rigid kind of defense that played directly into Soviet hands.

Hitler clung to his belief willpower could win out over all simply because—or at least it seemed so to him—previously it had. For two decades, as he'd first waged a political struggle for mastery over Germany and then a military struggle for mastery over Europe, others had cautioned that objective, material factors would never allow for success. But he had indeed succeeded in gaining control of Germany, and then overran most of Europe during the war's first 18 months.

The German triumph in the west in 1940 seems to have been the final factor in cementing Hitler's belief in the primacy of will over material. If some operation was stalled, go in again with more determination. If an assessment of the enemy strength was daunting, lower the estimate. For instance, about the time the dictator was splitting *Army Group South* in two, Gen. Franz Halder, chief of the army general staff, wrote in his diary: "The *Führer*'s underestimation of the enemy's potential is taking on such a grotesque form that serious planning for operations is no longer possible."

At Stalingrad the Germans lost about 25 percent of their operational strength in Russia, forever ending their hopes for any kind of final offensive solution to the war. At Kursk they threw away a last chance to create military stalemate. Real strategy was no longer a guiding principle of their war effort; what followed was only blind ardor, useless heroics and insane fanaticism.

Selected Sources

Clifford, M. Elizabeth, James F. Dunnigan, Virginia M. Mulholland, et. al., eds. *War in the East: The Russo-German Conflict, 1941-45*. New York: SPI, Inc., 1977.

Ellis, John. *Brute Force: Allied Strategy and Tactics in the Second World War*. New York: Viking, 1990.

Weinberg, Gerhard L. *A World at Arms: A Global History of World War II*. New York: Cambridge Univ. Press, 1994.

Ziemke, Earl F. *Stalingrad to Berlin: The German Defeat in the East*. Washington, DC: Office of the Chief of Military History, 1968.

_____ and Magna E. Bauer. *Moscow to Stalingrad: Decision in the East*. New York: Military Heritage Press, 1988.

Chapter XVIII

Blitzkrieg Army, Siege Führer
A Reinterpretation of World War II in Europe
by R.H.S. Stolfi

The reigning interpretation (or "received wisdom") about the course of World War II in Europe gives the Germans little possibility of winning. The role of Britain in the survival of the Allies during the first half of the war is over-emphasized, and Hitler's attack on the Soviet Union is presented as foredooming the Third Reich to defeat. This common school of thought credits Hitler with a blitzkrieg mentality during the offensives of 1939-41, and presents various combinations of Alamein, Stalingrad, and Kursk as turning points in the war.

This received wisdom fails to account for numerous data and events which remain unexplained by its interpretations. It represents, then, what we might call "Newtonian Historical Physics." In my book, *Hitler's Panzers East*, I've sought to develop a more advanced interpretation of the war. Similar to the case of today's quantum physics vs. Newton, the revisionist argument in the book explains more phenomena of the war more effectively than the old model.

In the broadest sense, the received wisdom view explains the war as one the Germans could not have won. Those interpreters acknowledge German tactical brilliance in the blitz victories of 1939-41, but present them as unfair exercises run against weak, unprepared, or inept opponents. The blitz campaigns are explained as succeeding only until the Germans met the determined and better-prepared resistance of Britain, the Soviet Union and the United States. In that view, the blitz campaigns were just incidental events in a German march toward destruction. In warring against the Allies, the overwhelming odds Germany faced in numbers of men and weapons preordained her defeat.

In the logical sense, this conventional reasoning actually falls into the category of an after-the-fact argument in which German defeat is assumed to have been predetermined by the fact of that defeat itself. Surrounded by such thinking, historians have failed to adequately address the individual campaign that was the turning point in the entire war, and the many salient lessons to be drawn from it.

The Defeat of France

In the planning and conduct of the French campaign, Adolf Hitler is generally assumed to have intended a lightning war ending in a quick victory over that nation. Historical evidence, though, including Hitler's oral statements and written directives during the prelude to the campaign, support a contrary view that his goal was merely to seize Belgium. Even after the destruction of the Allied armies there, strong supporting evidence indicates he then focused on assuring the capture of the Lorraine area in France, rather than the fall of the Republic.

Within the framework of the received wisdom of a fully intended blitz, Hitler's conduct during the campaign has remained poorly explained to the present day. The dominant historical interpretation of his decision to halt the panzers short of Dunkirk remains implausible, indeed, almost bizarre.

That is, Hitler is supposed to have spared the British forces in order to conduct more effective peace negotiations with London in the near future. This strained suggestion, and other similar ones, reveal a separation from reality between the received wisdom and the actual course of the campaign in the west. Simply put, we have no indication that in May 1940 Hitler believed the French campaign would be brought to so swift a conclusion, and with it an accompanying opportunity for peace negotiations with Britain. I believe the evidence suggests Hitler never intended the quick defeat of France, but rather just the certain conquest of Belgium.

The crucial strategic moment for Hitler was when he found himself, through brilliant diplomatic maneuvering (the Soviet-German Nonaggression Pact, 23 August 1939) followed by eventual miscalculation, thrust into a war with Britain and France. He then realized he had projected Germany into a great strategic siege his armed forces had little chance of breaking, but that Germany had every chance of enduring by means of cautious military adjustments to the siege lines.

With an iron consistency, Hitler pursued a strategy designed to ensure German control over economic resources that would guarantee the Reich's survival against Britain and France in an indeterminate and desperate siege.

Viewed this way, the entire war in Europe comes into clear focus. On 9 October 1939, Hitler ordered his army commander to prepare an attack in the west to be launched no later than 12 November. In retrospect, it must be admitted Hitler saw no chance for the defeat of France in such an attack by a German army precipitously retrieved from the Polish conquest and launched into a winter offensive in northwestern Europe. Based on document and word, Hitler can be seen as wanting the seizure of Belgium to ensure the security of the Ruhr, while also creating a more effective siege position for Germany, particularly against Britain.

From such a perspective, Hitler's two great, and apparently aberrant, decisions to halt the advance to the Channel on 15 May, and halt the advance toward Dunkirk on 28 May, can finally be understood. He feared if the *12th Army* continued its attack toward the Channel, strong French forces lying to the south would counterattack into its flank, defeat it, and stabilize the Allied positions in Belgium.

Hitler was thus not really concerned with cutting off the Allied forces in Belgium, nor in rapidly crushing them as part of a further decisive maneuver to defeat France in a lightning campaign. He was concerned with securing Belgium, and dedicated to a conservative, assured eviction of the Allies from that nation.

Hitler raged at Franz Halder, Chief of the General Staff, in words that remain inexplicable unless this revisionist view is taken: "[If we continue to push the armor forward toward the Channel], we are on the best way to ruin the whole campaign!" It is evident from these words Hitler equated the entire campaign with the seizure of Belgium.

When later on 28 May he halted the German armor before Dunkirk, that behavior can now be seen as part of a consistent pattern. Hitler remained fiercely determined to prevent any possible setback to the German field armies closing in on the huge Allied forces still fighting in Belgium.

With the destruction of the Allied armies in Belgium and the Netherlands, and the rapidly following defeat of France, the war entered a new phase. Here the received wisdom on World War II overrates the aerial battle over Britain and German preparations for seaborne invasion in the period from July 1940 through June 1941.

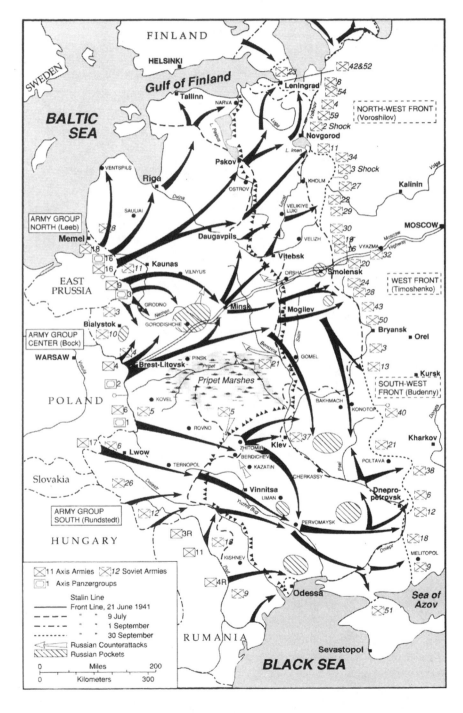

The same thinking suggests Hitler was driven by continued British resistance to knock Britain out of the war by an attack on the Soviet Union. Such interpretation demands we accept the argument Germany attacked a stronger opponent (the USSR) to force a weaker one (Great Britain) out of the war.

Raised in importance in my thesis is the fact European Russia contained resources of iron ore, coal and grain so vast as to make Germany self-sufficient and ensure a German victory in World War II in 1941. German victory over the Soviet Union in the summer of 1941 would have been the decisive event of the war in and of itself.

Barbarossa—Conjectures

The conventional interpreters of World War II claim that once Hitler attacked the Soviet Union he foredoomed Germany to defeat. Rarely has a historical event been so tarred by its outcome, while simultaneously being feathered by feeble analysis of the event itself. Confronted by the formidable dimensions of European Russia, and the fact of German defeat in the war, historians have rushed to agree that Hitler and the German army made a fatal mistake in attacking the Soviet Union.

My revisionist counterpoint is that the German mistake was not in attacking, but rather in losing. This generalization is more subtle than it may appear at first glance. It depends for its real impact on acceptance of the further revisionist generalization that Germany had the strength to defeat the USSR in the summer of 1941.

The central idea of *Hitler's Panzers East* is that the German army had "smashed" the main concentration of the Red Army defending the Smolensk land bridge to Moscow during July and early August 1941. German *Army Group Center* (AGC) had the numbers, weapons, logistical capability, and plan to seize Moscow before the end of August. I've held this view since the late 1950s, but had to wrestle in the intervening period with the challenge of establishing an argument in support of it that also provided a credible explanation for the historic German final defeat.

I have finally come to argue the case for German victory over the Soviet Union on the basis of nothing more remote than the actual performance of those invading forces in the Barbarossa offensive. I've also come to argue the case for German victory in World War II in Europe by showing that the defeat of the Soviet Union in the summer of 1941 would have been the decisive juncture in terms of German control over populations and resources on a continent occupied by the Axis from the English Channel to the Volga River.

These same arguments also prove realistically sensitive to time. The Germans had to move fast to get to Moscow, the communications and transportation center of European Russia and the political and psychological heart of the Soviet Union. Moscow was the point of no return for the communist party in terms of mobilization and political prestige. As the telephone, railway, and political center of the state, Moscow had to be held by the Soviet government.

I make this claim with trepidation because the road to historical hell is, of course, littered with similar self-confident generalizations. I can verify this one, however, because from the first day of the war, the Red field armies fought—seemingly instinctively—to hold on to every square meter of territory. Then, as the Soviet high command began to direct events more deliberately, it never wavered from a formula of defense based on the idea of holding as far west as possible while concentrating newly mobilizing forces between the Germans and Moscow.

For the Germans, who seized the initiative in the east with their vast surprise offensive, the greatest single issue—the grand uncertainty of the campaign—was whether the Soviets would defend as far west as possible or run for their hinterlands, trading space for time in order to mobilize forces deep within the state for an eventual strategic counteroffensive.

This great unknown, the crucial one for judging the fundamental capability of the German army to win immediately in the east, remains obscured by the faulty after-the-fact interpretation of the war. The Germans are assumed to have placed themselves in an impossible situation in Soviet Russia from the very opening of their attack. Intent on marshalling arguments in support of the historic end result, the conventional interpretation misses the epic potential of Operation Barbarossa to end the war in the east in the summer of 1941.

The German army did not attack the USSR to lose; it attacked to win, and it played out wargames, developed plans, and concentrated forces that its command judged would give it victory. The whole business, though—a surprise attack on the largest, most heavily armed, and third most populous state in the world—would necessarily be an adventure in uncertainty and chance. Halder, along with the key field commander Fedor von Bock, calculated that only if the

Soviets tried to evade decisive battle on the frontier would the outcome of the campaign become uncertain.

Barbarossa—In Fact

In the actual event, with little central direction in the first days of the campaign, the Soviet field armies not only tenaciously defended everywhere, but also launched major attacks westward. Then, as the Soviet high command began to regain contact with its hard-hit forces, it also enforced strategic and tactical formulas of resistance and attack to the west at any cost.

In the wargame played out by AGC headquarters at the end of 1940 for the attack against the Soviet Union, the great uncertainty centered on the question of whether the defenders would attempt to escape eastward. Maj. Peter von der Gröben, the assistant operations officer for AGC at that time, who was responsible for the conduct of the wargame, exclaimed to me in an interview that he could scarcely believe the German good fortune when, by the third day of the war, it had become evident the Red Army was stubbornly defending everywhere, while all newly mobilizing forces were also being fed westward into battle.

The great strategic question was thus quickly answered; the Soviets had selected the single strategic formula for survival best suited to hand victory to the Germans in Soviet Russia. Simultaneously driven by political and strategic necessity to defend Moscow, the Soviet command began to group the main concentration of the Red Army between AGC and their capital.

As the battle unfolded in June, fate presented the German army with the opportunity to defeat the main concentration of the Red Army before Moscow. By the magnitude, timing and location of that great battle, the Germans could have paralyzed the Soviet mobilization and thus essentially defeated them late in the summer of 1941.

These generalizations stand or fall largely on the basis of the performance of the German and Red armies in June and July 1941. Specifically, did the German divisions of AGC move at a pace fast enough to arrive at Moscow in late August while at the same time destroying the main forces of the defenders?

The advance of the *7th Panzer Division* of *Panzer Group Hoth* in AGC supports a picture of German victory. In one of the most astounding military achievements of World War II, this armored division ad-

vanced from the German border during the brief period from 0305 hours, 22 June, to 2300 hours, 25 June 1941 to cut the great highway between Minsk and Moscow. During its drive, the *7th* spent almost one entire day halted at Vilna, thus covering the road distance of about 390km to Minsk in three days of actual movement.

Halted from 26 June to 2 July to help ensure the destruction of the Soviet forces just trapped in two huge pockets west of Minsk, the *7th* resumed its advance toward Smolensk on that latter date. It cut the main highway and rail connection to Moscow, well east of Smolensk, at Jarcevo, on 16 July, having advanced 520km by road. At that moment the division was only 325km from Moscow.

The nearness of the German victory over the Soviet Union probably comes into clearest focus on that date in the middle of July. Then, based on its earlier performance in Soviet Russia, the *7th Panzer Division* lay only three days from Moscow. That division, of course, could not have continued its advance on 16 July because it was (temporarily) exhausted from the battles it had fought to get to Jarcevo and the tough fighting still involved in the destruction of the Smolensk pocket.

But by 4 August that pocket was burned out and the German mobile divisions were resting and rehabilitating for the advance directly against Moscow. If the German army plan for the invasion (the "Halder Plan") had continued to function, we can estimate AGC would have launched its final drive to Moscow on or about 12 August, and gone on to seize that city in a double envelopment similar to those earlier at Minsk and Smolensk by 28 August.

In actuality, Hitler refused to give the armor the "green light" for Moscow, debated for weeks with his generals over the further conduct of the war, and finally ordered about half the strength of AGC southward into the Ukraine on 25 August.

Hitler achieved a brilliant tactical success in that move. Gen. Heinz Guderian, probably the premier armor commander of the war, led the mobile divisions south and linked up with the tanks of Panzer Group Kleist shortly before noon on 15 September. At that moment, anti-tank and motorized infantry units of Guderian's *3rd Panzer Division* set lines of encirclement southeast of Lochwiza around a vast Soviet pocket in the central Ukraine. The Germans eventually took 665,000 prisoners out of that cauldron—seven times the number of Germans and Romanians who would be captured at Stalingrad early in 1943. But the effort and time expended in the south also lost World War II for the Germans.

In the meantime, *7th Panzer Division* would mark time around Jarcevo for an extravagant 78 days. The division was held there not due to logistics difficulties, casualties, or Soviet resistance, but because of Hitler's determination to assure immediate and certain control over the central Ukraine.

The enormity of the situation can be made clear by asking the question: what if the same division had been halted with the other German armor along the Meuse River in Belgium after 13 May 1940 for 78 days, while Hitler procrastinated about future objectives and then finally ordered a drive into Lorraine to assure the immediate and certain control over the iron ore of France? The answer, of course, is that the German army could scarcely have won the French campaign, let alone the larger Russian campaign, under such restrictive operational directives.

161

But perhaps the two most immediate and strongest arguments that support a picture of the German army overwhelming the Soviets in August 1941 are those based on the actual performance of the invaders in their advance south that summer, and in their following advance east at Vyasma and Bryansk in October. In the former case, powerful elements of AGC moved 550km south against strong Soviet resistance in the Ukraine. From that it's hard to escape the conclusion the same attacking mobile force, advancing earlier on 12 August along with the rest of AGC, would have been capable of an equally successful drive in a shorter period in the direction of Moscow.

The Vyasma-Bryansk battle of October similarly shows the epic possibilities of the first months of Barbarossa in terms of the defeat of the Soviet Union. On 2 October, *7th Panzer Division* and the other German divisions around it attacked along a main axis of advance through Vyasma toward Moscow. By that time the Soviet high command had already had more than two months to fortify a defensive front and mass its forces for the defense of Moscow.

It would seem, then, that AGC should have had little real prospect of a successful renewed advance to Vyasma, let alone Moscow. The new offensive had to be prosecuted against the main concentration of the Red Army, hunkered in prepared positions, with its psychological equilibrium regained and a clear mission to halt any German advance. Yet, in an astonishing and still largely undetailed example of operational prowess, *7th Panzer Division* advanced in a period of four days (106 hours) to Vyasma, and there linked up with *10th Panzer Division* to form a new pocket of approximately 55 Soviet divisions.

In fighting of gigantic proportions lasting from 2-14 October, AGC broke up and destroyed the mostly encircled forces defending Moscow, taking 650,000 prisoners in two pockets at Vyasma and farther south at Bryansk. But as the Red Army and Soviet government were revealed to be powerless to prevent a German advance to Moscow, the climatological circumstances of autumn rain and cloud cover that prevented the drying of the entirely unpaved road system halted the German mobile divisions.

Presented with yet another unearned opportunity to survive, and aided by the half-miraculous and also unearned circumstance of the coldest winter in the recorded climatological history of Europe, the Soviets survived Operation Barbarossa in 1941.

But the real point of recounting this battle of October 1941 is to illustrate and support the idea that much the same engagement fought

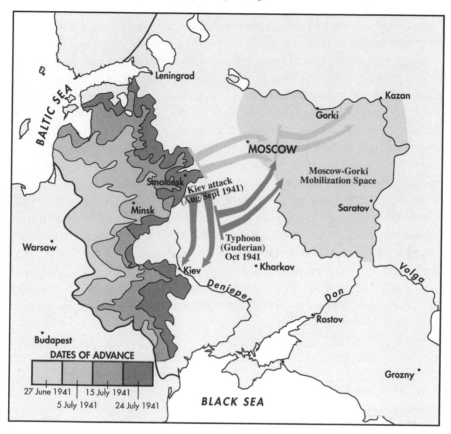

in the middle of August, by relatively stronger German forces against weaker and psychologically collapsed Soviet forces, would have had far more decisive results. In such a battle, with the German armies advancing over intact roads in late summer weather and with longer hours of daylight, they could have moved into the rail, telephone and command center of the Soviet Union and then even beyond it to occupy that country's last remaining significant mobilization area.

This surmise about an advance beyond Moscow is strengthened by the circumstance that the Germans would have been moving along the main arteries of the great rail system radiating out of the capital.

Such a late-summer chain of events equates with the defeat of the Soviet Union and the correlated German victory in the war in Europe. The German army had the fundamental capability—the command style, the numbers of men and tanks, and the logistical system—to win World War II during this brief window of opportunity in July-

August 1941—and they would never have it again at any other time or place in the war.

Conventional interpreters of the course of the Second World War have presented the battles of Alamein, Stalingrad, and Kursk, each alone or in various combinations, as turning points of the European war. But as turning points for that entire war, rather than just as important junctures leading to following distinct phases of the war, those battles fail to be realistic candidates.

Stalingrad fails as a turning point because in March 1943, one month after the German surrender there, Field Marshal Erich von Manstein's *Army Group South* launched a counteroffensive that momentarily regained the strategic initiative in the east. The Stalingrad battle can scarcely be the turning point in the war when its aftermath was the German Kursk Offensive of July 1943. At best, from the perspective of the great coalition ranged against Germany, Alamein and Kursk can be viewed as joint marker points along the road of Germany's defeat—Alamein from the standpoint of the West, and Kursk from that of the East.

Chapter XIX

Czechoslovakia '38
What If They'd Fought?
by Dr. Peter H. Gryner

"**O**peration Green," the German codename for their planned attack on Czechoslovakia in the fall of 1938, was an inevitable part of the political and military development of European affairs that led to World War II. Throughout this story, the paramount fact remains Adolf Hitler was an evil and ruthless politician, an unscrupulous nationalist, and a man determined to enforce his will and accomplish his goals by whatever means available.

Hitler had clearly defined his ideas in his book, *Mein Kampf* (*My Struggle*), and today we can only regret the democratic statesmen of his era didn't bother to read it. Those men lived in a world ruled by a system based on reason, traditional values, mutual understandings and political horse-trading. Hitler did not play his game by their rules. He set out to rearrange the map of Europe, retaliate against those who had humiliated Germany at Versailles, establish a new world order under Nazi rule, move east by force of arms to capture the breadbasket of Europe, enslaving any nations that attempted to stand in the way.

His plan might have been aborted without starting a general European war until the *Anschluss* of Austria. From that point on, Hitler's affairs ceased to be simply a matter of internal German politics. The annexation of Austria was the first step, a carefully prepared and well staged political move, a part of the planned "Drang Nach Osten" ("*Urge to the East*"). The Anschluss was aimed at upsetting the balance of power in the Danube basin, and at eroding the security of Czechoslovakia. To clear the road to the east, both Austria and Czechoslovakia had to disappear as independent political entities.

A few months after Austria's submergence, Hitler issued an ulti-

matum demanding the Czechs cede the Sudeten border area to the Reich. Prague declared a full mobilization of its armed forces on 23 September 1938. Other European countries followed suit: France ordered a partial mobilization, Great Britain called up its reserves, and even the Soviet Union declared its support for the Czechoslovakian cause. For a while it looked as if a great alliance had been formed to thwart the Germans.

But the rattling of swords proved misleading. The British Prime Minister, Neville Chamberlain, didn't want to go to war "for a quarrel in a far away country between people of whom we know nothing." A few days after that statement, the infamous Munich Conference was begun, and the treaty resulting from it sealed the fate of Czechoslovakia. The document was signed by the representatives of Germany, France, Britain, and Italy—the Czechoslovakians and Soviets were not even invited.

Abandoned by France, its primary ally, and virtually blackmailed by a Britain unprepared for war, Czechoslovakia was now effectively isolated. The Czechs faced a terrible choice: resist the Germans alone or capitulate.

The Prague government chose to capitulate. That decision was announced on 30 September, against both the will of the Czech general staff and people. On 1 October, the German army occupied the Sudentenland without having to fire a shot, and in doing so dealt the Czechoslovak Republic a virtual death blow. With the forfeiture of the Sudetenland, the Czechs suffered an irreparable loss of strategic territory, industry, resources and modern fortifications that were the key to the defense of the entire country.

Paris and London were overwhelmed with joy; Chamberlain and Daladier (the French Prime Minister) became the media heroes of the day—the champions of "peace in our time." But anti-Fascists all over the world wondered in dismay whether the sacrifice of democratic Czechoslovakia would truly prevent war. The question was answered in the negative on 14 March 1939, when the German army occupied the remainder of western Czechoslovakia, simultaneously abetting the creation of a puppet Slovak Republic in the east. All this happened in direct violation of the Treaty of Locarno and the Munich Agreement.

Only the Czech 3rd Battalion of the 8th Border Regiment put up a brief fight, trying to stop an advancing SS column. All other Czech soldiers laid down their arms, and their country ceased to exist. World War II had effectively begun.

Europe in the 20s & 30s

On 1 December 1925, an international treaty was signed in the Swiss town of Locarno. That signing finally and definitely ended the First World War; its repudiation 11 years later helped precipitate the Second. Locarno was, at least on paper, a good treaty. Peace between France and Germany was guaranteed by Great Britain and Italy. That pleased all four of them, especially Italy, which in signing gained greatly in status. France reaffirmed her existing alliances with Poland and Czechoslovkia, and it was further agreed French action under those alliances would not constitute aggression against Germany.

At the time, Locarno was widely considered to have made a new general European war impossible. It was expected the climate of mutual trust the document was aimed at fostering would lead to the withdrawal of Allied troops then occupying the Rhineland, and would later enable Germany to join the League of Nations. Both those expectations proved correct soon afterward.

The treaty, however, had one weak point; it did not address Germany's refusal to accept the *status quo* along her eastern frontiers.

Berlin had accepted the loss of Alsace and Lorraine, but its insistence on separate "arbitration treaties" with Poland and Czechoslovakia, leaving open the door to future negotiations and changes, was of great concern to the governments in Warsaw and Prague (which were not signatories to the main Locarno treaty). Those governments were also concerned with France's apparent renunciation of her right to go to war with Germany unless the League of Nations agreed some member state had been attacked without provocation. Both the Czechs and Poles, feeling their mutual defense treaties with France had suddenly declined in value, spoke of a "sellout."

The Czechoslovak Republic had always been accepted by the West as one of the most successful creations of the Paris Peace Conference. Her constitution, ratified in 1920, was a modern document of democratic principles even Thomas Jefferson would have admired. It included guarantees of personal liberty, equality and a balanced distribution of government powers. During the inter-war period, no questions were ever raised regarding the freedom or propriety of Czechoslovakian elections, the workings of its judiciary, or the authority of its National Assembly. The Czechoslovak Republic, in fact, established a reputation for democratic development, against a background of relative political tranquility, that contrasted strongly with the situation in the other countries of the area.

Polish democracy gave way to the coup of Gen. Pilsudski in 1926. In Bulgaria, progressive democratic developments were brought to a halt by assassination in 1923. In Austria, Engelbert Dolfuss imposed dictatorial measures in the early 1930s. Yugoslavia, in the midst of a crisis in Serb-Croat relations, became a virtual monarchist-dictatorship by 1929. Hungary was under the dictate of Adm. Horthy and his ultra-conservative elite. Romania had its political development stunted by the increasingly authoritarian King Carol. The fate of democracy in Germany and Italy is, of course, too well known to need rehashing here. But while all those countries succumbed to pressures from the far right (generated in response to the perceived threat of Communist revolution), Czechoslovakia continued to move slowly and cautiously along the path of democracy.

In the field of foreign policy, Czechoslovakia resolutely and consistently worked for peace, international arbitration, collective security and friendly relations with her neighbors. Czechoslovakia was a loyal member of the League of Nations, an original signatory of the Kellogg-Briand Peace Pact outlawing aggressive war, and stood ready at all times to fulfill her obligations resulting from the acceptance of the system of collective security. At the League's headquarters in Geneva, her representatives opposed the Japanese invasion of Manchuria and China, and the Foreign Minister of Czechoslovakia, Dr. Edward Benes, was also president of the Assembly of the League when it voted sanctions against Italy in response to that nation's invasion of Ethiopia.

From the moment the Nazis gained power in Germany, the Czechs recognized their final aims and the threat to European peace they represented. In early 1932, Benes warned the Italians their support of the Nazis' rise to power would eventually work against them. At the same time, he also conferred with Poland's Foreign Minister, Jozsef Beck, proposing revisions of the existing agreements regarding their frontiers and establishing a basis of military cooperation against Germany.

In July 1932, Benes returned to Prague from the World Disarmament Conference then being held in Geneva. He summoned the Czech general staff and the minister of defense to warn: "In spite of our efforts for the success of the Disarmament Conference, everything I have already seen and heard inclines me to...[believe it will fail]. A dreadful crisis is inevitable.... I give you four years. The crisis will probably come in 1936 or 1937. By that time the Republic has to be prepared militarily."

In October, Benes received a report on the "Volta Conference" just held in Rome. There Italy and Germany agreed to work toward large-scale revisions of existing peace treaties. Benes reacted by proposing closer military and political cooperation between his country, Romania and Yugoslavia. This was the so-called "Little Entente" that had been loosely formed in 1920-21. After the Volta Conference, the time seemed right to strengthen and intensify those agreements.

On 16 March 1933, the Little Entente pact was strengthened, but two days later, Mussolini proposed a new "Four Power Pact." Under its provisions, Germany, Italy, France and Britain would agree to allow the revision of earlier treaties. This act of revisionism was obviously directed against the Little Entente. To get Paris and London to agree to the general legitimacy of treaty revisionism, the Fascists and Nazis were maneuvering the two democratic powers to abandon their interests on the continent in favor of concentrating on the overseas affairs of their colonial empires.

The Four Power Pact was signed in Rome on 15 July 1933. It was strongly rejected by public opinion in both Britain and France at the time, and of course by the states of the Little Entente and Poland. The French and British parliaments, in fact, never ratified the treaty—but still, it can easily be seen as a precursor and model for the Munich Agreement of 1938.

In October 1933, Germany withdrew from the World Disarmament Conference and from the League of Nations. Czechoslovakia responded by stepping up her national defense program.

Czechoslovakia's Strategic Importance

Hitler had military, economic and political reasons for invading Czechoslovakia. Her geographic position made her the most important country in central Europe. Her territory was a gateway to the east as well as to the Danube basin. In 1868, after Prussia had defeated Austria in a war fought mostly in Bohemia, Otto von Bismarck warned: "Whoever is master of Bohemia is the master of Europe. Europe must, therefore, never allow any nation except the Czechs to rule it, since that nation does not lust for domination. The boundaries of Bohemia are the safeguard of European security, and he who moves them will plunge Europe into misery."

For offensive purposes, Czechoslovakia covered Poland's southern flank, and could also serve as a springboard for operations into the Ukraine and the Danube basin.

For defensive purposes, the western portions of the Czechoslovak Republic represented a deep wedge jutting into the Third Reich. Hitler saw clearly its potential as a possible Soviet army and air force base, bringing those forces within easy reach of the German heartland.

Economically, Czechoslovakia was one of Europe's industrial centers. In 1930, the population of the Czechoslovak Republic was 14.7 million, which ranked it ninth of 25 European nations. By 1938, the population had grown to 16 million, with Slavic Czechs, Slovaks, and Ruthenes accounting for 12 million of that total. A German minority of 3 million, plus smaller Polish and Hungarian minorities, played important roles in Hitler's plan of division and conquest.

In 1929, Czechoslovakia produced more pitcoal, lignite, pig-iron and steel than Italy. In 1938 she ranked third in central Europe in industrial capacity—behind only Germany and Italy. That relatively great capacity represented the real basis for Czechoslovakian national defense. Their light machinery and armaments industries were some of the best in the world. The Skoda Works, with plants in Prague, Brno and Zbrojovka, produced first-class weapons, cars, trucks, tanks and ammunitions. The Skoda Works in fact represented the third-largest national armaments complex in Europe, ranking only below the Krupp concern in Germany and Schneider-Creusot in France.

Politically, the Czechs were in the vanguard of various anti-German alliance systems. A strategically and militarily free Czechoslovakia represented the last obstacle to be overcome before the "Urge to the East" could be started in earnest. These, and not the propaganda facade provided by the Sudeten Germans, were the real factors providing the motive for Hitler's invasion.

Czech-German Relations, 1933-37

Shortly after he came to power, Hitler proposed a German-Czechoslovak bilateral non-aggression treaty. These overtures were immediately rejected by Prague on the grounds that Czechoslovakia was committed to the principles of the League of Nations, already had mutual understandings with other nations within the region, and had outright alliances with still others. Benes stated his country would be unable to enter into such a bilateral treaty with Germany without agreement from all other "interested" European states. He also informed Britain, Poland, France, and the countries of the Little Entente of Hitler's proposal.

In the fall of 1935, Hitler made another move toward a bilateral treaty with Czechoslovakia. He sent a diplomatic delegation to Prague with the following stated objectives: 1) get Benes (now president of Czechoslovakia) and Hitler to meet personally to agree on the final form of a new policy of friendship between their two countries; 2) work out a non-aggression pact similar to the one signed by Germany and Poland in 1934; and 3) remove all barriers to mutual trust that may have developed as a result of past relations.

The envoys further stated that when those three objectives were accomplished, Germany would recognize, affirm and guarantee the existing frontiers of Czechoslovakia. They also stressed Hitler's desire to negotiate these matters directly with Benes, in private and in absolute secrecy.

Benes agreed this time, stating he would welcome such a German-Czech treaty, and requested a detailed written proposal. By early the next year, he had such a document in hand, including a clause of recognition of the present frontiers of Czechoslovakia. Hitler only requested "cultural autonomy" be granted the German minority in the Sudetenland, and pledged—everything else being agreed upon—that he would never seek their "territorial autonomy."

But Benes brought the discussions to an end by pointing out that signing the bilateral agreement as it was written would actually require Czechoslovakia to renounce her earlier treaties with France and the Soviet Union. The German diplomats suggested Benes rewrite the agreement in a form that would not affect either nation's pre-existing treaties. The Czech president agreed and submitted his revised document to Berlin in January 1937.

Hitler, though, sent no answer to Benes' revised treaty, and he never allowed his diplomats to approach Prague on the subject again. What had changed was *Der Führer's* adoption of a new course toward relations with Czechoslovakia. Hitler, it seems, had rethought his attitude toward the Sudeten Germans and the excellent propaganda leverage their situation presented to him.

The Development of Operation Green

The actual blueprint for the Germans' plans of aggression against Czechoslovakia originated in June 1937 and was given the codename "Operation Green." On 24 June, Field Marshal Werner von Blomberg, the German Minister of War, issued a secret directive to the armed forces' unified preparation for a war in the east. The part of the directive concerning Operation Green suggested such an eastern war might start with a surprise invasion of Czechoslovakia to parry or forestall the imminent attack of a superior enemy coalition through the same area.

To justify such an action in the eyes of the international community, necessary preconditions had to be created politically. The task of the armed forces would be to break into Czechoslovakia quickly, by surprise and with the greatest force possible, leaving the minimum strength necessary as a border shield in the west. The final object of the attack was to be the complete elimination of Czechoslovakia as a military factor in any broader war, which would include denying the Soviet air force operational bases there.

In discussions throughout the autumn between Hitler and his generals, it was further determined the invasion was to be executed with the "speed of lightning." Concerns centered on the strength of the Czech border fortifications. Most disturbing, according to von Blomberg, was the fact the defense line in Northern Moravia was approaching the same magnitude and capabilities as the French Maginot Line. The Commander-in-Chief of the German Army, Gen. Werner von Fritsch, accordingly ordered a study of all the alternatives available for the attack, with a special emphasis given to the breaching of the fortifications.

The Czechs' Friends & Neighbors

Czechoslovakia's position between Germany and the Soviet Union was a difficult one. Germany coveted Czechoslovakia as a gate through which to expand to the east and southeast, while for the Soviets Czechoslovakia presented a natural buffer to such expansion.

There was another Great Power that had interest in Czechoslovakia: France. The French saw Czechoslovakia as a strong potential threat to the German rear in any new war Berlin might start in the west. By its mere existence, an independent Czechoslovakia also blocked direct German access to the raw materials and fuel resources of southeast Europe. Further, French leadership in continental affairs in the period between the two world wars was based on her influence over the small countries of central and eastern Europe. French withdrawal from those regions, Paris was certain, would bring on immediate German domination, thus reducing France to a secondary power.

Those were the great fundamental strategic considerations determining the foreign policy of Czechoslovakia in the late 1930s. In fact, Benes, who became the republic's second president, often summarized the "three pillars" of his country's foreign policy this way: 1) the League of Nations; 2) the Little Entente; and 3) the alliance with France.

The Little Entente had originally been formed to block Hungary's efforts to regain the territories lost at the end of World War I. Later, many attempts were made by Germany and Italy to break up that alliance so as to be able to deal with each of its member states separately. Those efforts in fact had some success as can be seen by the fact that even by 1938 the Little Entente had added no provisions for mutually resisting German aggression against any one of its members.

The story of the Franco-Czech alliance was different. The two countries were in fact linked by a bond stronger than any treaty: they both knew the defeat of one by the Germans would likewise be the death knell of the other.

It was a popular belief in Great Britain at the time that the French commitments in central and eastern Europe were a mistake and might lead to entanglements that actually helped bring on, rather than put off, a new European war. But the suggestion that France should have given up agreements essential to her security was as preposterous as the idea London should give up her interests in the Mediterranean to avoid possible conflict with Italy. Put more simply—Czechoslovakia was France's Gibraltar. The two nations concluded a treaty of alliance and friendship in January 1924, and the following year the agreement · was further strengthened by an annex to the Locarno Treaties, providing for mutual assistance in the case of a German attack on either.

Czechoslovakia's relations with the Soviet Union were not so clear-cut. In May 1935, the Czechoslovakians and Soviets concluded a pact of mutual assistance, and by its provisions the two were bound to go to each other's assistance without waiting for the League of Nations to certify the fact of aggression. However, Soviet military intervention in support of Czechoslovakia was tied to that of France. It was this clause that led to problems in the critical days of September 1938.

After the signing of the 1935 pact, friendly relations began to develop between the general staffs of Czechoslovakia and the Soviet Union, and the anti-Communist stance of the Prague government was put more and more into the background. Military delegations exchanged several visits, Soviet officers inspected the growing Czech border fortifications, some manufacturing license agreements for aircraft were made, and the question of wartime use of airfields in Slovakia by the Red air force was studied. More importantly, the Czech army shared the development of its 105mm field gun, the most modern artillery piece in the world at the time, and the Skoda medium tanks models 37 and 38 were tested at Soviet proving grounds. In the spring of 1938, a Czechoslovakian delegation went to the USSR to study defenses there.

All these activities, of course, were denounced not only in the Nazi press in Germany, but also on the floor of the Czechoslovak parliament, where the conservative parties came out in strong opposition to any kind of cooperation with the Soviet Union. Ultimately, though this dissent among Czech politicians regarding Soviet military help played only a minor role in Prague during the actual Munich Crisis, it did take on major significance in the minds of many British and French politicans, who considered any Soviet moves into Czechoslovakia as tantamount to a Communist invasion of central Europe.

German Army Opposition to Hitler

During the first years of Hitler's regime, he tried not to antagonize the German army's leadership. He claimed the only way to achieve the goals of National Socialism was with the army, never against it. But after 1937 he began to take the steps necessary to implement stricter control and, ultimately, complete subjugation of the armed forces. Those moves arose from Hitler's frustration with his generals over their seemingly increasing opposition to his policies—in rearmament and foreign expansion in particular. Those army leaders who in 1933 hadn't shown enough enthusiasm for the Nazis were soon dismissed, and the top defense posts were put into the hands of four men—von Blomberg, von Reichenau, von Fritsch, and von Beck—on whom Hitler thought he could depend fully.

Von Blomberg was a professional soldier with an impeccable career. But he was politically naive, and some who knew him felt he lacked firm character. He saw Hitler as a strong leader and the savior of Germany, and initially supported Nazi policies without hesitation.

Von Reichenau was also a first-class soldier and supporter of Nazi policies. However, he also was an aristocrat and a realist and didn't approve of the excesses and vulgarity of National Socialism.

In general, all four army leaders initially supported Nazi policies, though each for different personal reasons. The first change in attitude came with the risky and provocative occupation of the Rhineland in 1936; from then on it was von Beck in particular who cast himself against Hitler, and who conspired with the civilian opposition, such as it was, to change the political decision making process in Germany.

It was the hurried speed of rearmament, the apparent lack of planning and insufficient resources that most worried those generals. They were also concerned about Hitler's dangerous foreign policy and the increasing subjugation of the army to Nazi Party rules. Their protests to Hitler mounted.

Then in early 1938 came the "Fritsch-Blomberg Affair." Von Blomberg married a secretary who, it turned out, was a former prostitute, thus disgracing the honor of the German officer corps. Von Fritsch was falsely accused of homosexuality (the charges were trumped up by Göring and Himmler who, by dethroning generals, hoped to garner more glory and influence for themselves), and by the time he cleared himself it was too late to save his career.

Hitler mastered the affair brilliantly. Though at first hesitant, he moved ahead once he saw the opportunities the crisis presented. Von Blomberg and von Fritsch were forced to resign. They were replaced by opportunists completely subservient to Hitler. The news was announced over the radio on 4 February 1938 by Hitler himself.

It was a deep and crucial redistribution of power within the political structure of the Third Reich. Hitler personally took over command of the armed forces. The former armed forces office within the ministry of defense became the "High Command of the Armed Forces," with *der Führer* at its head. Once begun, the reshuffling was easy to continue: 16 other high-ranking generals were relieved of their commands and 44 more were transferred.

The annexation of Austria came in the aftermath of the Fritsch-Blomberg crisis and was organized primarily by the Nazi Party, with the general staff being practically shut out. It was the Austrian experience, combined with Hitler's initiation of the Operation Green planning, that finally moved von Beck to plan military resistance.

Von Beck, in cooperation with Carl Gördeler, the mayor of Munich and unofficial head of what civilian opposition there was to Hitler, intended to openly demonstrate that the generals could at least rein in Nazi policy excesses. He counted on the support of the army high command. Since the totalitarian regime had eliminated all other checks and controls, von Beck saw it as the army's proper role to change Hitler's course.

But his plan had a weak link: von Brauchitsch. Though he had agreed with von Beck's ideas and had promised to bring to Hitler's attention the material shortages and general unpreparedness for war, he lacked the courage to actually do so.

On 16 July 1938, von Beck wrote a memorandum wherein he urged von Brauchitsch to summon the top generals and together threaten Hitler with their mass resignations unless he ordered an immediate stop to all war preparations. A military *Putsch* was to be considered as a last resort. The plan failed because Brauchitsch never cooperated actively, and the faltering Western powers never acted strongly enough to bring matters to a head. Embittered and without support, von Beck resigned in August. Both he and Gördeler were executed during the purge following the July 1944 assassination attempt on Hitler.

More Planning for Operation Green

With those generals out of the way, Hitler had outmaneuvered the last possible domestic opposition, the traditional army officer elite. In gaining Austria, he had presented the *Wehrmacht* with an advantageous situation by maximizing Czechoslovakia's encirclement.

For the Czech army general staff the reality of the new extended border with Germany created a planning nightmare. They reacted by starting a new line of fortifications along the former Austrian border, and established plans for flooding areas in South Moravia, around the River Dyje.

The new strategic situation also allowed for some rethinking on the German side. On 22 April 1938, Hitler and Gen. Wilhelm Keitel, the head of the OKW, met for detailed discussions. The two agreed an out-and-out surprise attack on Czechoslovakia was probably undesirable because it would generate a hostile world reaction against Germany. Hitler suggested the attack be launched as the result of some trumped up diplomatic crisis or incident, such as the possible assassination of the German ambassador in Prague.

The two also decided to conduct the attack on several axes, with the objective of penetrating the Czech border fortifications at several points at once. Ground support from the *Luftwaffe* was to be provided for each attacking column, with the mission of aborting enemy counterattacks against the points of penetration, interdicting their flow of reserves and destroying their communication network.

Hitler also announced he had decided to exploit the internal situation within Czechoslovakia, to provide a basis for thwarting quick involvement by Britain and France. Thus a new propaganda campaign was begun against the Czechs soon after the *Anschluss*. Working under direct instruction from Berlin, Konrad Henlein, the leader of the Sudeten German Party, declared his organization could no longer tolerate the "persecution" of the German minority within Czechoslovakia and began agitating for complete autonomy.

The new composite draft of Operation Green was completed by Gen. Alfred Jodl. It concluded that if it came to war, a decisive German victory should be sought within four days to forestall Allied intervention. Toward that end, most of the army was to be deployed against the Czechs, with only light screening forces left in the west. A simultaneous north/south pincer operation was outlined, to link-up in the general area of Brno. With Czechoslovakia thus cut in half, the major portion of her armed forces would be encircled in the "Bohemian Cauldron." The new draft plan also called attention to the desirability of sparing Czech industrial centers so their potential could be added to the Reich's war economy.

The First Crisis, May 1938

The revised directive for Operation Green, drafted on 20 May 1938, was in effect only one day. On 21 May, Czechoslovakia declared a partial mobilization. All first-class reservists, anti-aircraft defense units, specialists, border regiments and fort garrisons were called up, and the air force was put on alert. The fortress battalions mobilized and moved into the still uncompleted bunkers of the "Little Maginot Line." Prague stated that German troop movements and concentrations in the border regions, as reported by the Czech intelligence service, were the reason for the surprise move.

Other documents indicate the mobilization was actually triggered by a warning from the British to the Czechoslovakian ambassador in London, Jan Masaryk. Other information was passed to Prague by members of the outlawed German Social-Democratic Party. As early as 16 May, reports from them indicated German officers and NCOs in Saxony were being given Czech language instruction. Other reports indicated weapons and ammunition were being distributed to members of the paramilitary *Sudeten Freikorps*. On the 20th, two Sudeten German couriers who failed to obey an order given by a Czech policeman were shot dead in Cheb (Eger). Riots broke out in the German-speaking areas of the Czech border regions.

As dawn broke on 21 May, then, Europe awoke to face an international crisis. Rumors of a pending German invasion continued to spread. But the central fact in the crisis was that Czechoslovakia, a minor power, had seized the initiative in continental politics. The mobilization was provocative toward Nazi Germany, a state extremely sensitive regarding its prestige, especially military prestige. Prague's decision was a dramatic demonstration to France and Britain that Czechoslovakia would not be a willing partner in their games of appeasement with Berlin. More than that, it forced them to play the Czechs' game, for the risk of immediate war would now be less if the

two Allied powers exerted pressure on Germany than it would be if they stood aside as they had with Austria.

Benes had declared shortly before the crisis that if Czechoslovakia and the Western powers stood fast together war could be avoided. But if Germany gained the resources of southeast Europe, they would certainly have to fight later on, and then under much more unfavorable conditions. It had to be made clear to the Nazis, he said, that another *fait accompli* would not be tolerated, as had been the case with Austria, since the entire continental balance of power was now at stake.

Under such circumstances, both the British and French governments played the role Benes had cast for them. On 21 May, the French ambassador to Berlin emphasized to that government the dangers that would follow from a German-Czech conflict because of the French-Czech alliance. Premier Daladier summoned the German ambassador to his office and indicated a mobilization order lying on his desk. He warned: "It depends on you, Excellency, whether I sign this document or not."

The reaction from London was even stronger. "Reports from central Europe," wrote the German ambassador there, "let loose such a panic as has not been seen here since 1914." The British ambassador in Berlin went to the Geman foreign office four times that day, warning if Germany attacked Czechoslovakia, France would undoubtedly be compelled to intervene, and Britain might therefore also be "forced to protect her interests."

It seemed war could come at any moment, but Gen. von Brauchitsch put a severe jolt into those debating in the Nazi government when he reported "categorically" that military preparations were not sufficient to face the risk of war at that time. The British and French then released word of their warnings to the press, which was already full of reports of ominous German preparations and Czech countermeasures.

The Germans, of course, did not attack, and there was elation in Czechoslovakia. The impression was spread in the world press that Prague, closely supported by the British and French (and perhaps by the Soviet Union) had compelled the Germans to call off a planned invasion. The would-be aggressor had been foiled by a "Grand Alliance."

Hitler reportedly fumed for days. It was a tremendous blow to his prestige, but he could not risk a war against Czechoslovakia with France and Britain, and possibly the USSR, also ranged against him. Even more maddening, France and Britain seemed to have been brought closer to agreement regarding central European security affairs than at any time since 1919. (It had been leaked that those two nations had agreed to resume regular military staff conversations.)

Hitler instructed Henlein to return to Prague and resume negotiations. Then he summoned his principal advisors to the Reichschancellery to hear a two-hour phillipic: "It is my unshakeable will that Czechoslovakia shall be wiped off the map... We shall tackle this situation in the east. Then I will give you three or four years' time, and then we will tackle the situation in the west." He went on, instructing that final military preparations be completed in four months, by 1 October.

Orders were also given for a crash program of construction for the "West Wall," a line of fortifications along the French border, to reduce the risk of interference from that quarter. (By mid-September, 600,000 men were working on those defenses.) Plans were laid to expand the army to 96 divisions.

As great a success as the first crisis had seemed to be for Czechoslovakia, it in fact paved the way for the Munich debacle of September.

Finalization of Operation Green

The Czech mobilization had caught Hitler off-guard. He had not been prepared, when his bluff was called, to launch an immediate strike against a strong and well-prepared opponent. But the first Czech crisis did stimulate in Hitler the fresh determination to crush Czechoslovakia at the earliest opportunity, and a still newer draft of the plan for Operation Green was put into effect.

By 30 May 1938, Gen. Keitel was able to provide the armed forces' commanders-in-chief a revised *Führer* Directive. The new order was to be carried out by 1 October at the latest. The document indicated a more direct approach was to be taken from its very first sentence: "It is my unalterable decision to smash Czechoslovakia by military action in the near future. It is the job of the political leaders to await or bring about the politically and militarily suitable moment."

More concretely, lightning-swift military and political action was to follow as a result of some incident in which Germany was seen to be provoked in some serious way. The element of surprise was also stressed so Czechoslovakia would not be prepared to resist the invasion militarily.

Just as in the 20 May draft, the revised plan still called for the German armed forces achieving decisive results within four days. This was deemed essential to deter any hostile nations that might help Czechoslovakia if the war went on too long. Still, Hitler judged correctly (as was shown later during the "Phoney War" period) that it would take "a while" before the Allies would launch any kind of serious ground action.

Regarding possible intervention by one or more eastern European nations, the following was emphasized:

> Among the eastern powers, Russia is not the most likely to intervene...[And if such intervention comes, it] will probably consist of reinforcements of the Czech air force and armaments. However, the decision must not be neglected concerning what measures are to be taken if Russia were to come to the point of starting a naval and air war against

us or even begin a penetration into East Prussia through the border states. In the case of a Polish attack we must hold the eastern fortifications and East Prussia, using the Frontier Guard and its formations until the conclusion of the action of Operation Green will give us freedom of movement.

On 12 July, the army high command distributed a new and highly secret schedule of summer maneuvers. This schedule was designed to meet the special needs of the army for Operation Green. That is, it put the involved units into favorable dispositions for launching the actual attack.

On 10 August, Hitler summoned the army and air force chiefs and delivered a three-hour speech bashing the officer corps' "defeatism." This tirade was prompted, according to Jodl's diary, by the remark of Gen. Adam that the West Wall could probably only be held for three weeks.

Later that same month, Hitler approved a new memorandum concerning the timing of the attack. The triggering incident had to be used in such a way that the war could begin during favorable flying weather to allow immediate and full-scale deployment of the *Luftwaffe*.

At another conference on 3 September, with the preparation for Green now well along, Hitler shared his final thoughts on the shape the war-to-come would probably take. He stressed the necessity of utilizing the motorized forces for flanking actions, and summarized the impending attack, in an almost train-of-consciousness monologue as follows:

> The 2nd Army Sector is the smallest. The strongest Czech defenses are in that area; thrusts in the 10th Army area are much more promising. Roadblocks are prepared everywhere. [But they are] no reason for hindrance. The Czechs will hold opposite the 2nd Army and keep an assault force ready east of Prague. A thrust against it into the heart of Czechoslovakia is to be made. The thrust in the 14th Army area will fail because of transport difficulties in Austria. Therefore assemble all motorized and armored divisions with 10th Army and employ them in the thrust there. Once we break through in that area, the southern front—which is built up opposite of 12th Army into three defense lines—

The German Plan of Attack

will collapse. An army in the heart of Bohemia will bring about the decision. There is a possible repetition of Verdun in the case of 2nd Army. To attack there would mean bleeding to death for a task that cannot be accomplished.

Thus it was agreed the invasion would be spearheaded by *10th Army* on the axis Klatovy-Pilsen-Prague. In cooperation with *12th Army*, the Czech fortifications in southwest and southern Bohemia would be breached in several places at once.

On 9th September, while in Nuremberg to attend the annual Nazi Party rally there, Hitler again summoned his generals. This time he placed emphasis on the necessity of preventing the Czech army from retreating intact out of Bohemia and Moravia into Slovakia. This was to be accomplished by grand pincer attacks from *2nd* and *14th Armies*. The earlier doubts about a "second Verdun" taking place in those sectors seem to have been forgotten; in his notes on the conference, Gen. Halder wrote: "This operation will definitely succeed."

On 16 September, the Germans began moving reinforced border guard battalions into positions along the Czech border. A secret order was issued to the German railroad administration to maintain its rolling stock in such a way as to allow its use in the concentration of the army on or around 28 September.

On 19 September, the armed forces high command sent word to the *Sudeten Freikorps* in Czechoslovakia to tone down its activities lest they give the Czechoslovakians a pretext to go to a state of alert again.

But the diplomacy of appeasement was also in operation during this period. Having been brought so close to the precipice in May, the French and British had no desire to look over the edge again. On 21 September, the German high command issued an order directing that preparations for the invasion be continued, but also stating the various services should be ready for a possible peaceful takeover.

On 28 September, Gen. Schmundt recorded the following in his diary: "At 1300 on September 27, the *Führer* and Supreme Commander of the Armed Forces ordered the movement of the assault units from their exercise areas to their jumping-off points. The assault units must be ready to start Operation Green and advance against Czechoslovakia on 30 September."

That same day, Gen. Halder wrote in his diary: "The staff reports about a conference with Göring, who states that a general war can hardly be avoided any longer. It may last seven years, but we will still win it."

But at about 5:00 p.m., there was a sudden relaxation in the tension. Hitler announced he had decided to accept the idea of a conference with Chamberlain, Daladier and Mussolini in Munich. The immediate danger of a new European war was thus aborted, and the Munich debacle was put in motion.

What If the Czechs Had Fought?

In 1938, Czechoslovakia's population was only one-fifth that of the Third Reich's. The annual output of steel in Czechoslovakia equalled one month's output in Germany. About 75 percent of Czechoslovakia's international trade had to pass through German territory. On the other hand, Czechoslovakia had an excellent armaments industry that could not only provide abundant arms and munitions to the Czech army, but to those of the Little Entente and other nations as well. (In 1935, Czechoslovakia had been the world's leading exporter of small arms.)

To ensure their defense, the Czechs enacted a series of far reaching measures beginning in 1933. They established a "Supreme State Defense Council," with almost dictatorial powers to coordinate economic affairs with defense requirements. In the following year conscription was extended from 18 to 24 months. In 1935 the fortification scheme was started. In 1936 the "State Defense Guards" were set up as paramilitary bodies to support the army in maintaining law and order in the troublesome Sudeten area.

In short, the process of the militarization of ordinary civilian life in Czechoslovakia was well along by 1937. It was with obvious pride and a sense of accomplishment that Benes would later write in his memoirs: "In the summer of 1938, our army was, despite all its shortcomings that I became very well aware of during the Munich Crisis, one of the best in Europe. Its morale and equipment, as demonstrated during the two mobilizations, were up to standard."

That optimistic view was largely supported by the French general staff and by the bulk of evidence reaching the British Foreign and War Offices from Czechoslovakia. The British military attache in Prague at the time, Lt. Col. Stronge, believed the Czech army was "well equipped" and it would be a "great mistake to underrate its value." He speculated that in the event of a serious German breach of the fortified border defenses, the Czech forces could retreat behind the River Vltava, and from there by stages back to the Moravian/Slovakian plateau. Bohemian geography offered, Stronge believed, "what must almost be a unique succession of natural rearguard positions right into Slovakia—still the last and least accessible stronghold."

Gen. Faucher, the head of the French military mission in Czechoslovakia, shared Stronge's views and expressed his belief in the great defensive value of the Little Maginot Line.

To Gen. Syrovy, the Inspector General of the Czechoslovak army, the most important tasks were to run a smooth and rapid mobilization and not to be taken by surprise.

On the other side, the senior officer corps of the *Wehrmacht* did not share Hitler's enthusiasm for a blitzkrieg against Czechoslovakia. Their opposition was exemplified by Gen. von Beck, who believed it would take at least three to four weeks to defeat Czechoslovakia. He repeatedly warned Hitler against the danger of a two- or multi-front war, since he was convinced France was bound to intervene in the event of a German attack on Czeckoslovakia. Thus a small war might be transformed into a general European war, with the difference being that Germany in 1938 was less prepared than she had been in 1914 to wage a long fight. Von Beck was supported in his arguments by Gen. Thomas, Chief of the Army Armaments Bureau. Thomas particularly criticized the inadequate provisions for the build up of strategic reserves.

Further, the successful execution of a blitz attack against Czechoslovakia would have depended on a number of imponderables. The blitzkrieg had not yet been tested in its entirety. The *Luftwaffe* required good weather. The timing of the "incident" within Czechoslovakia seemed to have misfired when Prague's forces quickly suppressed the unrest among the Sudeten Germans following Hitler's inflammatory speech on 12 September. The Czechs succeeded completely in their September mobilization, calling over a million men to the colors by 1 October. Thus the chief precondition for the execution of Operation Green, the element of surprise, was simply not available to the Germans on the date of the planned attack.

As for the Czech military leaders, they accepted the prospect of war with a sound professional confidence. That confidence was based, first of all, on the knowledge that due to Germany's only recent reintroduction of conscription in 1935, Berlin could not put more troops in the field than had been trained since. But an even more important element of their confidence lay in their belief the French and Soviets would help if called upon to do so.

When interviewed 30 years later in 1968, Gen. Krejci (Chief of the Czech General Staff in 1938) said he had estimated the total of Czech forces, including their reserves, would have roughly equaled the strength of the Germans in the expected areas of attack. He also confirmed the assumption the Czech army planned to stage a fighting retreat all the way back to Slovakia.

It appears that Allied assistance, at least in the form of the Soviet air force, would have been a reality. Late in September, preparations were already being made to accommodate between 450 and 600 Red Air Force fighters and bombers. Also, on 24 September, the Romanian government acceded to requests from Moscow to provide a ground and air corridor for the Red Army and Air Force to facilitate the transfer of machines and manpower to Czechoslovakia in case of a

German attack there. Bucharest gave permission for the Soviets to use a railway for the movement of two divisions, including 300 tanks and 700 artillery pieces, within the first two weeks of a German attack. A refueling airfield for Soviet planes was also prepared by the Romanian army near the Czechoslovakian border. The French, though, remained a big question mark.

At the time, both French and British military experts tried to answer the question of how long the Czechoslovakians could hold out alone against German aggression. Lt. Col. Stronge, in a memo dated 3 September 1938, rejected the idea the defenders would go down in three weeks or less. He observed that, on average, the Czech army and its equipment were equal to the Germans. He thought the decisive factor would be the morale of the Czechoslovakians. If that broke, the invasion and conquest would not take longer than a week or two; if it held, the defense might last for at least a month. A month would have been enough time for a determined Allied intervention to have made the difference.

German & Czech Strategic Concepts in 1938

The Germans

German strategy in World War I centered on their concept of *Vernichtungsgedanke*. It was the infamous Field Marshal von Schlieffen who had come up with the idea, after developing von Moltke's theory of flanking and encircling moves into a new, all-embracing doctrine of decisive maneuver. *Vernichtungsgedanke* tanslates as "idea of anni- hilation," and it has gone into military history as the term for what von Schlieffen believed to be the ultimate aim of any war effort: the total destruction of the enemy's forces by means of swift, decisive blows delivered from the front, flank and rear.

In 1914, the German army's modified version of von Schlieffen's original plan for a wide maneuver to turn the French flank and destroy them from behind almost succeeded. Only the physical exhaustion of the troops, logistical shortcomings resulting from the rapid advance, and a few critical mistakes by local commanders saved France, stopping the invasion on the Marne River.

During the following war years, as the deadly trio of trenches, artillery and machineguns ruled the battlefield, all attempts to break the stalemate in the west and return to swift and decisive maneuver failed. Though the Germans utilized the power of the defense there, the superiority of their mobile strategy was proven in 1915, 1916 and 1917 in the east, when first Serbia, then Romania, and finally Russia were knocked out of the war. Despite the ultimately failed experience on the western front, *Vernichtungsgedanke* remained the pillar of German strategy to the end of the war.

The final defeat in 1918 led to some uncertainty in the minds of many German military leaders. They compared their strategy of decisive maneuver with the doctrine of firepower-and-fortifications that had dominated the Western Front. Some of the German generals even supported for a time the French theory of the "Gradual Offensive," which was slow but safe. Attacks were to be made only with secured flanks, by infantry supported by tanks and artillery, and even the spearhead units were to be able to go over to the defensive at any instant.

The German debate was not finally resolved until Gen. von Seeckt, head of the Weimar Republic's army, offered his solution. He believed the experience of World War I had shown a need for greater mobility, not less, and that the failure of the German war effort had been caused by mistakes of command rather than by a failure of doctrine. He expressed his idea this way:

> The whole future of warfare seems to lie in the employment of mobile armies, relatively small but of high quality, and rendered distinctly more effective by the addition of aircraft and by the simultaneous mobilization of the whole force... The army of the future must satisfy three demands. First, it must have high mobility. This can be attained by employment of numerous and highly efficient cavalry units, the fullest possible use of motor transport, and the marching capacity of the infantry. Second, it must have the most effective armament. Third, it must have continuous replacement of men and material.

The strategic debate of the German army command was decided in the late 1920s. The successors of von Moltke and von Schlieffen won, and the idea of *Vernichtungsgedanke* survived. The doctrine was reaffirmed and given modern elaboration in a directive on troop command issued late in 1933. Its first page read: "Even war undergoes constant evolution. New arms give ever new forms of combat. To foresee this technical revolution before it occurs, to judge well the influence of these new arms on battle, to employ them before others, is an essential condition for success."

The directive also advocated the use of tanks and motorized transport for penetrations; in contrast to prevailing foreign doctrines it did not restrict those mobile forces to an infantry support role. On the contrary, it stressed that mobile units tied too closely to the infantry would lose their advantage of speed and thus eventually be knocked out by the defenders.

Still, the new doctrine was not truly revolutionary—it was really a modified version of the idea invented in the previous century. Infantry divisions on the march with horse-drawn guns and supply wagons were still seen as the decisive elements of encirclements; the motorized units and armor were to be subordinated to their ultimate needs. Armor was to be the cutting edge of the flanking attacks, help to penetrate enemy front lines, destroy enemy artillery, disrupt enemy reserves, and finally close the pincers—but the marching infantry would still be critical in tightening the ring and then destroying the encircled forces.

Such was the official thinking in the early 1930s, when Col. Heinz Guderian developed his more radical "armored concept"—what later became known as the "Blitzkrieg" (or Lightning War). The final directives for Operation Green indicate the attack on Czechoslovakia was planned in the Blitzkrieg fashion. The breakthrough of the fortified line was to be followed by *independent* panzer thrusts, penetrations and exploitations. The Czechs were supposed to be overturned by a lightning mechanized stroke that, it was hoped in Berlin, would not take longer than a week.

The Czechs

The war plans of Czechoslovakia were based on a doctrine very different from that of the Germans. It was a doctrine of defense conducted behind fixed fortifications, a doctrine heavily influenced by the French military thinking of the 1930s. However, this defensive attitude was somewhat modified by the lessons of mobile defense that had been used by the Czech Legion in Russia.

The basic concepts of the Czechoslovakian defensive doctrine ran as follows: defense behind fixed fortifications, flank counterattacks against penetrations into that first line of defense, mobile defense in the hills and highlands of Bohemia and Moravia during any retreat out of that area, a final halt along the western reaches of Moravia, or at worst, Slovakia.

To aid this strategy, by 1938 the Czechs had fortified their entire border with Germany, covering some parts of it with the strongest fortifications in Europe. Plans also existed to move western industrial centers to Slovakia for reconstitution there. Food supplies from within the rump-defensive area were deemed to be sufficient, and oil and gasoline were to be supplied by rail from friendly Romania.

But fortifications aside, if left alone to fight against Germany, Czechoslovakia's strategic position could hardly have been worse. Her sausage-shape formed a 1,000-kilometer corridor extending deep into German territory. The total length of her frontiers was over 4,000 kilometers, and only 200 kilometers of it bordered on a friendly neighbor, Romania. Half the border area, more than 2,000 kilometers, was shared with Germany; and almost 1,800 kilometers was shared with hostile and unpredictable Poland and Hungary.

Viewed only in the strategic abstract, Czechoslovakia actually appeared indefensible against her real and potential foes. The Czech general staff, then, chose an all-defensive doctrine out of necessity: it was really the only available strategy, regardless of the support that might have eventually been received from outside.

The Blitzkrieg Solution

The tactical doctrine of the German army emphasized the fundamental role of small combat teams using infiltration techniques to penetrate enemy lines. "Infiltration" had indeed become a scary word on the western front in 1918; for a while, it appeared as if the Germans had finally found a way to break the stalemate of trench warfare.

The essence of the new tactics lay in surprise, speed, and the flexibility inherent in well-trained and heavily-armed combat groups, the so-called *Stosstruppen* (Stormtroops). These were battalion-size units, armed with automatic weapons, light machineguns, hand grenades, flamethrowers and light mortars, and supported by light artillery. After a short but intensive barrage they moved forward to create narrow penetrations through enemy lines. Any defensive strongpoints were bypassed and left to the masses of regular infantry coming behind. Meanwhile, the stormtroopers continued their advance into the enemy rear area, destroying artillery positions, head-quarters, communications, supply facilities, and generally sowing chaos.

The confusion this caused among unprepared defenders often resulted in the breakdown of their entire command structure and the disruption of large units. Their morale was shaken by the surprise and violent attack. Combined with the other factors described above, such an attack could lead to the complete collapse of the defense along the front. The narrow gaps were thus turned into wide penetrations, and the mass of regular infantry moved forward to maintain the momentum.

That was the method Ludendorff used in his offensives of 1918. But the advantage was eventually lost, and the Allies gained enough time to move in reinforcements and restore their lines. That decisive loss of momentum on the German side was caused by the slow pace of their horse-drawn supply columns and the eventual exhaustion of the infantry after the initial penetrations. The postwar development of motorized and tracked vehicles, with their much greater range and speed, removed those shortcomings.

The genius behind the new Blitzkrieg theory that first supplemented and then supplanted the earlier footbound infiltration doctrine was Heinz Guderian. To quote the British author Len Deighton from his book, *Blitzkrieg*: "It is unique in military history for one man to influence a design of a weapon, see to training the men who use it, help plan an offensive, and then lead the force in battle."

But Heinz Guderian did just that. Born in 1881, he served in World War I with a telegraph battalion, and was in charge of a large wireless station that provided communications for the cavalry. He also served as a staff officer on the Eastern Front, and after the war was selected to join the Inspectorate of Transport Troops. It was this job that enabled him to study the tactical use of motorized infantry in combat, and elaborate on it from his experience with battlefield communications. All this came together to make him the German army's leading expert on mobile warfare in the early 1930s.

He read the works of British tank expert J.F.C. Fuller, and from them envisioned the idea of a fully mechanized force striking *independently* and deeply behind enemy lines. It was in making the mobile forces independent of the marching infantry that Guderian's thinking became truly revolutionary and distinct from the classic *Vernichtungsgedanke* concept.

Still, Guderian's basic theory of the Blitzkrieg was at first seldom challenged by his superiors simply because it did largely agree with the classic thinking on mobility, and worked well in the overall scheme of the *Vernichtungsgedanke*. He was first supported by von Blomberg, the German War Minister, and later also by Hitler. The latter, after seeing a prototype of the Panzer I tank at a demonstration in 1935, exclaimed: "That's what I need! That's what I want!"

In October of that year, Guderian was appointed Chief of Staff of the newly created armored forces. From that point on, he steadily elaborated his thinking into an all-embracing doctrine of victory through a mechanized indirect approach, which did generate serious opposition among more conservative elements of the high command.

The doctrine as it finally evolved had three main stages of execution. First, the armored forces, with strong support from the air, concentrates its attack on the weakest point of the enemy line. Taking advantage of surprise, ferocity, and local firepower superiority, it breaks through the enemy line on a narrow front, bypassing strongpoints, which are left to be cleaned out by the follow-on infantry.

Next comes the penetration. The armored force *independently* drives deep into the enemy rear areas, always moving as fast as possible from point to point of least resistance. New defense lines and strong points are again bypassed, and the true direction of the main thrust is disguised by constantly developing decoy penetrations. (Hence the "indirectness" of the approach to the final objective.) Speed and flexibility are the most important factors at this stage; the security of the flanks is at best secondary. The sheer momentum of the attack caused confusion among the enemy and disrupts his command system, preventing him from concentrating enough troops to reform an effective opposition.

The third stage is the exploitation of the tactical gains into a strategic advantage. This is done by a further extension of the indirect approach described above. Now, though, the enemy is eventually entirely destroyed by the disruption and loss of command-control over his own forces. As his units lose direction and coordination, fear, doubt, panic and uncertainty finally and fully shatter morale. The will to fight declines until all organized resistance ceases.

The German Army in 1938

In the summer and autumn of 1938, the German army (*Heer*) was not ready for a major European war. There were two main reasons for that unpreparedness. The first was the shortage of trained personnel. Though each successive six-month period increased the general level of individual training and the number of trained reservists, the German army had probably not yet reached the required level of overall proficiency necessary for defeating Czechoslovakia within a short time.

The second, more important, reason was the lack of all kinds of military supplies, including ammunition and fuel. Perhaps the most serious problem was the ammunition shortage. The army high command based its in-stock requirements on a hoped-for lightning war against Czechoslovakia not to exceed one month. In September 1938, however, there was an overall 50 percent shortfall of the called-for requirement, and in artillery and mortar shells that shortfall was even greater—a staggering 70 percent.

The army plan for 1936 called for a wartime army (*Kriegsheer*) of 41 regular and 25 reserve divisions. The latter would be brought up to strength only during mobilization. By the end of 1937 the army had 32 infantry, four motorized infantry and three panzer divisions, one incomplete mountain division, one cavalry brigade, and the 25 reserve infantry divisions, for a total of 66 major units.

Four of the reserve divisions were formed by cadres withdrawn from regular formations, and had reduced allotments of weapons and transport. The other 21 reserve divisions were *Landwehr*, formed from reservists aged 35 and older, veterans of World War I. The *Landwehr* divisions were equipped with obsolete weapons, and each had only one artillery battalion and practically no motorized transport. Further, their divisional and regimental commands were understaffed due to the acute shortage of commissioned officers.

By 1938 the situation had somewhat improved, at least on paper. Ten new divisions had been formed (or taken over during the *Anschluss*), of which six were motorized or mechanized. In actuality, some army headquarters and many support and administrative units simply did not yet exist. Even the formation of the regular army remained incomplete. In the first-line divisions, 34 infantry battalions of an authorized total of 315 (that is, a 12 percent shortfall) had still

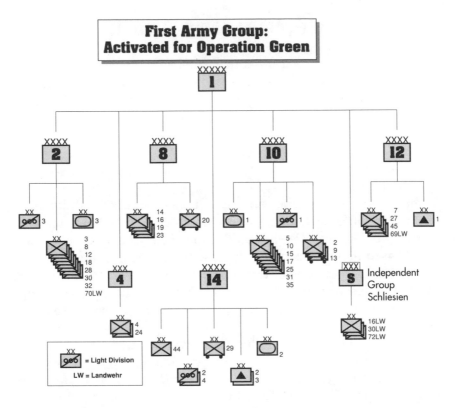

not been formed or completed. Approximately the same shortfall existed in the artillery arm.

The actual mobilization of the full paper-strength army would have required an addition of approximately 3 million men, 400,000 horses, and 200,000 motor vehicles.

On the positive side, the organization of the German army in 1938 was logical, simple and effective. The highest command was the army group, composed of two or more armies, each of which had two or more corps. A corps was formed of two or more divisions, which were the largest homogeneous field units capable of sustained independent action and command.

The most outstanding characteristic of this organizational scheme was its flexibility. Divisions, corps and armies were frequently shifted from higher command to another, swiftly and smoothly, according to operational requirements.

The division was the most important field unit of the German army. These units were self-contained formations with generally balanced

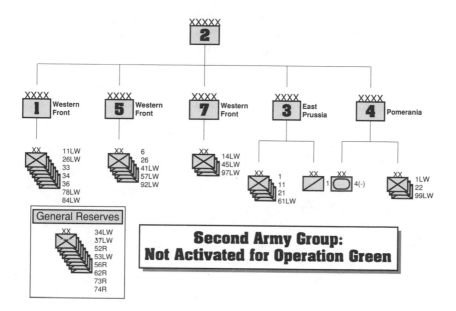

compositions of combat arms, though the mechanized units still needed adjusting. There were five types of divisions: infantry, motorized infantry, mountain infantry, light and armored (panzer).

The first-line infantry divisions had three infantry regiments, each of three battalions, an infantry gun company, and an anti-tank company. The battalions consisted of three infantry companies and a heavy weapons company. The division also controlled two artillery regiments, a reconnaissance battalion, a machinegun battalion, an engineer battalion, an anti-tank section, and an anti-aircraft section, plus supply, medical and administrative services, for a total strength of about 17,000 men.

The single combat-ready mountain division also had an authorized strength of about 17,000 men, but had a smaller artillery component than its regular infantry counterparts to facilitate travel across rugged terrain.

Only two of the four light divisions (the 1st and 2nd) were fully operational in September 1938. At the time they had a motorized reconnaissance battalion with 18 armored cars, two motorized artillery regiments with two sections each, a cavalry regiment of three battalions, a company of engineers, and an anti-tank section. Their cutting edge lay in their tank battalion, which consisted of three companies of light tanks (46 Pzkw Is) and one company of Pzkw IIs (22 tanks), for a total armor strength of 68 vehicles.

The three panzer divisions consisted of a tank brigade and an infantry brigade. The tanks were organized in two regiments of two battalions each, totalling about 330. One company in each battalion was supposed to have medium Pzkw III tanks equipped with 37mm guns. In actuality, though, each division possessed only one company of those machines per regiment (22 tanks). A fourth panzer division was forming at Paderborn, but at the time of Operation Green it had only one tank regiment and no artillery.

The infantry brigade in each panzer division was composed of a regiment of motorized infantry, a motorized artillery regiment, reconnaissance, anti-tank, engineer, and motorcycle battalions, and signals, medical and administrative units.

The 1938 panzer divisions' total manpower came to only 11,500.

The *7th Flieger* (paratrooper) *Division* had only begun forming in 1937, and in September 1938 there was only one battalion of paratroopers and one airlanding regiment ready for operations.

The quality of the army's weapons and equipment left much to be desired. The standard infantry rifle was the Mauser model 98, which was adequate but obsolete. Modern machine pistols and sub-machineguns were still only in development. Many units were still armed with World War I vintage light machineguns, and no modern heavy machinegun was yet available. Heavy mortars were practically non-existent, and the standard anti-tank rifles would have been ineffective against the armor of the Czech tanks. The only anti-tank gun in service was the 37mm PAK 35/36, and it was also ineffective against contemporary armor—it earned the derisive nickname "the army's doorknocker."

German artillery was divided between divisional and army support units. The standard weapon was a 100mm K18 gun, supported by 150mm and 170mm howitzers. A few 210mm howitzers were available, stationed mostly in the west. All these gun designs dated back to World War I.

The infantry support guns (a specialty of the German army) were produced in both light and heavy models (75mm and 150mm), and were considered adequate for their task.

The only anti-aircraft weapons issued to the army were the light 20mm FLAK 30, but they were not yet available in adequate numbers. The famous 88mm FLAK 18, models 36 and 37, were all under *Luftwaffe* control and only a few had made their way into the artillery regiments of the panzer division.

Chapter XX

Poland '39

by Pat McTaggart
with contributions by L. Dean Webb

On 3 November 1918, the Polish Republic was proclaimed in Warsaw. The creation of an independent Poland had recently become an Allied war aim, and with the end of World War I the victors went about the business of carving up eastern Europe. Poland's borders were fixed by the Treaty of St. Germain, the Versailles Treaty, and—after a bitter and see-saw 18-month war with the nascent Soviet Union—the Treaty of Riga.

The men who redrew the map of Europe tried to please everyone, and—of course—in so doing, actually pleased no one. Poland was given a land corridor to the Baltic Sea, thus placing thousands of Germans under Warsaw's control and separating East Prussia from the rest of the Weimar Republic. The German port of Danzig was declared a "Free City." Though Danzig was internally controlled by an overwhelmingly German city population and its legislature, the Poles were put in charge of its customs offices and foreign affairs, and maintained a military presence.

As Poland was coming into being, Adolf Hitler lay in a hospital recovering from blindness suffered in an Allied gas attack. Like most Germans, Hitler regarded the separation of East Prussia, along with the resultant "Polish Corridor," as a national disgrace. Twenty years later, as leader of the Third Reich, he sent his armies to avenge the "Shame of Versailles," and in so doing triggered the greatest conflict in history.

Prior to the 1939 invasion, reclamation of lost German territory was already a large part of Berlin's foreign policy. The Saar, Upper Silesia, Austria, Memel, the Sudetenland and Czechoslovakia were all incorporated into the Reich with little real opposition from the Allies. Accordingly, even though Poland had a defense treaty with Britain

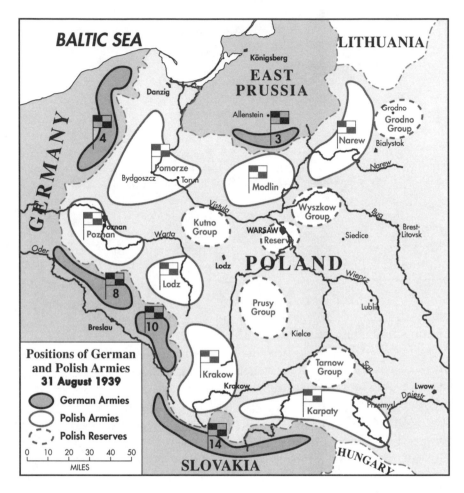

Positions of German and Polish Armies 31 August 1939

German Armies
Polish Armies
Polish Reserves

0 10 20 30 40 50
MILES

and France, Hitler did not believe the westerners would go to war to defend a country barely two decades old.

On 23 August 1939, the fate of Poland was sealed when German Foreign Minister Joachim von Ribbentrop signed a non-aggression pact with the Soviet Union. Included within the pact was a secret codicil dividing Poland between the two totalitarian powers. With the threat of a two-front war thus at least temporarily removed, Hitler issued instructions to his generals to proceed with the plan to invade Poland. He set 1 September as the date for operations to begin.

German planning foresaw the battle for Poland developing in the following manner. *Army Group North's 3rd Army*, attacking from East Prussia, would send the bulk of its forces directly toward Warsaw. One corps would swing west to link up with *4th Army*, cutting the

Polish Corridor. That combined force would drive south to link up with *Army Group South* at the juncture of the Oder and Vistula Rivers.

Army Group South's 8th Army would push toward Warsaw, while establishing contact with *4th Army* on its left flank. The *10th Army's* task was to sweep across central Poland and reach the Bug River, thus effectively cutting the country into northern and southern halves. Finally, the southern-most German army, the *14th*, was to attack through the mountainous region of southern Poland and capture the fortress town of Lvov, while at the same time preventing retreating enemy units from escaping to Hungary and Romania (then neutral countries).

The Polish commanders unwittingly helped the German planners by concentrating their forces near the border between their two countries. They did this out of a misguided political determination to hold all of Poland, rather than take up the excellent interior defensive positions provided by the Narew, Vistula and San Rivers.

Army Group North, 1-3 September

At 4:40 a.m. on 1 September 1939, *Luftwaffe* aircraft began the systematic destruction of the Polish air force. Five minutes later, the vintage (1906) battleship *Schleswig-Holstein*, which was officially on a "courtesy call" to Danzig, opened fire on the Polish fortress of Westerplatte in the harbor. Meanwhile, *Kriegsmarine* submarine and surface units blockaded Polish Baltic ports, preventing ships of the Polish navy from escaping to friendly countries. (Luckily for the Poles, their five-boat submarine fleet was already at sea.)

The opening minutes of the ground battle almost cost the Germans one of their best generals. Heinz Guderian, accompanying the forward elements of the *3rd Panzer Brigade*, came under fire from his own artillery. His command car ended up in a ditch, with shells exploding around it, but Guderian was not even scratched.

A dense fog kept the *Luftwaffe* from carrying out many planned close support missions. In many places that inactivity allowed the Poles to blow up bridges before German ground troops could capture them. Some artillery and *Luftwaffe* units mistakenly attacked their own troops, but German casualties remained light, and the errors did little to prevent the attackers from advancing in all sectors.

As troops of the Danzig Brigade fought for control of that city from

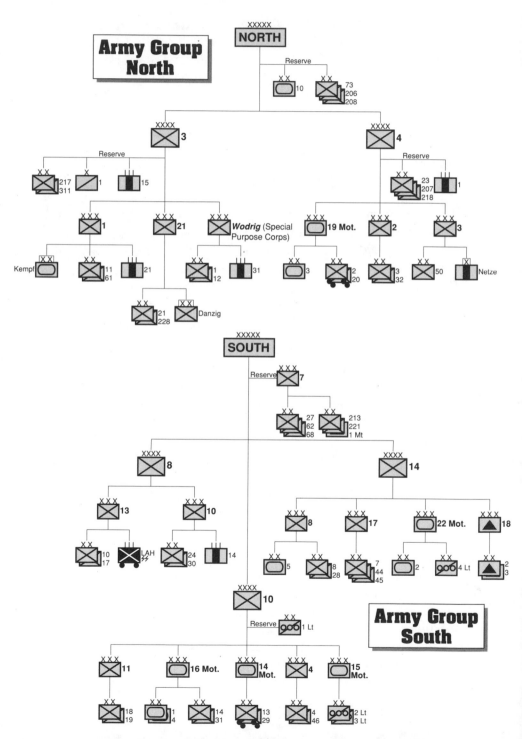

Organization of Polish Ground Forces for War, 1 Sept. 1939

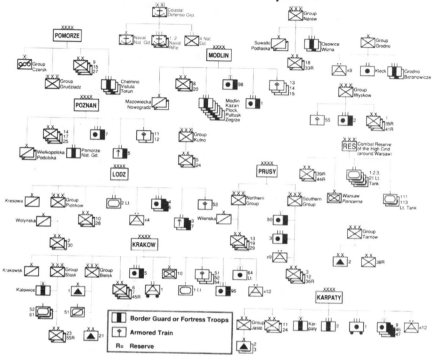

within, elements of the *3rd* and *4th Armies* began their drive to seal the Corridor.

Guderian's *19th Motorized Corps,* supported by an infantry corps on each flank, forced the Polish 9th Infantry Division and Pomorska Cavalry Brigade to withdraw behind the Brda River. Though the Poles destroyed the bridges spanning the river, the *3rd Panzer Division's* motorcycle battalion was able to establish a bridgehead on the eastern bank, using rubber boats to ferry the men across. By the end of the first day, engineers had built a pontoon bridge over the Brda, and motorized elements were rushing to meet their comrades from *3rd Army,* who were by then advancing from the east.

Though the Poles were generally stunned by the initial onslaught, a few Polish commanders quickly organized counterattacks. However, the Poles' tactics and weapons could not match those of the German mechanized units. The *3rd Panzer Division* reported a massed attack (probably from Pomorska Cavalry Brigade) on that first day. "It was like something out of World War I," an officer noted. "Massed

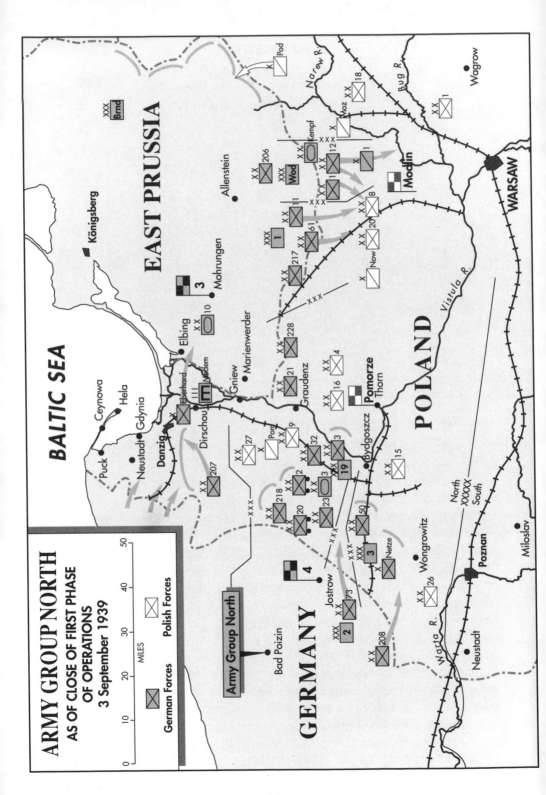

ARMY GROUP NORTH

AS OF CLOSE OF FIRST PHASE OF OPERATIONS
3 September 1939

MILES

0 10 20 30 40 50

German Forces

Polish Forces

Army Group North

BALTIC SEA

EAST PRUSSIA

POLAND

GERMANY

WARSAW

Königsberg

Puck
Ceynowa
Hela
Neustadt
Gdynia
Danzig
Elbing
Eberhard
Medem
Dirschou
Gniew
Marienwerder
Graudenz
Allenstein
Mohrungen
Thorn
Pomorze
Bydgoszcz
Netze
Wongrowitz
Poznan
Miloslav
Neustadt
Bad Poizin
Jostrow
Modlin
Wagrow
Narew R.
Bug R.
Vistula R.
Warta R.

Brnd
Pod
18
1
Kempf
206
Wod
12
1
1
11
1
8
1
61
217
20
Now
10
3
228
21
4
16
27
Pong
9
32
3
19
15
2
3
218
20
23
50
3
Netze
4
73
2
208
26
North
XXXX
South

A dead Polish tanker lies next to his burned out light tank, a PZI Tk.3, on the road to Mlawa.

squadrons charging with sabres drawn. Our machine guns decimated row after row of enemy riders. They would retire, regroup, and come again until none were left."

While *4th Army* moved eastward, *3rd Army* crossed the East Prussian border. Its *21st Corps* advanced southwest to meet *4th Army*, while *1st Corps* and *Corps Wodrig* moved south in the direction of Warsaw. The *1st Corps* immediately ran into stiff resistance from the Polish 1st Infantry Division and Nowogradzka Cavalry Brigade. The Poles fell back to a fortified area around the town of Mlawa, and waited there for the Germans to advance.

Panzer Division Kempf, an *ad hoc* unit centered around the *7th Panzer Regiment* and the *SS Motorized Infantry Regiment Deutschland*, ran straight into the withering fire from the Mlawa defenses. Polish bunkers and minefields dotted the landscape, and the defenders' interlocking fields of fire made open movement hazardous. SS assault troops suffered heavy casualties as they worked to breach the bunkers, and Polish anti-tank fire destroyed 7 panzers and damaged 32 more.

Kempf was forced to call for help from the *11th* and *61st Infantry Divisions*. Three days of heavy fighting were needed before the Poles were finally compelled to give up Mlawa. The stand at Mlawa had blunted what otherwise could have been a lightning German drive directly to Warsaw by the shortest route.

Meanwhile, the lengthy Polish mobilization plans had been wrecked, thanks to *Luftwaffe* strikes on rail and communications centers. But those troops who had been called up in the last days before the war started were for the most part able to reach their assigned positions.

One such unit, the 1st Reserve Cavalry Regiment, reached the northern front on 2 September. Due to German control of the air, the horsemen had been forced to use trails through wooded areas instead of the main roads. "The *Luftwaffe* was everywhere," one survivor recalled. "They hit us every place we went. We lost our field kitchen the first day. That was the end of hot meals for the rest of the campaign."

Despite the *Luftwaffe* attacks, though, the cavalry regiment was able to attack some German positions just across the East Prussian border. The attack met surprisingly light opposition from the frontier battalions of *Provisional Corps Brand*. "Most of the troops we encountered in our foray into East Prussia seemed over-age," that same survivor recalled. "They didn't want to stand and fight."

The Poles' cavalry probe into East Prussia was cut short, however, when other German units swung in behind the attackers in an attempt to cut them off. The 1st was able to retreat before the last exit closed, then headed south to join with the Nowogrodzka Cavalry Brigade, which had been mauled at Mlawa.

Gen. Anders, commander of Nowogrodzka, kept his unit moving south. They stopped in Warsaw for only one day before continuing their journey. Cavalry units would be of little value in street fighting, so Anders kept heading south toward the open Polish plain where his unit might do some good.

While *3rd Army's* left flank was still fighting near the frontier, its *21st Corps* continued moving southwest to link up with *4th Army*. On 2 September, the *21st* and *228th Infantry Divisions* advanced to within five kilometers of Grudziadz. There the Polish 4th and 16th Infantry Divisions were kept from retreating across the Vistula River by concentrated artillery fire, and were instead forced to fall back to the south.

Then, on the evening of the 2nd, the reconnaissance battalion of the *3rd Panzer Division* reached the Vistula from the west. The *20th Motorized Infantry Division*, after suffering setbacks the previous day

A destroyed Polish bunker at Mlawa.

from Polish cavalry attacks, provided flank cover for the rest of *3rd Panzer*, and by 3 September the forward elements of the *3rd* and *4th Armies* were firmly linked. That juncture trapped the Polish 9th and 27th Infantry Divisions, as well as the Pomorska Cavalry Brigade, north of the new German lines. Those units destroyed themselves in a series of desperate attacks against the German units holding the base of the blocking corridor.

Farther north, Polish forces still held the fortified Hela Peninsula, but they were also under constant attack by land, sea and air. Lt. Karl Hermann Lion, a Stuka pilot of *Attack Group 186*, sank the Polish destroyer *Wicher* and minelayer *Gryf* in Hela harbor on 3 September. Those ships, along with several coastal batteries, had given the Poles vital support against the German forces attacking across the peninsula. Even with that support destroyed, though, the peninsula would not be secured for several more days.

Battle for the Narew

With the former Polish Corridor now under German control, *Army Group North* was free to hurl the combined weight of its *3rd* and *4th*

Armies southward toward the Polish capital. The *4th Army* swung southeast, scattering the Polish 15th Infantry Division and taking the town of Bydgoszcz. At the same time, *3rd Army's 21st Corps* forced the remnants of the Poles' 4th and 16th Infantry Divisions to retreat toward Torun. Then *1st Corps* and *Corps Wodrig* continued their advance toward the Vistula and Bug Rivers, meeting only light opposition.

The Poles fought well, but with their supply columns continuously decimated by the *Luftwaffe*, and on-hand ammunition running out, there was little that could be done to stop the Germans. The Polish commander-in-chief, Marshal Rydz-Smigly, sent a message to Paris and London, underlining the disaster in the making: "The entire front has been broken. We can only retreat to a defensive line behind the Vistula and hope that it will be held."

Von Bock, *Army Group North's* commander, was quick to issue orders keeping his divisions hot on the heels of the weakening Modlin and Pomorze Armies as they retreated. The *4th Army* executed a wide sweep to the southeast with the bulk of its forces, while *3rd Army* pushed the Pomorze Army eastward toward Warsaw. Von Bock planned to trap and destroy the Poles north of the Narew-Vistula line, using *4th Army* as his hammer and the *3rd* his anvil.

But things did not go as planned. The *4th Army's* repositioning took extra time, allowing the majority of the Pomorze Army still in the field to retreat in good order. The Modlin Army, however, was exposed to continuous air attacks, which further disorganized its units. Ignoring their flanks, German motorized formations sped forward in an effort to split up the retreating Poles. Several Polish units were destroyed in the bitter race to the Narew River.

That running fight was not totally one-sided, however. As *SS Regiment Deutschland* closed on the Narew crossing at Rozan, it came under heavy machinegun fire from Polish fortifications on the east bank. Rozan was a former Imperial Russian fortress town, with four World War I forts the Poles had modernized.

Supported by elements of the *7th Panzer Regiment*, along with two battalions of artillery, the men of the *Deutschland Regiment* stormed forward. But the Poles that day were giving as good as they got. The *7th's* command post was hit, killing several headquarters personnel and wounding others, while small arms and machinegun fire raked the German infantry as it advanced. Panzers were brought up, and by firing into the bunkers at almost point-blank range, finally managed to silence the Polish forts. Several of the tanks were knocked out during the operation, but in the end the Germans took the town and crossed the river.

By the evening of the 6th, the Polish high command realized the Narew River line could not be held. New orders were issued for the Modlin Army and the Narew Operational Group to retreat to a new defensive position behind the Bug and San Rivers.

The Poles had destroyed most of the bridges spanning the Narew, but German engineer units quickly rebuilt them. The *61st Infantry Division* crossed the Narew at Pultusk, then pushed immediately toward the Bug, scattering the Polish rearguard units before it. That division, now guarding *3rd Army*'s right flank, became the pivot on which the *1st Corps* turned. Once across the Narew, *1st Corps* moved southwest toward Warsaw. With *4th Army* advancing from the west, the Polish capital was effectively isolated on two sides.

The *3rd Army*'s left flank was meanwhile reinforced by Guderian's *19th Motorized Corps*, along with the *10th Panzer Division*. Once in position, that flank began a wide sweeping maneuver. The *21st Corps'* *21st Infantry Division* breached the Polish line and fought its way to Nowogrod and Lomza, while *10th Panzer* crossed the Narew east of Wizna, driving into the Polish rear.

Guderian's corps then sliced through several elements of Operational Group Narew, continuing a wider sweep to the south. Guderian, ignoring his exposed flanks, never gave the defenders a moment to regroup. His motorized corps kept on the move, outpacing the footbound *21st Corps* and overturning all new Polish defense plans as fast as they were turned out.

While the Poles were no match for the panzers, they did slow the *21st Corps*. The *21st Infantry Division* was heavily engaged by the Pole's 18th Infantry Division in a wood just south of the Narew. But then the *20th Motorized Infantry* and *10th Panzer* were diverted to the area, inflicted heavy casualties on the 18th Infantry, thus clearing the way for the *21st* to resume its advance.

Beyond the Narew

As the *21st Infantry Division* marched south, it ran into a defensive line of bunkers and machine gun positions manned by the Polish 33rd Infantry Division. An additional surprise came in the form of an attack from the Podlaska Cavalry Brigade. Luckily for the Germans, their divisional artillery was in position to fire a devastating barrage that disrupted the cavalry and forced them back. The invaders then turned their guns on the bunker line. Soon, the *21st* was on the move again.

In the west, the operational area of *4th Army* was taken over by *8th Army*, which was simultaneously fighting a battle on the Bzura River with the Poznan and Pomorze Armies. But once *4th Army* was thus released, it moved eastward across East Prussia to establish new positions on *3rd Army's* left. From there, *4th Army* prepared a new attack designed to eliminate all Polish forces in the Bialystok/Brest areas.

While *4th* was still repositioning, Guderian's *19th Motorized Corps* continued its drive. By the evening of the 11th, the *20th Motorized Infantry Division* was engaged in a hard fight with the remnants of the Polish 18th Infantry Division, south of Zambrow. The corps' other units were even farther south, with *10th Panzer* at Bransk, and *2nd Motorized* and *3rd Panzer* near Bielsk.

The divisions comprising Operational Group Narew began to fall out of contact with each other because of Guderian's motorized exploitation. As *4th Army's* infantry hurried to catch up, they followed the paths torn open by Guderian, in the process destroying several more Polish units that had been left disorganized in the wake of the panzers' advance.

The *3rd Panzer* took Bielsk the following day, all but destroying the Polish 35th Infantry Division in doing so. The fall of that town opened the way for Guderian to concentrate his forces for an assault on Brest-Litovsk. There, Polish units that had escaped his initial onslaught were hurriedly digging in at the fortress city. As *3rd Panzer* sped toward the place, it ran into the remnants of the Polish 18th Infantry Division. In a brief, but violent, engagement, the troublesome 18th was finally destroyed, and its valiant commander, Col. Kossecki, was taken prisoner.

Farther east, *21st Corps* (*21st* and *216th Infantry Divisions*), along with *Corps Brand*, was moving on Bialystock. They took 6,000 prisoners in a fight near the village of Andrejewo before even reaching the larger town's main defense line.

On 14 September, Guderian received word from *10th Panzer* that it had reached the outer fortifications of Brest-Litovsk. An initial assault was successful in breaching that line, but was stopped short of capturing the city proper. The Poles retreated into the inner fortress, called "the Citadel," and awaited the next attack.

Shortly after the start of the campaign, German motorized infantry in southern Poland fire while still in their truck.

Guderian reacted by sending the *20th Motorized Infantry Division* to Brest, to provide much needed infantry support. After two days of heavy fighting, the Citadel was finally taken. Six-hundred Poles marched in to captivity with quiet dignity; the German troops saluted them as they marched out. The same day, 17 September, *3rd Panzer* reported it had contacted advance elements of *Army Group South* near Wlodawa.

Around Warsaw, *3rd Army* had taken most of the northern suburbs then formed a barrier preventing Polish units inside the city from escaping to the north and east. On orders from Hitler, who was worried about heavy casualties that could be suffered in house-to-house fighting, the city was to be bombed into submission.

Along the Baltic coast, the Poles continued to put up a fierce resistance at Gdynia. The backbone of that defense was the Polish Naval Infantry Brigade, under Col. Dabek. *Corps Kaupisch* (*207th Infantry Division* and *Brigade Eberhard*) paid for every gain with blood, as it slowly forced the Poles back against the sea. Aided by *Luftwaffe* bombers and the guns of the *Schleswig-Holstein*, the Germans managed to cut off the Polish forces on Hela by 12 September. Two days later,

Kaupisch captured Gdynia, forcing Dabeck's troops to retreat across a flat coastal area north of the city.

The Poles continued to fight stubbornly, but the destruction of their major ammunition depot by aerial attack finally put an end to organized resistance. Some 2,000 Poles surrendered, but Col. Dabeck was not among them. He chose suicide, rather than suffer the indignity of captivity. By the night of the 16th, the only Polish units left along the coast were the defenders of the Hela Peninsula.

Army Group South, 1-6 September

By 6:00 a.m., 1 September, advance elements of Gen. Gerd von Rundstedt's *Army Group South* had already driven four miles into Poland. It took the defenders several hours to recover from the initial shock, but by midday, von Rundstedt was receiving reports of cavalry counterattacks and the demolition of bridges and roadways—which slowed the advance considerably.

Gen. Blaskowitz's *8th Army* (the only German army made up entirely of infantry units) engaged the Lodz Army in a head-on attack. At the same time, Blaskowitz extended his left to prevent effective coordination and communication between the Lodz and Poznan Armies.

The *SS Leibstandarte Adolf Hitler Motorized Infantry Regiment (LAH)*, operating on *8th Army*'s extreme right flank, was able to capture several bridges by surprise in the opening hours of the battle. Soon after 9:00 a.m., however, Polish sniper fire slowed their advance. Enemy anti-tank guns destroyed two *LAH* reconnaissance vehicles near the village of Boleslawez, causing the first casualties of the war for what was to become one of Germany's premier units.

Despite growing Polish resistance, *8th Army* was able to reach the Prosna River by the end of the day, inflicting heavy casualties on the 2nd and 10th Infantry Divisions of the Lodz Army in the process.

Gen. Reichenau's *10th Army* held the bulk of the armored and motorized units of *Army Group South*. The *1st* and *4th Panzer Divisions*, forming the cutting edge of that army, engaged three Polish infantry divisions and a cavalry brigade in a drive that carried the panzers 15 miles into enemy territory in the first day. Most of the enemy units trying to make a stand were simply bypassed and left to the following infantry divisions.

The Poles, though, earned the respect of the tank crews early on

ARMY GROUP SOUTH
AS OF CLOSE OF FIRST PHASE
OF OPERATIONS
6 September 1939

German Forces   Polish Forces

that first day. A cavalry squadron of the Wolynska Cavalry Brigade held up a column of the *4th Panzer* with one anti-tank gun and a few machineguns. It was only after aerial and artillery bombardment, coupled with massed fire from the panzers, that the defenders were dislodged. The *1st Panzer Division* also ran into fierce resistance from the 7th Infantry Division.

That division had the misfortune to occupy positions at the boundary of *10th* and *14th Armies*. A key objective for von Rundstedt during the first days of the war was to separate the Polish armies facing him in the south, so they could be destroyed piecemeal. So, as the 7th fought with *1st Panzer*, units of the *14th Army* hit its flank and rear. The 7th was destroyed, opening a breach between the Lodz and Krakow Armies.

Farther south, other *14th Army* units coming out of Slovakia drove Polish defenders out of the Jablunka Pass and the town of Nowy Targ. The Krakow Army was already penned in from three sides by the evening of 1 September, and its divisions were in disorganized retreat toward their namesake city as the sun rose the following day.

During the night of 1-2 September, Polish forces facing the *8th* and *10th Armies* had a chance to regroup. They established defensive positions along the eastern bank of the Warta River, and occupied fortifications around Czestochowa, Katowice, and Nikotow. Polish engineers carried out demolitions of bridges and roadways, which made motorized movement through the area difficult. German aerial reconnaissance also reported a number of divisions from the Polish general reserve moving into the area.

At 6:00 a.m. on 2 September, von Rundstedt renewed his attack. The *4th Panzer Division*'s advance north of Czestochowa was halted by a counterattack by Uhlan (lancer) Cavalry Regiments 27 and 28, supported by an artillery battalion. The panzer division's unit history states the Polish "cavalry was armed with modern weapons, and their anti-tank unit was very strong."

On 3 September, von Rundstedt ordered his armies to break the Polish line at any cost. *Luftwaffe* bombers pulverized Polish positions as the units of *Army Group South* moved forward. The Poles, lacking any aerial reconnaissance, didn't discover which were the main German thrusts until it was too late.

German bridgeheads were soon established on the east bank of the Warta River. Armored and motorized formations crossed quickly, creating havoc among the Polish defenders. Czestochowa, Katowice and Nikotow were all taken, opening the way for a German advance across the southern Polish plain. The line had held for two days: Rydz-Smigly had hoped for ten, which would have been enough time for the Poznan and Pomorze Armies to reach new positions, and to complete the mobilization of the rest of the forces in the area.

While *10th* and *8th Armies* continued to advance in south-central Poland, *14th Army* fought its way through the mountainous terrain in the south. German troops of the *1st* and *2nd Mountain Infantry Divisions* battled the Polish 2nd and 3rd Carpathian Mountain Brigades for key access routes through the rough country. As the Poles retreated, *14th Army* advanced on Krakow from the west, while its right flank moved steadily to the north, cutting off any chance of escape for the Polish units being surrounded throughout the area.

Once the main Polish line was broken in the south, events moved quickly. The commander of the Lodz Army reported his right had been smashed, and that his 10th Infantry Division "has fallen to pieces. We are leaving the Warta line. … The situation is grave."

The *16th Motorized Corps* had already cut deeply into the Polish center. That corps' panzer units had taken Radomska by the evening of the 3rd, and two days after that were another 60 kilometers to the northeast, advancing on the town of Gora Kalwarja. Those panzers were, of course, followed by infantry units, which cleared the captured areas of bypassed Polish stragglers.

Beyond the Warta Line

On 6 September, von Rundstedt's forces continued their advance. The *8th Army* swung toward Lodz, with its left heading north, in the direction of Poznan. In the center, *10th Army*'s panzers set out for the town of Radom; intelligence had reported the remnants of the Krakow Army were attempting to rally there.

The strung out panzer columns made inviting targets for Polish counterattacks. Elements of the *1st Panzer Division* were hit in the flank by the Polish 29th Infantry Division. A running battle ensued for most of a day. Again and again, the Poles threw themselves at the Germans, only to be driven back each time with tremendous losses. The battle resulted in the virtual destruction of the 29th and the capture of its commanding general. As the day ended, the panzers were about 90 kilometers southwest of Warsaw, and the *14th Army* had taken Krakow.

That same day also marked the end of *Army Group South*'s first operational phase. The Poznan Army was retreating eastward; the Lodz Army was under heavy attack; the Krakow Army was being enveloped; and the Karpaty Army was withdrawing toward Lwow and Lublin.

In the early hours of 7 September, *1st Panzer Division* received its new order: "Forward to the Vistula." With *4th Panzer Division* on its left, *1st Panzer* swept aside the 13th Infantry Division and took the town of Rzeczyca after a bitter fight against entrenched defenders. Toward evening, the *1st*'s headquarters received more encouraging news from its mechanized neighbor: the *4th* had taken Balisk, a town less than 60 kilometers from Warsaw.

The *8th Army*, advancing northeast, was finding it increasingly difficult to keep up with the motorized elements of *10th Army* on its right. The *8th*'s left was also extending dangerously. Those infantry divisions, facing the Poznan and Pomorze Armies to the north, were occupying a considerably longer front per unit than was acceptable. Gen. Blaskowitz, *8th Army*'s commander, relayed his concerns to von Rundstedt, but was curtly told not to worry about it.

Looking at the overall picture, von Rundstedt had every reason to be optimistic. Elements of the *4th Panzer Division* were at the outskirts of Warsaw by 8 September, with the *LAH* providing flank cover. Polish forces had abandoned Lodz, and the city surrendered to the *17th Infantry Division* the same day.

The *10th Army*'s penetration into central Poland had destroyed any hope the defenders there might be able to regroup. The Germans' armored pincers were already closing the noose around five Polish infantry divisions (3rd, 7th, 12th, 19th and 29th), as well as the Krakowska Cavalry Brigade.

Further to the south, units of the *14th Army* fought a series of sharp engagements that drove the Poles north and east, opening the way for an advance on Lwow by elements of the *1st Mountain Infantry Division*.

The Poles seemed all but finished—but they still had a few surprises left.

Counteroffensive along the Bzura

Early on 9 September, Blaskowitz received word that divisions on his army's (*8th*) left flank were engaging Polish units of unknown strength. As more reports came in, it became apparent this was not just another desperate effort to escape, but an all-out counterattack.

Generals Kutrzeba and Bortnowski had moved most of the Poznan and Pomorze Armies into position along the Bzura River. Three divisions, supported by cavalry brigades on both flanks, crossed the Bzura and sent the *30th Infantry Division* reeling. (The *30th*'s commander lost an arm during the opening phase of the battle, but continued to direct his unit.) More Polish units entered the gap left by the *30th*, and soon Blaskowitz was in danger of having his left flank turned.

The Polish objective was to link up with the Lodz Army, thus forming a new defensive ring around the capital. As the attack continued, all three divisions on *8th Army*'s left flank were forced to give ground. The situation was viewed as "critical" by Blaskowitz, but von Rundstedt saw the Polish attack as a means to bring about the final destruction of all the enemy forces in the Kutno-Bzura area. He ordered the units of *10th Army* to head north to reinforce Blaskowitz's *8th*. At the same time, German divisions pushing from the north and west succeeded in breaking through the weakened Polish defense lines there, falling on the rear of the attacking force.

The *10th Army* also kept up pressure on the Lodz Army, and by 12 September, Gen. Kutrzeba had received word that Polish force was retreating north toward Modlin. Any cooperation with the Lodz Army was now out of the question, so the Polish commander was forced to call off his attacks. He then made new plans to head east, directly to Warsaw.

Elsewhere in the South

While the battle along the Bzura was in full swing, other elements of *Army Group South* continued to hammer at the Polish forces before them. The *4th Panzer Division* launched the first in a series of attempts to breach Warsaw's defenses, but was stopped by heavy enemy fire. After three hours of fighting, the *4th's* commander reported losses of 63 out of 120 tanks involved. He withdrew his battered division to its initial position and waited for infantry support.

South of Warsaw, *1st Panzer Division* had taken Gora Kalwarja, and had established a bridgehead on the eastern bank of the Vistula. The Poles fought like demons to eliminate the bridgehead, but *Luftwaffe* support prevented them from making headway.

At Radom, the encircled Polish units were through fighting. By 11 September, an estimated 60,000 prisoners had been taken; organized resistance there was at an end. The end of the Radom battle left *10th Army* with a powerful reserve, most of which was moved north to destroy the Lodz Army.

The *14th Army* crossed the San River on 10 September. Within two days, the Polish 24th Infantry Division was smashed beyond repair, and surviving elements of the 11th Infantry Division were forced into the fortress town of Przemysl.

A battlegroup of the *1st Mountain Infantry Division* was already approaching Lwow, over 90 kilometers east of Przemysl. The mountaineers captured the Zboiska Heights, which dominated the northern approach to Lwow, on 13 September. Despite several Polish counterattacks, supported by heavy artillery fire, the *1st* clung to the heights until other elements of *14th Army* arrived the following day.

Inside Przemysl, the Polish defenders maintained a stubborn resistance. Several German divisions had to be diverted from other areas for the final assault. The town finally fell on 15 September.

Except in Lwow itself, the fall of Przemysl put an end to organized resistance in the *14th Army*'s area of operations. As Lwow came under siege by the *18th Corps*, other German units fanned out and destroyed the isolated pockets of shattered Polish units still fighting in the south. The Germans also attempted to set up a screen to prevent fleeing Polish units from reaching safety in Hungary and Romania.

With northern and southern Poland basically secured, the Germans were able to concentrate their forces to destroy the Polish armies still operating around Kutno, on the Bzura River, in Warsaw, and in the fortresses of Brest-Litovsk, Lwow and Modlin.

Over one-third of the entire Polish ground force was encircled in the Kutno-Bzura cauldron. Twelve infantry divisions (2nd, 4th, 10th, 13th, 14th, 15th, 16th, 17th, 25th, 26th, 28th and 30th) and three cavalry brigades (Wielkopolska, Kresova, and Wolynska) were hemmed in by 29 German divisions. As the vice tightened, the *Luftwaffe* dropped over 328 tons of bombs.

By the night of 16 September, there was no longer any chance of escape for the Poznan and Pomorze Armies. Only two cavalry brigades and the remnants of the 15th and 25th Infantry Divisions managed to slip through the German lines and reach Warsaw before the iron ring finally closed. Gen. Kutrzeba was among those who escaped.

The Germans were on the threshold of victory, but the fighting in Poland was by no means over. The situation between the Vistula and Bug Rivers was still fluid. In the Lublin-Chelm area, remnants of the Prusy and Modlin Armies were still on the march; their objective was Romania. Further south, surviving elements of the Krakow Army fought a series of bloody battles in an attempt to break through the Germans and reach Hungary. A battlegroup of the Krakow and Karpaty Armies surprised *SS Motorized Infantry Regiment Germania*, forcing the Germans to retreat and clearing the way for several thousand Poles to reach the neutral countries to the south.

For all the surviving Polish units, movement to the south and east represented the only means of escape. On 17 September, however, the entire situation changed again when a strong Soviet force crossed the Polish border.

Operations, 17 September - 6 October

The first of the final series of German objectives to be taken was Brest-Litovsk on 17 September. The *10th Panzer* and *20th Motorized Infantry Divisions* made a final and victorious assault on the citadel just as the Polish garrison began an attempt to breakout. (Even though Brest-Litovsk was in the Soviet sphere, as laid down in the pact of 26 August, the German high command allowed their units east of the boundary to continue their missions.)

The *8th Army*'s operations against the Kutno-Bzura Pocket also met with success. On 17 September, over 40,000 Poles went into captivity. The *4th Panzer Division* and the *LAH* repulsed several attempts by the 17th Infantry Division to escape the encirclement. Another larger force managed to breach the German line and headed in the direction of Modlin. However, those Poles were intercepted and destroyed the next day by units of the *10th Army*.

No one could deny the bravery of the Poles. Time after time, they threw themselves at the German positions. But bravery and determination alone were no match for tanks, planes and artillery. Realizing the futility of sacrificing more men in a lost battle, Gen. Bortnowski surrendered his command on 19 September. In all, some 150,000-180,000 Poles were taken prisoner in the Kutno-Bzura pocket.

Lwow had been under siege since 13 September, and it seemed to the German troops surrounding the city the Poles' defenses would never crack. Sometimes the men of the *1st Mountain Infantry Division* found themselves under attack from two sides: as they attempted to break in, they were often also engaged from the rear, as Polish troops heading south crossed through their lines.

With the Soviet intervention, the mountaineers feared they might be robbed of their final victory. Lwow was in the Soviet sphere, and orders were already on their way to hand over positions around the city to the advancing Red Army.

But the Polish garrison in Lwow was also aware of the Soviet attack. After discussing the situation with his officers, the city commander sent an emissary to the Germans, offering to surrender to them before the Communists arrived. That offer was accepted, and the Poles marched into captivity on the 22nd. The mountain troops saluted the Poles as they laid down their arms—a sign of respect for soldiers who had fought one of Germany's elite divisions to a standstill.

The Polish government, along with Rydz-Smigly, fled to Romania the day after the Soviet intervention began. They left orders Warsaw should hold out until France and England could relieve the pressure with a massive attack on the western front—an attack the men giving the order must have known would never come in time to save Poland.

Once the pocket at Kutno was eliminated, *Luftwaffe* bomber formations returned to the sky over Warsaw. But the German command still ruled out a ground assault there as too costly. The 140,000-160,000 defenders inside Warsaw were firmly dug in. Aside from a few German probing attacks, the job of reducing the city was to be left to artillery and air power. The bombardment caused thousands of civilian casualties. The city water works, as well as most other utilities, were wrecked, but the Poles still resisted every German attempt to breach their defenses.

On 25 September, over 1,000 cannon began a massive bombardment of Warsaw. That artillery was joined by 240 Stukas and 100 Do.17 bombers, which unloaded more than 560 tons of explosives on the city. They were followed by 30 Ju.52 transport planes that dropped 72 tons of incendiary bombs.

The defenders had put up a gallant fight, but deteriorating medical and health conditions, coupled with mounting civilian casualties and a growing shortage of food, made further resistance futile. On the morning of 27 September, the Polish commander sent a delegate to *8th Army* headquarters to negotiate the city's surrender. At 2:00 p.m. that same day, the Warsaw garrison received the order to give up.

With the fall of Warsaw, only two organized pockets of resistance, Modlin and Hela, remained. At Modlin, about 35,000 soldiers, mostly survivors of the Modlin and Lodz Armies, occupied an extensive network of forts and other defensive positions.

Three German infantry divisions (*14th*, *32nd* and *228th*), along with *Panzer Division Kempf*, *1st Light*, and the *SS Motorized Infantry Regiment Deutschland*, were given the task of cracking the Polish defenses. *Luftwaffe* bombers and army artillery pounded the Poles day and night, but the old Russian forts had been built to last. In the end, Modlin had to be taken the old fashioned way—with infantry assault troops.

Supported by *Kempf*'s panzers, *Deutschland* breached the Polish lines east of the town on the 25th. At the same time, the *1st Light* and *32nd Infantry Divisions* began clearing the forts south of the Narew. It was tough fighting. Though many of the forts were surrounded, the Poles inside continued to resist, causing many deaths among the

GERMAN SITUATION
AS OF EARLY MORNING
17 September 1939

0   10   20   30   40   50
MILES

— — — German-Russian Demarcation
Line of 17 September

— — — — German-Russian Demarcation
Line of 1 October

attackers. The Germans called in combat engineers to help, and by the 28th, several key Polish positions had been captured. The formal surrender followed the next day.

The Poles at Hela surrendered three days later. That narrow peninsula was ideal for defense, and the Naval Brigade had fought with tenacity. Again, though, *Luftwaffe* bombardment, this time coupled with the heavy guns from two World War I era battleships, proved decisive. On 1 October, 5,000 Polish troops surrendered at Hela.

The End

There were still thousands of Polish soldiers at large in the countryside. Penned in by the Germans in the west and Soviets to the east, their only salvation lay in the south. They moved in formations ranging in size from small groups to multi-division conglomerates, fighting running battles with enemy troops as they attempted to reach the Hungarian or Romanian borders.

As soon as the Soviets had invaded eastern Poland, many individual Polish commanders had decided to take their men into neutral countries, in the hope of continuing the struggle at a later date. Thousands of Poles did manage to make it to safety, in at least one case, with the help of the Germans. After a meeting between a Polish cavalry commander (whose unit had been fighting Soviet forces) and the commander of the German *28th Infantry Division*, the Poles were allowed to continue south with a signed document stating "the *28th Infantry Division* guarantees the Polish free access to the south."

Most of the Poles, however, did not make it. The final stand of the Polish army took place between 4 and 6 October. The 50th and 60th Infantry Divisions, along with three cavalry brigades, were surrounded and destroyed by German motorized and panzer units in a forest north of Kock.

The results of the Polish campaign shocked the world. German losses were placed at 8,082 killed, 5,029 missing, and 27,278 wounded, along with 217 tanks (mostly Pz. Is and IIs) destroyed. Between 400-500 *Luftwaffe* aircraft were lost.

Against that, the German armed forces effectively destroyed the Polish army, navy and air force. The Polish army alone lost 123,000 killed and 133,700 wounded. Another 694,000 soldiers were taken prisoner by the Germans, and 217,000 more were lost to the Soviets. About 60,000 made it across the borders of Hungary and Romania, while another 15,000 crossed into Latvia and Lithuania. Three Polish destroyers and two submarines escaped to England; three other submarines were interned in Sweden.

Poland itself was dismembered. It would be five long years before a new Polish state emerged, and 45 years beyond that before the Poles again achieved a truly independent nation.

To and Fro, Back and Forth

The actual military offensive against Poland was to have begun precisely at 4:30 a.m. on Saturday, 26 August. That was Hitler's original plan, and up until 6:00 p.m. on the 25th it was also the plan the entire *Wehrmacht* was expecting to carry out. The point-of-no-return deadline for calling off the attack (if there were some radical change in the diplomatic scene) had been set for 3:00 p.m. That deadline had come and gone when *der Führer* received a piece of news that made him rethink the invasion's entire rationale.

The news was from Mussolini. It was not good. Italy would be unable to go to war against France and Britain unless it immediately received huge and impossible amounts of supplies from Germany. Failing that, the Italians recommended the whole thing be postponed until 1942. In light of all this, the message concluded, if Germany went ahead, Rome would provide moral and political support for Berlin, but little else.

Hitler had been counting on the threat of Italian participation in the war to hold off Britain while Nazi forces overran Poland. With that aid no longer forthcoming, the dictator fell into a crisis of self-doubt. The order to halt troop movements toward the border was given at 7:30 p.m., only nine hours before the offensive was supposed to start.

Totalitarian governments are usually thought to be run on the principle that once the supreme leader gives an order, it is carried out as fast as the speed of communications permits. Hitler's government, however, was in reality not a well-oiled machine, and neither was the German high command. That body was an odd mix of old Prussians, "young Turks," and Nazi Party hacks—none of whom particularly liked the others. Gen. Franz Halder, chief of the Führer's military headquarters, got the order about an hour after it was first issued, and he took another hour or so to pass it before the various service chiefs to get their nods.

Once the various military staffs knew for certain the invasion was called off, it became their job to inform the lesser headquarters throughout eastern Germany about what was going on. It proved almost impossible, though, to get in contact with the units already in the field and rolling toward their jump-off points. For instance, the *1st Corps* headquarters in East Prussia only got the cancellation order at 9:37 p.m., after several of its units were already beginning their final moves to cross the border. Several staff officers were frantically rushed toward the front, and they just managed to stop the infantry and tanks in time.

A few units didn't get the word until after they'd actually begun to engage Polish forces with small arms fire. Their rear-area artillery units had already been stood down, so it appeared no full-fledged campaign was really beginning. The eager-for-peace Polish government explained away all the incidents as the work of "marauding German bands" that had merely roughed up some frontier customs guards.

Of course, Hitler soon regained his initial resolve, figured Germany could win without Italian help, and ordered a new start date of 1 September. That time, of course, it went ahead as planned.

—L. Dean Webb

The Western Front

Despite binding treaties and a declaration of war on 3 September, Britain and France did little to help their Polish allies. During that autumn, British unpreparedness for war was matched only by French incompetence in waging it.

Gen. von Leeb, commander of *Army Group C* on the western front, was a defensive expert. On 1 September, he had 34 divisions (made up mainly of reservists) with which to guard against an Anglo-French attack. The Germans' vaunted Siegfried Line was strong in places, but was still largely unfinished.

France's mobilization gave that nation an army of 81 infantry (7 motorized), 3 cavalry, 2 mechanized, and 13 garrison divisions. Of those, 23 divisions were either on duty in the colonial holdings or guarding the frontier with Italy.

The British Expeditionary Force was still crossing the Channel when Gen. Gaston Prételat, commander of the French 2nd Army Group, ordered his forces to attack into the Saar region on 7 September. Nine divisions of his 3rd and 4th Armies cautiously advanced on a 15-mile front. They encountered only light opposition at first.

Though practically the entire *Luftwaffe* was engaged in Poland, the French air force was nowhere to be seen.

Prételat had picked one of the strongest and most defensible parts of the Siegfried Line to attack. As the French moved forward, they ran into minefields, boobytraps and concentrated fire from German bunkers and artillery.

As soon as casualties started returning to the French rear areas, their commanders began to display extraordinary degrees of caution. That mood, of course, soon spread to the soldiers in the field. In one case, a single German machinegun nest stalled an entire French division for a day. Von Leeb used the opportunity the French timidity provided to reshuffle his troops, reinforcing the threatened sector with more artillery and reserve divisions.

French press communiques, meanwhile, made wild claims to upgrade the offensive in the public's perception. They spoke of capturing "100,000 acres" of German territory—a figure that sounds impressive until one realizes it only represented a 1.5x15 mile area of little strategic significance.

The French advance stopped dead even before it reached the main Siegfried Line defenses. Prételat claimed he needed more time and troops: his timetable set 17 September as the earliest possible date for renewing the offensive.

Long before that, though, the Germans had massed 17 divisions to repel the push. The Soviet intervention in Poland on the 17th put an end to any hope of survival for that nation. The same day, the French command ordered their troops to give up the captured German territory and move back to the safety of the Maginot Line.

The failure of the French can be blamed on a number of factors—poor planning, general incompetence, low morale, and—perhaps most of all—nightmare visions of the millions who died during the years of trench warfare in World War I. Whatever the primary cause, there was really no effective way the western Allies could have fulfilled their treaty obligations to Poland. The speed with which the Polish resistance collapsed under the new Blitzkrieg style of warfare psychologically cowed the Allies into a completely defensive posture. That posture would last until Hitler directed his combat-proven armies against them in the spring of 1940.

Chapter XXI

Counterattack at Arras

by Michael K. Robel

Highly mobile attacking forces moving along an unconventional and unanticipated avenue of approach have broken through a thin crust of defending units and are driving deep into the friendly communications zone. Local reserves attempting to attack the attackers in their flanks, or in desperation head on, are easily brushed aside or destroyed.

Countering the thrust is made more difficult because it occurs near a national boundary in a coalition army grouping, and had split the defending forces in two. Because of the tempo of the enemy offensive and the close support of their field artillery and aviation, disrupted friendly communications and dwindling supplies, the defending command is incapable of determining where, when, or how to commit its slim reserves to have the best chance to stop the attack. Finally, a small counterattack unexpectedly paralyzes the high command directing the enemy forces, giving the friendly side an opportunity to stabilize the front and the ability to launch a major counteroffensive.

That's a description of the Battle of France as it might have been had the Allied command been able to take full advantage of the effect of the Anglo-French counterattacks at Arras on 21-22 May 1940.

Arras, in size only one minor battle during the Allied debacle, contributed to halting the German advance for two-and-a-half days, thus giving the British Expeditionary Force (BEF) time to make its escape to and through Dunkirk. In fact, this little-studied fight contains many lessons about how to engage mobile, tank heavy forces—lessons that may still be of use today.

To counter the German invasion of the low countries, the completely motorized BEF, commanded by Lord Gort, and the French 1st Army Group, commanded by Gen. Billote, rushed into Belgium

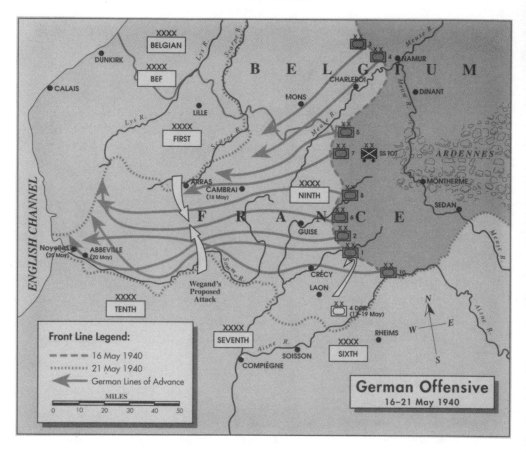

German Offensive
16–21 May 1940

Front Line Legend:
- – – – 16 May 1940
- ·········· 21 May 1940
- ← German Lines of Advance

MILES
0 10 20 30 40 50

covered by the French Cavalry Corps (2nd and 3rd DLMs—Division Légeres Méchaniques, or Light Mechanized Divisions). Then, totally surprising the Allies, who still relied on traditional (slow) methods of analyzing the enemy course of action, the German tank spearheads advanced through the Ardennes, brushed aside the French and Belgian cavalry screens and drove toward the sea.

Only too late did Gort finally determine what was happening. The Germans had deliberately refrained from engaging his units moving to the north. By not doing so, they had encouraged the separation of the Allied front. As the panzers emerged from the Ardennes, their mere presence astride the Meuse split the Allied armies. The BEF's lines of communications were in danger of being cut, and all of Belgium might soon be separated from Allied territory. Surprised by their own success, the Germans halted to allow their infantry to catch up with the armor spearheads along the Sambre and Oise Rivers.

Belatedly, the Commander in Chief of the Allied Forces, Gen. Gamelin, ordered attacks to close the gap between his northern and southern forces, and simultaneously sever the German spearhead at its base. The only immediate response to his order came from Charles DeGaulle's newly organized, under-equipped and untrained 4th DCR (Division Cuirassées Rapides, or Fast Armored Division). Even that unit only managed three small and abortive counterattacks against Gen. Heinz Guderian's *19th Panzer Corps* from 17-19 May.

The DLMs in Belgium, which had been dispersed along the front to provide tank support to the infantry units, were meanwhile ordered to concentrate around Cambrai and prepare to attack south as part of this same order from Gamelin.

The major German units in this battle were the *7th Panzer Division*, commanded by Erwin Rommel, and the *SS Totenkopf* (motorized infantry) *Division*. Those units made a preliminary effort against Arras on 20 May, but were halted by stubborn British resistance. The Germans then formulated a plan to hit Arras the next day at 3:00 p.m.. This time they would send the *7th* and the *SS* northwest around the town, while the *5th Panzer Division* attacked from the east, thus taking the place in a classic double envelopment.

Frankforce Is Born

While all this was going on, British Gen. Sir Edmund Ironside, Chief of the Imperial General Staff, arrived in France and immediately ordered Gort to launch a major attack south toward Amiens. Gort felt such a move was impossible, however, and talked his superior into accepting a plan for a more limited counterattack aimed simply at clearing the enemy from around Arras. This push was to be under the control of Maj. Gen. H.E. Franklyn, commanding the British 5th Infantry Division. Ironside accepted all this, then left to discuss operations with Billote at Lens.

At Lens, Ironside talked the French into launching a two-division counterattack toward Cambrai on the 21st, to be coordinated with Gort's move at Arras. From this it appears Ironside had persisted in seeing the coming attack as at least a beginning for a concerted effort to drive south and close the gap between the northern and southern Allied armies; however, Franklyn's orders were never changed to reflect this reaffirmation.

On their own, the French asked Franklyn if he would continue his

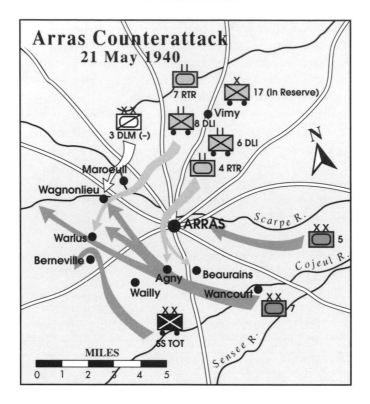

Arras Counterattack
21 May 1940

7 RTR

17 (In Reserve)

Vimy

3 DLM (–)

8 DLI

6 DLI

N

Maroeuil

4 RTR

Wagnonlieu

ARRAS

Scarpe R.

5

Warlus

Berneville

Cojeul R.

Agny

Beaurains

Wailly

Wancourt

SS TOT

MILES

0 1 2 3 4 5

Sensee R.

counterattack past Arras. Franklyn declined, claiming his orders didn't authorize such an extension, but then countered by offering to relieve the French Cavalry Corps (along the Scarpe River east of Arras), enabling those units to move west. The French agreed, and also allocated the 3rd DLM from the cavalry corps to assist in Franklyn's counterattack by committing its 60-70 Somua tanks to cover his western flank.

This unevenly assembling counterattack group, now christened "Frankforce," also came officially to include the British 50th Northumbrian Division, commanded by Maj. Gen. L. Martel, and the 1st Tank Brigade, led by Brig. Douglas O. Pratt.

In actuality, though, the bulk of the 5th Division remained tied down defending the Scarpe River to the east of the proposed counterattack area, and its remaining brigade (the 17th) was kept in reserve. One brigade of the 50th Division (the 150th) also got pulled into the Scarpe battle. Finally, late on the 20th the French reported the 3rd DLM would not be ready and they therefore did not want to go until at least the 22nd. Franklyn, however, was determined to attack on schedule.

Thus what had been intended as a four-plus division force became one barely equaling one good brigade: the 6th and 8th Durham Light Infantry (DLI) Battalions from the 151st Brigade of the 50th Division, and the 4th and 7th Tank Battalions of the Royal Tank Regiment of the 1st Tank Brigade.

A Slow Start

To reach the proposed battle area, the British tanks had to travel 120 miles on their own tracks. The roads they used were subject to enemy air attack and were crowded with retreating units and refugees. Still, at 5:00 a.m. on the 21st, the tanks of the 4th and 7th battalions arrived at the Vimy assembly area, having lost only 12 of their number along the way. The counterattack would have a total of 58 Mk Is, 16 Mk IIs, and 14 Mk VIs, split evenly between the two battalions.

Martel ordered his units to rest, conduct maintenance, and "not worry about impending operations."

Coordination for the attack was chaotic throughout Frankforce. Radio problems hampered communications. Intelligence indicating German units were already operating north of the Scarpe River departure line was only partially disseminated. Only one out of every eight tanks had detailed maps; the rest used Michelin touring maps or went without.

Though Franklyn wanted to attack as soon as possible, both Martel and Pratt insisted on time for maintenance and rest. The final attack order was therefore not issued until 7:00 a.m. Originally planned to begin at 1:30 p.m., the operation finally began at 2:30. Frankforce went forward without air or artillery support. Unintentionally, but effectively, it did succeed in spoiling the planned German attack that was itself just ready to go off.

Frankforce was divided into two columns (each led—tellingly—by the *infantry* battalion commanders) on parallel routes about three miles apart. On the east, 4 RTR and 6 DLI were to penetrate along a route through Achicourt to Wancourt. On the west, 7 RTR and 8 DLI were to move from Maroeuil to Wailly and Berneville. The French Division (when it finally joined in) was to drive from north of Maroeuil toward Warlus.

After clearing German forces between the Vimy assembly area and the line of departure along the Scarpe (a surprise), the two columns crossed the river and pushed toward their initial objective, the Cojeul River. After the Cojeul was reached, the plan called for the releasing of the reserve 17th Infantry Brigade, which would push toward the Sensee River three miles beyond the Cojeul.

At the tactical level, the British used their Mk IIs to overwatch and support-by-fire their Mk Is, while the Mk VIs were used for command, control and reconnaissance.

A Good Beginning

The 4th RTR crossed the Scarpe behind the *25th Panzer Regiment* and destroyed some German transport units. Continuing to Achicourt, it engaged the *7th Panzer Division*'s artillery and elements of its *6th (Motorized) Infantry Regiment*, throwing both into confusion. By coincidence, Rommel was at the scene, trying to hurry the *6th*'s infantry along to join the *25th*'s tanks, and took personal command of the situation.

Hurrying from gun to gun, Rommel directed their fire without, at first, any visible effect. He ultimately had to commit the 88mm guns of his anti-aircraft unit to penetrate the thickly armored British tanks. During this time his aide de camp was killed, and Rommel frantically informed his chain of command he estimated he was being attacked by "at least five divisions" and "hundreds of tanks."

The other column didn't move as fast; the *7th Panzer*'s *7th (Motorized) Infantry Regiment* managed to hold it for a time in the vicinity of Warlus. But later the *SS Totenkopf* was also engaged, and some of its elements panicked and surrendered outright, or fled southward.

Seeing that the eastern column had got ahead and out of support range of the western, Martel ordered it to secure Beaurains and wait there for further orders.

At about 4:00 p.m., both British tank battalion commanders were killed while riding in their Mk VIs. But both their executive officers, one of whom was later captured, took command smoothly in each unit.

French tanks advancing near Warlus then mistakenly engaged some British anti-tank guns, killing some of their crews. The English fired back, destroying four French tanks before both commanders realized their mistake. Those same French also later engaged elements of the *Totenkopf*.

A Bad End

By 6:30 p.m., as casualties and confusion mounted, it became obvious the attack would not reach its objectives, and Martel became increasingly concerned about the possibility of a German counterattack. He ordered Frankforce's two columns, both already stopped, one at Beaurains and the other at Warlus, to dig in and make those places "tank proof."

Between 6:00 and 7:00 p.m., Rommel ordered the *25th Panzer Regiment*, which had managed to push through all this to reach its own offensive objectives for the day, to turn back and strike the British in their flank and rear.

German air and artillery began to register among the British in Beaurains at 6:15, driving 6 DLI out of position. It was then struck by returning elements of the *25th Panzer Regiment*. The 4th RTR came to the support of 6 DLI, and both units managed to withdraw to Achicourt.

Other elements of the *25th* attacked 7 RTR and 8 DLI in Warlus, losing three Panzer IVs, six Panzer IIIs and some light tanks for anti-tank fire.

The German attacks at both places began to develop so much strength that Franklyn ordered his columns (and the French 3rd DLM) back to the start line. This phase of the battle lasted until about 1:00 a.m. on 22 May.

Elsewhere on the 21st, Gen. Maxime Weygand, newly appointed C-in-C of the French army, met with representatives of his 1st Army Group and the Belgian army to discuss developing a further counterattack south. Unfortunately, the other key player, Lord Gort, didn't arrive at the conference site until 8:00 p.m., thus missing the others by three hours. More importantly, Gort had by that time made up his mind to evacuate the BEF, but said nothing to Billote, who had remained behind to brief the tardy Englishman on the conference. While this was going on, lead elements of Guderian's panzer corps had reached Abbeville, only a few miles from the Channel coast.

On the morning of 22 May, the French belatedly launched their own counterattack toward Cambrai. Like the British attack the day before, it was whittled in size before starting until it finally amounted to just one regiment from a DLM. It pushed into the *32nd Infantry Division*, but by 10:00 p.m. had ground to a halt and been ordered back to its start line.

German Reaction & Assessment

The *7th Panzer Division*'s casualties at Arras were reported as 89 killed, 116 wounded, and 173 missing. The *Totenkopf* admitted to 19 killed, 27 wounded, and two missing. (Those figures are almost certainly in error, since the British claim to have taken 400 SS prisoners.) German tank losses amounted to over 20 vehicles of all types.

Though Rommel claimed 43 British tanks destroyed, actual losses were more likely to have been 26 Mk Is, two Mk II Matildas, and several light tanks and personnel carriers. The French 3rd DLM was rendered virtually combat ineffective during the final stages of the operation, when its tank complement was almost totally destroyed.

Rommel's apprehension and on-scene but misinformed reports had been passed quickly up the German chain of command. The *1st, 2nd* and *10th Panzer Divisions* were all pulled into reserve. An outright halt order was issued on the 23rd, all of which gave the BEF time to begin its evacuation through Dunkirk.

Conclusions

The Arras counterattack seems to have had two effects. First, it led the Germans to call a three day halt, though other factors contributed to that order: 1) the Germans realized the campaign in the low countries was ending, and wanted to conserve and redeploy their armor to finish off the French; 2) the ground became less suitable for tanks nearer the coast; 3) the number of mechanical breakdowns was mounting; and 4) Göring boasted his *Luftwaffe* could finish the job alone.

Second, the quick failure of the Arras counterattack, along with his continued dissatisfaction with the French command, convinced Gort that evacuation of the BEF was the only logical course left.

At the tactical level, the successes the British gained were due less to speed and shock action than to their vehicle's thick armor. For example, one machine took 14 hits and still remained battle-worthy.

The 1st Tank Brigade had been trained almost exclusively in infantry support tactics. Pratt later wrote of the unit in this operation:

> Had we only been allowed to stage a methodical battle with

a series of reasonable short objectives, with some artillery support and even a little air support, and no frantic rush, we should have done far better and saved many lives of fellows we could not afford to lose.

In his memoirs, Guderian stated:

The English did not succeed in breaking through, but they did make a considerable impression on the staff of Panzer Group von Kleist, which suddenly became remarkably nervous. Subordinate units, however, were not infected by this.

Field Marshal von Rundstedt said of the attack:

A critical moment in the drive came just as my forces had reached the Channel. It was caused by a British counter-stroke southward from Arras toward Cambrai, on 21 May. For a short time it was feared that our armored divisions would be cut off before the infantry divisions could come up to support them. None of the French counter-attacks carried any serious threat as this one did.

Martel, writing after the war, echoed Rundstedt:

As it was, the attack probably delayed the main enemy movement via Calais by two days, which may have had a considerable effect on the success of our operations to cover the evacuation from Dunkirk.

Finally, Rommel's conduct during this battle was especially interesting. He did not project the ideal of the cool, calculating commander to which his popular image later gave rise. Still, he was already demonstrating his famous tendency to lead from the front while exercising direct command of units in critical situations.

In any event, the Arras counterattack made an impression on the German command far out of proportion to its actual size. But because there were already German units on the coast when it began, it remains doubtful if a more full-blooded effort could have changed the final outcome of the campaign. It is certain a greater Allied success at Arras would have created time for even more units to be evacuated from Dunkirk.

"Typical" German Panzer Division, 1939/40

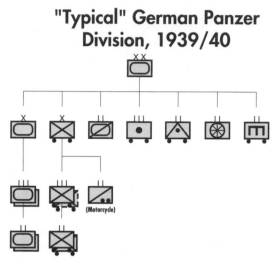

German Armor Organization at Arras

Like tank design itself, the organizational structure of armor units was evolving at the time of Arras. Most tank formations of the day were tank-heavy, without enough infantry to properly support their armor operations. That lack was keenly felt by the Allies at Arras.

Along the entire front, Allied armor actually outnumbered German by 3,401 to 2,570 deployed vehicles. The crucial difference lay in the fact the Germans concentrated 70 percent of their tanks for their main thrust through the Ardennes, while the Allied armor was dispersed across the entire front.

The German 1939/40 panzer divisions were the best armored organizations of the period. They were extremely flexible because of the widespread use of radios, which enabled their sub-units to be directed and redirected quickly, at tempos never approached by their French and English counterparts.

The German army mustered 10 panzer divisions for the invasion of the west. Not all those divisions were organized the same way: six had two panzer regiments of two battalions each, three had one regiment of three battalions, and one (Rommel's 7th) had a regiment consisting of only two battalions. Total authorized tank strengths varied from 274 to 416 AFVs, including expropriated Czechoslovakian machines.

Infantry and support strength also varied: no two panzer divisions in the campaign had exactly the same organization. Unlike the Allies, however, infantry and support strength in the panzer division was generally sufficient to support the tank battalions.

Chapter XXII

Smolensk-Yelnia
Blunting the Blitzkrieg

by Pat McTaggart

When the Germans launched Operation Barbarossa on 22 June 1941, they hoped for a short campaign. Two weeks into the invasion, even the most skeptical observers were beginning to think they might get it. Hundreds of thousands of Soviet soldiers were already being herded west as prisoners of war, and a large portion of the Red Army's pre-invasion order of battle had been severely mauled or destroyed outright.

However, the very rapidity of the Germans' advance brought with it the problems all invaders of Mother Russia had faced for centuries. The vastness of the land, coupled with a deplorable road system, limited the avenues of attack available. Within the German high command there was also a growing conflict over strategic goals. These had already been evident during the pre-attack planning, and they were never really resolved before the campaign began.

One faction regarded the mineral- and grain-producing regions of southern Russia and the Ukraine as the primary objective to be secured; another group believed the rapid capture of Leningrad, Moscow and other western Russian cities held the key to victory. Destruction of the Red Army was held critical by the adherents of both approaches, but it seemed none of them had taken into account the enormous human resources Stalin had available to flesh out, build and rebuild his order of battle.

On 8 July, the commander of *Army Group Center*, Field Marshal Fedor von Bock, issued an "order of the day" that forecast the imminent collapse of the Red Army. Von Bock's forces had just completed the destruction of four enemy armies in the Bialystok-Minsk region. Twenty-two Soviet infantry, seven armored, and three

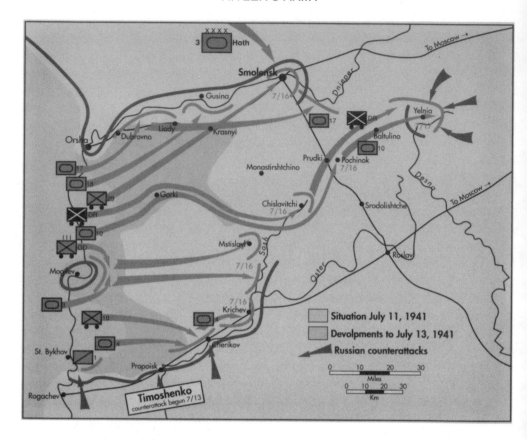

cavalry divisions, and six mechanized brigades, had been wiped out. An estimated 287,704 Soviet soldiers had fallen into German hands in the encirclement.

Even before the annihilation of the Soviets in the Bialystok-Minsk pocket had been completed, units of Gen. Heinz Guderian's *Panzer Group 2* had crossed the Berezina River. Disregarding his exposed right flank, he ordered a further advance to the Dnieper River, the last natural defensive barrier before Smolensk.

As Guderian's men and tanks approached the river, his Red Army counterpart, Marshal Semyon K. Timoshenko, was rushing units and materiel to its eastern bank in an effort to halt the Germans there. STAVKA (the Soviet high command) had ordered Timoshenko to gain time on his "Western Front" to allow the mobilization of the nation's 16 million military-age males to get into high gear.

Both Guderian and Timoshenko knew the significance of the city of Smolensk. For the German, Smolensk's capture would provide the staging point for the frontal advance on the Soviet capital, less than 200 miles farther on.

With Guderian's forces approaching head on, Timoshenko also faced a threat on his northern flank. There armored units of *Panzer Group 3*, commanded by Gen. Hermann Hoth, were advancing on Vitebsk, a gateway to Smolensk. As Hoth's panzers advanced, Timoshenko shoved unit after unit forward to that area in another desperate attempt to buy time to fortify the Dnieper line.

Across the Dnieper

Despite Timoshenko's efforts to delay them, by 10 July Hoth's units had seized Vitebsk and Guderian was poised on the western bank of the Dnieper. The Soviet commander had worked his men feverishly to fortify all the likely crossing points along that stretch of the river, and he'd also labored administratively to bring together what he hoped was a force large enough to stymie any German attack. On that date his Western Front deployed 31 infantry, seven armored, and four motorized divisions.

Luftwaffe reconnaissance gave the two German commanders a fairly accurate picture of what they faced. Guderian also sent his own ground reconnaissance units along the western bank to probe for Soviet weak spots—and they found them. On the day Vitebsk fell, he ordered his units to cross the river at three points, while bypassing strongly fortified areas at Mogilev, Orsha and Rogachev.

At Stary Bykhov, *24th Panzer Corps* (*3rd Panzer, 4th Panzer,* and *10th Motorized Infantry Divisions*) sent grenadiers and engineer units across the river in the early morning. A bridge was completed by nightfall, and armored elements of the corps were soon headed eastward across it.

Meanwhile, *46th Panzer Corps* (*10th Panzer* and *2nd SS "Das Reich" Motorized Infantry Divisions,* and *Motorized Infantry Regiment "Grossdeutschland"*) crossed at Shklov, just north of Mogilev, where they met with fierce resistance from a unit of Soviet officer cadets. Eventually a machinegun company of the *Grossdeutschland* succeeded in driving the defenders out of their entrenchments and secured a bridgehead in that area.

Still further north, at Kopys, *47th Panzer Corps* (*17th* and *18th Panzer Divisions* and *29th Motorized Infantry Division)* ran into heavy Soviet artillery fire, and even some air attacks, as their grenadiers started to cross the river. Several assault boats were blown from the water as they sped toward the eastern shore. However, with the help of some self-propelled artillery firing from the western bank, and smothering Stuka attacks on Soviet artillery positions, the *29th* gained enough ground to allow the armored divisions to begin crossing over.

In the north, Hoth's *Panzer Group 3* began its attack at 3:00 a.m. Under cover of artillery fire, armored and motorized units of his *57th* and *39th Panzer Corps* tore holes in the lines of the Soviet 19th, 20th and 22nd Armies, overrunning entrenchments as they advanced toward the motor highway to Moscow.

By the evening of 10 July, Timoshenko's Dnieper line was in a shambles and German units were sweeping east out of their newly won bridgeheads. The Soviets' fortified river-line positions between the bridgeheads were for the most part bypassed. For the next two days the two panzer groups continued their advance, smashing through hastily-assembled defensive positions and routing several Soviet divisions in the process.

During this fighting, German observers noted that the average Soviet soldier, though typically a fearless and savage fighter, lacked the training and organization necessary to counter the blitzkrieg tactics of the attackers. There was a tendency among the Soviets, as soon as the grenadier-laden German panzers appeared, to bunch up for safety near artillery and anti-tank positions. Of course, that only created gaps in the defensive lines through which the German forces could pass.

Gen. Andrei I. Yeremenko, Timoshenko's deputy, tried to counter the German tactics by ordering the artillery to concentrate exclusively on the panzer columns. At times this idea proved successful, but as long as the *Luftwaffe* controlled the skies above the battlefields, Soviet artillery positions were destroyed at a rate that prevented their contribution from being anywhere near decisive. It was another two years before massive Red Army "PAK Fronts" (anti-tank concentrations) would prove capable of consistently stopping German armor in its tracks.

By 13 July, Soviet resistance began to stiffen. As more reinforcements arrived, Timoshenko threw them directly into the path of the advancing Germans. *Luftwaffe* reconnaissance flights radioed a constant stream of reports describing new Soviet units moving toward the front. German intelligence and operations officers shook their heads in amazement as Red Army tank columns seemed to appear from nowhere. Panzer units had to be constantly redeployed to counter probes and attacks on the flanks of the German drives.

Unfortunately for Timoshenko, however, his many counterattacks were never properly coordinated. His commanders persisted in throwing their armor into battle piecemeal, where they were soon blown to bits by the efficient German war machine.

Even during this chaotic period, the Soviets were not complete strangers to flexible improvisation and the unexpected rewards such measures could yield. For instance, completely by chance, Yeremenko learned there was a quantity of highly flammable gasoline-phosphorus mixture called "KS" stored at Gomel, not far from the front. He had his supply units transport the stuff directly to the frontline infantry units with orders to distribute and use it immediately.

The panzer units were taken unaware by the new weapon. When bottles containing KS were thrown against the sides of the German tanks, exposing the mixture to air, combustion was immediate. In the first few days of its use, several panzer crews died screaming in agony when the liquid fire found its way inside their machines. Thus the "Molotov Cocktail" was introduced into the Russo-German War. German commanders were forced to counter the new threat by detailing squads of panzer grenadiers to accompany all tank units and keep the Soviet infantry at a distance.

Soviet Counterstrike

However helpful such stop-gap measures might be, Timoshenko knew that only a massive counterattack could really halt the German advance. He therefore ordered Yeremenko to strike at the extending right flank of Guderian's units with a force of 20 divisions. The attack, on 13 July, caught Guderian's forces in full stretch and threatened to disrupt the entire operational plan of the panzer group.

Yeremenko could not have chosen a better time to hit back. Gen. Geyr von Schweppenburg's *24th Panzer Corps* (which had picked up the *1st Cavalry Division* in the last few days) had been charged with guarding the panzer group's right flank. Many elements of the corps were still far to the rear, however, fighting Lt. Gen. Gerasimenko's 13th Army holding out in and around Mogilev. Those units had to hold their positions there until German infantry divisions could slog forward to replace them.

Yeremenko's divisions attacked from the Gomel area and succeeded in recapturing Rogachev and Zhlobin in their initial assault. Schweppenburg hastily diverted some elements of the *4th Panzer* and *10th Motorized Infantry Divisions* to counter the Soviet push, but the main burden fell on Brig. Gen. Kurt Feldt's *1st Cavalry.*

As the Soviets advanced, Feldt's reconnaissance units were able to get between their columns and into their rear areas, disrupting supply and communications. Before long, Yeremenko's attack had fallen into disarray. Panzer and motorized infantry units set up defensive positions at key road junctions, while their cavalry counterparts continued to slice through and past Yeremenko's battalions. But even as the attack bogged down, Yeremenko pressed his commanders to advance.

While Schweppenburg's corps was tied up repelling the Soviet flank threat, Guderian ordered the bulk of his panzer group to continue east. His objective was to get a bridgehead on the eastern bank of the Desna River, around the town of Yelnia. The high ground there would provide a perfect springboard for the final assault toward Moscow.

Timoshenko also recognized Yelnia's importance. As Guderian's panzers approached, units of the 19th, 24th and 28th Armies were already preparing defensive positions there under orders to hold "at all costs." At the same time, Timoshenko continued to throw fresh troops into the flank counterattack. Between 12 and 14 new divisions were deployed to defend the approaches to Smolensk, and other Soviet forces already surrounded continued to fight. The 13th Army constantly probed the German lines around Mogilev, in an effort to link up with Yeremenko's attack force.

The Smolensk Pocket Forms

Disregarding the situation on his flank, Guderian continued to push toward Smolensk and Yelnia, while Hoth's panzer group made a wide swing around Smolensk from the north. There was little the Soviets seemed able to do as the panzers crashed through their lines. On 15 July, Orsha fell to the *17th Panzer Division*, opening the way for the *29th Motorized Infantry Division* to move directly to Smolensk. Farther south, the towns of Gorki and Mstislavl were captured by units of the *10th Panzer* and *Das Reich Divisions* after bitter fighting.

On the same day, the *7th Panzer Division* cut the road and rail lines running between Smolensk and Moscow. Though Smolensk was now effectively cut off, Guderian and Hoth were unable to completely close the gap between their two panzer groups. An estimated half-million Soviet troops were within their grasp, but counterattacks to their flanks continued to draw off the men and materiel needed to complete the encirclement.

While Soviet units outside Smolensk fought desperately to stave off that final closing, the *29th Motorized Division* made ready to assault into the city proper.

Timoshenko had already issued the standard "hold at all costs" order to the defenders of Smolensk, and the militia there feverishly built barricades and fortified buildings in preparation for the on-slaught. Units of the 16th Army were sent streaming into the city through the gaps in the German lines to provide the necessary regular-army backbone to the local defenders.

Early on 15 July, the *29th*'s *71st Infantry Regiment* got inside the main Soviet defenses by means of a little-used trail on the southwest of the city. By midday they had captured several heavy artillery batteries and seized a key enemy position at Konyskhovo, a suburb of the city. As night fell, the *71st* was already fighting well within the southern bounds of Smolensk.

The next day, the *15th Infantry Regiment* joined the *71st* for a strengthened assault. It began at 4:00 a.m., and by noon the southern half of the city was in German hands. But Soviet sappers had managed to destroy all the bridges leading across the Dnieper to Smolensk's north side.

This fighting, though going in the Germans' favor, was different in that it reached a level of intensity not previously experienced during the invasion. One soldier of the *29th* wrote: "It was a ghostly picture that we saw in this dead city. The destruction was far worse than at Borisov or Minsk. Dead lay everywhere, houses and bridges destroyed, and on the far shore, the northern part of the town was in flames."

At 4:30 p.m., the combat engineers of the *29th* launched their rubber rafts, full of infantry, into the river and headed toward the enemy shore. An artillery and *Luftwaffe* strike kept Soviet fire to a minimum, and a bridgehead was soon established. While reinforcements were still coming across, the lead German elements broke through the river defenses and started their final drive into what remained of Soviet Smolensk. By 5:30 p.m., the railway station was under German control.

Every intersection was barricaded. Many buildings had been for-

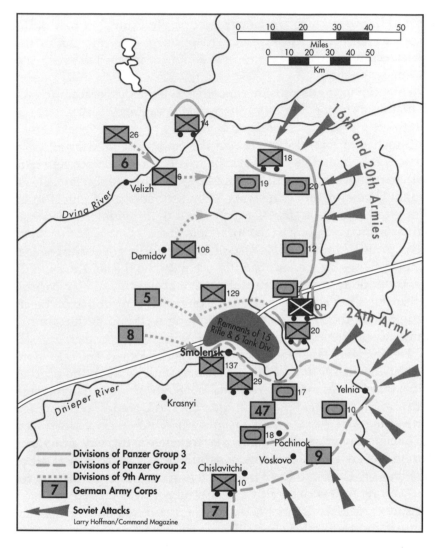

Larry Hoffman/Command Magazine

tified from their cellars to their attics, and all were stubbornly defended. But no matter how bravely the mixed militia/army units fought, they were no match for German assault tactics.

By 7:00 p.m., forward German elements reached the northern limits of Smolensk. Several desperate Soviet counterattacks, from various directions, were foiled by combined infantry and artillery fire as the Germans strove to broaden their control. At 8:00 p.m., the *29th*'s commander reported to his superiors that Smolensk had been brought entirely within the Third Reich. One of the primary objectives of Operation Barbarossa had been achieved.

Complete Fluidity

Guderian had little time to savor his victory at Smolensk. Yeremenko's attack on the southern flank continued without respite. Schweppenburg was hard pressed to keep his supply lines open, and several motorized detachments were still tied up around Mogilev, where they waited for infantry from the *2nd Army* to relieve them. At the same time, the *1st Cavalry* and *10th Motorized Infantry Divisions*, along with parts of the *4th Panzer Division*, were kept constantly on the move, blunting Soviet attacks and sealing off their penetrations.

The German high command wanted the Soviet troops in the Smolensk area destroyed as quickly as possible, but the pincers of *Panzer Groups 2* and *3* could not yet be closed. Soviet attacks on the flanks, as well as fierce resistance inside the pocket itself, prevented a link up.

Guderian's forces were spread too thinly to complete all the tasks they needed to perform. There simply were not enough units to take Yelnia, defend the group's southern flank, close the gap in the Smolensk pocket, and pin down all the Soviet forces in the pocket until the infantry armies arrived.

The panzer leader had planned to use the *Grossdeutschland Regiment* to link up with Hoth east of Smolensk, but that outfit was still engaged with Soviet units north of Roslavl. The force supposed to relieve *Grossdeutschland* there, the *18th Panzer Division*, was tied down along the Dnieper and could not get underway before infantry units came up to take its place. Meanwhile, though, the *10th Panzer* and *Das Reich* divisions fought their way toward Yelnia.

In addition to battling the Soviets that blocked their way, the German armored and motorized elements became increasingly plagued by mechanical breakdowns. In less than a month, these mobile units had driven over 600 miles into the Russian Motherland. They had far outpaced their supply columns, and the lack of maintenance and spare parts for the vehicles was taking a heavy toll. For example, most of *10th Panzer*'s Mk IV tanks were already out of commission, due in about equal measure to enemy action and breakdowns.

Still, despite supply, casualty and wastage problems, the *10th Panzer Division* kept moving. On 19 July, Yelnia fell to its forward elements. The division's *69th Panzer Grenadier Regiment* suffered severe casualties storming an anti-tank ditch that protected the town, but by nightfall those men had forced the Soviets entirely out of Yelnia and pressed on to positions east of the place.

That same night, the Soviet area commander, Gen. Konstantin K. Rokossovsky, sent several regiments forward in an attempt to recapture Yelnia. But the *10th* fought that effort to a standstill, and the next day *Das Reich* arrived to stiffen the German positions. Together, those two divisions formed the easternmost spearpoint of *Army Group Center*'s advance—they were only 185 miles from Moscow.

With the capture of Yelnia, Guderian began to press von Bock for more units to exploit the potentials opened by that success. But the army group commander replied the only thing that mattered at the moment was sealing and eliminating the Smolensk pocket. He also told Guderian categorically that another push farther to the east was "out of the question" for the time being.

While the German generals debated, Yeremenko and Timoshenko continued to hammer at the extended flanks of the panzer groups. In the south, von Schweppenburg's corps was stretched to the limit. The *1st Cavalry Division* was desperately trying to contain yet another Soviet breakthrough southeast of Stary Bykhov, while the *10th Motorized* reported its ammunition almost completely exhausted after heavy action near Propoisk. Elements of the *3rd* and *4th Panzer Division*s had to be thrown into the line piecemeal at critical points to prevent a major break in.

At what was almost literally the last minute infantry from Gen. Wilhelm Fahrmbacher's *7th Corps* finally reached Mogilev, thus releasing the motorized units that had been surrounding that place. The Soviet garrison there was now firmly entrenched, and Fahrmbacher's initial attacks met with little success and severe losses. It took a week of heavy fighting before that city was finally secured.

At the same time, von Bock was coming under increasing pressure from the high command to eliminate the Soviets in the Smolensk pocket. In turn, von Bock demanded Hoth and Guderian complete their link up east of the city and finish the whole affair as quickly as possible.

Then Soviet forces inside the encirclement began heading east, trying to slip through the gap between the panzer groups. The German infantry fighting to prevent those units from escaping were simultaneously hit by attacks from Red Army units outside the pocket trying to link up with their trapped comrades.

Army Group Center Tank Wastage by Panzer Division

Pz. Div.	Operating Tanks 22 June 1941	Operating Tanks 31 August 1941	Percent Lost*
3	198	41	79
4	169	49	71
7	299	130	57
10	206	159	23
12	231	96	58
17	180	38	79
18	200	62	69
19	239	102	57
20	245	88	64
Total	1,967	765	61

*About half these losses were due to mechanical breakdown; those machines eventually returned to service.

Finale Around Smolensk

As long as there were Soviet units still trying to escape the Smolensk encirclement, Timoshenko used everything at his disposal to help them. On 23 July, he unleashed yet another counterattack—this one aimed at nothing less than the recapture of Smolensk and the cutting off of the spearheads of the two panzer groups.

The already overburdened German divisions reeled before the new offensive. Then the infantry divisions Guderian and Hoth had been screaming for began to arrive on the scene, and they were immediately thrown into the line, but the situation remained critical.

Rokossovsky's forces managed to break through the thinly-held German perimeter around the pocket and succeeded in freeing some of the trapped units of the 16th and 20th Armies. As the offensive continued, both panzer generals were forced to deploy and redeploy their mobile units daily in an effort to prevent their lines from cracking completely.

In *Panzer Group 2*, the *3rd* and *4th Panzer Division*s were sent to Krichev to fend off a strong Soviet attack there. At Yelnia, *Das Reich* and *10th Panzer* beat back several attacks, but suffered considerable losses themselves. The new eruption of fighting at Yelnia forced the diversion of *Grossdeutschland* and all of the arriving *9th Corps* toward that critical sector. However, those relief forces were pulled into the fighting around the Smolensk pocket and could not disengage—the Germans in Yelnia had to continue to fend for themselves.

Far to the rear, the 13th Army was finally battered into submission at Mogilev by the infantry of the *7th Corps*. Thirty-five thousand prisoners were taken, but their stubborn defense had prevented four sorely needed German infantry divisions from reaching the forward area for over a week.

As the survivors of the 13th trudged into captivity, their comrades inside the Smolensk pocket continued to stream eastward through the six mile gap that remained between *Panzergroups* 2 and 3. Many of those who could not make it through to the east went into the vast surrounding forests instead, there forming the cadre of partisan units that would plague the German rear area for years to come.

Hoth's forces, spearheaded by *7th Panzer Division* and *20th Motorized Division*, kept inching their way toward Yelnia from the north in an effort to seal an even larger Smolensk pocket. The *7th* fought off attacks from two Soviet rifle divisions. Elements from Hoth's group and *Das Reich* finally met on 27 July.

This re-encirclement was tenuous at best. The German lines were still too thinly held to totally seal the pocket. As late as 2 August, von Bock received a report from his aerial reconnaissance stating "the Russians have built a bridge on the eastern side of the Smolensk pocket and are streaming out to their own lines." Between 100,000 and 150,000 men escaped, forming a valuable reserve of manpower for the subsequent battles for Moscow.

New Directions

While these battles raged along *Army Group Center*'s front, decisions were being made in Berlin that would have far reaching effects on their ultimate outcome. Guderian was surprised to learn that once the Smolensk pocket was eliminated, his panzer group was to swing southwest in an effort to encircle approximately 10 Soviet divisions in the Gomel area. Flying to army group headquarters, Guderian told von Bock he could not carry out any new operations until his mobile units were rested and refitted. He also argued against the Gomel operation in general and in favor of a continued advance toward Moscow.

But von Bock had anticipated Guderian's objections. He told the irate panzer general that the overall army commander, Field Marshal

Top: The Moscow highway in July and August of 1941.
Bottom: The Moscow "highway" in October 1941, after the rainy season had begun.

von Brauchitsch, had visited his headquarters earlier that day. Those two agreed that instead of using Guderian's forces at Gomel, as Berlin wanted, they should be committed against the Soviet forces operating in the Krishnev-Roslavl area. That still wasn't the move toward Moscow Guderian wanted, but the change was better than nothing, and he flew back to his command somewhat mollified.

Guderian's troops at Yelnia were meanwhile under constant attack as Timoshenko tried to eliminate the salient. The area began to draw in units from both sides like a magnet. The *Das Reich Division*, forming the left flank of the bulge, suffered several severe attacks. But then the *268th Infantry Division* entered the lines, freeing elements of the *10th Panzer Division* to form a "fire brigade," roaming the perimeter to reinforce the battered defense at critical points. Eventually, nine German divisions got a taste of battle at its worst around Yelnia.

By the end of July, the eastward advance of *Army Group Center* had been halted temporarily for rest and regrouping. This allowed the infantry corps to finally finish catching up to their motorized compatriots. They were able to take over the task of rounding up what remained of the Soviet units inside the deflating Smolensk pocket, as well as relieving some of the armored units on the front line.

Guderian's armored forces desperately needed overhaul. On 29 July, he reported his panzer group had only 263 entirely dependable tanks—he had started the campaign with 953. It was only the arrival of the infantry that enabled the maintenance personnel to get his armored units ready for the planned offensive at Roslavl.

That new encirclement battle began on 1 August. Its two-pronged attack proceeded with textbook efficiency, and within eight days the Germans captured about 38,000 Soviet troops, and captured or destroyed about 200 tanks, and 200 artillery pieces. By 14 August, the Krichev pocket was also cleared, yielding another 16,000 prisoners and 76 artillery pieces.

But those successes had also pulled some of Guderian's panzer units south, off the Moscow axis. Von Bock then ordered the group further south to help *2nd Army* in the Gomel area. Guderian realized the moves were needed to finally and firmly shore up his southern flank, but still, they were moves that took him away from—not toward—Moscow.

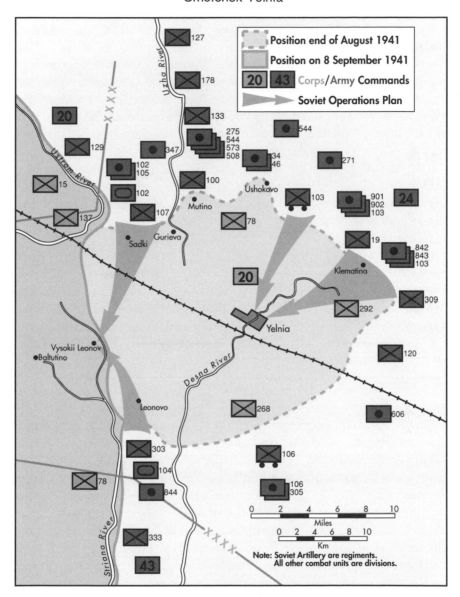

Yelnia

While Guderian slid away from Smolensk, the battle for Yelnia reached new levels of ferocity, and on 5 August the battle of the Smolensk pocket was finally declared won by *Army Group Center*. In an order of the day to his troops, von Bock announced a total of 309,110 prisoners, 3,205 tanks, 3,000 artillery pieces, and 314 Soviet aircraft destroyed.

But those figures meant little to the Germans at Yelnia. The enemy in front of them was nothing like the beaten and demoralized rabble that Radio Berlin spoke about. Stalin had personally promised Timoshenko he could have all the troops and equipment he needed to retake Yelnia, and the Soviet commander used those resources to attack the German lines incessantly.

The reason for the constant pressure was simple. Even though Guderian's forces were presently moving south, Stalin knew the Germans would eventually turn north again. Then they would want to use Yelnia as a forward jump off point for a renewed drive on Moscow.

On the German side, infantry units of the *4th Army* streamed toward Yelnia to bolster the salient. The *Das Reich Division* and the *Grossdeutschland Regiment* were still engaged in heavy fighting on its left flank. As new battalions arrived at the front, they were immediately committed to fill the ever-thinning ranks of the defenders. The battle for Yelnia gave the German army its first full-blooded taste of the savagery of total war to come on the Eastern Front.

Enter Zhukov

The Soviet high command had a trump card to play. Gen. Georgi K. Zhukov was given command of the "Reserve Front" that had taken over operations around Yelnia in late July. His orders from Stalin were clear: eliminate the threat at Yelnia by any means possible. Zhukov planned an offensive designed to push the Germans back across the Desna River and stabilize the entire area.

Guderian's slide south had pulled much of the *Luftwaffe* with him. The infantry at Yelnia were thus left to their own devices as the Soviet pressure increased. In mid-August the *Das Reich Division* and *Grossdeutschland Regiment* were also withdrawn from the area. Only a few detachments from the *10th Panzer Division* were left behind to support the infantry and counter any Soviet breakthroughs.

Zhukov gave the Germans no respite. The German *20th Corps* had been in the area just one week when it reported the loss of 2,254 men. Each division in the salient was suffering daily losses of between 50-150 men.

For his finale at Yelnia, Zhukov used the 24th Army, composed of

13 divisions, as his main assault force. They were supported by over 800 artillery pieces, as well as several "Katyusha" mobile rocket launchers.

Early on 30 August, the *137th Infantry Division* came under attack by elements of the Soviet 102nd Tank Division and the 100th and 107th Rifle Divisions. As the first cracks began to appear in the German line, the Soviets increased the pressure with a three-hour barrage.

Zhukov had fought and defeated the Japanese at Khalkhin-Gol in Mongolia in 1939. There he had demonstrated an expertise at handling combined-arms forces. When his infantry battalions succeeded in creating a gap in the German defenses, he immediately ordered formations of tanks forward to widen the breach. Without significant armored support, there was little the Germans could do to stop Soviet penetrations.

On the southern flank of *20th Corps*, Zhukov sent his 106th Motorized and 303rd Rifle Divisions against the German *268th Infantry Division*. Though that attack was only a diversion, it drew off German reserves that might otherwise have been used in the north.

Meanwhile, the eastern part of the salient, defended by elements of the *78th* and *292nd Infantry Divisions*, was hit by the Soviet 103rd Motorized, and the 19th and 309th Rifle Divisions, supported by six artillery regiments. Their task was to break through the German lines and head for the town of Yelnia, splitting the salient in two.

By 2 September, the German units around Yelnia had been decimated. During the first three days of Zhukov's final offensive, the *137th Infantry Division* reported the loss of 1,200 men. Other divisions fared no better. The commanders inside the salient reported their units were at the limit of their endurance, and that if something weren't done soon, both the *9th* and *20th Corps* would be used up.

The high command finally agreed the Yelnia position was no longer tenable. Another great battle of encirclement was underway around Kiev, and there were no reserves left to help the forlorn infantry of the *4th Army*. The German evacuation was helped by a sudden onset of bad weather, and by 6 September all units inside the Yelnia salient had been pulled out.

Lessons Learned

The battle around Smolensk and the subsequent fight for the Yelnia bulge taught both sides valuable lessons. Soviet tacticians learned the importance of massed artillery at key sectors of the front. They refined those methods, and in later war years Red Army artillery was used with devastating effectiveness. Zhukov's use of a combined-arms force to obtain a breakthrough demonstrated to other Soviet generals that they could beat the Germans at their own game. Finally, the Red Army showed that the German war machine could be stopped.

The failure to completely close the Smolensk pocket in a timely manner pointed up to the German command that mobile forces by themselves could no longer provide a strong enough ring to overcome an encircled enemy. Yelnia was the first real setback for the *Wehrmacht* in the east. The fierce Soviet defense and counteroffensive signaled that the Soviet soldier was not yet a defeated enemy. Yelnia, then, became a taste of things to come.

Chapter XXIII

Krim
The War in the Crimea, 1941-42
by Pat McTaggart

Barely two-and-a-half months after the start of Operation Barbarossa, the armies of Field Marshal Gerd von Rundstedt's *Heeresgruppe Süd* (*Army Group South* or AGS) had advanced hundreds of miles into the Soviet Union. Along the way several enemy armies had been destroyed, and tens of thousands of prisoners were languishing in German POW camps. On the surface it seemed the Red Army was all but finished, and in Berlin General Staff officers were already congratulating each other on another successful campaign.

The ordinary German *Landser* (infantryman), however, saw the situation on a different level. His Soviet counterpart, though poorly equipped and badly led, was a fierce opponent. So while the high command celebrated, the soldiers at the front noticed a marked increase in the will of the Soviet soldier to resist.

Far to the rear of the frontline, Soviet General I.E. Petrov's Coastal Army still held the port of Odessa against a Romanian siege. On AGS's right flank, the remnants of Colonel-General F.I. Kuznetzov's 51st Army were dug in on the Isthmus of Perekop—the gateway to the Crimea.

As his generals prepared for the next—and what was supposed to be the final—phase of Barbarossa, Adolf Hitler became increasingly anxious about the danger presented by a Soviet-controlled Crimea. The critical Romanian oilfields at Ploesti were within reach of Red Air Force bombers operating from the peninsula, and Hitler also feared the area could be used as a staging zone for an attack on AGS's lines of supply and communication. Therefore, on 12 August 1941, he ordered Gen. Ritter von Schobert's *11th Army* to prepare for an operation to clear the Crimea.

Von Schobert was killed in an airplane accident before the attack

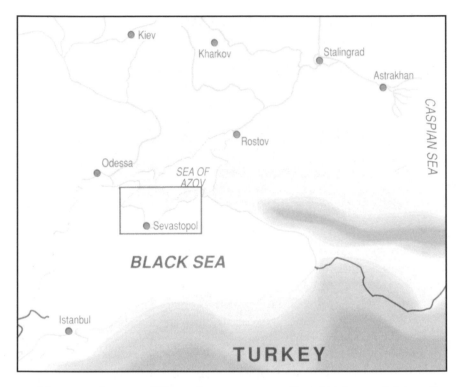

could get under way. His replacement was Gen. Erich von Manstein. He possessed one of the keenest strategic minds in the German Army, and had formulated the basic operations plan that led to the fall of France in 1940. During the opening stages of Barbarossa, he showed his grasp of mechanized warfare as he led *56th Panzer Corps* on an amazing 200-mile dash to the Dvina. In the Crimea, he would prove himself one of the finest *Feldherrn* (army commanders) of the war.

Perekop

Von Manstein had a difficult task. *11th Army* faced not only the Perekop Isthmus position, but was also responsible for a sector of the main front to the east. The isthmus itself was a defender's dream. Only four-to-five miles wide, the Soviets had the time to prepare extensive defenses. In this they were aided by extensive pre-war study of the area—during the Russian Civil War, the Red Army had successfully stormed through the isthmus, and that operation was studied by Soviet officers in the inter-war years. The lessons learned from it proved invaluable to the soldiers working on the line in 1941: trenches, pillboxes and minefields covered every avenue of approach.

Two other routes were available into the Crimea, both of which crossed the *Sivash*, a saline marsh east of the Perekop that separated the Crimea from the mainland. Just east of the isthmus was a railroad line, while farther east was the Arabatskaya Spit, a land corridor only a few hundred yards wide. Neither was particularly useful to an invading army.

The first German soldiers who had the chance to observe the defense on the isthmus at close range knew instantly a surprise attack could never work against such positions. Old hands now, veterans of the lightning summer advances, they prepared for a bloody head-on clash with an enemy determined to resist to the death.

Von Manstein's attack opened on September 24th. The plan was for Eric Hansen's *54th Corps* (*46th, 50th* and *73rd Infantry Divisions*) to seize the Perekop positions, after which Ludwig Kubler's *49th Mountain Corps* (*1st* and *4th Mountain Infantry Divisions*) and "Sepp" Dietrich's SS motorized division *Liebstandarte Adolf Hitler* would exploit the breach, fanning out into the peninsula.

Hansen's men moved out in the early morning, supported by every available artillery and engineer unit in *11th Army* and by the guns of *Sturmgeschütze Abteilung 190* (*Assault Gun Battalion 190*). For three days the Soviet 156th and 276th Rifle Divisions fought desperately to hold their positions. Finally, though, the relentless shelling and non-stop attacks of Hansen's infantry forced the shattered divisions back to the town of Ishun. Kuznetzov committed four divisions (40th and 42nd Cavalry, 106th and 271st Rifle) to hold the town. In spite of this, everything seemed to be going according to von Manstein's plan. The *Gebirgskorps* and the *Liebstandarte* had already begun moving south for the anticipated exploitation when a new development radically upset the German timetable.

On 26 September, the Soviet 9th and 18th Armies attacked the German and Romanian lines between Melitopol and Nikopol on the Ukrainian mainland. Von Manstein was forced to throw his would-be exploitation troops back into the front line to stop this new threat. Hansen had to halt his attack while the situation in the north was restablized, which took three weeks.

Kuznetzov used the respite to improve his defenses and reorganize his forces. On 16 October, the Soviet defenders received another unexpected reinforcement—Gen. Petrov's Coastal Army began evacuating Odessa by sea. By the time the Germans resumed their Crimean attacks, an additional 70,000 to 80,000 Red Army soldiers had landed in Sevastopol and were on their way to the front.

The German forces were restructured prior to resuming the offensive into the Crimea. *11th Army* gave up *49th Mountain Corps* and the *Liebstandarte*, but also gave up its share of the main front. It would now be concerned solely with the Crimea. Manstein commanded two corps with six infantry divisions and a battalion of assault guns, later reinforced with another corps of two divisions.

At 0510 hours on 18 October, *11th Army* returned to the attack. The Soviet positions at Ishun were subjected to a rolling bombardment, followed by assault troops who stormed the Soviet trenches. Kuznetzov had used his time wisely, though; the barrage had only minimal effects on the reinforced bunkers and pillboxes that dotted his lines. German assault platoons were shot to pieces in front of the heavily-mined and wired entrenchments.

For eight days, *54th Corps'* divisions bled themselves white in an effort to take the Soviet positions. The Russians fought ferociously, but eventually the battle turned in the Germans' favor.

On 22 October, STAVKA (the Soviet High Command in Moscow) replaced Kuznetzov with Lt. Gen. P.I. Batov, but the change in command could not alter the outcome of the battle. Even the arrival of some of Petrov's Coastal Army units did little to stop the German advance. By the 27th, Hansen's infantry, along with 24 assault guns from the *190th*, had broken through the final Soviet line, and the door to the Crimea was open.

54th Corps counted 1,920 dead and 7,273 wounded during the Perekop operations. Thousands of Soviets died and 26,000 were taken prisoner. Manstein's troops had all but destroyed nine rifle and four cavalry divisions during the battle.

Into the Crimea

Though his men were exhausted, von Manstein planned to smash the remnants of the 51st Army on the 28th. But as dawn broke, the lead German battalions found the Soviet positions empty. Batov's forces, moving under cover of darkness, were already headed south and east in an effort to regroup. Petrov, knowing a pitched battle on the Crimean plain would be disastrous, ordered his units to fall back toward Sevastopol.

Von Manstein reacted quickly to the new situation. With the bulk of his army now free to maneuver, he issued new orders to his commanders. Hans von Salmuth's *30th Corps* (*22nd* and *72nd Infantry Divisions*) turned southwest and made for Yalta and Sevastopol by way of Simferopol. Hansen's *54th Corps* (*50th* and *132nd Infantry Divisions*) advanced directly toward Sevastopol, while Hans Graf von Sponeck's *42nd Corps* (*46th*, *73rd* and *170th Infantry Divisions*) headed east toward the Parpach peninsula.

By 1 November, Simferopol had fallen and *30th Corps* was advancing on Yalta, while *54th Corps* was steadily moving down the western coast toward Sevastopol. Reconnaissance units advanced at lightning speed, surprising enemy formations miles to the rear of the front lines. In the east, von Sponeck's divisions had reached the Parpach region before most of Batov's units, thus cutting the vital Soviet supply line from Kerch. On 3 November, the *170th Infantry Division* took Feodosiya by storm. To many of the men of the *11th Army*, it appeared to be a repeat of the first days of Barbarossa.

By the second week, most of von Manstein's objectives had been taken. The *46th* and *170th Divisions* assaulted the Soviet defenses across the isthmus at Parpach. Russian fire caused heavy casualties among the German regiments, but by the 15th the entire Kerch peninsula had been conquered.

Further south, units from *72nd* and *22nd Divisions* took Yalta, then turned west to link up with *54th Corps*, which was approaching Sevastopol from the north. It seemed the Crimean campaign was all but over.

On to the City—Almost

Gen. Petrov, however, had other ideas. As his Coastal Army retreated toward Sevastopol, he was already working on plans for the defense of the city, one of the most heavily fortified in Europe. STAVKA sent Vice Admiral Oktabryski, a proven combat leader, to assume overall command of Sevastopol, while Petrov remained in command of the Coastal Army itself. As German reconnaissance units came closer to the outer defense ring of the city, they noticed a strengthening of resolve in the Soviet defenders. Red Navy officer candidates, guarding key approaches to the port, refused to yield an inch. Old fortifications were manned by Red Army units that were determined to hold at all costs. *Luftwaffe* bombers were already flying

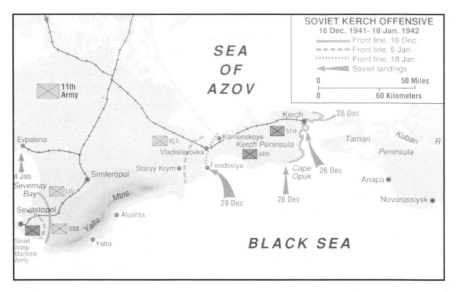

sorties against the city, but it took a few more precious days before the German regiments formed a perimeter around the fortress.

Petrov and Oktabryski had their men working day and night to improve the already formidable city defenses. Three defense lines surrounded Sevastopol. The outer perimeter was 27 miles long. The second (main) line ran for 23 miles, while the inner covered 18. Each line was protected in depth with machine gun and artillery positions. Mines and a series of massive bunkers covered the main approaches. Petrov's artillery included several naval batteries (152-305mm) which were zeroed in on all likely avenues of attack. The Soviet commander had also ordered his engineers to remove turrets from damaged Red Navy ships in the harbor, creating additional bunkers with them.

The Black Sea Fleet, operating out of Novorossisk, made daily runs to Sevastopol, bringing ammunition and new battalions into the city. *Luftwaffe* anti-shipping units were hampered by the weather and could do little to stop the flow of supplies. By the time the Germans finally began their assault, they were met by 60-70,000 naval and Red Army defenders, augmented by several thousand members of the Young Communist Organization.

The German situation was complicated by two other factors—Russian weather and their own high command (OKH). Crimean winters are usually mild, but 1941 was not a usual year. Like their brothers in the north, the men of the *11th Army* had little winter clothing. By mid-November, the temperature had already fallen to 10 degrees

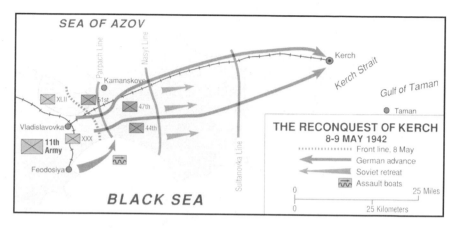

SEA OF AZOV

Parpach Line
Nasyt Line
Kamanskoye
Kerch
Kerch Strait
Gulf of Taman
Taman

Vladislavovka
51st
47th
44th
11th Army
XXX
Feodosiya
Sultanovka Line

THE RECONQUEST OF KERCH
8-9 MAY 1942
················· Front line, 8 May
German advance
Soviet retreat
Assault boats
0   25 Miles
0   25 Kilometers

XLII

BLACK SEA

Fahrenheit—not as cold as it was before Moscow, but bad enough—and that cold cut through their thin uniforms. Rain and snow storms also prevented any early assaults. OKH did more damage—the apparent ease of Manstein's campaign caused them to transfer most of *73rd Division* to the Rostov area.

Nevertheless, von Manstein was confident of a quick victory—he expected to capture Sevastopol no later than New Year's Day. Leaving only the *46th Division* and three Romanian brigades to guard the 180 miles of coastline between Yalta and Kerch, von Manstein put the rest of his army into position for a two-pronged attack. He set the morning of 17 December as the start-date for the offensive.

The deplorable road conditions in the Crimea forced the bulk of the German army and corps artillery to be situated on the northern front, so the main effort would have to come in *54th Corps'* sector. There, *22nd Division*, supported by a Romanian motorized regiment, was given the task of breaking into the Belbeck Valley and destroying the gun emplacements guarding Severnaya (North) Bay. Hansen's other three divisions (*24th, 50th* and *132nd*) were to advance through the scrub-covered hills east of the city. *30th Corps* (*72nd Division* and *1st Romanian Mountain Brigade*) had the job of diverting Soviet reinforcements by making a frontal assault on the southeastern sector of the enemy line.

At 0610 hours on the 17th, 25 artillery batteries opened fire on the Soviets. As shells were still falling, the assault groups of *54th Corps* moved forward. Overhead, von Richtofen's *VIII Fliegerkorps* dropped tons of bombs on Soviet secondary targets.

The *16th Regiment/22nd Division*, commanded by Dietrich von Choltitz (who would later surrender Paris to the Allies), attacked through the fortified zone east of the Belbeck Valley. Despite many casualties, the *16th* penetrated deep inside the defensive line. Its brother regiments (*47th* and *65th*) and the other attacking divisions did not fare as well. Superbly camouflaged entrenchments, coupled with minefields, heavy artillery fire and reinforcements from the 388th Rifle Division, which had landed the previous night in Sevastopol, slowed the German advance to a crawl. As the first day of the battle ended, *54th Corps* reported 306 dead, 1,342 wounded, and 50 missing. It had been, as one member of the *22nd Division* stated, "One hell of a day," but it was only the first of many.

While Hansen's attack was stalled in the north, von Salmuth's *30th Corps* successfully broke through the outer perimeter on the south-eastern sector. The regiments of the *72nd Division* and the *1st Romanian Mountain Brigade* encountered heavy fire as they stormed the Russian-held heights that controlled the area. Grenades rained from above as the infantrymen clawed their way to the top. By the 19th, the *105th Regiment/72nd Division* had captured Chapel Mountain, which gave them an excellent observation post for calling in artillery fire on the Soviets' secondary positions. The next day, the *105th* repelled several Russian counterattacks, aided by air strikes and effective artillery fire. But the savage fighting took its toll on the regiment—by 21 December, it was down to an effective strength of only 7 officers and 260 men.

Back on the northern sector, *22nd Division*, supported by heavy artillery fire, finally broke through the defenses two days before Christmas. The Soviet 40th Cavalry Division put up a gallant fight on the Mackenzie Heights before being forced to abandon them. The Germans were only a few kilometers from Severnaya Bay when they ran into the Soviet 79th Independent Naval Infantry Brigade, which had been brought into Sevastopol by the Black Sea Fleet only hours before. The timely arrival of the 79th brought the Germans to a halt.

The German *24th*, *50th* and *132nd Divisions* still faced serious opposition as they advanced from the east. Thick brush and mounds of rubble made every step a nightmare for the *Landser*. The Soviet art of camouflage was used to perfection in the rugged terrain, and squads of German soldiers found death was only a few yards from their jump off positions, as they were cut down while approaching concealed enemy positions. But despite this tenacious defense, it seemed Sevastopol would soon be within von Manstein's grasp. Slowly, methodically, the Soviets were being pushed back. Von Salmuth's corps was on the move again, and Hansen's units systematically neutralized several of the great forts that were an integral part of Petrov's defense.

German losses were serious. For example, the *2nd Battalion/16th Regiment/22nd Division* had 49 men left out of 500. The troops remaining were worn out from months of marching and fighting. In addition, *11th Army* was aware of major Soviet offensives on the mainland. There, attacks along the entire front were forcing the generals at OKH to consider the heretofore impossible—retreat or be destroyed. The surprise "Stalin Offensive" had caught Hitler and his commanders completely off guard. The capture of Sevastopol became only a secondary consideration.

But fresh units of *170th Division* were finally arriving after a difficult march from Feodosiya, and von Richtofen's planes kept up the pressure by continuous strikes on convoys of the Black Sea Fleet as they tried to slip into Sevastopol with men and supplies. Von Manstein felt one final effort was all that was needed to achieve victory, and ordered his commanders to continue the attack.

The painful German advance continued. Several key positions were taken. Von Choltitz and the soldiers of the *16th Regiment* were already in front of Fort Stalin, preparing for the final assault on the bunkers that would open the way into the city—when disaster struck.

The Stalin Offensive in the Crimea

In planning their winter offensive, STAVKA had not forgotten the Crimea. Oktabryski had been at Novorossisk, planning an amphibious operation to retake the peninsula, when von Manstein's attack on Sevastopol opened. He hurried back to the fortress as the situation there worsened. The planned invasion, originally scheduled for 21 December, had to be put off for a few days because reinforcements were sorely needed in the beleaguered fortress.

Christmas night found units of Pervushin's 44th and Lvov's 51st Armies filing aboard Black Sea Fleet ships in Novorossisk and other Caucasian ports. They sailed out in gale force winds, headed for landing areas on the Kerch coast. The weather was both a blessing and a curse for the Soviet commanders. It prevented the *Luftwaffe* from discovering the flotilla, but at the same time it hindered the off-loading of men and materials.

Lvov had 3,000 men ashore at Kerch by midday on 26 December. Scattered units of *46th Division* were soon locked in combat with elements of the 244th, 302nd and 390th Rifle Divisions. The German corps commander, von Sponeck, stripped his other coastal defenses to the bone and sent all available men to hold Lvov's infantry. German forces gradually began to get the upper hand, even though Soviet reinforcements continued to pour onto the beachheads.

Just when von Sponeck thought the situation was under control, he received word of a second landing at Feodosiya on 29 December. More than 40,000 men, along with tanks and artillery, landed at the port in less than two days. Romanian troops in the area were quickly overwhelmed, some units disintegrating altogether. Max Schmidt, a German survivor of the *46th Division*, states that the Romanians were truly useless, and several companies of them were integrated directly into German battalions as the only way to keep them together.

Repeated German/Romanian counterattacks were beaten back with the help of Black Sea Fleet destroyers and cruisers firing from just outside Feodosiya harbor.

Faced with a large enemy force so far to his rear, von Sponeck ordered the *46th* to break contact and retreat to the narrow Parpach line. Von Manstein countermanded the order almost immediately, but it was too late. The division commander had already issued orders to his units, and soon the roads were crowded with German troops heading west in sub-zero temperatures. Their path was littered with abandoned guns and vehicles, but most of the infantry managed to make its way back. Part of the Soviet 63rd Rifle Division managed to position itself across the line of retreat, but was quickly overrun.

So, just as the assault on Sevastopol was reaching its crisis, von Manstein was forced to cancel the operation in order to stop the Soviet advance from Kerch. This was the second time in three months he had been forced to cancel an offensive on the verge of success because of a threat elsewhere. The German Army was simply stretched too far, trying to take too many objectives simultaneously.

Some Romanian units and the *213th Regiment/73rd Division* were sent to reinforce *46th Division*. Other units were pulled from the Sevastopol fight in order to form a defensive line from which a counterattack could be launched.

Though the Red Army had conducted two successful landings, the local Soviet commanders failed to follow up their initial victories. Lack of initiative and a rigid operational doctrine prevented the kind of lightning blow that might have shattered *11th Army*. The slow-moving Soviet forces gave the Germans time to occupy a defensive line across the narrowest part of the Parpach isthmus. When the lead elements of Lvov's and Pervushin's armies finally moved into the area, they were stopped dead in their tracks by German fire.

Back at Sevastopol, Petrov decided this was the time to start his own limited offensive. Only days before, von Choltitz's men had taken Fort Stalin. Now they were forced to give it up as their undermanned battalions were hit by the relatively fresh troops of the Coastal Army. Positions that had been paid for in blood had to be abandoned as Petrov's men reclaimed most of their defensive perimeter. Knowing the shortcomings of his command, Petrov ordered his troops to dig in once their limited objectives had been achieved. By New Year's Day, the lines at Sevastopol were back to where they had been on 17 December. Except for a Soviet parachute drop at Evpatoria, which was quickly destroyed, and a few feeble attempts by the Red Navy to create new beachheads on the southern coast, the Sevastopol area remained quiet for the moment.

The Situation Stabilizes

With matters still in doubt on the mainland, von Manstein had to rely on his own resources to bring the Crimean situation under control. Von Sponeck, blamed for the loss of Kerch, was relieved of his command. Court martialed for failure to obey orders, he was eventually implicated in and shot after the failed July 1944 bomb plot against Hitler. Fretter-Pico took over the *30th Corps*.

With the Sevastopol front stabilized, *11th Army* prepared to deal with the Soviet forces facing them at Parpach. However, Lvov and Pervushin had their own plans, though they ran into trouble with them almost immediately. An attack by the Soviet 157th Rifle Division, supported by an armored column, was smashed by the *213th Infantry Regiment*. The three still-serviceable guns of the *190th Assault Gun Battalion* destroyed 16 Soviet tanks.

Von Manstein marshaled his forces for a counterattack, but once again uncontrollable factors intervened. Temperatures rose to above the freezing mark, turning frozen roads and trails into impassable quagmires. The general was forced to wait another two weeks before he could act.

It was still fairly muddy on 15 January 1942, but von Manstein could not afford to wait any longer. At 0600 hours, German artillery began a thunderous barrage, while three and a half understrength divisions moved forward in the early morning light. More than eight Soviet divisions, supported by tanks, stood ready to meet them. Luck favored von Manstein that morning. A *Luftwaffe* attack hit Peruvshin's 44th Army headquarters, seriously wounding the general and killing several of his key staff officers.

On the southern flank, *170th Division* and *105th Regiment* punched a hole through the Soviet line and headed for Feodosiya. In the center, the *132nd Division* advanced ten kilometers the first day and took control of the heights overlooking the important communications hub at Vladislavoka. In the north, *46th Division, 213th Regiment* and the assault guns advanced to within 12 kilometers of Parpach, destroying several Soviet tanks along the way. Romanian troops followed closely behind the German divisions, consolidating the flanks as von Manstein's men slogged forward.

Temperatures fell below freezing the following evening and remained so for the next few days, which improved the maneuverability of the few motorized units. Feodosiya fell on the 18th, yielding more than 10,000 Soviet prisoners. Vladislavoka was captured the same day by a combined infantry and assault gun attack. The Soviets, stunned by the rapid German advance, retreated to the defensive line at Parpach, where they hastily reoccupied strongpoints left from the 1941 fighting. The sub-zero temperatures had frozen the Kerch Straits, so Soviet reinforcements crossed the ice to strengthen the new line.

Von Manstein needed one more push to regain the Kerch Peninsula, but a *panzer* detachment promised to *11th Army* was diverted to another sector two days before the scheduled assault on Parpach. The German infantry was forced to dig in.

The Soviets Try Again

During the first two weeks of February, the Soviets transferred vast quantities of men and material across the frozen straits. The headquarters of the newly created Crimean Front (Gen. Kozlov) was ordered to prepare for an all out offensive designed to crush von Manstein's forces before spring. Nine rifle divisions, two infantry brigades, two tank brigades and a new army HQ (47th) made up the new Soviet strike force along the Parpach line.

Red Air Force fighters and bombers flew hundreds of missions over the German lines in preparation for the new attack. Kozlov was ordered to start the offensive on 13 February, but operational difficulties forced him to postpone it for two weeks. Stalin sent Political Commissar Lev Mekhlis to oversee the preparations and make certain the army commanders obeyed all instructions to the letter.

The Soviet buildup did not go undetected. German aerial reconnaissance gave von Manstein an excellent picture of the enemy preparations, while radio intercepts even provided him with the exact start date of the attack.

The stabilization of the situation on the mainland allowed OKH to send *11th Army* its first reinforcements in months. Two divisions, *28th Jäger* and *22nd Panzer*, were on their way to the Crimea. The assault gun battalions assigned to *11th Army* were also brought back up to strength. By the time the Soviets were able to attack, they faced a revitalized enemy.

Despite warnings from army and front commanders, Commissar Mekhlis demanded the offensive go ahead. At 0600 hours on 27 February, 70 batteries of Soviet artillery hit German and Romanian positions north of Vladislavoka. The *46th Division* and *Assault Gun Battalion 197* repulsed numerous tank and infantry attacks in the first few hours of the offensive. Farther north, however, the *18th Romanian Infantry* fled as infantry-laden T-34s slammed into its forward positions.

The Soviets followed up their success by sending several infantry units into the gap. By 3 March, parts of the 47th and 51st Armies had occupied a seven-mile-deep bulge. Luckily for Manstein, *213th Regiment* was in position to reinforce the Romanians before their retreat became a rout. Before Kozlov could exploit his attack further, the Crimean weather intervened, this time in the Germans' favor. Rain slowed the Soviet armored columns so much Kozlov was forced to call off his offensive, at least for the moment.

Both sides used the ensuing 10-day respite to regroup and reinforce their units. Though the Soviet success in the north had been substantial, the cost in men and material was heavy—*46th Division* alone destroyed 41 Soviet tanks. The Soviets still had not learned to use their armor properly. STAVKA sent still more reinforcements to the Crimea, giving Kozlov 13 rifle divisions, one cavalry division, three rifle and four armor brigades.

Mekhlis renewed the pressure on Kozlov to resume the offensive, which he did on 13 March. Artillery and bombers pounded the German and Romanian lines, but the assaulting units ran into immediate difficulty. In the south, waves of Soviet infantry threw themselves time and again against the German line. Local breakthroughs were dealt with by reserve companies as Fretter-Pico's *30th Corps* clung to its positions. Overhead, *Luftwaffe* and Red Air Force fighters duelled in the cold Crimean sky.

Kozlov continued to push the attack. His soldiers suffered dreadful casualties, gaining very little in the process. In one week, 136 Soviet tanks had been destroyed by well-directed assault gun and artillery fire. One platoon of six assault guns under Lt. Hans Spielmann accounted for 49 of them. But the Germans also paid a price for their tenacious defense. Mattenklott's *42nd Corps* alone suffered over 1,700 casualties between 13 and 20 March.

As the Soviet offensive ran out of steam, von Manstein hoped to catch Kozlov off guard by launching a counter-offensive with units of the newly arriving *22nd Panzer Division*. That division, equipped with outdated French and Czech armor, ran headlong into a Russian tank assembly area. As the T-34s opened fire, the surprised Germans beat a hasty retreat. Out-gunned and under-protected, 30 German tanks were left burning on the Crimean countryside.

Both sides were worn out by the continuous fighting, but their masters in Moscow and Berlin refused to allow a respite. More reinforcements reached Kozlov, and by 26 March he was ready to strike again. The *46th Division* came under heavy attack from four Soviet rifle divisions. The division commander was wounded during the first hours of the assault, but his unit conducted a skillful holding action until reinforcements arrived. The attack ended in failure.

Once again, Kozlov was forced to request reinforcements for his battered armies, but von Manstein had no intention of awaiting yet another Soviet attack. He planned an offensive of his own, codenamed *"Trappenjagd"* (Bustard Hunt). He pulled the *22nd Panzer* out of the line and replaced it with fresh units of the *28th Jäger Division*. The *22nd Panzer* was reequipped with German tanks and was ready to meet the Soviets on more equal terms.

Before the Germans could attack, Kozlov, pressed by Mekhlis, made one last attempt to break the German line. In the early hours of 4 April, six rifle divisions, supported by 150-160 tanks, launched the last Soviet assault of the campaign. They were met with concentrated artillery fire that disrupted their advance almost immediately. By day's end, Mattenklott's corps had destroyed 56 Soviet tanks and killed hundreds of Red Army soldiers. German losses were 70 killed and 174 wounded or missing. Kozlov called off the offensive on 11 April.

Bustard Hunt

German reconnaissance kept von Manstein informed of Soviet troop movements. During the last week of April, *11th Army* intelligence reported an estimated 17-21 rifle divisions, 2 cavalry divisions, 3 rifle and 4 tank brigades under Kozlov's command.

The Soviet general had more than enough forces to man the three positions that formed the backbone of his defense. His first line (Parpach) extended across the narrowest part of the isthmus. A second line (Nasyr) was established several kilometers to the east. The final line (Sultanovka) was built along an ancient fortification known as the "Tatar Wall." It was some 40 kilometers to the east of the Parpach position.

Von Manstein decided to strike on 8 May. The Soviet bulge north of Vladislavoka presented the most tempting target, so *42nd Corps* was ordered to fake preparations for an attack in that sector. The Soviet command fell for the deception and immediately began moving reserves to the area. The actual German attack was launched by *30th Corps* (*28th Jäger, 50th, 132nd Infantry, 22nd Panzer*) on the southern part of the front. Kozlov and Makhlis were caught completely off guard.

Von Richtofen's bombers cleared the way for the advancing infantry, while artillery disrupted Soviet assembly areas and lines of communication. An *ad hoc* group of German and Romanian motorized units under von Groddeck burst through the line and headed east, followed by the bulk of *30th Corps'* infantry. By nightfall, Fretter-Pico's troops had advanced six miles. The next morning, the Germans swung north and demolished the left flank of the Parpach defenses.

Soviet counterattacks were disrupted by Stukas, and by the 12th the Soviet command had lost control of the battle. The roads were soon clogged with Red Army soldiers fleeing east, trying to reach Kerch before *22nd Panzer* and *Group Groddeck*. In the north, several divisions were pinned against the Sea of Azov.

STAVKA ordered Kazlov to pull back to the Sultanovka line, but it was too late. The Germans gave Kozlov no time to reorganize. The final blow came on 15 May, when German tanks and infantry captured Kerch.

In little more than a week, the Kerch Peninsula had been entirely recaptured. The *11th Army* claimed the Soviets lost 170,000 prisoners, 1,133 guns and 258 tanks. Kozlov and Mekhlis were removed from their commands and called back to Moscow in disgrace. The loss of three armies was a heavy blow to the Soviet effort in southern Russia. AGS was already preparing for its advance toward Stalingrad, and the divisions of the Crimean Front would be sorely missed as the Soviets attempted to defend the Caucasus.

Operation Sturgeon Catch

While the battles had been raging around Parpach, Oktabryski and Petrov had worked to strengthen the lines at Sevastopol. The bunkers and gun emplacements recaptured from the Germans in December had been rebuilt and reinforced. Lessons learned during the previous year were studied and new defensive networks were constructed, making it more difficult for the Germans to use the same avenues of attack. Reinforcements brought Petrov's strength to more than 106,000 men, though he was short of aircraft (55) and tanks (38).

The German *54th Corps* had kept the fortress surrounded during the winter and spring—there was no question of attacking while the fate of the eastern Crimea was still in doubt. After the successful completion of the Kerch operation, the *22nd Panzer Division* was transferred out of the Crimea. Kerch and the southern coast were garrisoned with a combined German and Romanian force while the majority of the German infantry divisions set out for Sevastopol.

Von Manstein's plan basically followed the lines of his December assault. In the north, *54th Corps* (*22nd, 24th, 50th* and *132nd Divisions* and *213th Regiment*) would again bear the brunt of the fighting. General Lascar's *Romanian Mountain Corps* (*1st Romanian Mountain* and *18th Romanian Infantry Divisions*) was to secure positions on Hansen's left flank. *30th Corps* (*28th Jäger, 72nd* and *170th Divisions*) would attack along the southern front, preventing Petrov from shifting his units northward.

The infantry would be supported by over 600 aircraft from *8th Fliegerkorps*, by the assault guns of *Assault Gun Battalions 190, 197* and *249*. Guns from several FLAK regiments were also placed in forward areas to provide additional artillery and anti-aircraft firepower.

The main support for the assault would come from artillery. The *11th Army's* artillery chief, Johannes Zuckertort, was in charge of the largest concentration of artillery used so far during the war. In addition to regular army and corps units, Zuckertort's arsenal included a dozen 11-inch coastal howitzers, a dozen 14-inch howitzers, and three colossal siege guns: Gamma (17-inch), Karl (24-inch), and Dora (31.5-inch).

The *11th Army* also received a number of remote-controlled "Goliath" demolition vehicles. Packed with 150 pounds of explosives, these two-foot-high vehicles could blow a path through Soviet minefields or knock out a tank at close range.

Operation *"Störfang"* (Sturgeon Catch) began in the pre-dawn hours of 3 June with an ear-shattering barrage that lit up the sky surrounding Sevastopol. Within minutes, Soviet artillery in reinforced positions was answering the German fire with an effective counterfire. The artillery duel continued for five days, while the infantry on both sides lay crouched in their foxholes, not daring to raise their heads.

Von Richtofen's bombers added to the carnage by bombing Sevastopol day and night. *Luftwaffe* pilot Werner Baumbach later recalled, "From the air, Sevastopol looked like a painter's battle panorama. The early morning sky swarmed with aircraft hurrying to unload their bombs on the town. Thousands of bombs were dropped on the fortress. A single sortie took no more than 20 minutes. By the time you gained the necessary altitude you were in the target area."

At 0350 hours on 7 June, special sections of German reconnaissance platoons started moving toward the Soviet line. Outposts were silenced before they could give alarm, and as the sun began to rise, the main body of infantry was already closing on Petrov's outer perimeter. The veterans of the '41 campaign moved forward cautiously. They remembered their dead comrades, cut down the year before by fire from the Soviet's superbly camouflaged positions.

The *22nd Division* moved back into the Belbeck Valley, assisted by *50th Division*. But this time, as soon as it had penetrated the forward Soviet line, the *132nd Division* moved through to continue the assault. The Soviets resisted to the death, taking many Germans with them.

By late afternoon, Hansen was forced to report that only some of the preliminary objectives had been taken. Murderous fire from the Soviet line had blunted his attack along the entire front. Cursing God, the *Luftwaffe*, and the high command, German infantrymen dug into the rocky Crimean soil in an effort to escape the shells flying overhead. The *50th Division* reported over 600 casualties on the first day; other divisions sent in similar figures.

Another attempt to break the line was made the following morning. *Stukas* roared overhead, dropping bombs with pinpoint accuracy, as the *Landser* again pressed forward. Supported by assault gun platoons, the German infantry finally made a penetration in depth. By the 9th, the first of the great bunkers was under attack. Von Choltitz's *16th Regiment* attacked Fort Stalin, but was repulsed with frightening losses. Engineers were called in to help take the fort, but intense Soviet artillery and small arms fire stopped them cold.

With negative reports coming in from almost every sector, Hansen finally ordered his divisions to halt their attacks. The *54th Corps* had tried its best, but the Soviet positions were too strong. The men needed rest before a new effort could be mounted.

Von Manstein was forced to shift the focus of his attack southward. The *30th Corps* assaulted on 11 June, and secured several key positions over the next few days. Temperatures of over 100 degrees Fahrenheit plagued attacker and defender alike as they fought for control of Ruin Hill and Chapel Mount. The outcome was finally decided by German air and artillery support. The Soviet commander could not reinforce his position because of the accuracy of the German bombardment. His men fought to the death, but in the end *30th Corps* finally gained control of these important observation posts.

The push in the Belbeck Valley resumed on the 13th. Fort Stalin came under heavy attack by the aircraft of *Stuka Wing 77*. One of the pilots, Werner Weihrauch, scored a direct hit on the massive artillery cupola, rendering it inoperable, for which he received the Knight's Cross. The *16th Regiment* finally captured the fort after fierce hand-to-hand fighting. The *132nd Division* continued to advance across the Belbeck Valley, taking near-crippling losses as it overran the last positions of Petrov's outer line.

Casualties mounted during the next two days, but the Germans kept up the pressure along the entire front. The *30th Corps* broke through the outer perimeter and took up a position at the foot of the Sapun Hills. The *54th Corps* was now in the midst of the northern main defense belt, and Sevastopol was under constant attack from aircraft.

On 17 June, Zuckertort's artillery started the day with another massive bombardment. The fighting reached a new level of intensity as German assault units captured the approaches to several of Petrov's concrete forts. Armed with flamethrowers and satchel charges, the *Landser* managed to overcome heavy Soviet resistance. Assault guns from the *190th* and *197th* shot point-blank into firing slits, while infantry squads charged through holes blown in the thick walls and fought with the Soviet defenders inside. Forts "Volga," "Ural," "Cheka," "Siberia," "GPU," "Molotov," and "Bastion I" were in German hands by the end of the day, and Schmidt's *50th Division* was in position to attack the "Old Fort" and the Mackenzie Heights.

Casualties during the fighting were so heavy von Manstein was forced to pull the *132nd Division* out of the line. It could no longer be considered an effective combat unit. The Romanian *4th Mountain Division* was brought forward to fill the gap.

There was still one holdout in the main defense line. Fort "Maxim Gorky I," a 300-yard-long concrete giant, continued to fire 14-inch shells at German troop concentrations. The *213th Regiment* was called on to capture it. Accompanied by engineers, the troops advanced through a withering fire. The 1,000-man garrison inside "Maxim Gorky I" beat back every attack. Stukas were called in for support and one plane, flown by Lt. Georg Studemann, matched Weihrauch's skill by scoring a direct hit on one of the gun cupolas, putting it out of action. Two more days of desperate fighting ensued before the Germans could claim victory. Only 50 defenders came out of "Maxim Gorky I" alive—a grim testimony to the determination of the Soviet defense.

Oktabryski and Petrov were flooded with reports of German advances from every sector. The Black Sea Fleet made a renewed effort to continue the hazardous run into Sevastopol harbor, quickly unloading reinforcements and supplies before the *Luftwaffe* could attack. *Kriegsmarine* motor torpedo boats dueled with Soviet destroyers in an effort to stop the convoys, but the Black Sea Fleet managed to keep the route open. As soon as reinforcements were unloaded, they headed directly to the front in an effort to save the disintegrating situation.

On the 19th, the day "Maxim Gorky I" finally fell, German troops pushed forward to Severnaya Bay, while Romanian units, after days of heavy fighting, took control of the eastern end of it. The following day, Sevastopol harbor was effectively closed to surface shipping when the "North Fort" was seized by troops from *54th Corps*. Petrov, knowing further defense of the northern shore was futile, abandoned his positions there in order to make a stronger stand on the bay's south side.

As the fighting raged in the north, *30th Corps* continued to advance on Sevastopol from the south. *170th Division*, reinforced with the newly arrived *420th Regiment*, fought for control of the heavily fortified Sapun Hills. The Soviet troops of the 386th Rifle Division put up an heroic defense which lasted several days.

By 26 June both sides were too exhausted to continue. Von Manstein's forces controlled virtually all of Petrov's main line, but it had been a costly affair. Several regiments, decimated by weeks of fighting, were down to battalion strength, and no new reinforcements could be expected—OKW was much too preoccupied with the developing Stalingrad offensive.

Final Push

While his men rested for the next two days, von Manstein moved his artillery into new positions closer to the fortress. He kept up the pressure on Petrov by sending waves of bombers to attack Sevastopol's inner defense belt. The situation in the city grew worse when the Black Sea Fleet finally gave up on further surface sorties. Submarines, with their limited supply carrying capacities, were henceforth the only means of bringing in materials. Petrov received his last reinforcements, the 142nd Infantry Brigade, on the night of the 26th.

The final phase of the battle for Sevastopol began in the opening hours of 29 June. Units of the *22nd* and *24th Divisions* crossed a 1,000-yard stretch of North Bay shortly before midnight. With von Richtofen's bombers covering the noise of the assault boats, *16th Regiment* landed and swiftly overran several key sectors along the southern shore. By noon, five regiments were across, and reconnaissance units were already advancing well into the rear of the Soviet line.

At 1:30 a.m. of that same morning, *30th Corps* renewed its push in the south. Its right flank was secured when units of the *50th Division* captured Inkerman, neutralizing the northern portion of the Sapun line. Bitter fighting took place as *420th Regiment* broke through the Soviet line and advanced to the English Cemetery. There, German and Soviet soldiers killed each other among the graves of men who had died fighting for Sevastopol nearly a century earlier.

While that battle was raging, *170th Division* smashed a larger hole in the Sapun line, allowing *28th Jäger* and *72nd Division* to follow up with successful attacks on the Soviet flanks.

The *11th Army* artillery, firing from frontline positions, was able to blast numerous passages through the Soviet defenses. By the 30th, *30th Corps* was in the process of cleaning out the last pockets of Soviet resistance in the south. The *54th Corps*, now fighting in Sevastopol itself, was meeting a mixed reaction from the Soviet defenders. In some areas, Red Army troops surrendered by the hundreds, while in others; they resisted until they were killed.

Oktabryski and Petrov were ordered to leave the city by STAVKA, and under cover of darkness they made their way to the coast where they were picked up by a ship that carried them to safety.

On 1 July the announcement of the fall of Sevastopol was broadcast over German national radio. For the men of *72nd Division*, that proclamation was a little premature. Even as German troops staged a victory parade in the ruins of Sevastopol, the *72nd* was still fighting significant Soviet forces on the Kherson Peninsula, including the defenders of fort "Maxim Gorky II." On 4 July the costly assault on "Maxim Gorky II" ended when its 1,500 starving and thirsty defenders gave up. Five days later the Kherson Peninsula was finally secured.

Besides unknown thousands of dead, the Soviets lost 95,000 prisoners at Sevastopol. The Black Sea Fleet lost four destroyers, four submarines and several smaller vessels. Von Manstein reported *11th Army* losses at 4,337 killed, 18,183 wounded, and 1,580 missing.

The successful assault on the fortress at the end of a six-month campaign earned Manstein his Field Marshal's baton. It was one of the most varied and brilliant campaigns of the war, but would soon be overshadowed by the titanic struggle at Stalingrad.

Chapter XXIV

The Demyansk Pocket
by Milton Goldin

Histories of what Soviet historians used to call "The Great Patriotic Fatherland War," and what English-language readers more commonly refer to as World War II's eastern front, tend to devote their attention to the most titanic battles: Moscow, Stalingrad, Kursk, Berlin. Yet dozens of other actions profoundly affected the course of the war. In that secondary category, no battle deserves more consideration than the 1942-43 *Kesselschlacht* (pocket battle) around Demyansk, a village located half way between Moscow and Leningrad in the area of operations of the *Wehrmacht's Army Group North*.

Demyansk marked the first time the Soviets encircled major German formations, and the first time aircraft were used to supply over 95,000 men. After the many sackings of senior German army officers in December 1941 and January 1942, the handling of Demyansk from Berlin also marked Hitler's debut as sole and supreme warlord of Nazi Germany. Further, the later battles around Stalingrad can actually be viewed as larger scale repeats of Demyansk.

Hedgehogs

On 16 December 1941, as the German forces in the east began to reel under the pressure of an expanding Soviet counteroffensive, Hitler issued an order forbidding retreat: "The enemy will gradually bleed themselves to death with their attacks. They are hurling their last available forces into battle."

Obstinate as he was, though, the *Führer* knew his forces were stretched too thinly for them to hold a continuous line. Instead, strongholds ("hedgehogs" to those who manned them) were to be established in key locales such as Rzhev, Gzhatsk and Vyazma. The defenders in those bastions would not attempt to block Soviet advances past their positions; they were simply to hold until circumstances again swung in favor of the Germans. Then the hedgehogs would become springboards for the counterattacks that would cut off and annihilate the Soviet salients among them.

Meanwhile, in the area opposite the boundary between *German Army Groups North* and *Center*, Soviet Gen. Pavel Kurochkin's Northwest Front began active offensive operations on 7 January 1942. German reconnaissance teams reported enemy motorized convoys and ski troops equipped with sleds were moving southeast across frozen Lake Ilmen. By daylight on the 8th, two Red Army divisions had crossed the ice pushing south.

West of Ostashkov, on *16th Army*'s extreme right flank, the 3rd and 4th Shock Armies went over to the attack on 9 January, driving into the *123rd Infantry Division*. That unit's strongpoints were so widely separated the Soviets simply moved between them. During the next three days a 30-mile-wide gap was opened in the German front in that area, seemingly demolishing Hitler's hedgehog theory. To the German high command, this Soviet breakthrough raised the possibility the Soviets might succeed in encircling *Army Group Center* by pressing down from the north.

Neither was the command of *Army Group North* confident of its position. During the afternoon of 12 January, AGN's commander, Field Marshal Wilhelm von Leeb, ordered Gen. Ernest Busch, commanding *16th Army*, to prepare to pull back his *2nd Corps*, which was the army group's southeasternmost formation. Leeb next called Hitler and proposed a general withdrawal of his entire command to a line south and west of Lake Ilmen. Hitler denied the request, responding that he had to think in terms of the ill effect such a retreat would have elsewhere along the front. The *Führer* then summoned the field marshal to his headquarters at Rastenburg in East Prussia.

No give and take was injected into the situation during those talks. Hitler wanted Leeb not only to stay put, but to find enough replacement manpower from within the army group itself to counterattack and close the gaps recently opened by the Soviets.

Leeb had hardly returned to his own headquarters, however, when he learned the southern wing of the Soviet drive against his army group had reached the critical Kholm-Molvotitsy-Demyansk road. Convinced his front south of Lake Ilmen was now in imminent danger of collapse, he asked Hitler to either relieve him or grant him the authority to order a general retreat. The *Führer* responded by sending a message to Leeb's chief of staff, Gen. Kurt Brennecke, reaffirming the order for *Army Group North* to stand. On 17 February, Hitler would finally relieve Leeb for "reasons of health," putting Gen. Georg von Küchler, a more dedicated Nazi, in his place.

The Bigger Picture

During January 1942, Stalin believed a general Red Army offensive across the entire front would rout the German armies in Russia. After all, the invaders' morale had already been lowered by their failure to take Moscow, and they were presently reeling under the impact of the severe winter weather. On the other side, Hitler can at best be described as ambivalent. He remained steadfastly convinced any large-scale German withdrawal would turn into a rout all along the front. At the same time, though, he maintained that the Soviets lacked the skill and manpower needed to turn the setbacks suffered by his armies into anything remotely resembling a disaster on the scale of Napoleon's 1812-13 experience.

As January had ended with none of the grand encirclements his generals feared having actually taken shape anywhere, it seemed to Hitler the rightness of his stand-fast order was proven. The Soviet 11th Army was barely in contact with the critical Staraya Russa-Molvotitsy-Demyansk road, while farther south 3rd and 4th Shock Armies were being frustrated in their attempts to drive a wedge between *Army Groups North* and *Center*. Three foot deep snow and sub-freezing temperatures were in fact hampering the operations of both sides. In places, artillery barrages barely chipped the hard frozen ground.

Another real problem for both sides at this point lay in the fact neither had the needed numbers of men or weapons to gain the local superiority necessary to mount strong attacks with reasonable chances for success. Though the Soviets certainly held the initiative, they still generally lacked the degree of professional military skill needed to transform opportunities into actual triumphs.

During early February the Soviet attacks south of Lake Ilmen even seemed for a time to decline in strength, and the German command began to have hope the acute phase of the crisis there was over. But records show that Brennecke in particular feared the wedges driven into the German line north and south of Demyansk might still be turned into Soviet pincers to encircle *2nd* and *10th Corps* around that

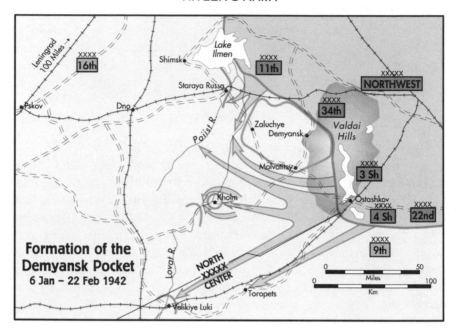

Formation of the Demyansk Pocket
6 Jan – 22 Feb 1942

village (prewar population 2,472). Brennecke, of course, was indeed on the mark with his fears. Kurochkin proposed to Moscow that he destroy the exposed German corps in an encirclement east of the Lovat River.

Demyansk Encircled

On 9 February 1942, the Soviets cut the Demyansk salient's last supply route, thereby turning it into the Demyansk pocket. Inside, the six divisions of *2nd Corps* (headquarters of *10th Corps* had been outside the perimeter when the pincers closed, so *2nd* took over all command responsibilities inside) were commanded by Gen. Walther von Brockdorff-Ahlefeld, who set up his headquarters in Molovtitsy, near the defense's southern rim. From the outside, Stalin, intensely interested in the great prize to be gained here, immediately began radioing specific instructions to Kurochkin on how to reduce the pocket as quickly as possible.

During the next week, the advancing Soviets closed another, though much smaller, pocket to the southwest of Demyansk around the village of Kholm. It contained approximately 3,500 German troops from several German divisions. At the same time, the perimeter around Demyansk was made tighter.

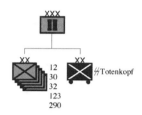

German Forces Cut off in Demyansk February 1942

On 19 February, Hitler designated Demyansk a "fortress" to differentiate it from a *Kessel*, or pocket. A fortress, unlike a pocket, was viewed to be the result of a deliberately adopted strategy rather than a misfortune of war caused by enemy action. At the same time, the Nazi warlord began to look around for the ways and means to launch a rescue attack across the roughly 80 miles that separated his new fortress from the main front.

Kurochkin meanwhile received orders from Stalin to "squeeze out" the Demyansk pocket within five days. But against Brockdorff-Ahlefeld's determined troops, only minimal progress was made toward that goal.

Supplying the Pocket

During the last week of February, Brockdorff-Ahlefeld felt compelled to explain to Hitler what should have already been obvious: while able to hold off the Soviets, the defenders in the pocket only survived from hand to mouth, completely dependent on the success or failure of each day's airlift. Surprisingly, Hitler received the message calmly, along with a report of similar problems from the nearby Kholm pocket. He even admitted in his reply to the corps commander that he was aware Demyansk wasn't really a fortress despite the earlier declaration.

But then he also declared he'd selected 13-16 March as the jump off period for the Demyansk relief operation. Despite the continued lack of manpower for renewed attacks, the *Luftwaffe* was to provide enough ground support aircraft that the effect of "escort artillery" would be achieved, enabling the infantrymen to blast through the blocking Red Army formations.

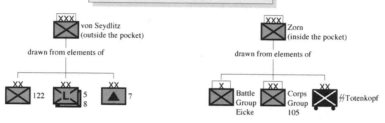

The German Force for Operation "Bridging Strike" March/April 1942

von Seydlitz (outside the pocket) — drawn from elements of — 122, 5/8, 7

Zorn (inside the pocket) — drawn from elements of — Battle Group Eicke, Corps Group 105, SS Totenkopf

To supply Demyansk, every Ju-52 transport plane then assigned to *Army Groups North* and *Center,* along with half those operating behind *Army Group South,* had to be pressed into service. Each day, on average, some 350 German aircraft attempted to fly in and out of the encirclement to provide the 300 tons necessary to sustain the next 24 hours of combat.

Of course, given the desperate situation, priority had to be given to delivery of munitions rather than to food and clothing. One German medical report filed in early March from inside the pocket reported the soldiers lived in dark, damp, badly ventilated and cramped bunkers, where they breathed foul air and had no chance to wash themselves or their clothes. All were infested with lice and many suffered skin infections. The cold also led to soaring incidences of frostbite, while the lack of hygiene caused great numbers of bladder infections. The lack of reserves inside the pocket also meant long hours on duty, with some men stricken by exhaustion and others developing nervous disorders.

Rescuing Demyansk

The planned Demyansk relief operation was codenamed *Brückenschlag* (Bridging-Strike). Combat elements from six divisions, three driving in from the outside and three attacking from inside the pocket, were organized under two senior division commanders. Gen. Walther von Seydlitz-Kurzbach led the outsiders (*Group von Seydlitz*), while Maj. Gen. Hubert Zorn commanded the effort from within the pocket (*Group Zorn*).

The effort was delayed for a few weeks while von Seydlitz put his troops through an intensive training program in the kind of open-or-

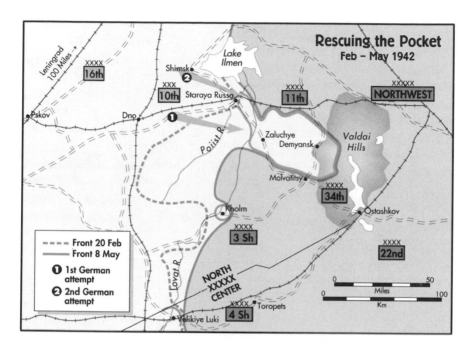

der, forest oriented, infiltration tactics the Finns had used so successfully against the Communists during the 1939-40 Winter War. He
chose that method because the armor upon which the the Germans
normally liked to stake their offensive successes would be notably
absent from this attack. The panzer-impoverished *Army Group North*
had few fighting vehicles to spare and, anyway, the terrain over which
Group von Seydlitz would have to fight was heavily wooded, far from
ideal tank country.

A further delay in Bridging-Strike's start was caused when the
Luftwaffe ground support aircraft earmarked to make up for the lack
of tanks got held up in another operation going on farther north. Then,
on 21 March, when the outside force did finally get moving, the planes
proved of little help, since through the dense canopy of woods their
pilots could hardly see any men on the ground, let alone tell Germans
from Soviets.

In fact, the only heavy weaponry von Seydlitz's men could depend
on came in the form of the first large-scale issue of the new *Panzerfaust*
(armored fist) rocket-propelled anti-tank grenades. Though those
weapons would later evolve into formidable heavy infantry weapons,
these were early models that had a maximum range of only 50 yards.
Again, the dense trees limited their utility.

The plan called for the inside group to hold off while von Seydlitz pushed strait in from the west. After two days, however, temperatures climbed above freezing and stayed there even at night, turning the three feet of snow that had been on the ground into slush. The advance slowed, with the lead units unable to reach the Lovat River, which was to have been the signal for the inside group to begin its attack.

The Soviets, meanwhile, were also honing the skills they would use during the many other pocket battles to come. For instance, on 29 March, Stalin split the command of the Red Army forces engaged around Demyansk by putting Lt. Gen. N.F. Vatutin in charge of those units on the perimeter of the pocket (the "inner" ring), thus leaving Kurochkin to concentrate on resisting von Seydlitz's rescue attack (the "outer" ring).

By the end of April, the German expedients had proved more powerful than those of the Soviets. On the 29th, after redeploying northward to attack along the Staraya Russa-Demyansk road, *Group von Seydlitz* and *Group Zorn* were able to link up on the Lovat River. (On 5 May a similar rescue mission broke through to the smaller Kholm pocket to the south.) A 25-mile-long corridor, nowhere more than three miles wide, was thus created that reunited *2nd Corps* with its parent *16th Army*.

At times afterward, the Soviets would succeed in thinning that corridor to little more than the width of a one-lane road, while at other times Mother Nature would sink even that slender lifeline under two feet of muddy water. But the pocket was never really in danger of annihilation again before Hitler authorized its abandonment early in 1943.

The Importance of Demyansk

During the period of the Demyansk encirclement in 1942, the *Luftwaffe* flew 64,844 tons of materiel into the pocket. Some 30,500 men were also flown in as replacements, while 35,400 wounded and sick were evacuated.

Viewed from the prospective of the flyers, a total of 32,427 sorties were flown to Demyansk, consuming 42,155 tons of aviation fuel and another 3,242 tons of lubricants. Also consumed were 265 aircraft, along with 385 *Luftwaffe* ground and flight personnel killed. Those losses had the immediate effect of completely aborting the German transport pilot training program for four months. In fact, the losses in machines, skilled pilots and air crews generated at Demyansk were never completely made up before the end of the war.

Without doubt, it was the "success" scored by the *Luftwaffe's* transport arm at Demyansk that a few months later led Reichsmarshal Hermann Göring to boldly assure Hitler the *6th Army*, newly cut off at Stalingrad, could be kept supplied by aircraft. But in making that claim Göring failed to consider the number of men to be supplied at Stalingrad was over three times that at Demyansk; the distance to fly to get there was greater, and the number of planes available only marginally increased.

At Demyansk, the Germans in the pocket required 300 tons of supply to sustain themselves each day. Though they fell below that target on some days, by the time the operation there was over the figure for average daily deliveries had been pegged at 302 tons. At Stalingrad the daily requirement figure was 500 tons. Such an operation would have required at least 1,050 transport planes; at the time there were only 750 such craft in the entire *Luftwaffe*. On its best day, the Stalingrad airlift delivered only 290 tons.

Gen. Fritz Morzik, chief of the *Luftwaffe's* air transport arm, writing shortly after the war, probably best summed up the overall negative impact of the German "success" at Demyansk:

> Demyansk, as it turned out, provided a rather dangerous illustration of the potential usefulness of air transport. For from that time on German military leaders were inclined to be indiscriminately enthusiastic regarding its employment. The extraordinary success of that first attempt at supplying an encircled force by air quite naturally implied that air transport could be utilized with equal success in any similar situation in the future. German leaders were convinced that they could compute the scope of such an operation on the basis of the need for supplies and the number of transport aircraft available for employment. The basic thinking behind this decision was to lead to seriously detrimental consequences as the war progressed.

How Long Was the Eastern Front?

British military historian Basil Liddell Hart once described the eastern front of early 1942 by writing that it was "so deeply indented as to appear almost like a reproduction of Norway's coastline, with fjords penetrating far inland."

Even that vivid prose hardly did the situation justice. In *Army Groups North* and *Center* in particular, Soviet salients and pockets were faced by German bulges and fortresses, alternately peppering the landscape from south of Moscow to Leningrad. Among and behind the German hedgehogs, the remnants of Red Army units earlier bypassed by Nazi troops, prisoners of war escaped from German pens, and civilian partisan fighters all struggled to sabotage the invaders' communications and supply lines. Such Soviet "formations," of course, had no fixed bases and so are hard to pin down on smaller maps.

It is therefore difficult to estimate the front's true length that spring. The most often found estimate—2,000 miles—seems close enough when viewing maps of the scales usually found in history books and articles. But when looked at on maps of a scale more commonly used by the actual command staffs of the time (say, for instance, 40 miles to 3⅛ inches), the impression is totally changed. In fact, the entire battlefront may have been as long as 4,000 miles when taking into account all the situations described above.

The significance of Hitler's decision to man such ridiculously convoluted lines in front of the two army groups can really only be appreciated by what happened when he finally, during the spring of 1943, authorized the abandonment of the Demyansk, Rzhev, Gzhatsk and Vyazma salients to free more troops for the projected Kursk offensive that summer. After those moves were made, 21 German infantry divisions became available for redeployment outside the salients. Those same 21 divisions had just months before sat out the entire Stalingrad campaign in useless positions while *6th Army* perished. We can only wonder what the course of the fighting would have been had those German divisions been in positions around *6th Army* in November 1942 in place of the underequipped Hungarian, Romanian and Italian forces actually there.

The Ju-52, Workhorse of the Luftwaffe

A total of 4,850 Ju-52 three-engined transports were built between 1932 and 1944. Specifications included a wing span of 96 feet, length of 62 feet, gross weight of 24,317 lbs., and three 575 horsepower engines giving a maximum speed of 178 miles per hour. A typical load was about 6,600 lbs., or 17 fully equipped soldiers. The design's most outstanding feature, apart from its general robustness, was probably its ability to operate from extremely short runways (1,300 feet).

Though the Germans fielded a variety of other air transport craft, and often improvised by pressing into service models not designed for the role, the Ju-52 was without doubt the workhorse of the *Luftwaffe*'s air transport arm throughout the war. At Demyansk the Germans used some 500 Ju-52s organized into 15 "Special Bombardment" groups.

Sources

Erickson, John. *The Road to Stalingrad*. New York: Harper & Row, 1975.

Morzik, Fritz. *German Air Force Airlift Operations*. New York: Arno Press, 1961.

Suchenwirth, Richard. *Historical Turning Points in the German Air Force War Effort*. New York: Arno Press, 1968.

Uebe, D. Klaus. *Russian Reactions to German Airpower in World War II*. New York: Arno Press, 1968.

Werth, Alexander. *Russia at War, 1941-1945*. New York: Avon, 1964.

Ziemke, Earl F. and Magna E. Bauer. *Moscow to Stalingrad: Decision in the East*. New York: Military Heritage Press, 1988.

Chapter XXV

The Battle of Narva, 1944
by Pat McTaggart

The German army of 1944 was no longer the seemingly invincible military force that had conquered most of Europe in the first years of World War II. In the previous year the Red Army had pushed the German *Army Group Center* back over 400 miles, from Voronezh to Kiev. Another 400 miles had been lost by *Army Group South* when the Soviets forced it to abandon the rich lands between the Don and Dniepr Rivers. The only relatively static German front was in *Army Group North*'s sector.

There the siege of Leningrad was in its 28th month. Apart from occasional probing attacks, the Germans were content to shell the city with artillery and maintain patrolling along the perimeter. Overall, it had become a quiet sector. However, Josef Stalin and the Soviet High Command (STAVKA) were planning a series of hammer blows designed to break that siege and eventually move the Red Army to the frontiers of Germany itself.

In the opening weeks of January, two Soviet Fronts (army groups) prepared massive assaults. Gen. L.A. Govorov's Leningrad Front was to strike out from the city with the 42nd and 67th Armies, while the 2nd Shock Army attacked from the Oranienbaum pocket.

Gen. Kiril A. Meretskov's Volkhov Front was to hit the enemy with another three armies; the 8th at Mga, the 54th on the Volkhov River, and the 59th around Novgorod. Between those two fronts, the Soviets hoped the entire German *18th Army* would be enveloped in a Stalingrad-like pocket offering no hope of escape. They were confident the superiority they had in arms and men would smash the Germans.

On the other side, Adolf Hitler was not worried about the position of *Army Group North*. In fact, on 28 December 1943, while looking for units to strengthen the battered corps of his other east front armies,

Map 1
The Soviet Offensive from Leningrad-Oranienbaum
January 1944

German:
Division HQ
Surrounded Units

Soviet:
Divisions
Corps HQ
Army HQ
Initial Assaults
Exploitation

0   40
Km

he told his army chief of staff, Gen. Zeitzler, "Even now we can get 12 divisions out of *Army Group North* to send elsewhere." He ordered plans made to start transferring the first of those divisions in early January.

Hitler may have had confidence in the army group's defenses, but the commander of *Army Group North*, Field Marshal Georg von Küchler, was not as certain. He felt his *16th* and *18th Armies* could ill afford to lose the units being taken from them. Even before the withdrawals, there were not enough combat troops to properly man the positions.

A secondary line, known as the Panther position, had been under construction since the fall of 1943. It ran from the Gulf of Finland, along the Narva River and Lake Peipus, south through Pskov and beyond Vitebsk. This was to be the fall-back position in case the army group was forced to retreat. Hitler's plan for depleting von Küchler's forces would, however, stretch the defenders to the absolute limit. The stage was thus being set for a possible major disaster.

The Offensive Begins

On the night of 13/14 January, the Soviet attack began. From the Oranienbaum pocket, over 100,000 shells fell upon the divisions of the *3rd SS Panzer Corps*, while the Leningrad Front attacked with 42 infantry divisions and 9 tank corps. The *SS Corps* was composed of the *9th* and *10th Luftwaffe Field Divisions*, the *11th SS Nordland Division*, and the *4th SS Nederland Brigade*.

The first German unit to be caught in the Soviet onslaught was the *10th Luftwaffe Field Division*. It instantly fell apart, leaving a gap through which the Reds poured with tanks and infantry. The *9th Luftwaffe* fared no better. Two days later, the commander of *18th Army*, Gen. Georg Lindemann, was forced to use his only reserve, the *61st Infantry Division*, to try to plug the gap left by the shattered *Luftwaffe* units.

The next morning, Govorov's artillery unleashed a barrage that dropped over 220,000 shells on the German *50th Corps* in front of Leningrad. Gen. Masslenikov's 42nd Army then overran the German defenses, and by the end of the day achieved a penetration of 2.6 kilometers.

Meanwhile, Meretskov's Volkhov Front assaulted the Germans at Lake Ilmen. It was clear to von Küchler the Communists had opened a major offensive, but had weather on the 15th worked to restore some of his confidence, since the Red Air Force became temporarily grounded. Further, some reinforcements were made available to the army group and the movement of divisions to other fronts was halted. The German command was temporarily under the impression their forces could hold the present positions and cut off the Soviet penetrations into their lines. The next day, though, the Russian skies had cleared and the might of Soviet airpower was again felt along the entire front.

Under the protective cover of their airpower, Soviet forces pushing out of the Oranienbaum pocket raced to meet the Leningrad units. There seemed to be no way for the German units on the coast to escape. The men of Gen. Steiner's *3rd SS Panzer Corps* were driven to ground by the Soviet artillery and the guns of the Baltic Fleet. Scattered pockets of resistance held the attackers in some places, but Soviet armor and air superiority made the overall situation hopeless.

Heroes on Both Sides

The Soviets had learned their lessons well from their German teachers, and their soldiers had adapted the principles of the *Blitzkrieg* to their own kind of fighting. In the first two weeks of the offensive, 12 Red Army officers and enlisted men won the coveted title, Hero of the Soviet Union. For example, 2nd Lt. Volkov of the 131st Guards Regiment, Sgt. Skuridin of the 98th Infantry Division, A.F. Tipanov, of the 64th Guards Infantry Division and Pvt. I.N. Kulikov gave their lives by blocking the slits of German pillboxes with their bodies, allowing their comrades to successfully attack the positions. Sgt. Morozov, of the 90th Infantry Division repulsed a German counterattack, even though his comrades were all dead and he was badly wounded.

The Germans had their heroes, too. Maj. Fritz Bunse, commander of the *11th SS Engineer Battalion*, and Lt. Col. Hanns-Heinrich Lohmann, commander of the *3rd Bn./Norge Regiment* of the *11th SS Division*, both received the Knight's Cross for leading their units in successful, though ultimately futile, holding actions. On 16 January, 2nd Lt. Georg Langendorg's *5th Company* of the *11th SS Reconnaissance Detachment* met a Soviet column of 54 tanks. With only six anti-tank guns, Langendorf's company destroyed 48 of the enemy vehicles and forced the others to retreat.

The Retreat Begins

Despite their high casualties, the Soviets were more than able to make good their losses with reserve troops. By 18 January, von Küchler reported to Hitler his entire line from Leningrad to Novgorod was collapsing. The Soviet 58th Rifle Brigade had crossed the ice of Lake Ilmen and broken through German positions south of Novgorod. Troops of the 2nd Shock and 42nd Armies had linked up at Ropscha, and the German units on the coast could be written off.

Von Küchler gave orders for his *26th Corps* to withdraw almost 20 miles to new defensive positions. But Hitler took his usual hold or die attitude and forbade the movement of the corps, though his will alone was no longer enough to stop the Soviets. At any rate, the order for withdrawal had already been implemented, and it was too late to countermand the retreat. After almost 900 days, the siege of Leningrad had been broken.

While Hitler and von Küchler argued over the retreat of one corps,

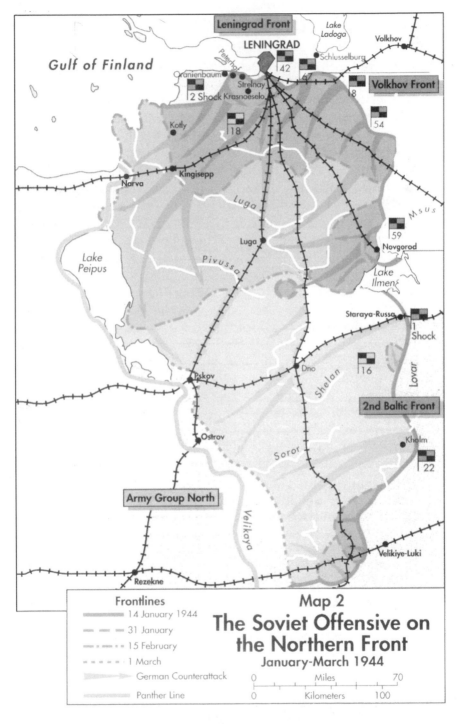

Gulf of Finland

Leningrad Front
LENINGRAD
Lake Ladoga
Volkhov
Schlusselburg
42
Oranienbaum
Peterhof
Strelnay
Krasnoeselo
2 Shock
Volkhov Front
8
Kotly
18
54
Narva
Kingisepp
Luga
Msus
Luga
59
Novgorod
Lake Peipus
Pivussa
Lake Ilmen
Staraya-Russa
1 Shock
Dno
Shelan
16
Lovar
Pskov
2nd Baltic Front
Ostrov
Soror
Kholm
22
Army Group North
Velikaya
Velikiye-Luki
Rezekne

Frontlines
14 January 1944
31 January
15 February
1 March
German Counterattack
Panther Line

Map 2
The Soviet Offensive on
the Northern Front
January-March 1944

0   Miles   70
0   Kilometers   100

Army Group North's lines were being shattered everywhere. Partisan units attacked supply columns and destroyed rail lines and bridges. Many German divisions were down to regimental strength, and regiments had worn away to company size. For example, on 19 January, the *503rd Grenadier Regiment* of the *290th Infantry Division* reported a strength of only 3 officers and 100 men.

By 24 January, units of the Soviet 42nd Army had reached Krasnogvardeysk and were heading for the Luga River. Von Küchler had no choice but to order a full retreat to the Luga in the hope his troops could hold there. But again, Hitler rejected the proposed withdrawal and von Küchler was forced to appear before him personally to plead his case. He told Hitler the *18th Army* had already suffered 40,000 casualties and only a fraction of those had been replaced, but the *Führer* remained firm in his demand for no retreat. The dictator had lost all confidence in von Küchler and was already looking for a replacement; but events on the northern front would wait for no man—not even for Hitler.

By the 30th, the situation had become even more desperate for the Germans. Soviet forces continued their advance under the protection of the Red Air Force. Their tank and motorized units fanned out and spread havoc in the German rear areas. Once more von Küchler appealed to Hitler for permission to retreat. Though it was already too late for some of his units, the field marshal also knew any further delay could cost him his entire command.

The advancing red lines on the map finally convinced Hitler *18th Army* had to withdraw to the Luga River line, but he had delayed that decision for too long. Enemy spearheads had already crossed the river north of the town of Luga. A day later, Hitler relieved von Küchler of command and replaced him with Gen. Walter Model.

Model was a strong defensive tactician and a favorite of the *Führer*. He issued his first order, which—of course—merely echoed the wishes of the supreme commander: Not a single step backward will be taken without my express permission. That attitude, along with having Hitler's confidence, allowed Model to exercise a greater degree of independence than his predecessor. Model, too, soon realized the Luga line could not be held, so he carefully formulated a plan of defense that would bring his troops back to the Panther Line step by step.

To Narva

The *3rd SS Panzer Corps* had been in the thick of battle since the opening of the offensive. Its *9th* and *10th Luftwaffe Field Divisions* were shattered, and the remaining units (*11th SS Nordland Division* and *4th SS Brigade Nederland*) were sorely understrength. Steiner's men had been on the move constantly, always just one step ahead of the Soviets, but as soon as the panzer corps reached the Luga River, new orders were received.

After a retreat of over 150 miles, they were ordered to dig in and make a stand at the Narva River. The orders were crystal clear—Narva had to be held at all costs.

Hitler was determined to hold the Narva line for political as well as military reasons. Foremost was that his far-northern ally, Finland, was growing weary of the war, and several peace initiatives had been passed between officials in Moscow and Helsinki. Hitler could not afford to lose Finnish support for his forces fighting on the arctic Murmansk front. If Finland quit the war, German units there would be in jeopardy, and the loss of the Baltic states might be the thing to make Finland finally sue for peace.

Second, if Narva were taken by the Soviets, they would, in one stroke, succeed in penetrating the Panther Line's far left flank. Such a move would put them in place to flank the entire fortified position, thus rendering the German expenditure of time and engineering resources a complete waste.

Further, the ebb of the front elsewhere in the Soviet Union had given Narva a symbolic importance beyond that indicated by logical strategy alone. That is, the town had suddenly become one of the *Wehrmacht*'s last toe-holds inside the boundaries of Old Russia. Once Narva was given up (along with some other small bits and pieces around Pskov, just south of Lake Peipus), the fighting would have moved entirely into areas—the Baltics, Belorussia, the Ukraine—outside the Russian ethnic heartland. That benchmark would be a first-class propaganda coup for Stalin—one Hitler was loathe to concede.

Whether aware of all that or not, Steiner's men (barely) won the race to the Narva River for their *Führer*. Interestingly, the SS units that did the racing were composed mostly of volunteers from countries other than Germany. For example, 40 percent of the soldiers of the *Danmark Regiment* of the *11th SS Division Nordland* were recruits from

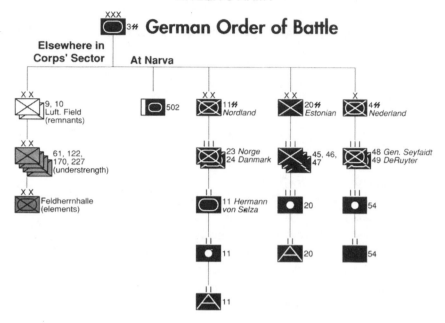

XXX

⬤ 3 ✠ **German Order of Battle**

Elsewhere in Corps' Sector | **At Narva**

Denmark. A large number of Norwegians served in the *Norge Regiment* of the same division. Further interspersed with those contingents were men from Finland, Sweden, Holland, Belgium and Estonia, along with a German cadre. The corps' *Nederland Brigade* was mainly composed of Dutch volunteers.

If those troops could not pin the Soviet advance, the attackers might swing south, behind Lake Peipus, and cut the rail lines at Riga and Dvinsk, leaving *Army Group North* and much of *Army Group Center* without supply routes. The only other combat units in the area were some half trained Estonian security forces and the *SS Kampfgruppe Kueste*, which until then had only been used for coastal defense.

By 2 February, the *11th SS Division* and the *4th SS Brigade* had established themselves along the Narva line. At Narva itself, a strong bridgehead was formed on the eastern bank. (Beyond complying with the Führer's will, that move was also in accord with German military doctrine, which called for bridgeheads to be maintained on the enemy-controlled side of rivers, as possible jump-off points for later counteroffensives.) The frontline of the Narva bridgehead ran for over seven miles, from above the village of Lilienbach in the north, to the village of Dolgaja Niva in the south.

The town itself had known war almost from its birth. Denmark controlled it in the mid-13th century. Then Teutonic knights fought

Soviet Order of Battle at Narva

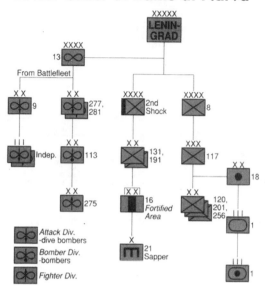

for, and gained control of, the rich lands surrounding it. Hermannsburg, their castle on the west bank of the Narva River, had been one of the keystones of their eastern kingdom. The forces of Peter the Great and Charles XII of Sweden fought around Narva during the Great Northern War. Czar Ivan III built Ivangorod, the Russian counter to Hermannsburg, on the east bank of the river, directly across from the Teutonic castle.

Rag-tag survivors from smashed *Luftwaffe* and army divisions were thrown into the line north and south of the city to hold the western bank of the river. At first the river itself was the only defensive position the Germans possessed, but as the Soviets started to mass on the eastern bank, SS engineers worked frantically to provide bunkers and trenches. Inside the bridgehead itself, engineers of the *54th Nederland Pioneer Battalion* worked with frontline troops to provide crude but effective barricades and connecting trenches to stop the Soviets.

On the outskirts of Narva, Maj. Wilhelm Schlütter was supervising the placement of his batteries from the *Nederland* artillery detachment. Although an officer, Schlütter and his staff worked side by side with the enlisted men, since he knew time was essential to get his unit ready. The quick arrangement of camouflage, trenches, bunkers and hundreds of smaller details was necessary to insure the safety of his guns, but there was little time to make sure the emplacements were laid out by the book.

While Schlütter's artillery was digging in, the men of the *Nederland Brigade* and the *Nordland Division* hastily prepared defenses on the eastern bank of the river.

On the southern sector of the bridgehead, the Danes of Lt. Col. von Westphalen's *24th Regiment* were under constant artillery fire. In the center and the north, *Nederland* units reported large concentrations of enemy infantry and armor.

Soviet-German Strength Ratios / Army Group North Sector / January 1944

Category	Sov: Ger
Leningrad Front	
Men	2.7:1
Artillery	3.6:1
Tanks	6.0:1
Volkhov Front	
Men	3.3:1
Artillery	3.5:1
Tanks	11.0:1
Overall	6.0:1

The Fight for Narva

On 3 February, the Soviet commander attempted to establish a bridgehead on the western bank of the river north of Narva. This attempt ended in failure when tanks of the *11th SS Panzer Battalion*, commanded by Lt. Col. Paul-Albert Kausch, and a platoon of Tiger tanks under Lt. Otto Carius, attacked and destroyed the Soviet units that had crossed the river.

But three Soviet armies, the 8th, 47th and 2nd Shock, continued to probe for weak spots in the German positions. Finally, they managed to secure a bridgehead at Siversti on 12 February. More troops and equipment were sent across the river as the Soviets expanded and consolidated their tenuous foothold on the west bank.

South of Narva, the 8th Army also achieved some success. There, Soviet troops pushed across the river and established a dangerous bridgehead that threatened to cut off the entire *3rd SS Panzer Corps*, as well as two army divisional battlegroups. To oppose the 8th Army, the German commander mustered battlegroups from the *170th, 227th,*

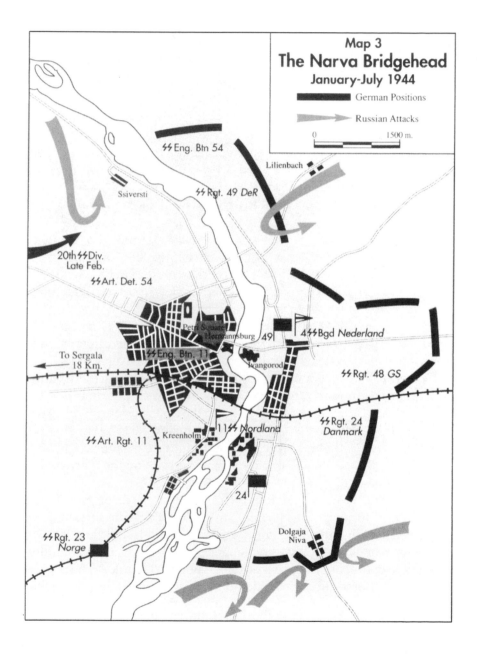

Map 3
The Narva Bridgehead
January-July 1944

German Positions

Russian Attacks

0   1500 m.

SS Eng. Btn 54

Lilienbach

Ssiversti

SS Rgt. 49 *DeR*

20th *SS* Div.
Late Feb.

SS Art. Det. 54

Petri Square
Hermannsburg   49

4 *SS* Bgd *Nederland*

To Sergala
18 Km.

SS Eng. Btn. 11

Ivangorod

SS Rgt. 48 *GS*

11 *SS* *Nordland*

SS Art. Rgt. 11

Kreenholm

SS Rgt. 24
Danmark

24

Dolgaja
Niva

SS Rgt. 23
Norge

and *61st Infantry Divisions*. But he also had elements of the *Feld-herrnhalle Panzer Grenadier Division* and Tiger tanks from *Battalion 502*.

The Tigers, under the command of Maj. Willy Jähde, proved invaluable during the coming months. Jähde's tanks were again and again placed in key positions in the line, where probing Soviet armor soon found that the combination of artillery and tank fire made moving in the open a deadly proposition.

Gen. Lindemann's *18th Army* was slowly bleeding to death. In one month, *Army Group North* had been pushed back about 150 miles. Three divisions had been wiped out, and the Soviets claimed 7,200 prisoners, 189 tanks destroyed and 1,800 artillery pieces captured. At the same time, *18th Army* reported 35,000 wounded and 14,000 killed. Hitler finally had no choice but to agree to Model's request for a total withdrawal of all units to the Panther Line.

At the same time, Soviet forces allowed the Germans no respite at Narva. While their 8th Army prepared to assault the southern flank, the 47th and 2nd Shock Armies kept up the pressure in the north. The Siversti bridgehead was reinforced, and a new crossing was made even farther north.

To strengthen their line, the Germans rushed units of the *20th SS Estonia Division* from their training centers in Germany directly to the front. That unit, commanded by Maj. Gen. Franz Augsberger, was composed mainly of Estonian volunteers. They reached the fighting on 20 February, and in nine days of combat, forced the Soviets on the west bank north of Narva to withdraw to the eastern side. (A company of Tigers from *Battalion 502* also played a major part in that success, and Maj. Jähde ultimately received the Knight's Cross for his leadership during the battle.) The first of many crises for the Germans at Narva had passed.

Though the Soviets had lost their foothold north of Narva, the German line south of the city was still vulnerable. The terrain there was ideal for defense, but the German divisions holding it were divisions in name only. It was no longer possible for them to maintain a solid line of defense in the dense forests and marshlands. The Soviets perceived that and therefore ordered their 8th Army to move quickly, before the Germans could consolidate their positions.

After the usual pre-assault bombardment, the Soviets attacked. Their troops stormed forward from the bridgehead west of Kriwasoo. By 24 February, Soviet units had reached the main railway supplying the Narva area, and only two battalions of the German *61st Infantry*

Division were available to meet them. Despite dogged resistance, the Soviets pushed ahead. STAVKA's plan was to force a wedge in the German lines and drive to the coast, totally isolating the *3rd SS Panzer Corps* at Narva.

Fierce fighting raged for days, as units of the *61st* and *Feldherrnhalle Divisions* counterattacked. Elements from *Battalion 502* were also used as a mobile fire brigade to bolster any place in the line that seemed in danger of caving in. Again, Jähde's Tigers finally helped turn the tide of battle in favor of the Germans. Lt. Carius' platoon played a major role in destroying Soviet armor that had broken through the defenses.

The Soviets were finally driven back with heavy losses, but the German lines remained strained. Units from the *Norge Regiment* at Narva were called in to help strengthen them.

Constant Soviet probing actions kept the Germans on alert. At Auwere, the *122nd Infantry Division* repulsed a heavy Soviet attack. The Reds suffered such massive losses that, according to divisional accounts, "they did not bother us again, but looked elsewhere for an easier way through our lines."

While the 8th Army attacked in the south, the Narva bridgehead was receiving its own taste of hell. Though the Soviet attacks to the north of the city had been partially successful, Front Commander Govorov realized the German bridgehead on the eastern bank had to be crushed before a decisive breakthrough could be achieved. He therefore ordered a heavy assault in the Lilienbach area, held by Lt. Col. Hans Collani's *49th SS Regiment*, composed of Dutch volunteers.

As Collani's men lay in their trenches, Soviet infantry advanced under the cover fire of several Red Army artillery batteries. The Soviet barrage let up only when their troops were directly in front of Collani's positions. Collani in turn called for fire support from Schlütter's artillery, and after hours of savage hand-to-hand fighting, the attackers were forced back.

The *49th* was subjected to strafing attacks and artillery fire during the next few weeks, but Govorov decided to use his main forces elsewhere for the time being. During that welcome respite, engineers of the *Nederland Brigade* continued to strengthen the defenses with barbed wire and mines.

Another Try

During the first week of March, the German troops at Narva could sense something was coming. Soviet units were on the move, and the roar of tank engines could be heard from beyond the enemy lines. In the sky, the Red Air Force roamed at will, strafing anything that moved in the defenders' positions. Finally, on the night of 6/7 March, the storm broke. Soviet bombers turned Narva into rubble as they dropped their explosives with devastating accuracy. There was hardly a building left standing in the city. After the bombing, the Soviet artillery added to the carnage with another barrage. The town was left completely to the soldiers as the civilians fled west.

Govorov kept the Germans off balance by bombarding the *Danmark Regiment* on the southern flank of the bridgehead. At the same time, though, he ordered his troops to attack the center, held by Col. Wolfgang Jörchel's *48th Regiment*. The Soviets forced Jörchel's Dutch troops back, and a breakthrough seemed imminent. By summoning his last reserves, however, Jörchel was able to lead his men in a counterattack that caused the Soviets to retreat yet again. The *48th Regiment* regained its lost trenches, but the cost had been high.

Undaunted, Govorov switched to the Lilienbach area once more. His men attacked the *49th Regiment*'s positions after another huge artillery strike, and achieved success as they battled their way into the Dutch defenses. After some minor setbacks caused by German counterattacks, Govorov ordered his reserve tanks and infantry into the breach. Schlütter's artillery and Jähde's tanks caused many casualties among the attackers, but the Soviet commander kept up the pressure. His tanks were now on an all-out drive to the Narva bridges. If they could be secured, the entire bridgehead would be without supply.

As the Soviet tanks moved south, Gen. Steiner called on Kausch's panzers to counterattack. While SS and Soviet infantry fought in the forward areas, the panzers and Govorov's T-34s played a deadly game of cat and mouse at the approaches to Narva. The hulls of burned out vehicles littered the landscape as Soviet and German fought each other, often at point-blank range.

The Soviet commander, realizing the bridges were beyond his reach, ordered his tanks to retreat and dig in. Kausch's panzers followed, but were met with a withering fire that then forced them to halt. Even though the bridges were safe, the breach in the German lines still threatened to unhinge the Lilienbach area.

By this time Collani knew his battered regiment could not hold out any longer in front of Lilienbach. His companies had taken heavy casualties and the survivors were at the end of their endurance. If the Soviets attacked in force again, there would be little hope of repelling them. In the end, there was no real choice. Collani ordered his troops to prepare to withdraw to new positions farther south. The shorter line of defense would compensate somewhat for the gaps in the ranks left by the violent fighting of the last few days.

But the Soviet commander was also aware of the situation and immediately brought up reinforcements to attack the retreating Germans. If his men could catch the enemy unaware, the retreat could be turned into a rout.

Shortly after midnight on 14 March, the Soviets pounded the grenadiers of the *49th* with a short but heavy artillery barrage. While exploding shells kept the SS men huddled in their trenches, Soviet infantry moved out of their forest positions and crept silently toward the German lines. Before the Germans could recover from the barrage, the Reds were upon them. Cries of alarm rang through the German positions as Soviet soldiers spilled into the trenches.

The Soviets had caught Collani's men flat-footed. Soviet units raced to intercept and surround the dazed German forces as they tried to withdraw. 2nd Lt. Helmut Scholz, leader of the *7th Company*, saw the danger immediately. As the Soviet barrage lifted, he formed an assault group from the survivors of his unit and pushed forward to counter-attack the enemy who were infiltrating the German lines.

Scholz's men fought with desperate energy, knowing SS prisoners were not given a good chance of survival in Soviet POW camps. The confined area of the trenches left little room for sophisticated weapons. Bayonets, spades and bare hands became the main instruments of destruction. Step by step, Scholz's men drove the Soviets back. Finally the trenches were cleared, and the enemy were all either dead or back in the forest—but that was still not the end of Scholz's fighting for the day.

The *2nd Bn./49th Regiment* had been surrounded by enemy forces as it withdrew from the Lilienbach line. Capt. Karl-Heinz Ertel had taken over command of the battalion when his commander was killed in the fighting. Ertel realized the danger that faced his men, but the Reds were masters of night fighting, and as the Germans made their way back to new positions, the Soviets seemed to be everywhere at once.

Scholz's depleted company then formed a wedge and sliced through the encirclement. In heavy fighting, they formed a corridor through which the battered *2nd Battalion* escaped. Once the new positions were reached, a coordinated artillery and heavy weapons barrage drove the remaining Soviets to ground.

Again a Pause

For a week the sector remained relatively quiet as both sides caught their breath. The spring thaw was fast approaching; with it would come rains that would turn the ground into a sticky morass, making the movement of heavy vehicles all but impossible.

Govorov gave his subordinates orders to break the *49th*'s lines before the thaw set in. So on 22 March, Soviet artillery fired a barrage that signaled the start of yet another attack. Red Army soldiers stormed the German lines in waves, shouting their ancient war cry, "Urra!" The brunt of the attack hit the *5th Company*, and Soviet soldiers soon broke into the trenches and overran several outlying positions. The company was virtually wiped out as the Soviets continued on to the rear of the *49th Regiment*'s lines. Capt. Carl-Heinz Frühauf had just replaced Ertel as commander of the *2nd Battalion*, and upon hearing of the breakthrough, he formed an assault group from his headquarters personnel and immediately launched a counterattack.

His men hit a 150-man Soviet force head on, and in savage fighting lasting for over half an hour, destroyed them. Frühauf then reformed his men and led them in an attack that pushed the Soviets completely out of the German trenches, forcing them to retreat to their own lines. For the time being, the Narva bridgehead was again safe.

For over a month, Soviet and German soldiers had fought each other in the swamps and forests around Narva. It was a precarious time for the defenders, whose only means of supply was the railroad and highway leading west. The Soviets had severed those lines several times during March, but German counterattacks had each time managed to restore them.

For the men of both sides, the fighting became a struggle for personal survival. Some *Luftwaffe* planes from *Bombardment Squadron 3* harried Soviet armor and infantry columns with dive bombing attacks, while Red Air Force squadrons continued to bomb and strafe the German positions without let up. Both sides constantly and effectively used their artillery to bombard enemy positions. The bloody fighting can best be summed up in the strength report of the *1st Bn./399th Rgt./170th German Infantry Divison*. Toward the end, it had an effective strength of only 69 men—barely half a company.

Finally, in late March, the *Norge Regiment* recaptured the vital area around Sergala, far to the rear, ending that threat to Narva's supply lines. It was then immediately sent back to the river line, with its last units arriving there in early April.

Along the entire front of *Army Group North*, the Russian weather turned in favor of the Germans. That is, the early spring thaw turned the marsh and lake areas into impassible terrain for tanks and heavy equipment. The Panther Line had been strengthened south of Lake Peipus, and enough forces had been gathered there to halt the Soviet advance. STAVKA, however, still hoped for a breakthrough at Narva, so they kept the pressure on the German bridgehead east of the city. Heavy artillery pounded the defenders daily, accompanied by flights of Red Air Force bombers.

On the German side, men braved the Soviet fire as they worked to strengthen bunkers and lay mines. The bridge at Narva came under attack from Soviet aircraft and artillery every day, but engineers of the *Nordland Division* kept it in operation. It required constant labor to keep it strong enough to carry supplies across to the bridgehead.

On the southern sector of the eastern bank, the men of the *Danmark Regiment* fortified their lines and established outposts to warn of any impending attack. Soviet artillery made life dangerous and many casualties were suffered by the Danes, including their commander, Graf von Westfalen.

Schlütter's *Nederland* artillery, along with the *Nordland* divisional artillery, formed the defensive backbone of the line. Soviet fire was answered with swift counterfire, while infantry small arms kept Soviet reconnaissance patrols from getting too close to the German positions. Snipers roamed the area searching for targets, and anyone unlucky enough to be caught in the open soon found himself the object of accurate rifle fire. But despite the enemy fire, the men inside the bridgehead managed to use this brief respite to rest and regain strength for the next round of the battle.

Govorov was also regaining his strength. His troops had suffered heavy casualties during the previous month; Kausch and Jähde's panzers had been effective against the Soviet armor, and time was needed to replace the losses. Replacements for the infantry were also sent, but it took weeks of training to properly integrate them into the veteran divisions. Meanwhile, the Soviets continued to harry the Germans with probing attacks and heavy patrols.

On one occasion, Red troops made an amphibious landing miles behind the front on the shore of the Gulf of Finland, causing some panic among the defenders. Those Soviets, however, were destroyed by the quick action of SS and coastal defense units.

Then Govorov, under pressure from STAVKA, resumed his attack on the bridgehead. The Germans now held a front of approximately seven miles on the east bank of the river. On the north side of the bridgehead, the Dutch regiments of the *Nederland Brigade* held off several determined attacks around the village of Lilienbach. Savage hand-to-hand fighting made for heavy casualties on both sides.

The Soviet commander then turned his attention to the southern flank of the bridgehead held by the *Danmark Regiment* of the *Nordland Division*. The Red Air Force kept the Danes huddling in their trenches until attacking ground forces were almost on top of them. Wave after wave of Soviet infantry rushed toward the SS positions, but for all their courage, they gained little ground.

As his attacks smashed against the German lines, Govorov ordered his air units to concentrate on bombing the town of Narva, hoping to disrupt the flow of supplies to the east bank. Narva was bombed around the clock, until there were no more targets to be found. German forces inside took heavy losses, but the flow of supplies continued.

After another few day's respite, the Soviets attacked the Lilienbach area once again. The *Nederland* defenders had been so weakened by the previous attacks there was little hope for them against this new offensive. The order to retreat was given and, under the cover of Schlütter's artillery, the troops withdrew to new positions south of the village.

Operation Bagration

Meanwhile in Moscow, STAVKA was working on another operation, code named Bagration, that promised to break open the eastern front once and for all. With the attack in the north stalled, the Soviet strategists planned to shift the bulk of their forces south and use them to destroy *Army Group Center*. Nineteen Soviet armies, as well as numerous independent and support units, stood ready to launch an offensive that would eventually annihilate two-thirds of the 38 German divisions facing them. Narva was now reduced to a secondary, yet still important, objective.

As preparations for Bagration continued, Govorov was once again ordered to start operations against the Narva position. The ground was now dry enough to allow tanks and heavy vehicles to attack. His new replacements had been put through combat training and were assimilated into his battle-hardened divisions.

During the past two months, artillery and small arms ammunition had been stockpiled, while the Soviet commander made plans for an attack meant to finally break the German line. Preliminary operations, scheduled to begin two weeks before the great offensive further south, were planned to focus German attention on the Narva front and thus draw reinforcements away from *Army Group Center*.

On 7 June, the German-Danish units on the southern flank of the Narva bridgehead were subjected to a murderous barrage. Low-flying Soviet ground attack aircraft pummeled their positions with fragmentation bombs and heavy machine gun fire. At the village of Dolgaja Niva, men clawed their way deeper into their foxholes, trying to escape the deadly fire. In the trenches and outposts, casualties mounted at an alarming rate, even though the positions had been reinforced with tree trunks and mounds of earth.

When the artillery fire lifted, hordes of Soviet infantry rushed to the attack. The shell-shocked Danes had little time to coordinate their defenses. Amid the dead and dying, groups of men manned machine guns and laid out grenades in preparation for close combat. The artillery of the *Nordland Division* was called in for support as the Reds advanced.

For several days the Soviets threw regiment after regiment against Dolgaja Niva. Finally, on 12 June, they achieved success and broke through the main trench system. As the Danes began pulling back, Soviet forces gathered to make a drive toward the Narva bridge.

Amid the chaos, Danish Sgt. Egon Christopherson led an assault group against the Soviet flank. With his handful of men, Christopherson charged through the enemy, firing automatic weapons and tossing grenades as they went. Luck was on the Dane's side. The Soviets panicked at the unexpected assault and pulled back toward their own lines, leaving many dead and wounded behind.

The men of the *Danmark Regiment* settled back into their old trenches, but their losses had been heavy. The gaps in their ranks could not be filled with reinforcements as easily as the enemy filled theirs. At his battle headquarters, Steiner read every report coming from the bridgehead. He knew his men could not hold for much longer, so he ordered a new defensive line to be constructed west of Narva. This so-called Tannenberg Line would take time to become operational, however, and that time would have to be paid for with more blood from Steiner's men.

Meanwhile, the Soviets again stepped up their assault. Govorov had his units continually switch their focus of attack at the bridgehead, keeping the Germans guessing as to where they would strike next. Soviet units once again established lodgements on the west bank of the river, and the German commander was forced to order Kausch and Jähde's panzers north to counter that threat. The defenders were stretched to the limit all along the river, and the meager replacements they received had to be thrown piecemeal into the line to hold the massive Soviet forces threatening to break out onto the German side.

Inside the bridgehead on the eastern shore, Soviet attacks were met with aggressive German counterattacks. Engineers of the *Nederland Brigade* fought tanks with flamethrowers and bundles of grenades, while the Soviet infantry was engaged in close combat by Dutch and Danish infantry waiting in the trenches. Casualties on both sides mounted as the see-saw battle continued. Small groups of men fought for mere yards of land, and entire platoons sometimes disappeared in the mighty air and artillery bombardments that swept the front.

For over a month, the German forces held their ground. Maj. Schlütter moved his artillery observation post into the Narva courthouse, one of the few buildings left standing in the city. From a turret overlooking the town, he was able to direct accurate support fire that broke up several Soviet attacks, but he also knew time was running against the defense. The volunteer regiments of the *SS* were down to little more than battalion strength.

Hitler was still demanding Narva be held, but on 22 June events in the south changed the entire shape of the German front. Operation Bagration, the long-planned Soviet offensive against *Army Group Center*, began with a gigantic barrage of artillery and air strikes. Red Army units broke through several areas in the German lines, and were followed by reserve forces that opened the gaps even wider. German regimental and divisional commanders pleaded for reinforcements, but there were none left.

Five German divisions were lost at Vitebsk, while many other units simply disappeared as the Soviets drove deep into the Nazi rear areas. Untold numbers were trapped in pockets by advancing Soviet armor, to be captured later by oncoming infantry units. Within days, long lines of German prisoners were heading east to uncertain futures as POWs.

At Narva, news of the breakthrough raised Soviet morale and made Govorov even more determined to achieve success. He increased his air and artillery attacks, and concentrated a force of 20 divisions for yet another assault.

The German forces along the river watched events in the south with great apprehension. Soviet bridgeheads on the west bank were being reinforced daily, and Steiner knew an attack would not be long in coming. There was no doubt a withdrawal would have to be carried out, with or without orders from Berlin. Steiner gave the order, and by 23 July several units inside the Narva bridgehead had begun to withdraw to the western bank.

Maj. Schlütter ordered his artillery to cover the retreating infantry, then began making his own plans for moving his batteries. He had orders to remain in position on the west bank until the final remnants of the east bank defenders had crossed the bridge. When that was accomplished, the bridge was to be blown by the same engineers who had maintained it for so many months.

Govorov's reconnaissance, of course, immediately showed a withdrawal in progress. On 24 July, he ordered his forces to attack along the entire front. Strong Soviet units charged from their footholds on the west bank, driving the depleted *Estonian SS Division* before them. On the line south of the city, Red armor drove toward the main highway connecting Narva to Tallinin. There was little the Germans could do.

As the Soviets advanced under the protection of the Red Air Force, the *Luftwaffe* took to the skies in a final effort to slow the enemy spearheads. Several Soviet aircraft were shot down, but it was not enough to make a difference. *Luftflotte 1, Army Group North's* air force command, could only muster 137 aircraft of all types to fight the more than 800 planes of the Soviet 13th Air Army of the Red Air Force.

End of the Bridgehead

Schlütter watched from his observation post as the final companies of Dutchmen and Danes moved across the Narva River. His radioman stood by, ready to transmit the order to blow the bridge as soon as the last troops had crossed. Suddenly, his post came under artillery fire. Soviet troops were seen edging toward the bridge even as the engineers completed their final demolition preparations. Schlütter could not afford to wait any longer. He gave the order and, with a deafening crash, the bridge that had supplied the Narva position for so many months collapsed into the river.

With his main mission accomplished, Schlütter and his observation team faced another difficult task—survival. Soviet artillery was bombarding Narva with incendiary shells, and what little was left of the town quickly turned into an inferno.

Schlütter's command post was already burning when he left the observation turret. Downstairs, he found his men trying to evacuate the building. With burning timbers crashing around them, Schlütter and his men forced their way through the wreckage and finally made it outside. Slowly they passed through the ruined town until they reached the batteries of the *Nederland* artillery.

It was well into the afternoon before Schlütter received word a narrow trail was open for his guns to pass through. The horses were hitched, and the *Nederland* batteries began their journey westward. In that retreat they joined soldiers from half-a-dozen countries who had fought to protect the Narva line for the past six months. They would continue to fight in the Baltic states for almost another year before surrendering to the Soviets in May 1945.

Chapter XXVI

Aachen '44

by Dirk Blennemann

The Allied pursuit of the German army across France and Belgium reached its zenith from 1 to 11 September 1944. During those 11 days, the British advanced approximately 250 miles, and the U.S. 1st Army covered about 200. As the first Allied soldiers crossed the German border on the 11th, they reached the line D-Day planners had originally expected they wouldn't gain until May 1945. The advance was thus 233 days ahead of schedule.

But fatigue, stretched supply lines, increasingly difficult terrain, stiffening German resistance, worsening weather and the (at least seemingly) fearsome Westwall were all working to apply the brakes to what had been a glorious and dizzying race. In the north, British Field Marshal Bernard Montgomery was preparing for Operation Market-Garden, while in the south Patton was fuming about his army's lack of supplies. But Lt. Gen. Courtney H. Hodges, 1st Army's commander, was still hoping his forces could break through the fortified line in the center and drive on at least to the Roer River. Perhaps the Roer could even be crossed and the advance pushed clear to the Rhine. Then, who could say, maybe home by Christmas?

As noted by Field Marshal Gerd von Rundstedt, the German commander in chief in the west, during the first week of September, most of his units along the front actually existed only on paper. The German army had lost about 27 divisions (67 regiments) on the western front during the previous three months. While Allied units were operating at about 80 percent of their authorized strengths, hardly a single German division was anywhere near that level. Most had incurred severe losses in both men and equipment, and many of their soldiers were badly demoralized. Von Rundstedt estimated his forces were equivalent to about half their number in Allied units.

Allied superiority in artillery was at least four to one, and in armored fighting vehicles it was about 50:1. Most importantly, the attackers' aircraft had total control of the daytime skies.

Allied Plans

The Allied planners at SHAEF (Supreme Headquarters Allied Expeditionary Force) looked to Berlin as their ultimate objective. But on the way to that capital they wanted to seize an intermediary objective, the loss of which, according to their main planning document, "would rapidly starve Germany of the means to continue the war"—the Ruhr industrial area.

Before the D-Day landing, the Allied supreme commander, Gen. Dwight D. Eisenhower, had agreed with his planners that the main advance into Germany should be directed toward the northeast, with the idea of entering the Ruhr along a route north of the Ardennes. But he also wanted a subsidiary drive south of the forest to provide a threat coming through Metz and the Saar area. That decision actually called for a broad—rather than a narrow—front advance, and meant the Allied forces had to spread out as they neared the German border early in September.

At the same time, SHAEF had to face the fact that there was going to have to be some kind of deviation from the original concept of the broad front advance because there were neither the vehicles nor the road net needed to continue the pace of the late summer along such lines. In addition, equipment that had been worn out during the summer fighting and pursuit had to be replaced, and the men equipped with heavier uniforms because winter was fast approaching.

Montgomery continued to push his own idea the advance should be consolidated into "one powerful, full-blooded thrust across the Rhine and into the heart of Germany, backed by the whole of the resources of the Allied armies."

That would have meant relegating the units across large sectors of the Allied front to purely static roles. Though Eisenhower rejected that notion in general, he did agree to a temporary pause across much of the front while Montgomery pushed ahead with his northern front to gain a bridgehead across the lower Rhine in the Netherlands (Operation Market-Garden). To support that offensive, parts of the

U.S. 1st Army were directed to swing northeast to more closely parallel the British moves.

That turn resulted in the 1st Army swinging through Liege. There J. Lawton Collins concentrated the three divisions of his 7th Corps into a compact formation covering about 15 miles of front. The 1st Infantry Division was less than 10 miles from Aachen; the 3rd Armored Division was in Eupen in the border area Germany had ceded to Belgium in 1919; and the 9th Infantry Division was moved into assembly areas at Verviers, halfway between Liege and the German frontier.

Having obtained permission to "reconnoiter the Westwall in force" on 12 September, Collins wanted to launch a strong surprise attack that might breach the fortified line in one push, before the Germans could man it adequately. The 1st was to move through the Westwall in front of Aachen, taking that place on the move, while the 3rd was to drive into the Stolberg Corridor by moving around Aachen on the south. If the armored division was able to easily cross the Westwall, it would circle around Aachen to Eschweiler, while the 9th would sweep through and secure the forests on the extreme right. Even if 7th Corps then had to pause to regroup and resupply, the Westwall would already be behind it when it resumed its attack.

German Plans

The German army had been forced onto the general defensive, and its operations had degenerated into nothing more than large-scale delaying actions. The front was too fluid for von Rundstedt to accomplish much toward actually forming one of the new lines Hitler kept designating on maps with feverish frequency. But on 11 September the high command ordered the Westwall be used as the prepared position along which the battered remnants of the armies in the west would make their stand, and to which arriving reinforcements would be sent to join their effort. The line was to be held "under any conditions," and von Rundstedt and his staff made honest efforts to do so.

The field marshal's most urgent problems came first from the threat posed by the Allied advance toward the Ruhr via the Aachen Gap, and second from the enemy's still uncommitted airborne reserves. At that moment, the only German reserves available for use were the reforming *9th Panzer Division*, along with one heavy tank and two

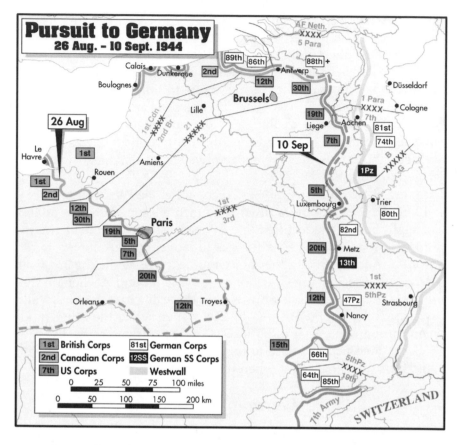

Pursuit to Germany
26 Aug. – 10 Sept. 1944

1st	British Corps	81st	German Corps
2nd	Canadian Corps	12SS	German SS Corps
7th	US Corps		Westwall

assault gun battalions. All those units were understrength, but were already on their way to the Aachen area.

The German commander directly responsible for defending the Aachen area was Gen. Friedrich August Schack, whose *81st Corps* was part of Gen. Erich Brandenberger's *7th Army*. On paper at least, it seemed Schack could base his hopes for blocking the Aachen Gap on six divisions. But northeast of Aachen, two of those divisions (the *49th* and *275 Infantry Divisions*) were so occupied resisting the approach of the U.S. 19th Corps that neither would be able to contribute to the fight against U.S. 7th Corps.

South of Aachen, Schack had the *526th Infantry Division*, backed by various local defense forces and *ad hoc* emergency units. In Aachen itself, and to the east of the city, was what was left of the *116th Panzer Division*. Schack's fifth formation was the *9th Panzer Division*, already earmarked by higher command to hold the front of the Stolberg

Corridor, but it was still in transit on 11 September. The sixth division, the *353rd Infantry*, was in reality no more than a weak regiment. Schack assigned it to the secondary band of the Westwall east of Aachen.

Schack anticipated the 7th Corps' main effort would be made against Aachen itself. He therefore turned over command of the city to the *116th*'s experienced commander, Lt. Gen. Gerhard Graf von Schwerin. In addition, Schack attached his corps artillery to von Schwerin's division. Beyond that, the corps commander could do nothing but wish Godspeed to the reinforcements the high command was promising were on the way.

U.S. 7th Corps Penetrates the Westwall, 12-16 September

The U.S. 1st Infantry Division spent the greater part of 12 September deploying for combat adjacent to the Westwall in front of Aachen. A battalion of its 16th Infantry Regiment worked its way into the fortified line south of there, but a counterattack by the engineer battalion of the German *526th Infantry Division*, supported by four assault guns, threw them back, discouraging further efforts that day.

After losing three tanks to the guns of a well concealed German anti-tank strongpoint, the left flank of the U.S. 3rd Armored Division stopped for the night 1,000 yards short of the Westwall. The 3rd's right flank reached Rötgen, also just short of the Westwall. In the center, a task force formed around the engineer battalion reached the pillboxes south of Schmidthof, but too late to make an attack that day.

Thus 7th Corps failed to accomplish Collins' goals. Road blocks, difficult terrain and unexpected German resistance had held both his armor and infantry outside the Westwall. In addition, the execution by the various American units had been slow, particularly in the 1st Infantry Division's sector, and most actions had been lacking in coordination and command control.

The next day Collins changed his plans, deciding to try to bypass Aachen. The 7th Corps scheme of maneuver was changed into what was basically a frontal attack into the Westwall south of the city, with the armored division flanked on both sides by the infantry. Collins ordered the 1st to avoid entering Aachen, instead surrounding it on three sides while giving direct support to the armored division with one of its regiments. The 3rd Armored was to proceed as before to penetrate both bands of the Westwall, take Eschweiler, then turn east

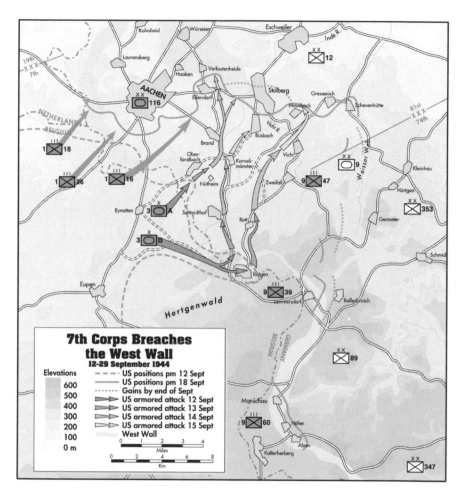

**7th Corps Breaches
the West Wall**
12-29 September 1944

Elevations	
600	
500	
400	
300	
200	
100	
0 m	

– – – US positions pm 12 Sept
——— US positions pm 18 Sept
·········· Gains by end of Sept
▷▷▷ US armored attack 12 Sept
▷▷▷ US armored attack 13 Sept
▷▷▷ US armored attack 14 Sept
▷▷▷ US armored attack 15 Sept
West Wall

0 1 2 3 4
Miles

0   2   4   6   8
Km

toward the Roer River. The 9th Infantry Division would protect the right flank of the armored drive, also lending the 3rd one of its regiments.

The new attack began at dawn on 13 September, when the 3rd Armored Division's Combat Command B (CCB) blasted a path through the dragon's teeth north of Rötgen, then moved into the town of Rott. Effective German resistance failed to materialize, and CCB thus penetrated the first band of the Westwall with one quick blow. But the picture at Rott suddenly changed when an SS sharpshooter unit of about 30 men opened fire. During the next few moments, CCB's lead tanks and halftracks lost a dozen crew members who had been advancing with their hatches open. The advance came to a standstill for the night.

In the meantime, the attempt by the 3rd's Combat Command A to breach the Westwall northeast of Oberforstbach failed due to German artillery fire and a 60-man counterattack backed by three assault guns and a Panther tank.

The Westwall was also penetrated farther south in a small sector attacked by a battle group built around the division's reserve and backed by an attached infantry battalion from the 1st Infantry Division. But because the hour was late, that column stopped for the night.

To the northwest, the 1st Infantry Division was frustrated in its attempts to advance along the flank of the armored drive. Its 16th Infantry Regiment had to fight its way past road blocks and delaying detachments, while absorbing dozens of small-scale counterattacks from the German *536th Reserve Grenadier Regiment* of the *526th Infantry Division*. A full-blooded attack by the 16th into the Westwall therefore had to wait one more day, after parts of the 26th Infantry Regiment took over an area on the 16th's left, and the 18th Regiment moved up even farther left.

Despite the various problems and delays, 7th Corps had created two ruptures of the Westwall's first band. That both were achieved along the face of the Stolberg Corridor, rather than farther south of Aachen, went a long way toward convincing the German corps commander he had erred in his earlier estimate of U.S. intentions. Schack ordered the *116th Panzer Division* to counterattack and destroy the American spearhead southeast of Oberforstbach. At the end of that counterattack, the Germans claimed they had resealed the gap south of the city. In reality, however, the *116th* only succeeded in driving back U.S. patrols.

In addition, Schack directed the headquarters of the *9th Panzer* and *353rd Infantry Divisions* to alert their units because "the enemy will probably launch a drive bypassing Aachen toward the second band of defenses."

The 7th Corps did indeed strike again on 14 September. As on the previous day, 3rd Armored Division's CCB made the most spectacular advance. Continuing from Rott, that unit drove across more than four miles of rolling country to approach Vicht, southeast of Stolberg, just as night came.

For their part, the various German commanders in the area didn't intend to fall back on the second band of Westwall fortifications without a fight. But they were unable to generate any activity on the ground that amounted to anything more than a withdrawal. Cratered roads, road blocks and small delaying detachments were all that got in the way of the Americans. Though parts of the *9th Panzer Division* were beginning to move into the eastern band of the Westwall by this time, repulsing U.S. attacks in the area of Büsbach, the sector opposite the U.S. 3rd Armored Division's CCB was held only by the *547th Security Battalion* of the *353rd Infantry Division*.

When CCB/3 attacked again around noon on 15 September, German resistance remained weak. All the firing pillboxes were silenced within an hour. Driving up the road toward Eschweiler, CCB passed the last bunkers of the Westwall's second band: they were completely through the Siegfried Line.

Elsewhere on the the 14th and 15th, the 3rd Armored Division's CCA began to exploit the penetration made in the Westwall's first band at Oberforstbach. By nightfall on the 14th, CCA had overrun a weak battle group of the *116th Panzer Division* near Brand, then advanced to the fringes of Eilendorf. There CCA/3 paused to await the arrival of the 1st Infantry Division's 16th Regiment, which was to seize the ground east of Aachen to protect the tankers' left flank in the coming drive to Eschweiler.

After days of frustration among outlying obstacles, the 16th Infantry Regiment at last launched a well prepared attack against the Westwall's first band on 14 September. Though skirmishes with elements of the *526th Infantry Division's 253rd Reserve Grenadier Regiment* and other local defense forces prevented them from reaching Eilendorf that day, the 16th entered the town late in the next morning. Fanning out to secure the area, the regiment's command was able to report it had completed its mission by nightfall. The U.S. 1st Infantry Division now ringed Aachen on three sides.

Upon the arrival of the 16th Regiment, CCA/3 renewed its drive northeast toward Eschweiler. After easy going through the first pillboxes halfway between Eilendorf and Stolberg, CCA was counter-attacked by the *2nd Battalion/11th Panzergrenadier Regiment* and the *50th Tank Destroyer Battalion*, both part of *9th Panzer Division*. The Germans brought seven assault guns into action, quickly knocking out a half-dozen Shermans. The fighting was some of the fiercest in 7th Corps' five-day-old push into the Siegfried Line, but by nightfall the U.S. tanks and infantry had penetrated almost a mile beyond the forward-edge pillboxes of the Westwall's second band. Only a few fortifications remained in front of CCA/3 before it, like CCB, would be through the entire Westwall.

At the same time, the battle for the Stolberg Corridor was broadened by the commitment of the U.S. 9th Infantry Division's 47th Regiment close along the right flank of 3rd Armored Division. Early on 14 September the 47th moved out of Rötgen behind CCB/3. The next day the regiment started to roll up a portion of the Westwall's second band by outflanking Zweifall and Vicht to the east. That area was defended by the weak *313th Grenadier Replacement and Training Battalion* of the *353rd Infantry Division*. Still, it took a full day to eliminate those Germans, primarily because of the difficult terrain they were holding.

From the German viewpoint, the advance of the 16th Infantry and CCA/3 beyond Eilendorf was all the more distressing because it severed contact between the *116th* and *9th Panzer Divisions*. Schack was reluctant to move the former fully into the Stolberg Corridor because the continuous pounding U.S. artillery had begun giving Aachen made him believe the city was going to be hit with an all-out assault on the 16th. Thus the German defense remained divided.

In the late afternoon of 15 September, Schack ordered the *9th Panzer Division* to counterattack. The first effort was made by a battle group of the *1st Battalion/10th Panzergrenadier Regiment* near Zweifall. It failed due to heavy American mortar and artillery fire. But a second, two-pronged attack by two battle groups organized from *2nd Battalion/11th Panzergrenadier Regiment, 9th Armored Reconnaissance Battalion, 1st Battalion/33rd Panzer Regiment*, and *50th Tank Destroyer Battalion* against CCA/3 and CCB/3 quickly knocked out over two dozen tanks and a dozen halftracks. The 3rd Armored Division was forced to stop for the 15th.

These events would have been encouraging to the Germans even if they hadn't been informed that night of the impending arrival of the fresh and powerful *12th Infantry Division*. Its first contingents were scheduled to reach the combat area during the night, and the entire division would arrive over the next 30 hours.

Unaware of the enemy reinforcements, the divisions of 7th Corps renewed their drives on the 16th. CCA/3 tried to continue northeast through the industrial suburbs of Stolberg. To the east, CCB/3 shifted the direction of its attack to the southeastern edge of that town. Both combat commands stalled due to concentrated German machinegun and mortar fire, and the 3rd Armored Division made no progress that day.

The difficulties of the 3rd Armored Division were offset by the spectacular advance achieved by the 9th Infantry Division's 47th Regiment. With the aid of a captured map, the 47th cleared Vicht and mopped up the nearby pillboxes during the morning. Then it pressed northeast through the Wenau Forest to Schevenhtte. This late-comer to the Westwall fighting thereby penetrated deeper into Germany than any other Allied unit, and was less than 10 miles from the Roer River.

But indications were beginning to appear of stirrings on the German side of the line. The following night almost every American unit along the front reported hearing the noise of heavy vehicular traffic, and a German colonel was captured who had been found reconnoitering—presumably for an attack—a little too close to American lines.

While events around Stolberg gave evidence of moving toward some kind of climax, on the left of 7th Corps, at Aachen, the 1st Infantry Division, supported by the 1106th Engineer Group, threw up a wall of defenses while awaiting the arrival of the 19th Corps to assist in encircling the city. By the evening of 16 September, the basic form of the wall around Aachen had been set as a half-moon arc extending from the 18th Regiment southwest of the city to the 16th Regiment's advanced position at Eilendorf. The command of the 1st Infantry Division had no intention of becoming embroiled in fighting through the streets and bomb-gutted buildings of Aachen, but was forced into fighting off local counterattacks from elements of the *526th Infantry Division*.

The German command was astounded the 7th Corps would stop short of trying to seize the city. To add to their problems, the panic that had first struck Aachen's populace during the night of 12 September returned when U.S. artillery began pounding their homes. By 16 September, civilian evacuation was in full swing and conditions inside Aachen became chaotic.

Positional Warfare, 17 September to 1 October

The situation changed rapidly for 7th Corps early on the afternoon of 17 September, when the Allies launched Operation Market-Garden some 50 miles northwest of Aachen. The corps' supply situation deteriorated, especially in regard to fuel and artillery ammunition, and its tactical air support simply disappeared to the north. The 7th's various formations were in the delicate situation of being through the Westwall in places, being half through in others, and at some points not having penetrated at all. The line was full of extreme zigs and zags. From an offensive standpoint, the penetrations made so far were too narrow to serve as the base for further operations toward the Roer or Rhine Rivers, and from a defensive standpoint the corps was potentially open to German infiltration and counterattack.

On the German side, the newly arriving *12th Infantry Division* was used to relieve the remnant of the *353rd Infantry Division*. The latter unit was then moved to the relatively quiet *74th Corps* sector farther south. Gen. Brandenberger ordered Schack to use his new division in "the best Prussian military tradition," meaning an all-out counterattack. Therefore at dawn on 17 September, the *12th Infantry Division's 27th Grenadier Regiment*, supported by remnants of the *9th Panzer Division's* armor, attacked in the direction of Münsterbusch. Their objective was to eliminate the bulge at Stolberg.

After initial progress, the counterattack was stopped by heavy fire from nearly all of 7th Corps' artillery, then repulsed by CCB/3. The *12th Infantry Division* continued its efforts to reclaim the Westwall's second band, but the result was an eruption of fierce, close-in fighting that brought no real gain for either side.

Late on 19 September, CCA/3 and CCB/3 started a methodical, costly mop up of the last German defensive positions inside Stolberg. Fighting without air support and lavish artillery preparation was a new experience for the Americans, and the learning cost was high.

At dawn on 22 September, the *27th Grenadier Regiment*, supported by the newly arrived *1012th Assault Gun Battalion*, counterattacked again, this time into central Stolberg, which was occupied by CCB/3. The 3rd Armored Division's commander authorized a withdrawal, and the combat command dashed back to Münsterbusch under cover of a smoke screen. There it found sanctuary, thanks to CCA/3's efforts to hold the German counterattack inside Stolberg.

That was about all either side was able to accomplish in the Stolberg Corridor for the time being. The Germans had effectively used terrain and small-unit maneuver to thwart 7th Corps' attacks. After 22 September the fighting died down. As the month drew to a close, 7th Corps shifted to the defense all across its front as it ran low on fuel and ammunition. In addition, the loss of air support to the Market-Garden operation had been a real blow to its combat efficiency.

Before 7th Corps could resume its attack, it had to shuffle units to release one for redeployment. The logical place for that shuffle was in the defensive arc around Aachen, for the next fight was not to be to the east or northeast, but was to be made directly against the city in conjunction with 19th Corps.

On 20 September, because of Gen. Schack's connection to von Schwerin and his unsatisfactory, piecemeal commitment of *12th Infantry Division*, Brandenberger relieved him of command. Gen. Friedrich Köchling took over *81st Corps*.

As the fighting subsided in the Stolberg Corridor, more German reinforcements began to arrive. The first major unit was the *183rd Volksgrenadier Division*, which was employed north of Aachen against 19th Corps. After shoring up the line there, Köchling pulled out the depleted *275th Infantry Division*, except for its fusilier battalion, and sent it south for refitting and reorganization. The fusiliers were put into corps reserve.

On 23 September, another full strength division, the *246th Volksgrenadier*, entrained in Bohemia with the mission of relieving what was left of the *9th* and *116th Panzer Divisions*. Those two units were put in reserve to refit and reorganize for the planned winter counterattack in the Ardennes (the Battle of the Bulge). The *246th* was therefore deployed into the center of the *81st Corps'* zone, where it took over the task of defending the city of Aachen in conjunction with the remnants of the *526th Infantry Division* and other local defense units. Lt. Col. Maximilian Leyherr, one of the *246th*'s regimental commanders, became the new commander of Aachen.

In addition to those reinforcements, *81st Corps* also received a regiment of bicycle infantry, another assault gun battalion, a Tiger battalion, and a tank destroyer battalion.

The Germans had in fact become stronger than at any time since 7th Corps opened its attack on 12 September. But the fighting to date had cost them dearly. In the week from 16 to 23 September, for example, the *12th Infantry Division* alone lost half its combat strength, a reduction from which it was not to recover throughout the rest of the autumn fighting. At the same time, *9th Panzer Division* lost two-thirds of its combat strength. But one needed commodity had been bought by all the sacrifice: time.

Closing the Circle, 2-16 October

During the second half of September, the U.S. 9th Army concluded its campaign in Brittany and began moving into the Ardennes-Eifel area. As that army arrived, it allowed Courtney Hodges to regroup his 1st Army. He reduced the size of 7th Corps' front around Aachen, and sent two divisions (7th Armored and 29th Infantry) to 19th Corps. But before Hodges could renew his drive to the Rhine, he had to attend to two items of unfinished business: capture Aachen and put 19th Corps through the Westwall north of that city.

Hodges decided to work toward both tasks at the same time. He ordered 19th Corps to penetrate the Westwall north of Aachen and then move to complete 7th Corps' partial encirclement. The penetration of the fortified line was to be carried out by 19th Corps' 30th Infantry Division. The hole would be exploited by 2nd Armored Division, which was to cross the Wurm River, then drive nine miles eastward to jump the Roer. Meanwhile, the infantry was to strike south to link with 7th Corps northeast of Aachen. To assist the new Westwall assault, the 29th Infantry Division was to make limited attacks along 19th Corps' northern flank. The final capture of Aachen was to be left to 7th Corps' 1st Infantry Division.

The 30th Infantry Division's commander, Maj. Gen. Leland Hobbs, chose to strike into the Westwall on a front little more than a mile wide along the Wurm River north of Aachen and southeast of Geilenkirchen. His choice of jump off sites was governed by his desire to avoid denser Westwall and urban areas to the south. In general his approach was probably best, but it was unfortunate for the attack's efficiency that he and his staff based their orders on map studies, without conducting any personal reconnaissance. As a result, to give one example, Hobbs ordered assault boats forward for the Wurm River crossing, only to find out from the report of a last-minute patrol the river was only two to four feet deep and 15 to 18 feet wide. Duckboard footbridges were hurriedly substituted for the boats.

The men of the 30th were organized into special pillbox assault teams equipped with flamethrowers and a variety of demolition charges. Tank destroyers and self-propelled 155mm guns were readied to pump direct fire into German positions, and an air-ground liaison officer was to accompany each infantry battalion. In addition, the regiments rotated their battalions through the line, enabling all to

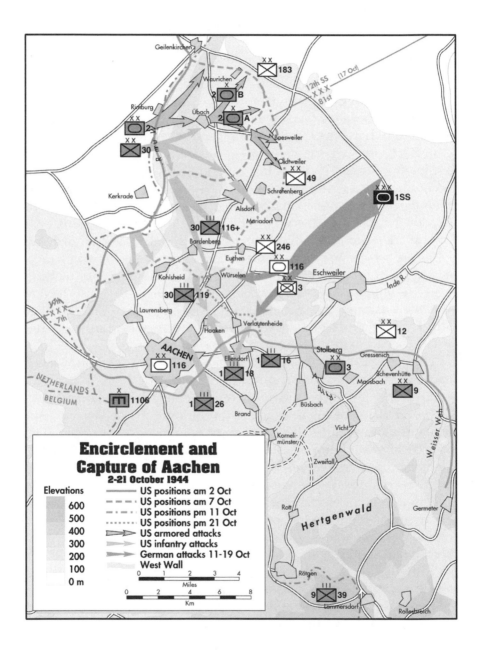

Encirclement and Capture of Aachen
2-21 October 1944

Elevations
600
500
400
300
200
100
0 m

US positions am 2 Oct
US positions am 7 Oct
US positions pm 11 Oct
US positions pm 21 Oct
US armored attacks
US infantry attacks
German attacks 11-19 Oct
West Wall

get refresher training in fundamental, combined-arms pillbox assault tactics.

On the other side, German intelligence officers were predicting a major attack on the first clear weather day. They most feared an offensive on a broad front southeast of Aachen, with the Roer River towns of Düren and Jülich as first objectives. They also anticipated a possible large-scale Allied airborne operation between the Roer and Rhine Rivers as a corollary to the new ground drive. With all that in mind, Köchling wrongly assumed the U.S. 1st Army would make a strong push through the Stolberg Corridor during the first days of October. As a result, he and his staff spent the end of September overseeing feverish preparations to strengthen the sector of the *12th Infantry* and *246th Volksgrenadier Divisions* immediately in and to the southeast of Aachen.

The U.S. 1st Army started an elaborate preparatory artillery program on 26 September. By 29 September, the shelling and ground support activity reached such a level that all daylight troop and supply movements in the German *81st Corps* sector had to be halted. Still, except for clearing away the camouflage, all the shelling, bombing and strafing was found to have little effect on the pillboxes and strongpoints themselves. The attack was then set back several times due to poor flying weather, finally kicking off on 2 October with an air strike.

The *Luftwaffe* showed no signs of reviving, and German anti-aircraft artillery was virtually nonexistent. Yet somehow this climactic strike was a complete failure. Some Germans taken prisoner even claimed they'd slept through it. Some observers reported the air effort had no real effect beyond providing the German infantry with new craters from which to fight. A real note of tragedy occurred when some medium bombers mistakenly struck a Belgian town 40 miles west of their assigned targets, inflicting hundreds of casualties on the civilians and Allied soldiers there.

Of course, despite the disappointing performance of the aircraft, 19th Corps remained committed to its ground attack. From the start, though, 30th Infantry Division's assault regiments (117th and 119th) met with difficulties. German resistance proved much tougher than had been expected, with one attacking company, for example, losing 87 of its men in an hour. The coordination between the attackers' infantry and armor completely failed, but the corps artillery saved the day for the U.S. riflemen. By nightfall, the two regiments had managed to create small bridgeheads across the Wurm.

That evening the men of the 30th waited for a German counterattack to materialize, but that reaction was delayed due to their surprise as to the location of the American effort. Deceived by diversionary attacks launched elsewhere by the 29th Infantry Division and the 30th's 120th Infantry Regiment, the German commanders of the *49th Infantry* and *183rd Volksgrenadier Divisions* failed to realize the narrow-front effort of the 117th and 119th Regiments was the real thing.

Shortly after dark, a battalion of Volksgrenadiers was ordered to counterattack in conjunction with the *902nd Assault Gun Battalion*, but murderous U.S. artillery interdiction delayed their jump off for three hours. At midnight the attack went in, but only a few of the infantryman and two assault guns were able to move forward. The counterattack ended as a complete failure, and Gen. Köchling ordered the *183rd* to thereafter confine its operations to merely trying to seal off the enemy penetration until stronger forces could be assembled to launch more effective countermeasures.

On the second day, 3 October, cooperation between the American tanks and infantry suddenly turned excellent. After clearing about a dozen pillboxes, the 119th broke through the band of fortifications, but still not fast or far enough to begin any substantial new advance. Once again the Germans brought the attackers to an abrupt halt after gains of only a few hundred yards, by launching numerous small-scale counterattacks. By the end of the second day, the depth of the 119th's bridgehead across the Wurm was still no more than 1,000 yards.

In the meantime, the 117th Regiment attacked in the direction of Übach, where tedious house-to-house fighting quickly developed. Some of the American riflemen involved described it as the heaviest fighting they'd seen since Mortain in Normandy. The tanks and halftracks of CCB/2 then rolled into the Übach maelstrom, since they were scheduled to cross the Wurm River at noon. The armor got into the town, but due to the congestion on its streets, the heavy German shelling, and the continued house-to-house fighting all around, no further progress was made. By nightfall neither armor nor infantry had progressed beyond Übach's northern and eastern edges, with many buildings in the town still in German hands.

By dawn on 4 October, Köchling had maneuvered five infantry, one engineer, a Tiger and two assault gun battalions into position to

Aachen '44

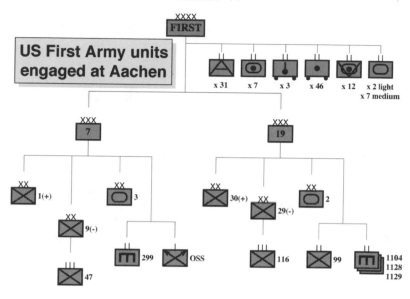

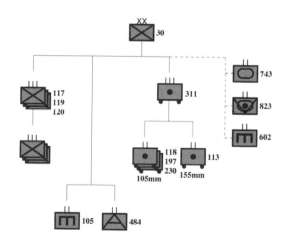

counterattack the 119th. Their main effort pushed into the center of that regiment, and as the U.S. riflemen saw the Tigers they panicked and fell back. But then shortfalls from the Germans' own artillery began to throw the counterattack into disarray too. By the time the Germans had sorted things out, the 119th was again stabilized, reinforced with tanks and tank destroyers. Only one German infantry battalion actually reached Übach, where it was completely smashed, reduced to only 25 men.

The force that had been so difficult to assemble and looked so impressive to Köchling on paper had been reduced to impotence in a matter of hours. Von Rundstedt and Brandenberger, who visited Köchling's headquarters during the counterattack, both came away with the impression the forces available around Aachen were insufficient for a successful defense. They ordered Köchling to send every available unit within his corps to the threatened sector, and promised reinforcements.

Though the German counterattack had failed, it did delay U.S. operations on the 4th, with no appreciable American advances achieved that day. Resuming the attack on 5 October, the 2nd Armored and 30th Infantry Divisions found the pattern of German resistance unchanged. But this time the advance moved more quickly, since the coordination among the various ground combat arms and supporting aircraft worked perfectly. By the end of the day, Übach was completely secured and three villages beyond it were also seized. Even if the U.S. riflemen had paid for the advances with heavy casualties, the developments seemed encouraging.

At the same time, Köchling continued his efforts to set up a greater concentration of defending units opposite the American drive. But just like the force assembled for the 4 October counterattack, these newly arriving units were more impressive on paper than they were on the ground. Once again assembling units from various sectors of the front to execute a coordinated counterattack proved a difficult task. The Germans failed to strike on 5 October, thereby losing their chance. Köchling was forced to commit his units piecemeal, in reaction to the pattern of U.S. attacks.

The U.S. 19th Corps expanded the bridgehead in the directions of Waurichen, Baesweiler and Alsdorf on 6 October. The attackers repeated the combined arms techniques used so successfully the day before and made good progress. The Germans reacted by moving tanks and anti-tank guns into position late in the day, finally stopping the U.S. advance with dug-in infantry backed up by direct-fire heavy weapons less than a 1,000 yards short of the line Baesweiler-Alsdorf.

Also as on the day before, the Germans conducted numerous small-scale counterattacks of roughly battalion size, supported by a handful of tanks and assault guns. During those efforts, German artillery hammered the bridgehead with some of the heaviest concentrations the U.S. troops had ever experienced. Köchling, in fact, massed all his *81st Corps* guns against the bridgehead. Even the *Luftwaffe* got into the act, launching one strike with good results.

During the afternoon of 6 October, the commander of *German Army Group B*, Field Marshal Walter Model, visited the command post of *81st Corps* to lend his weight to the effort to assemble sufficient forces for launching a decisive counterattack against the Westwall bridgehead. But Model was too late; 6 October proved to be the high water mark of the German resistance against 19th Corps. Every unit the German command had seized upon for movement into the threatened sector was simply absorbed into the defense by the unremitting pressure of the 2nd Armored and 30th Infantry Divisions.

The 19th Corps was in fact preparing to exploit through and beyond its bridgehead. The fight to breach the Westwall was ending, and the planned juncture with 7th Corps to encircle Aachen became the new goal. The weight of American armor, and clear skies that allowed for great air activity, provided the margin of success on 7 October. Baesweiler, Oidtweiler, and Alsdorf fell, and by late in the day 30th Infantry Division was only about three miles away from Wrselen, the planned point of contact with 7th Corps. Further heavy losses were inflicted on the Germans when their line collapsed and numerous overruns were made by the Americans.

For their part, the Germans continued to try to assemble an effective counterattack force, this time in the vicinity of Alsdorf. The main components of the new group consisted of the *Regiment von Fritzschen*, made up of bicycle infantry, the *1st Assault Regiment*, a battle group from the *108th Panzer Brigade*, plus about 40 tanks, tank destroyers and assault guns drawn from various other units. Any real hope of denying Aachen to the Americans lay not with this small force, but with von Rundstedt's promise to commit his theater reserves: the *3rd Panzergrenadier Division* and the now-refitting *116th Panzer Division*.

Attaching those two divisions to the headquarters of the *1st SS Panzer Corps*, von Rundstedt ordered a major operation to restore the situation around Aachen. But those potentially decisive reinforcements were still in transit on 7 October because Allied air attacks on the railways imposed serious delays. Köchling feared Aachen would fall before they could arrive.

Events at Alsdorf on 7 October convinced the U.S. 1st Army command the time had come to force the issue at Aachen. On the morning of the 8th, the 117th Regiment moved to seize the high ground east of Würselen. The attack progressed steadily until about 9:30 a.m., when a German counterattack erupted. This was the *von Fritschen* force trying to retake Alsdorf, thereby closing the gap that had opened in the lines of the *49th Infantry Division*. After heavy fire began from the giant guns of the *723rd Railroad Artillery Battery*, panic spread among the Americans, who thought they were being hit by some new kind of secret weapon. Then the U.S. line collapsed completely when five Hunting Panthers of the *519th Tank Destroyer Battalion* appeared, allowing some of the German armor and infantry to break into Alsdorf. There the German attack ran out of steam, but the 117th's progress had again been blocked, and in such a way that it seemed possible the regiment might be surrounded southeast of Alsdorf.

While this was going on, the U.S. 1st Infantry Division's 18th Regiment attacked north toward Verlautenheide. In a cleverly run night attack, the place was secured with no difficulty. Again, small-scale German counterattacks began on 8 and 9 October, but since the *246th Volksgrenadier Division* was now having to absorb punishment on two fronts, from the 18th Regiment's northward push and the southward attacks of 19th Corps, the Germans found it almost impossible to release any troops for counterattacking.

The one strong suit the Germans showed during this period was their artillery. Because the American attacks were being delivered on a narrow front no more than five miles across, the defenders were able to concentrate their shelling to good effect. Still, the 18th Infantry Regiment took Haaren on 10 October. (Again, the seizure was relatively easy, but with a more difficult mop up and defense against counterattacks following.) The final closing of the ring around Aachen seemed to be in sight.

On 10 October 1st Division headquarters sent an ultimatum to the commander of the German garrison in Aachen. He was warned if he failed to capitulate unconditionally within 24 hours U.S. forces would pulverize the city with artillery and bombs, then seize the rubble with a ground assault. In fact, units from the U.S. 26th Infantry Division had already begun preparations to move into the tangle of factories lying between Aachen proper and Haaren.

The German military commander in Aachen, Leyherr, dutifully rejected the ultimatum in accord with Hitler's last-stand orders. Two days later, Leyherr was relieved in deference to his division commander, Col. Gerhardt Wilck. Then on 10 October, von Rundstedt gave final authorization for commitment of the *1st SS Panzer Corps*. He attached a proviso to the authorization ordering that the force not be committed piecemeal, but as a whole and concentrated corps. But the further assembly the proviso required meant delaying the new counterattack until 12 October.

The German 8 October counterattack had almost completely stalled further offensive movement by 30th Infantry Division. Only 117th Regiment made some gains on the 9th, when the 7th Corps' drive northward against Verlautenheide diverted German attention. Later that same day, parts of the 120th Regiment took the high ground near Würselen, while elements of the 119th Regiment occupied Bardenberg. But both objectives had to be given up to a late-afternoon counterstroke delivered by the *108th Panzer Brigade*.

The 30th Infantry Division renewed its efforts to secure Bardenberg soon after daylight on 10 October. But the Germans had spent the night converting the town's cellars into pillboxes, and fought back fiercely from those new positions. Concealed automatic weapons thwarted all the Americans' attempts at infiltration. At nightfall 30th Division's headquarters ordered a complete withdrawal from Bardenberg to permit artillery to pummel the defenders without concern for hitting friendly troops.

Early the next day a fresh battalion from the 120th Infantry Regiment again attacked into Bardenberg. This time there was hardly any resistance from the remnants of the German *49th Infantry Division* still there. By last light on the 11th, both Bardenberg and the route to Würselen were clear of Germans.

Late that same day, the first of the *116th Panzer Division*'s regimental combat teams, primarily from the *60th Panzergrenadier Regiment*, arrived along with two hybrid SS battle groups that in happier times had belonged to the *1st SS Panzer Division "Leibstandarte Adolf Hitler."* Given the emergency situation at Bardenberg and the growing pressure on Würselen, the units of the *116th*, against von Rundstedt's proviso, were employed immediately as they arrived.

Brandenberger further reinforced *60th Panzergrenadier Regiment* with the SS battle groups, the remnants of the *108th Panzer Brigade*, and various small units drawn from all along the line during the night. This force began to attack toward Bardenberg just after dawn on 12 October. Its mission was to push back 19th Corps, widening and then defending the German corridor leading into Aachen.

During the morning a crisis came upon the headquarters of the

U.S. 30th Infantry Division when its commander was told the latest German prisoners taken had been identified as belonging to the *116th* and *1st SS Panzer Divisions*. The officers at the American headquarters began talking in terms of "another Mortain," and the need to commandeer all available artillery, anti-aircraft and service troops to back up the line. The 30th's commander claimed: "This is one of the decisive battles of the war!"

Even though anxiety was high at its headquarters, the men of the 30th contained every German thrust made that morning. The Germans continued to look for a way in during the afternoon, but were frustrated because the return of sparkling clear weather brought back hordes of enemy aircraft. As night came, the situation across 19th Corps was again under control.

Despite its defensive success, however, it was becoming clear the 30th couldn't finish the job of encircling Aachen on its own. Elements of 2nd Armored Division and some corps engineers were rushed in as reinforcements. In addition, the 29th Infantry Division's 116th Regiment was freed to move by placing other engineers into the line near Kerkrade.

On 13 October, the U.S. 116th Infantry Regiment launched an attack through the streets and buildings of Würselen. Because coordination between the 116th's infantry and the 2nd Armored Division's tanks proved hard to achieve, only snail-like progress was made that day and the next. Also, by this point Würselen was being defended by the entire *60th Panzergrenadier Regiment*, along with elements of the divisional engineer and reconnaissance battalions. Tanks were dug into houses and concealed positions all through the town.

Even three dive-bombing missions and a time-on-target artillery barrage on 15 October failed to do the trick for the attackers. In three days the American attack at Wrselen gained no more than 1,000 yards; a gap of more than a mile still lay between 19th and 7th Corps.

Soon after the surrender deadline expired in Aachen on 11 October, air strikes from fighter bombers opened the assault on the city. A huge artillery bombardment was also begun, with both efforts continuing on the 12th and 13th. But U.S. patrols testing the defenses found no lessening of German defensive fire. At the time about 27,000 civilians were still in the city, and their presence seemed to stiffen the soldiers' determination to hold the place. The U.S. bombardment also generated lots of rubble that made operating motor vehicles difficult inside Aachen.

The U.S. command wanted a quick victory at Aachen, but not if it had to be a Pyrrhic one. During the next few days the ground assault was begun with the 26th Infantry Regiment nibbling away at the eastern suburb of Rothe Erde. Its actions there were supported by an OSS (Office of Strategic Services - the organizational ancestor of the CIA) company. That small unit was made up of U.S. soldiers dressed in German uniforms and carrying German weapons. After some initial success, nearly the entire company was captured. (But unlike Otto Skorzeny's similar "Operation Greif" teams used during the Battle of the Bulge, the Americans of the OSS units were not shot, but treated as regular POWs.)

The Germans missed a chance for success at this time by failing to detect the weak condition of the 18th Infantry Regiment's defenses to the northeast of the city. Attacking to try to enlarge the corridor into Aachen early on the morning of the 15th, the Germans missed an extremely weak spot in the 18th's lines by some 400 yards, moving instead against Verlautenheide. Forewarned by reports of the German assembly, both the 1st Infantry Division's and the 7th Corps' artillery was ready.

The American defensive fire stopped the bulk of the attacking infantry, but a handful of Tigers got through, spreading panic among the defending riflemen. Several companies were overrun. The timely arrival of air support saved the day for the 16th, completely collapsing the German effort. Some close-quarter fighting continued for the rest of the day, but continued heavy shelling prevented all German attempts to reinforce their effort.

To the U.S. troops involved, this German attack appeared to be a powerful and well-prepared push; it shattered nerves among the commanders in more than one echelon of command. In reality, the thrust was a hasty compromise brought on after the capture of an American officer the night before. He was carrying several maps and other revealing documents, and Gen. Brandenberger immediately seized on them as reason enough to justify a quick effort against the 16th Regiment before the information became stale. Thus what had been a comprehensive German plan forming for a large, coordinated counterattack became infected with the fungus of counterattack-by-installment, which soon frittered away what could have been an effective counterattacking force.

The headquarters of the *1st SS Panzer Corps*, which had just arrived on the scene on 11 October to oversee the operations of the *3rd*

Panzergrenadier and *116th Panzer Divisions,* quickly became superfluous, and was sent back on the 19th. The various German counterattacks had no common goals or coordination.

At intervals throughout 16 October, *3rd Panzergrenadier Division*'s formations continued to probe the U.S. 16th Infantry Regiment's sector, but always just with small units of infantry supported by at most a handful of armor. Mounting losses then prompted the *3rd* to suspend its efforts until the division could regroup. In two days of fruitless fighting, the *3rd* had lost a third of its combat strength.

After seven frustrating days, 19th Corps formed yet another plan for a link up attack on the 16th. Instead of repeating the main attack with the 116th Infantry Regiment inside Würselen, the 30th Infantry Division launched diversionary efforts all along its front at 5:00 a.m. The Germans turned more and more of their guns and reserves against the 117th and 120th Infantry Regiments during the morning, while at 10:30 a.m. Köchling committed his last reserve, *SS Battle Group Bucher,* against the 117th at Alsdorf.

But the main U.S. effort that day was unleashed by the 119th Infantry Regiment at Kohlscheid, then moving on to Wrselen. There the attack was stopped by the *6th Luftwaffe Fortress Battalion* when the American tanks became stuck in the mud and the infantry couldn't go on alone. Again U.S. close air support saved the American riflemen from being pushed back by a counterattack. After another afternoon of back and forth fighting, the 119th got moving again and at 4:15 p.m. achieved the long sought junction with 30th Division troops, closing the German corridor into Aachen.

Assault on the City, 17-21 October

Von Rundstedt knew unless the *3rd Panzergrenadier* and *116th Panzer Divisions* could quickly break the encirclement, Aachen was lost. Radioed cries of anguish from Wilck about the weakness of his garrison only heightened the old field marshal's concern.

Nazi propaganda broadcasts began declaring Aachen would become the "Allied Stalingrad," but there were only 4,393 German effectives inside the pocket. Most were from Wilck's own *246th Volksgrenadier Division,* since the *526th Infantry Division* had practically ceased to exist. In addition, there were some local defense units, four tanks, eight assault guns, and *SS Battle Group Rink,* which had been rushed into the city on 15 October to bolster the morale of the defenders by adding the presence of a few "elite" troops. Attempts by the Germans to break the encirclement on 17, 18 and 19 October again lacked coordination. Though some hard fighting occurred around Verlautenheide, no chance for a genuine breakthrough ever developed.

On the German side, losses continued to be severe during this phase. For example, one company of the 1st Infantry Division reported counting 250 German dead in front of its positions during a single day, a daily figure previously unmatched in the division's history.

Attempts by the Aachen garrison to support the attacks from outside the ring also got nowhere. By nightfall on 19 October, von Rundstedt concluded the defenders of Aachen had to be left to their fate, and ordered the *3rd Panzergrenadier Division*, by this time down to half-strength, to get ready to pull out.

Even the most fanatic German defenders inside the city now understood it was only a matter of time until Aachen's fall. The U.S. 26th Infantry Regiment in fact conducted a slow and methodical advance, dividing its men into small assault teams, a tank or tank destroyer accompanying each platoon. The armor kept each building under heavy fire until the riflemen could move up to it and inside. Buildings strong enough to withstand tank fire were targeted with 155mm guns.

After one bitter experience in which some bypassed Germans in cellars and storm sewers emerged in the rear of a U.S. attack team, the riflemen learned speed was less important than persistence. They no longer waited for actual targets to appear; each building, they assumed, was a nest of resistance until proved otherwise. The sewers proved a special problem because each manhole had to be located, thoroughly blocked and covered. The litter and rubble made other problems, since handling vehicles inside the city became difficult, with tires on jeeps and trucks frequently going flat.

During 19 and 20 October, German resistance inside Aachen began to crumble when the central part of town was cut off from the western residential sectors. Thereafter German resistance was based only on unconnected local strongpoints, and by 12:05 p.m. on 21 October it was over. Because Wilck's communications had broken down, by that point he had definite knowledge of the whereabouts of only about 500 of his men. U.S. troops therefore had to continue to sweep back and forth through Aachen, rounding up other German defenders as they found them. The Germans admitted to 5,100 casualties of all types inside Aachen, including 3,473 taken prisoner.

Aftermath

Though the Germans were forced out of the Westwall in several places, had failed to prevent the encirclement of Aachen, and held out within the city for only five days after it was surrounded, the true measure of the battle from their standpoint came from the telling, costly delay inflicted on the American advance toward the Roer and Rhine Rivers. In so doing, the Germans lost two divisions and had eight more mauled, including three fresh infantry and one newly refitted armored divisions.

Still, the overall recovery of the Germans after the massive disasters of the summer must be rated as only a little short of miraculous. The expenditure of replacements and artillery ammunition around Aachen had worried the German high command, which was desperately trying to build up stocks for the planned Ardennes offensive. But it was worth it in that the U.S. 1st Army was held up for a month and a half, and was made to suffer significant losses as well.

The events of the previous weeks had demonstrated to the Germans that during clear weather, large-scale ground movement, troop assembly, attack, counterattack and mobile defense operations were nearly impossible due to Allied air superiority and artillery strength. In such situations, local counterattacks proved to be the only way to stop an attacker superior in numbers and materiel.

But that reliance on local counterattacks also demonstrated how attrition had robbed the German army of its formerly outstanding field leadership. The equivalent of 20 battalions were used in counterattacks against the U.S. 30th Infantry Division alone, yet in only one or two cases did any single effort involve more than two reinforced battalions. In addition, *81st Corps* failed totally in trying to assemble and launch a single large counterattack, though at least two real opportunities occurred to do so.

A "Home for Christmas" drive to the Rhine and beyond was rendered totally impossible for the U.S. Army during September and October 1944. But 7th Corps could have taken Aachen in mid-September, against only weak German opposition, had it gone directly in rather than trying to maneuver around it and into the Stolberg Corridor.

Besides the unexpected heavy losses in men and materiel suffered at Aachen, which delayed the next planned Allied offensive operations and had a direct impact on the Battle of the Bulge, the fighting for that German city demonstrated to the U.S. high command its forces still suffered from shortcomings in the execution of combined-arms operations. The overall conduct of operations was disconcertingly slow and conservative. As a result, 19th Corps' commander, Maj. Gen. Charles H. Corlett, was relieved by Hodges.

The battle for Aachen clearly illustrates the problems that beset a military force weakened by lengthy pursuit, restrained by tightening supply lines, and confronted by an enemy who turns to fight inside strong natural and manmade barriers.

Aachen itself, since it was the first German city to fall to the Allies, was also the first to experience Allied military government. To assist them, they appointed an attorney, Franz Oppenhoff, as Burgermeister. He took the job even though he knew he would be considered a traitor by the Nazis until Germany was entirely conquered. His apprehensions proved correct, as he was found murdered in his own home by a *Werwolf* commando in March 1945.

Finally, in May 1945, Aachen became part of the British zone of occupation, and so began yet another foreign occupation of Charlemagne's historic city.

The German Army at Aachen, Autumn 1944

The German army lost some 75 infantry divisions (totaling 229 regiments) during 1944. The autumn of 1944 therefore represented a period of transition from good to bad quality infantry units. German survival that autumn depended on nothing so much as improvisation, but that very characteristic was their strong suit: the German army remained proficient at small unit tactics and rapid formation of *ad hoc* battlegroups. At every unit level the German army was fully committed to the idea of "mission tactics" (*Auftragstaktik*). That is, all unit and command structures were considered to be changeable according to circumstances. All command structures and the soldiers within them had to be prepared to take the initiative in any unexpected situation—and to do so without waiting for orders from above.

Within such a system, the ideal German soldier viewed the war as a clash of national and individual wills, to be conducted with maxi-

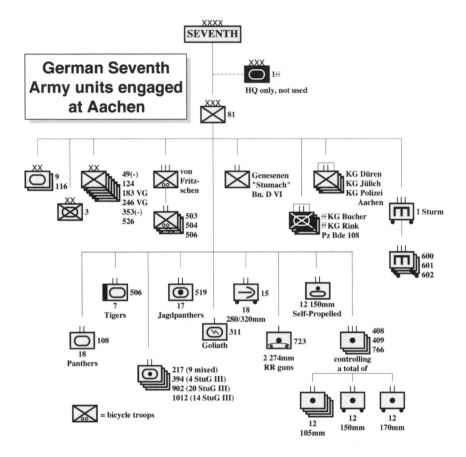

mum ferocity and efficiency. In combat, *Kampfkraft* (combat power, or fighting ability) was the sole judge of a soldier's or unit's worth.

By the fall of 1944, however, the training edge that had made the crucial difference in the German army's abilities in relation to its opponents could no longer be maintained. When SS Chief Heinrich Himmler was given command of the replacement army in August 1944, a number of changes were put in place. Daily training hours were lengthened, while training periods were reduced from 12 to 16 weeks down to an average of about six. Navy, air force and labor service personnel were shifted into the army, and the *Volkssturm* (People's Force, or militia) was created.

Many of the new German formations that resulted from those changes lacked the basic training necessary to carry out any missions calling for more initiative than static defense. But what the new units lacked in leadership and administrative ability, they tried to make up for with *Härte* (hardness)—the determination to hold on and fight to the very end. In general, though, such methods failed to change the course of battle, only succeeding in increasing German casualties. A few of the new formations still managed to achieve the old levels of excellence because they had received a veteran cadre from whom the newer soldiers could learn—such cadres often made all the difference.

By the autumn of 1944, the German army had also been reduced to fighting a poor man's war. Sufficient allocations of ammunition and fuel to carry out missions were becoming increasingly unavailable. Five years of savage combat and the increasingly intense and effective Allied strategic bombing campaign had the effect of steadily sapping the flow of supplies to German forces in the field. The way the German infantryman saw it at the time was the U.S. Army was inferior to his in the qualitative sense, but the GIs had more fuel, ammunition, tanks, artillery and planes. The Germans called the Allies' use of that logistical superiority to achieve their victories *Materialschlacht* (battle of attrition). Regardless of how they viewed it philosophically, all of them understood it was winning the war for the Allies.

The most important advantage the German army still had in 1944 lay in its leadership. The German concept of leadership and officer promotion was superior to that of all other armies. Officers were encouraged to be solicitous of their men's opinions and condition, with units and replacements deliberately set up on a territorial basis. German officers were expected to be masters of innovation and improvisation, doing much more with less than those who opposed them. Considering the supply and material difficulties under which the Germans operated, the accomplishments of the German army during the battle for Aachen are all the more remarkable.

German Units at Aachen

The *12th, 49th, 353rd* and *526th Infantry Divisions* were the primary German non-motorized units engaged at Aachen.

Only the *12th* was at full strength (12,352 men), because it had just undergone refitting and regrouping before being sent to the city. This veteran unit was organized as a standard 1944 infantry division, with some 4,137 riflemen in 21 companies. It consisted of three infantry regiments of two battalions each, plus an independent fusilier battalion, for a total of seven infantry battalions. Artillery support included three battalions of 105mm howitzers and one of 150mm guns. Engineer, anti-tank and anti-aircraft battalions were also organic to the division, but all such units were horse drawn. Only the fusilier battalion was truck borne (or sometimes bicycle-borne), and was usually in reserve or used for pursuit. It generally received the best soldiers and equipment.

The *49th Infantry Division* was nearly destroyed as it fell back in front of the 19th U.S. Corps between the Albert Canal and the Westwall. In a period of about two weeks the division absorbed 4,326 replacements in the form of 10 independent battalions (two infantry, one replacement, two fortress machinegun, one fortress infantry, four air force fortress). Two of the regiments in the division simply ceased to exist, and it fought thereafter without any regimental organizations within it.

Even divisions considered completely destroyed often had a core of survivors—mainly staff, rear echelon personnel and specialist troops—and that was indeed all that was left of the *353rd Infantry Division*, when to that core was added a conglomeration of five independent battalions (one training, one replacement, one security, one air force fortress, one battle group) to allow the unit to go on fighting. In reality, though, this "division" had been reduced to nothing more than a weak regiment, lacking virtually every kind of support.

The *526th Infantry Division* had been a reserve formation, originally charged with handling the training of various units in the Aachen-Cologne area. But as the front reached the western German border in September, the *526th* was transferred to the field army to be used as a regular combat formation. It consisted of three infantry regiments of three or four battalions each, for a total of 11 weak infantry battalions. This division had an engineer battalion, but artillery support was limited to a single battalion of 105mm guns, and nearly all heavy and signals equipment was lacking. Total strength was 8,400 on 10 September. Originally set up as an administrative formation, the *526th* and its component units were inexperienced and ill-prepared to carry out front line combat duties.

In August 1944, a new type of infantry division—called *Volksgrenadier* (People's Infantry)—was introduced by the Germans. The creation of this new type of unit stemmed from the increasing manpower shortages. With an authorized strength of 10,072 men, the *Volksgrenadier* divisions' organization consisted of three infantry regiments of two battalions each, for a total of six infantry battalions. Front line infantry strength was drawn from 18 companies fielding a total of 3,616 riflemen.

This reduced manpower naturally decreased the staying power of the *Volksgrenadier* divisions in combat. There was an attempt to compensate for the smaller numbers by increasing the issue of such items as submachineguns and assault rifles, but such additions could never completely make up for the loss in personnel, especially during mobile operations.

Artillery support in the *Volksgrenadier* divisions included a battalion of 75mm guns, two battalions of 105mm howitzers, and a battalion of 150s. An engineer and a mixed anti-tank/anti-aircraft battalion were also standard elements, but all were horse drawn, and signals equipment was lacking.

The *183rd* and *246th Volksgrenadier Divisions* belonged to the first series of this new type of infantry unit. Unlike some of the later formations, these divisions contained cadres of veterans, and therefore their performance in combat came close to those of standard German infantry divisions. The two divisions were lacking their fusilier and field replacement battalions, along with their assault gun company (14 armored fighting vehicles). In addition, their authorized battalions of 75s were replaced by rocket projector battalions (18 launchers). Each was minus one 105mm and the 150mm battalion.

The 1944 panzer division got a good mix of infantry and armor from its one armored and two armored infantry regiments, for a total of 13,725 men. The allotted armored strength was set up in two battalions, one each of Mark IV and Mark V (Panther) tanks. The armored infantry regiments each had two battalions for a total of four, but only one battalion in the division was actually mounted in halftracks (the others were in trucks). The artillery was usually self-propelled, and consisted of three battalions of 105mm howitzers. Reconnaissance, armored engineer, and anti-tank battalions were organic to the divisions, along with anti-aircraft and service elements. The reconnaissance and armored engineer battalions played particularly important roles because they were often used to form the core of battle groups.

The elite status of the panzer divisions within the German army meant the best trained and more motivated individuals were usually found there. These units represented the most capable forces still available to the Germans, and even after long years of war the panzer division was still a match for its armored foes.

The *9th Panzer Division* had been reorganizing in a rear area when von Rundstedt ordered it into the Aachen Gap—at that time it was the only sizeable reserve available along the entire western front. Because the refitting and regrouping process was not yet complete, when the *9th* arrived in the combat zone it was merged with the remnants of *Panzer Brigade 105* and other diverse battalion-size reinforcements. During the battle for Aachen, then, the title *"9th Panzer Division"* was really only a term of convenience describing a hodge-podge of armor, infantry and artillery. The division never exceeded half its authorized strength, with a maximum of only about 50 armored fighting vehicles on hand.

The *116th Panzer Division* was one of the *Wehrmacht*'s truly elite formations and had an outstanding reputation based on its performance in both Normandy and Russia. But due to severe losses suffered during the withdrawal from the Falaise Pocket, the *116th* consisted of only two small battlegroups by the time the fighting around Aachen began. These battlegroups were organized around the division's former armored infantry regiments, and were supported by what was left of the armor (about 20 armored fighting vehicles of all kinds). The division's artillery units had ceased to exist, but two battalions of 105mm howitzers from the *81st Corps* were attached.

At the end of September, the *116th* was passed into reserve to be brought up to strength for the German counterattack in the Ardennes that December. But events forced it to be sent back into the Aachen gap in October. In the three week interim, the division was rebuilt to a strength of 11,500 men. This amazing rebuilding was possible only because the *116th* was run by experienced officers who had good personal connections to those in the German army high command, thereby getting top priority. In addition, as the reader should expect by this point, the *116th* also maintained a veteran enlisted cadre, as well as its own training and replacement units and combined-arms school.

A German *Panzergrenadier* (armored infantry) division was more a kind of motorized infantry outfit than it was a true armored formation. Its two armored infantry regiments were each made up of three battalions, for a total of six. Compared to a panzer division, these two additional armored infantry battalions tended to give the *panzergrenadiers* more staying power in defensive engagements while also allowing them to hold more frontage. Authorized strength was 13,876, but due to shortages of armored personnel carriers, all riflemen rode into battle on trucks. These divisions contained a single armor battalion, which was usually equipped with assault guns rather than tanks. The other elements of *Panzergrenadier* divisions were organized similarly to those within *Panzer* divisions, but with fewer self-propelled and armored components.

Having recently been in combat in Italy and Lorraine, the *3rd Panzergrenadier Division* was run down when it arrived in the Aachen sector in October. Its rifle strength was down by about half, and there were only 16 assault guns and nine tanks available. The artillery regiment had been reduced to two mixed battalions, both towed rather than self-propelled. The shortage of motor transport, particularly in the *3rd*'s support and supply services, was particularly acute.

The Germans also committed many independent, battle group and *ad hoc* units to the fighting around Aachen. These included tank, tank destroyer, assault gun, combat engineer, infantry, bicycle infantry, and convalescent battalions, as well as several kinds of artillery units. The tank and tank destroyer battalions were always understrength, with five to 20 operational vehicles.

The quality of the independent formations varied greatly. Some, like *Panzer Battalion 506* (Tigers), *Tank Destroyer Battalion 519* (Hunting Tiger tank destroyers), and two SS battle groups, were excellent units. Others, like *Convalescent Battalion D-6*, or *Police Battle Group "Aachen,"* were little more than armed mobs. In theory all the various independent units were under command of *81st Corps*, but in practice they were attached to the various divisions.

These independent and *ad hoc* units represented the beginning of the wave of cannon fodder formations Hitler threw together during the closing months of the war. A good example here is provided by the two battle groups from the NCO training schools at Düren and Jülich, committed to help hold the line against the U.S. 19th Corps offensive in October. Instead of using these highly motivated and experienced cadres as a core around which to rebuild other units, or as replacements for them, they were formed into a poorly equipped infantry battalion.

Also typical for the German army, a conglomeration of rare weapons could be found among the independent units. *Railroad Battery 723*, for example, was equipped with two Soviet-built 274mm railroad guns. Other units were based on crazy ideas, such as *Wireless Panzer*

Battalion 311, which was equipped with radio-controlled "tanks" (actually self-propelled demolition charges). They were to be directed into enemy lines and exploded there by remote control. But the machines' poor mobility and general unreliability, as well as their vulnerability to smoke (which made it impossible for their controllers to keep track of them as they advanced), rendered them almost totally ineffective.

Sources

Amberg, J. *Es kamen die schlimmsten Tage unseres Lebens. Der Raum Wuerselen im 2. Weltkrieg.* Wuerselen, 1986.

Bryant, A. *Sieg im Westen, 1943-1945.* Duesseldorf, 1960.

Christoffel, E. *Krieg am Westwall, 1944-45.* Trier, 1989.

Ewing, J.H. *Let's Go! A History of the 29th Infantry Division in World War II.* Washington, 1951.

Guderian, H.G. *Das letzte Kriegsjahr im Westen.* Sankt Augustin, 1994.

Hewitt, R.L. *Work Horse of the Western Front: The Story of the 30th Infantry Division.* Washington, 1946.

McDonald, C.B. *The U.S. Army in World War II: The European Theater of Operations.* Washington, 1963.

Poll, B. *Das Schicksal Aachens im Herbst 1944.* Aachen, 1961.

Trahan, E.A. *Hell on Wheels. A History of the Second United States Armored Division, 1940 to 1946.* Evansville, 1978.

Whiting, C. and Trees, W. *Wie Aachen 1944 erobert wurde.* Aachen, 1975.

Chapter XXVII

Budapest '45

by Pat McTaggart
with contributions by Peter B. Zwack

Hungary had been an active ally of Germany in the war against the Soviet Union since shortly after Operation Barbarossa began in June 1941; by October 1944, it was one of the few German allies left. It was not, however, faith in an eventual Axis victory that kept German and Hungarian soldiers fighting side by side.

Early in 1944, German intelligence had learned that Hungary's head of state, Adm. Nicholas Horthy, had begun secret negotiations with the Allies. Within days of that discovery, German forces had occupied most of the country in what was officially called in Berlin a "protective measure," forcing Horthy to break off his efforts at a separate peace. But as German fortunes continued to decline over the summer, Horthy once again put out feelers, hoping to end his country's involvement in the war before the fighting actually passed through it. The Hungarian army, the *Honved*, was being steadily decimated by the Soviets, and a few units had already defected to the advancing enemy.

August 1944 brought a devastating attack on the German and Romanian forces of Gen. Johannes Friessner's *Army Group South Ukraine*, which was occupying defense lines in northeastern Romania. During the ten days from 20 through 29 August, the Soviet 2nd and 3rd Ukrainian Fronts, (under Marshals R.Y. Malinovsky and F.I. Tolbukhin, respectively) knocked Romania out of the war and destroyed a large part of Friessner's army group. Red Army communiques claimed 150,000 German dead and 106,000 prisoners.

The situation in southeast Europe became even more critical for the Germans when the Communists swept across the Hungarian border in early October. Horthy was now more than ready for direct

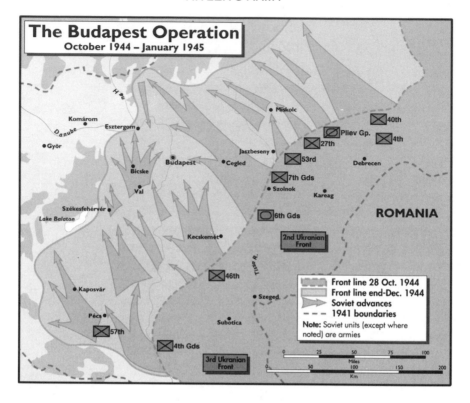

The Budapest Operation
October 1944 – January 1945

armistice talks, but once again German intelligence thwarted his efforts.

SS Maj. Otto Skorzeny—the commando who had earlier rescued Mussolini—was sent by Hitler to Budapest with a small detachment and told to correct the situation there. In a daring operation, Skorzeny and his men kidnapped Horthy's son Milos and spirited him away to Vienna. With Milos hostage, Horthy abandoned peace negotiations and surrendered his leadership of the Magyar state.

While German authorities took direct control of the Budapest government and its armed forces, Ferenc Szalasi, leader of the fascist Hungarian Arrow Cross Party, was installed as puppet leader. The destiny of Hungary was now completely bound to that of the Third Reich.

Advancing on Budapest

Though Skorzeny's actions somewhat stabilized the political situation in Hungary, the military position of Friessner's army group, which had been renamed *Army Group South*, remained shaky. With Tolbukhin's 3rd Ukrainian Front driving northwest from Romania, and Malinovsky's 2nd Ukrainian Front sweeping westward into Hungary, Friessner was forced to spread thin his already depleted units.

During the afternoon of 29 October, Malinovsky began an attack on the German line that he hoped would bring about the swift fall of Budapest. At the time, 2nd Ukrainian Front had at its disposal 600,000 Soviet and 35,000 Romanian troops, 750 tanks and 1,100 aircraft. Friessner's forces consisted of 330,000 German and 150,000 Hungarian troops. Several understrength panzer, panzer grenadier and Hungarian tank divisions contributed approximately 500 tanks to the Axis defense. Soviet artillery superiority was 4.5:1.

Even with such a healthy superiority over his opponents in men and equipment, Malinovsky had some apprehension about his assignment. His orders from Stalin were to capture Budapest as quickly as possible, at the latest by 3 or 4 November. But Malinovsky's units had been on the move for weeks, and the Marshal had wanted four or five days to consolidate and redeploy for a concerted drive on the city. Thus the Soviet field commander was caught in the tug of war that has plagued military men throughout the ages. The political leadership wanted a quick victory, and nothing would change that mindset. Disregarding Malinovsky's purely military concerns, Stalin ordered him to proceed on the 29th with whatever forces were on hand and ready to go.

Gen. I.T. Schlemin's 46th Army was picked to lead the way to Budapest via Kecslement. The 7th Guards Army (Gen. M.S. Schumilov) was ordered to establish bridgeheads on the western bank of the Tisza River, and the 40th, 27th and 53rd Armies were to advance toward Miskolc to tie down German forces in the north. The 7th Guards Army was supported by Gen. Pliyev's Mechanized Cavalry Group (4th and 6th Guards Cavalry Corps and 23rd Tank Corps), while 27th Army would have 5th Guards Cavalry Corps and 7th Mechanized Corps at its disposal.

The *3rd Hungarian Army* received the brunt of 46th Army's attack. The generally ill-equipped Hungarian units fought well in some sectors, but were no real match for the Soviets. By 1 November, the *3rd Army* was shattering, while the soldiers of the 46th Army had already advanced 20 to 40 kilometers along the entire sector of the attack.

The 7th Guards Army also made good progress during the first days of the offensive, securing a bridgehead 10 kilometers deep and 30 wide on the west bank of the Tisza. German and Hungarian forces, intermingled and fighting for their existence, could only reel with the blows as Soviet mechanized forces tore through their positions.

German *6th Army* Commander, Gen. of Artillery Maximilian Fretter-Pico, consolidated all German and Hungarian units in his sector (which was now redesignated *Army Detachment Fretter-Pico*) and desperately tried to stem the 7th Guards' advance. He was, however, in a truly untenable position, having already been forced to take some units out of the Tisza River line and send them south to battle 46th Army. That forced redeployment in turn allowed the 7th Guards to break out of its bridgeheads and push farther west. There was nothing for the German commander to do but abandon the Tisza line and retreat toward Budapest.

Malinovsky's main objective seemed to be within his grasp. Schlemin's 2nd and 4th Guards Mechanized Corps were fast approaching the southern suburbs of Budapest on 2 November, followed closely by the infantry of the 23rd Rifle Corps. The 7th Guards Army also continued to make good progress as it pursued retreating German and Hungarian units west of the Tisza. However, by moving back from the irregular Tisza line, Fretter-Pico was able to shorten his entire defensive position, thereby giving him the reserves necessary to launch a series of counterattacks against Schlemin's right flank. Armored battle groups from the *23rd* and *24th Panzer Divisions* caused serious losses to the 2nd and 4th Guards Mechanized Corps, which were both down to about 100 tanks.

Some Soviet tank units actually entered the suburbs of Budapest, where they were met by *ad hoc* German defense groups. The inhabitants of the eastern portions of the Hungarian capital were suddenly shocked at the sight of T-34s blazing away at Panzer IVs and Tigers literally outside their doors. A near panic ensued when a demolition charge went off accidentally, destroying several spans of one of the city's historic Danube River bridges.

By 5 November, the Soviet units inside the capital city were almost out of ammunition. Fretter-Pico's spoiling attacks continued to divert Schlemin's reserves to the flanks, leaving little hope for a quick capture of Budapest. The next day, Schlemin ordered a withdrawal to regroup and bring up supplies. Malinovsky's apprehension had been justified. With a little more time and planning, the Hungarian capital might have fallen easily. Now another solution would have to be found to capture the prize Stalin wanted.

Fretter-Pico had reprieved Budapest by deftly switching his mobile forces to the most critical areas of the Soviet offensive. In doing so he gave his infantry units time to dig in and construct a formidable new defensive position south of the city. Those units were then fleshed out with stragglers from the *3rd Hungarian Army*, who were rounded up by field police combing the area.

The Soviet commanders realized the enemy defenses south of Budapest would be a tough obstacle to overcome; Malinovsky therefore decided to redeploy in an effort to form an envelopment in the north. He ordered 4th and 6th Guards Cavalry Corps, 23rd Tank Corps and Pliyev's Cavalry Mechanized Group to the Cegled area, where he planned to begin a new drive on 10 November.

The start was delayed one day due to attacks from battle groups of the German *1st, 13th, 23rd* and *24th Panzer Divisions*, supported by heavy panzer battalions *503* and *509* (both fielding King Tigers). Meanwhile, as Soviet forces got into their jump off positions, the German and Hungarian troops in front of them worked feverishly to build "hedgehog" all-around defensive positions behind the front line.

Malinovsky's attack began on the 11th, but instead of the hoped for lightning armored thrust, the effort quickly turned into a plodding battle of attrition. The Axis soldiers fought for every kilometer of ground, retreating from one prepared defensive position to the next. Still, the weight of Soviet men and material began to tell, and the Axis line bent to the breaking point. By 15 November, the Soviets had gone about 40 kilometers. At the same time, 3rd Ukrainian Front began operations, with Gen. N.A. Gagan's 57th Army pushing across the Danube and establishing bridgeheads on the west bank south of Budapest. Reinforcements were immediately sent across the river to consolidate and expand the lodgments.

In the north, Schlemin's 37th Guards Rifle Corps crossed the eastern channel of the Danube, and after two days of heavy fighting against the Hungarian *1st Cavalry Division* occupied Csepel Island. Malinovsky's other forces continued to take Axis defensive positions, threatening Miskolc. Meanwhile on 26 November, 57th Army, supported by the newly arrived 4th Guards Army, attacked from its bridgeheads, drawing German armor southward in an effort to contain that advance.

The last week of November saw the 2nd and 3rd Ukrainian Fronts work in concert to encircle the Hungarian capital. On 28 November, Gagan's 57th Army (64th and 75th Rifle Corps and 6th Guards Rifle Corps) was fighting for control of Pecs, a town about 80 kilometers south of Lake Balaton. By 30 November, 3rd Ukrainian Front had occupied the west bank of the Danube to within 80 kilometers south of Budapest, while the 2nd Ukrainian continued to advance, driving back Axis forces northwest of the city.

Malinovsky halted his offensive briefly to redeploy, but Tolbukhin continued to push, reaching the southern shore of Lake Balaton on 4 December. *Army Group Fretter-Pico* suddenly faced the real possibility of being surrounded and destroyed by the armored pincers of the two fronts.

Malinovsky used the respite in his attack wisely. He brought Lt. Gen. A.G. Kravchenko's newly refitted 6th Guards Tank Army (5th Guards Tank Corps and 9th Guards Mechanized Corps) in beside the Pliyev Group, now composed of 4th Guards and 6th Guards Cavalry Corps along with 4th Guards Mechanized Corps. The 7th Guards Army would provide the infantry support for the mechanized units.

The 2nd Ukrainian Front resumed its offensive on 5 December in a sector held by three understrength German divisions (*357th Infantry*, *13th Panzer* and *18th SS Panzer Grenadier*). With a force of more than 500 tanks and self-propelled guns, the Soviets breached the line in several places, pouring reinforcements through the gaps. By 8 December, 6th Guards Tank Army was within striking distance of Estergom, 30 kilometers northwest of Budapest.

South of Budapest, Schlemin's 46th Army sent its 37th Rifle Corps against a line held by the *271st Volksgrenadier Division*. But those German infantrymen proved a hard nut to crack, holding on grimly, making the Soviets pay for every meter of ground. Their efforts allowed Fretter-Pico to build yet another defensive line using elements of the *8th Panzer Division*, the *1st Hungarian Tank Division* and an SS police regiment. That line, which ran from Lake Valencse along the rail and road system northwest to the town of Erd, brought the Soviet southern attack to a grinding halt as the 37th Rifle Corps was pummeled by counterattacks from *8th Panzer*. An NCO of the *8th*'s reconnaissance battalion, Sgt. Maj. Walter Böhm, later wrote a description of the high morale of his unit at the time: "No one thought of giving up. We attacked again and again, destroying several Soviet infantry units and stopping others dead in their tracks."

Budapest '45

German and Hungarian Forces Engaged Around Budapest January 1945

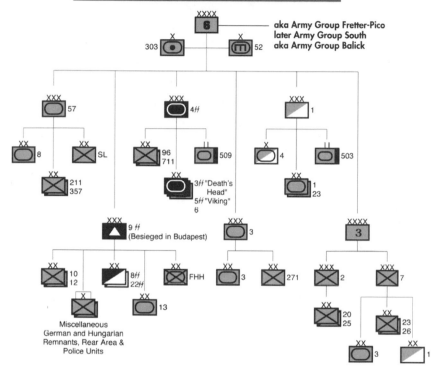

aka Army Group Fretter-Pico
later Army Group South
aka Army Group Balick

Arriving later as Reinforcements

Malinovsky tried shifting the axis of the southern attack to 4th Guards Army sector, which had been placed under 2nd Ukrainian Front's command. The 4th Guards advanced, only to be stopped on a defensive line running from Lake Velencse to Lake Balaton that was occupied by the *1st* and *23rd Panzer Divisions*.

Stymied in the south, Malinovsky looked to his northern armies, hoping for success there. Indeed, 6th Guards Tank Army, supported by infantry from 7th Guards Army, was gaining large amounts of territory, but none of it was significant. Also, as the drive fanned out it became overextended, inviting still more German counterattacks. The German defense, coupled with the effects of the hilly terrain there,

349

finally slowed 6th Guards. Malinovsky reacted by once again shifting his mechanized spearheads, hoping to obtain the decisive break-through. He sent 5th Guards Tank Corps to join 9th Guard Mechanized Corps in a combined assault into the Hron River valley.

By 13 December, the two corps were entering the valley when Fretter-Pico countered by moving most of *8th Panzer Division* to the area to bolster the defending units already there (*2nd Hungarian Tank Division, 357th Infantry Division* and the *SS Dirlewanger Brigade*). Still, the corps continued to advance during the following days, threatening to sever the communications between *Army Group Fretter-Pico* and the forces to the north. More German reinforcements (*3rd* and *6th Panzer Divisions*) were rushed in as a result of the dangerous situation, then split into several combat groups in an effort to defend both flanks of the beleaguered army group.

But 6th Guards Tank Army continued its westward movement, establishing bridgeheads across several minor rivers that flowed through the area. Whenever possible, local German commanders would attempt to destroy such positions before they could be expanded. Individual tactical successes, however, could not stop the Soviet steamroller everywhere. While elements of the *3rd* and *6th Panzer Divisions* were still heading north, 6th Guards Tank Army finally broke through the lines of the *357th Infantry Division*. Group Pliyev moved to exploit the gap.

The same day, 20 December, Schlemin's 46th Army and Galanin's 4th Guards Army renewed their attacks on both sides of Lake Valencse. The Axis positions there, weakened by the absence of the units just sent to the north, were pierced in several places.

The Soviets advanced relentlessly during the week that followed. On 21 December, 6th Guards Tank Army wheeled south, followed by Group Pliyev, while 46th Army, supported by 2nd Guards Mechanized Corps, advanced toward Val. Meanwhile, 4th Guards Army and 76th Mechanized Corps battled elements of *3rd Panzer Division* for the vital communication center of Szekesfehervar.

Two days later both those places were in Soviet hands, and the 18th Tank Corps, which had been brought up to reinforce 46th Army, was fighting for the key road junction of Bicske. The offensive continued without let up as the northern and southern Soviet pincers drove toward each other. On 24 December, 18th Tank Corps took Bicske and, with infantry units following closely, fought north toward Estergom to meet forward elements of 6th Guards Tank Army.

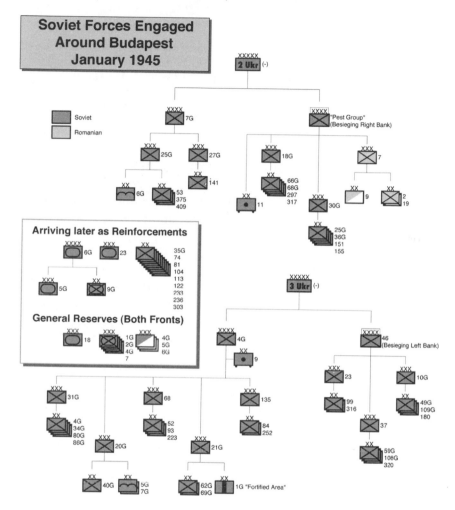

Budapest Encircled

The encirclement of Budapest was completed on 26 December. Inside the city, 70,000 German and Hungarian troops were trapped. Gen. Karl von Pfeffer-Wildenbruch, commander of *9th SS Mountain Corps*, was appointed overall commander of what was now renamed "Fortress Budapest." His forces consisted of the *13th Panzer, Feldherrnhalle Panzergrenadier, 8th SS Cavalry*, and *22nd SS Cavalry Divisions*, elements of the *4th SS Panzergrenadier* and *271st Volksgrenadier Divisions*, and several smaller independent units.

The Hungarian forces present, about 55 percent of the garrison's personnel, were under the command of Lt. Gen. Ivan Hindy. The *10th* and *12th Infantry Divisions* formed the bulk of Hindy's forces; the rest were units from the *1st Tank Division, 1st Cavalry Division, Guard Battalion Budapest,* an engineer battalion, a battalion of university students, and the city police force. Artillery support was provided by an anti-aircraft group of 160 guns.

As the Soviets had crossed the Hungarian border in the fall of 1944, the stockpiling of weapons, ammunition and other supplies had begun in Budapest. A network of trenches and strongpoints were built along the outlying areas of the city, and buildings in the city proper were turned into fortresses.

Appeals for the civilian population to evacuate had been received mostly with indifference by the city's million-plus inhabitants. Not fanatics, most simply wanted the war to pass them by and be over without their having to become refugees. Feeding that population became suddenly more difficult when, on 26 December, the Soviets captured one of Budapest's huge supply depots. Some 300,000 daily rations and 450 tons of ammunition were lost. Thus, as the new year approached, the citizens of Hungary's capital found themselves increasingly without fuel, water, electricity and food. It was the beginning of more than a month of suffering and death.

While the Soviet ring had been closing around Budapest, changes were occurring in the German command structure. Incensed by the continuous Soviet advances, Hitler sacked Friessner and Fretter-Pico. Gen. Otto Wöhler took over *Army Group South* and Gen. Hermann Balck replaced Fretter-Pico as commander of the German *6th* and Hungarian *2nd Armies*. It was to be up to those two men to reestablish Budapest as part of the main front. To assist them, Hitler transferred the elite *4th SS Panzer Corps*, consisting of the *3rd SS* ("Death's Head") and the *5th SS* ("Viking") *Panzer Divisions*, to Hungary on 24 December.

In setting up this New Year's scenario, the Soviets had rerun the classic double pincer maneuver they had used so successfully at Stalingrad two years earlier. Budapest itself was surrounded by the 7th Guards and 46th Armies, while almost 40 kilometers to the west the new front line ran from Lake Balaton in the south to the Danube between Komarno and Estergom in the north.

As the *4th SS Panzer Corps* moved south, the battle for Budapest itself had already begun. During the final days of December, three corps of the Soviet 46th Army (23rd, 37th and 10th Guards) engaged the *8th SS "Florian Geyer" Cavalry Division* and units from the *271st*

Volksgrenadier Division in the hilly suburbs of Buda, on the river's left bank.

Sgt. Friedrich Buck, then 22 and commanding a 400-man battle group of the *8th SS*, later recalled that early stage of the street fighting: "It was the most savage [fighting] I had ever seen. We fought man to man with bayonet, entrenching tools and grenades. The Soviets hit U.S. night and day without let up."

Buck's group held its own against combined armored and infantry attacks, often outnumbered 15 or 20:1. But no matter how many casualties the Soviets took, their superiority in men and equipment allowed them to fill the gaps in their ranks and attack again.

While Schlemin's units edged forward in Buda, the 7th Guards Army struck at the *1st Hungarian Tank Division* defending the southern sector of Pest, on the east bank. At the same time, the 18th Independent Guards Rifle Corps battled the Hungarian anti-aircraft guns arrayed along the main rail line, and drove the *22nd SS "Maria Theresa" Cavalry* and *12th Hungarian Infantry Divisions* from the outlying areas of Veceses and Rakoszsaba.

The Axis forces in Budapest fought hard for every block. Red Army Col. M.M. Malakhov later recalled: "The closer the Soviet troops drew into Budapest, the more desperate the enemy resistance became . . . The advancing troops had to overcome a maze of trenches, wire entanglements, anti-tank ditches and concentrated fire from all [kinds of] weapons. They had to take each building by storm and blast their way through roadblocks and barricades."

Inside the Axis lines the agony grew as unburied bodies lay rotting in the streets. Soviet artillery added to the carnage already being caused by the Red Air Force. Wood, coal and heating oil quickly became scarce, and many older people and young children froze to death. *Luftwaffe* pilots, flying Ju-52 transports, were able to bring in some ammunition and fuel, while He-111 bombers were used to drop other supplies by parachute. Soviet anti-aircraft guns brought down several of the planes every day, but enough got through to keep the garrison fighting. The morale of the fighting men remained high even though they were encircled. Garrison scuttlebutt told of a coming relief attack.

Soviet intelligence also knew an attack was coming, but they didn't know exactly where or when it would hit. Anticipating incorrectly, Malinovsky shifted his reserves and mobile forces south to bolster the area around Lake Balaton. He felt the German attack would surely

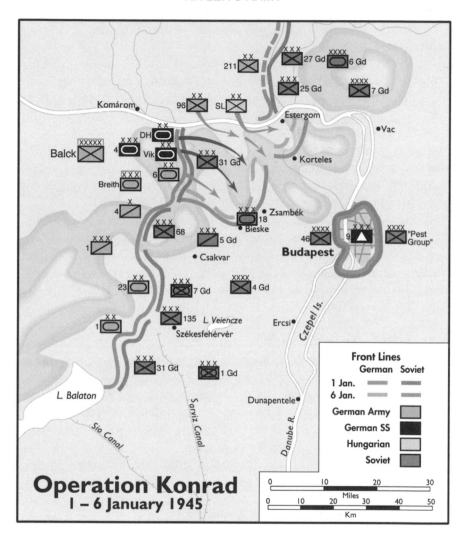

Operation Konrad
1 – 6 January 1945

Front Lines
German   Soviet
1 Jan.
6 Jan.
German Army
German SS
Hungarian
Soviet

| 0 | | 10 | | 20 | | 30 |
Miles
| 0 | 10 | 20 | 30 | 40 | 50 |
Km

have to come from that direction instead of through the wooded hills that dominated the northern approaches.

Operation Conrad

The relief operation, codenamed "Operation Conrad," began on New Year's Day 1945. While units of the *4th SS Panzer Corps* were still detraining, assault groups from the *96th Infantry Division* crossed the ice choked Danube eight kilometers west of Estergom under cover of darkness. By midday, those men were striking into the rear areas of the 31st Guards Rifle Corps.

At 10:30 p.m., *4th SS Panzer Corps* (now with the *96th* and *711th Infantry Divisions* attached) hit the already rattled 31st Guards with more than 250 panzers. The Soviets, caught flat-footed by the attack, were forced to retreat eastward. South of the *4th SS*, battle groups of the *6th* and *8th Panzer Divisions* ("Group Pape") hammered the 34th Guards Rifle Division, achieving a breakthrough there as well.

To further confuse Soviet intelligence, the *3rd Panzer Corps* and *1st Cavalry Corps* also opened an attack at 11:30 p.m. in the area just west of Szekesfehervar. Luckily, Malinovsky had armored reserves (1st and 7th Guards Mechanized Corps) close to the frontline in that sector. As the panzers battered their way through the forward Soviet trenches and anti-tank positions, orders were already being transmitted for the two Guards corps to move up and engage the attacking enemy.

The next day saw the German advance continue in the north. The 18th Tank Corps, hampered by snow covered roads and hilly terrain, moved slowly forward to meet the *4th SS Panzer Corps*. Malinovsky also sent two divisions from around the Budapest perimeter to support the wavering 31st Guards Rifle Corps. Despite those moves, and the German gains northwest of Budapest, Soviet intelligence remained convinced the diversionary attack toward Szekesfehervar was actually the main relief attempt.

On 3 January, the tempo of the *4th SS Panzer Corps'* advance increased as battle groups from *"Viking"* and *"Death's Head"* breached hastily erected Soviet defenses. House to house fighting raged in the villages lying across the attack sector.

Alarmed at those successes, Malinovsky ordered the 7th Guards Mechanized, 1st Guards Mechanized, 5th Guards Cavalry and 21st Rifle Corps away from the Szekesfehervar area and sent them north to stop the SS. After that the Germans in the north continued to make some progress, but there always seemed to be just enough fresh Soviet units arriving to prevent a clean breakthrough.

Soviet air power also became a factor in slowing the German drive. When the weather permitted, Red Air Force planes roamed the daytime skies at will, strafing and bombing German columns on the ground. With the Ardennes offensive still in full swing on the western front, the *Luftwaffe* was a rare sight in the Hungarian skies. The stubbornness of his front line soldiers' resistance gave Malinovsky time to form a second defense position. Coupled with the arrival of

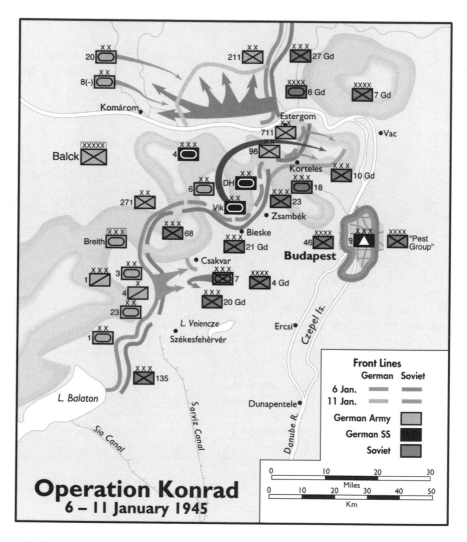

Operation Konrad
6 – 11 January 1945

reinforcements from the south, the shattered divisions of the 31st Rifle Corps managed to hold on.

On 4 January, the *Viking Division* was able to advance only five kilometers. Outside the key road junction at Bicske, 25 kilometers east of Budapest, they ran into a strong line of anti-tank and machinegun emplacements manned by the 41st Guards Rifle Division. The SS grenadiers charged those positions time and again, but the Guardsmen held and the attack ground to a halt.

In an effort to bypass the block, the commander of *Viking*'s panzer regiment, Lt. Col. Fritz Darges, led a battle group to probe for weak spots. In the dead of night they managed to breach a thinly held section of the line. The battle group then surprised a Soviet column, destroying a dozen trucks, four 122mm cannon, four 76mm anti-tank guns and large number of horsedrawn supply wagons. Continuing, Darges and his men assaulted Regis Castle, located on a commanding hill two kilometers northwest of Bicske. The Soviet garrison there retreated, but reinforcements were already rushing to the area to retake the position from the infiltrating Germans.

Darges organized his unit into an all-around defensive posture, firing on enemy supply columns on the road below and fighting off concentrated Soviet armored and infantry attacks. The battle group held against the Soviet assaults for three days. Around the castle walls and inside the courtyard, fierce hand to hand combat and grenade duels were waged. The battle group was finally relieved by other elements from *SS Viking Division* during the night of 7 January. In the snow surrounding the castle, 30 Soviet tanks lay burned and blackened.

But Malinovsky continued to funnel more units into the Bicske area, and soon even the most optimistic German commanders began to see a penetration was no longer possible there. Wöhler ordered Balck to give the southern force the go ahead for an all out assault to Szekesfehervar.

Once again Malinovsky was forced to redeploy his mechanized forces to meet a new threat. The new push by units of the *3rd* and *23rd Panzer Divisions* and the *4th Cavalry Brigade* forced back the 20th Guards Rifle Corps and part of the 7th Guards Mechanized Corps. But the momentum of the German attack was lost as the panzers came up against a strong Soviet secondary line.

Faced with another failed attack, Wöhler ordered Balck to make a final attempt in the north. *Viking Division* was pulled out of the line in front of Bicske and moved north, reassembling on the left flank of the *96th Infantry Division* just south of Estergom. At 10:30 p.m. on 10 January, *Viking* hit the defensive positions of the 86th Guards Rifle Division. The Soviets were again taken completely by surprise. As the Guards reeled under the assault, units of the 2nd Guards Mechanized Corps were sent to try to contain the German breakthrough, but the attacking SS could not be stopped.

Many of *Viking*'s soldiers had friends in the encircled units in Budapest. One member of the division, wounded early in the fighting, wrote: "My wound is not especially painful. I want to go back to the

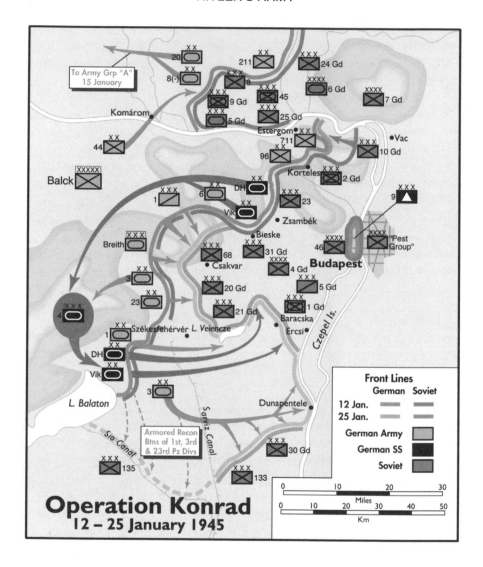

Operation Konrad
12 – 25 January 1945

Front Lines
German   Soviet
12 Jan.
25 Jan.

German Army
German SS
Soviet

troop, for I know Maj. Gen. Jochen Rumohr, commander of the *8th SS Cavalry Division*, and I am very eager to help him."

The attack continued to make progress. On 12 January, *Viking Division* took Pilisszentkereszt. By the next day, advanced elements of the division were within 21 kilometers of the Hungarian capital. It seemed success was just one day away; from one hill the SS men could see the steeples of Budapest through their field glasses.

Then the inexplicable happened. At 10:00 p.m. on the 13th, *4th SS Panzer Corps'* commander, Gen. Herbert Gille, received a message from *Army Group South* ordering him to abandon the attack. The men of *Viking* were stunned when Gille relayed the order. "I am certain the [northern] relief effort would have been a success," recalled Fritz Darges. "The [men at the] head of our assault unit could see the panorama of the city in their binoculars. We were disappointed and we could not believe the attack was stopped. Our morale was excellent, and we knew we could free our comrades the next day."

Gille echoed Darges' surprise and anger. He appealed to Balck and Wöhler to retract the order, but to no avail. The appreciation of the situation "at the highest levels" (that is, Hitler's headquarters) was that the northern effort had run its course and nothing decisive could be expected there. In direct contradiction of the German offensive doctrine that stressed the importance of relying on the judgment of subordinates on the spot, *4th SS Panzer Corps* was directed to redeploy southward to new positions near Lake Balaton. From there they would launch yet another attempt to lift the siege of Budapest. Hitler also added a new element to the plan. Not only was Budapest to be saved, but the bulk of the Soviet 4th Guards and 46th Armies was to be destroyed.

Fall of Pest

While the panzers rolled south, the noose around Budapest continued to tighten. Constant bombing and shelling made the streets impassable. Ammunition was at a premium and casualties were mounting at an alarming rate. On 12 January, the Soviets breached the main defense line on the outskirts of Pest. Their units rushed through the gaps, and hand to hand fighting became the order of the day across that side of the city. Using everything from pistols and hand grenades to bayonets and flame throwers, Soviet, German and Hungarian soldiers fought block by block and room by room.

By the 17th, it was clear to Pfeffer-Wildenbruch that Pest could no longer be held. He ordered an evacuation, and during the night the remnants of the Pest garrison crossed the Danube to the dubious safety of Buda. By 7:00 a.m. on the 18th, the evacuation was completed and the remaining bridges spanning the Danube were blown up.

Attack in the South

At 5:00 a.m., just two hours before the bridges were destroyed, a brief artillery barrage signaled the beginning of the new German offensive. The *4th SS Panzer Corps*, together with *3rd Panzer Corps*, smashed into the Soviet line from Szekesfehervar to Lake Balaton. In the Bicske area, the recently redeployed *1st Cavalry Corps* also began an attack.

That day the 62nd Guards Rifle Division, defending the Bicske road junction against *1st Cavalry's* assault, fought with outstanding bravery. Attack after attack withered in front of their defensive positions. Once again German plans were disrupted by nothing more than the steadfastness of the Soviet soldier.

But south of Szekesfehervar, the combined punch of four panzer divisions (*1st, 3rd, 3rd SS* and *5th SS*) produced wide gaps in the lines of the 135th Guards Rifle and 7th Guards Mechanized Corps. The panzers were able to advance as much as 25 kilometers on the 18th. The German attacks were also supported by 135 aircraft from the *Luftwaffe*—a rarity at this stage of the war. Though Soviet hedgehog defenses dotted the landscape, the *3rd Panzer Division* led the way by making the initial outflanking move that opened the enemy defenses.

Malinovsky felt confident enough about the 62nd Guards' defense of Bicske to take the 18th Tank Corps away from there and send it south. He also ordered 5th Guards Cavalry Corps to head that way and set up a new defensive line running from Lake Velencse to the Danube town of Adony. Another rifle corps, the 133rd (21st, 122nd, and 184th Rifle Divisions) was taken out of reserve east of the Danube to form a line west of Dunapentele.

But the reinforcements coming from the east bank didn't have time to form a cohesive defense. Forward elements of *3rd Panzer Division* reached the outskirts of Dunapentele on the 19th, while the *Death's Head* and *Viking Divisions* got into a running battle with the 18th Tank Corps. The fluidity of the situation in the south allowed German battle groups to forge ahead, bypassing many strong Soviet defensive positions. By the 21st, some 20 kilometers of the west bank of the Danube north of Dunapentele was in German hands, but fighting also continued to rage far to the west.

Soviet units that had been bypassed held out in their fortified positions in villages and crossroads. German units following their armored spearheads had to fight their way through those hornets' nests at every turn. Key villages changed hands daily as Soviet forces appeared out of nowhere, overwhelming small German garrisons.

While most of *4th SS Panzer Corps* engaged in a wild melee near the river, *1st Panzer Division* fought a fierce battle for control of

Szekesfehervar. There 69th Guards Rifle Division withstood the on-slaught for three days before being forced out of the town. With Szekesfehervar under German control, Malinovsky felt compelled to pull back his entire line in that area by five kilometers. That movement in turn allowed *23rd Panzer Division*, until then engaged north of the town, to take over *1st Panzer's* sector, which released it for the battle going on farther to the east.

By 22 January, the entire Soviet position between Lake Velencse and Adony was cracking. The 5th Guards Cavalry Corps had been reinforced by 1st Guards Mechanized Corps, but the line continued to be pushed northward. The *Viking Division* had captured another 10 kilometers of the Danube's west bank north of Adony. To that division's left, *Death's Head* and *1st Panzer* had secured the key town of Kapolnasnjek on Lake Velencse. The entire Soviet position west and south of Budapest was in jeopardy.

Malinovsky's problems were not confined to the southern sector. Battle groups from *6th Panzer* and *3rd Cavalry Divisions* made a successful push east of Bicske, forcing a break in the Soviet line at the junction of 4th Guards and 19th Rifle Divisions. About 25 kilometers was now all that separated the Germans' northern and southern advanced units. If they could meet, a large portion of the 4th Guards and 46th Armies would indeed by cut off, just as Hitler had planned.

There were several factors, though, that began to hamper the German advance. Air support remained spotty at best, and the deep snow and narrow roads made movement difficult. But the two most important factors were the lack of adequate infantry support to cover the panzer units' flanks, and the masterful way Malinovsky kept shuffling his reserves from one crisis to the next.

On 20 January, that Soviet commander had already ordered 30th Guards Rifle Corps out of Pest to reinforce 133rd Rifle Corps near Dunafoldvar. Units from the 68th Rifle Corps were sent to bolster the 5th Guards Cavalry Corps near Baracska. The Marshal also detached the 233rd Rifle Division, 236th Rifle Division, and 32nd Guards Motorized Rifle Brigade from the 57th Army and placed them under the control of the 135th Rifle Corps south of Lake Balaton.

While Malinovsky moved again to counter the Germans, the two lead panzer corps pressed their attack. On 23 January, the left flank of *1st Panzer Division* drove farther along the northern shore of Lake Velencse. The rest of the division joined with *Death's Head* to crack the strong Soviet defenses south of Baracska, while *Viking* redeployed north of Adony, probing for new weak spots.

The next two days saw the fighting reach even higher levels of intensity as *4th SS Panzer Corps* sought to break through the Baracska line. Southeast of that town a combined thrust by the *1st Panzer* and *Death's Head Divisions* pushed units of the 5th Guards Cavalry Corps toward the Danube. But the dug in Soviets exacted a heavy toll from the attackers. The battles raged under heavy snowfall and in temperatures as low as -5 C. Supported by *Heavy Panzer Battalion 509*'s King Tiger tanks, the Germans gained more ground. In one 20 minute action, the *509* destroyed 15 Soviet tanks and 50 anti-tank guns.

Still attempting to find a way around or through the Baracska defenses, Gen. Gille ordered *Viking* to relieve *Death's Head* south of the town. On 25 January, a new attack force put together from the *1st*

Panzer and *Death's Head* divisions swept aside the 223rd Rifle Division and advanced to the southwest bank of the Vali Canal, the last geographic barrier of any significance on the road to Budapest.

But as their attack in the south seemed to be making headway, the German effort in the north ran out of steam. The fierce defense of the 62nd Guards Rifle Division at Bicske, coupled with Soviet reinforcements arriving from other sectors, had forced *1st Cavalry Corps* to go over to a defensive posture.

After almost a month of continuous combat, Gille's corps had been reduced to a shadow of the force he commanded on New Year's Day. On the evening of the 25th, he reported to *Army Group South* his command had a strength of only five Panzer IIIs and IVs, 27 Panthers, 11 Tigers and King Tigers, and seven assault guns—a mere 50 machines in an entire corps.

Still, in the early hours of the 26th, the attackers pushed forward again. As dawn broke, the area southwest of the Vali Canal was cleared of defenders and a bulge was formed in the Soviet lines on the other side. The panzergrenadiers managed to advance to the outskirts of Val before being stopped by a combined infantry/mechanized force. The Germans could go no farther—Budapest was only 20 kilometers away and the northern pincer of *1st Cavalry Corps* only about half that distance. Charred hulls of Panther and Tiger tanks dotted the Hungarian landscape, intermingled with T-34s and American lend-lease Shermans.

Malinovsky had indeed shown himself to be a master of maneuver. As the Germans approached Val, he sent the 23rd Tank and 104th Rifle Corps into the area as reinforcements. At the same time, the German reconnaissance units holding the *4th SS Panzer Corps'* front around Dunafoldvar began to receive probing attacks from the 18th Tank, 133rd Rifle and 30th Guards Rifle Corps.

With the *4th SS* stalled before Val, and their southern flank dangerously weak, Malinovsky felt it was time to go over to the offensive. That attack, which began on 27 January, quickly overcame the weak German defenses near Dunafoldvar. In another week of heavy fighting, 26th, 46th and 4th Guards Armies regained all the territory lost during January. By 3 February, the Germans were back to their original December positions. Malinovsky could now focus his attention on destroying the garrison in Budapest.

Fall of Buda

Even while the *4th SS* had been trying to reach the capital, the city's defenders were steadily being squeezed into an area surrounding the hills of Buda. Once Pest had fallen, Malinovsky was able to concentrate his forces on the western side of the Danube. The German relief effort drew units from the siege, but never enough to bring the Soviet attacks there to a halt.

By 19 January, the garrison held a line that ran a little more than a kilometer along the Danube. The main defenses inside Buda centered on Castle Hill, a heavily fortified area that reached out about a kilometer in every direction from the center of that promontory. Inside and around that cauldron, Soviet and Axis soldiers paid in blood for every small advance and retreat.

The last week of January brought first hope, then despair, to the garrison. The final collapse of the *4th SS Panzer Corps'* relief attempt put an end to all illusions outside help was on its way. Air drops were still being carried out by the *Luftwaffe*, but the Axis perimeter had become so small most of those supplies landed behind Soviet lines. The increasing lack of food, water and fuel began to affect soldiers and civilians alike. The freezing temperatures added to the misery of those huddling in cellars for protection against Soviet artillery and bombers.

Street by street, the Germans and Hungarians retreated. Casualties were so severe the *9th SS Mountain Corps'* diary entry for 29 January noted the number of wounded would soon surpass the number on duty. Daily rations for the garrison members had by that time fallen to five grams of lard and 75 grams of bread, supplemented by a bowl of horsemeat soup.

The Soviet attacks continued unabated. They drove wedges into the Castle Hill position on 3 February. Reserves were then pushed into the gaps; soon several key positions, including some on the hilltop itself, were in Red hands. The south railway station fell on the 7th after prolonged hand to hand combat.

During the next two days, Soviet troops captured still more territory in the western and southern areas of the city, overrunning the artillery positions there. The *Luftwaffe* was no longer of any practical use, and only a lucky few were still able to find anything to eat.

Pfeffer-Wildenbruch knew the end was near, but was determined not to surrender. He called his divisional commanders together and announced his intention to break out of the city with or without outside help or approval. (Hitler wanted the siege broken and the city held, not the garrison to escape.) The men were to be divided into battle groups that would infiltrate their way through the encircling Soviet units while a picked rearguard kept enemy at bay as long as possible.

The breakout began during the night of 11 February, when lead elements of the *8th SS Cavalry* and *13th Panzer Divisions* pierced the lines of the 180th Rifle Division. Approximately 20,000 to 30,000 men took part in the attempt. Half of the original garrison had already been killed, and about 10,000 of the seriously wounded were left behind.

Soviet reinforcements immediately rushed to the area. The Red Army artillery that had been pounding Buda for weeks rained tons of shells upon the desperate escapees. The commanders of the *8th SS, 22nd SS* and *13th Panzer Divisions* were all killed in action before the sun rose, while Pfeffer-Wildenbruch was wounded and taken prisoner a few hours later.

The battle groups shrank steadily as they ran into more and more Soviet units. The Axis soldiers had abandoned their heavy weapons to gain mobility, but without them the German and Hungarian troops were no match for the Soviets blocking their path. Machineguns, artillery and air strikes all took their toll during the next few days. Of the original 70,000 man garrison of "Fortress Budapest," only about 700 made it safely back to the main German front.

Postscript

Soviet and Axis forces continued to fight in Hungary throughout February and March. Hitler's obsession with defending what was left of the country finally led to one of the largest tank battles of the war fought out in the mud around Lake Balaton in early March.

The Soviets finally succeeded occupied all of Hungary in April and then swept north, taking Vienna. A quicker Soviet victory might have been achieved in southeast Europe if the Red Army units tied down in the siege of Budapest had been available continuously along the main front. In that respect, then, the Budapest garrison did its job. However, the Germans' repeated efforts to relieve the city cost them most of what was left of their mobile forces in the area—strength sorely missed when the Soviets later advanced into Germany proper.

But the suffering endured by the civilians of Budapest, as well as that of the soldiers of both sides who fought to control the city, was perhaps the greatest tragedy of all.

The Defenders of Budapest

The most formidable element of the Axis garrison of Budapest was undoubtedly the *Feldherrnhalle Panzergrenadier Division*. A regular-army formation, the *FHH* had been constituted around the remnants of the *60th Panzergrenadier Division* annihilated at Stalingrad. The veterans evacuated by plane out of the cauldron on the Volga two years before found themselves once again encircled in Budapest. The division had about 8,000 effectives in the pocket (part of one regiment and some divisional artillery were not ensnared), and was equipped with 25 Panther and Mk. IV tanks, along with a full battalion of superb 150mm Hummel self-propelled howitzers. The *FHH* fought mostly in Pest until the evacuation into Buda on 17/18 January. The bulk of the breakout survivors (about 170) came from the *FHH*.

The other principal German army formation in Budapest was the *13th Panzer Division*. It had led the spearheads into the Caucasus in 1942, and distinguished itself in the following two years of defensive fighting. Heavy losses east of the Danube reduced its strength to approximately 3,000 men, mostly tankers, artillerymen and support troops, with about 20 Panther and Mk. IV tanks plus the bulk of the division's Hummel battalion.

Heavy anti-aircraft and gun support was provided by the *12th Flak Regiment*, consisting of sixty 88mm guns, four batteries of heavy 105mm guns, and eight Mk. IV mounted 20mm Vierling anti-aircraft guns. The remaining German formations were of the *ad hoc* type so common in the latter part of the war. Among these was an 800-man battlegroup, *Kampfgruppe Kundinger*, from elements of the *271st Volksgrenadier Division*. There were also a number of *Splinterverband* (splinter units), including four "alarm" battalions put together from sick and lightly wounded soldiers who were used to man relatively quite sectors.

The Waffen SS contributed two cavalry divisions. The *8th SS Cavalry Division "Florian Geyer"* had fought well in Russia since 1942. With a nucleus of tough and experienced German officers and NCOs, about half the 8,000 men were ethnic-Germans from Hungary, Bessarabia,

Transylvania and the Banat. Key combat multipliers were its anti-tank battalion, which included 10 Hetzer assault guns, and one 150mm and two 105mm towed artillery battalions. This division also had an effective flak battalion comprised mostly of the dreaded (towed) 88mm guns that would prove deadly in the final Buda hill fighting.

The *22nd SS Cavalry Division "Maria Theresa"* had been formed in the late summer of 1944, mostly of ethnic-German draftees from western Hungary fleshing out a cadre from the *8th SS*. About the same size as its brother division, though with older weapons, *22nd SS* was blooded in the defensive fighting on the approaches to Pest and performed well. Within the city, its troopers had excellent relations with the populace due to their Hungarian background (many spoke little or no German).

The Hungarian army provided a substantial portion of the defense, a fact overlooked in many accounts of the Budapest battle. The largest Hungarian fighting unit present was the *10th Infantry Division*. This veteran unit was well equipped, but heavy losses reduced it to 8,000 men by the time the siege began. Its backbone was its artillery regiment, which provided effective fire support to the very end.

The Hungarian *12th (Reserve) Infantry Division*, about 6,000 strong, had been organized in the late summer of 1944 when it became apparent the Red Army was about to break into Hungary. Weak, poorly trained and unreliable, this division fought feebly in most instances and suffered from desertions.

There was also a significant Hungarian armored component in Budapest. Remnants of the *Honved's 1st Tank Division*, with about 20 Hungarian Turan and German Mk IV tanks and approximately 2,000 men, were combined with a formidable assault gun group. Though the Turans were lightly armored and gunned, the Hungarian Zrinyi assault gun was a dangerous foe in urban terrain because it had a low silhouette and hefted a massive 105mm short barreled howitzer. The assault gunners of the group were a proud lot, having several times earlier given Soviet T-34 brigades bloody ripostes. There were about 40 operational Zrinyis in the group, and they fought with distinction.

On Csepel Island about 700 troopers of the *Hungarian Cavalry Division*, along with 2,000 men of the *Hadik Armored Hussar Regiment* fought hard to keep the Soviets from capturing the huge Weiss Company munitions works there.

Other unusual units, many *ad hoc*, filled out the Hungarian order of battle. There were five battalions of Gendarmes (4,000 total);

comprised mostly of former World War I NCOs, they were a tough group. The *Budapest Watch Battalion* (600 men) and the *Royal Guards Battalion* (600) added more solid infantry to the garrison. The *Guards*, picked for their height and fierce features, looked distinctive in their plumed helmets and old fashioned uniforms. Other regulars included the 3,000 men of the *Budapest Engineer Regiment*, and the *Budapest Air Defense Regiment*, which added 144 flak pieces (about eighty 80mm and 40mm Bofors guns, a dozen "88s," and many captured Soviet pieces that had been reconfigured to use Hungarian ammunition). Most of the Hungarian and German flak guns were deployed in Buda to protect Castle Hill and the critical makeshift airfield there.

Some unique paramilitary units also fought in Budapest. Foremost was the 1,000 strong *Vannay Battalion*, raised from scratch by Lt. Col. Laszlo Vannay during the autumn of 1944. This unit was composed mostly of World War I veterans now working for the city: firemen, subwaymen, sewer workers, engineers, etc. It was well equipped with weapons scrounged from all over Budapest, including several 75mm anti-tank guns on loan from the *22nd SS*. The *Vannay* men proved to be excellent fighters in the urban battlefield and particularly distinguished themselves during the fighting in Buda.

Other unusual units were the *1st* and *2nd Technical University Assault Battalions*, formed of highly motivated students who either wanted to fight for their homes against the Soviets or avoid being sent to Germany as laborers. Both units were barely trained; the *2nd* mostly consisted of high school students and had few weapons. The *1st* was the formation that halted the initial Soviet encroachment into Buda from the west. About 40 of these students fought to the last in the Ministry of Defense building on Castle Hill as part of the breakout's rearguard.

Rounding out the defense were the approximately 1,500 men of the Arrow Cross militia who stayed behind after their party leadership fled Budapest in November. These poorly-disciplined Hungarian fascists fought ferociously, knowing they would probably be hanged if captured. They were well armed; all carried the excellent Hungarian Kiraly machine pistol, and they were often committed against enemy tanks and infantry that penetrated the defense's forward line. Unruly off duty, a number of these thugs in uniform terrorized the Jewish ghetto until finally stopped by regular Hungarian and German troops.

Despite its unusual mix, the garrison proved a cohesive force: the Russians have still not released their casualty figures for the battle.

—Peter B. Zwack

A Strategic Overview of the Siege of Budapest

By October 1944, it was clear to everyone but a fanatic few that the Allies were going to win World War II—but the final shape of the coming postwar Europe was yet to be determined. Across all the remaining fronts, remnant German armies were chased back to the borders of the Reich and its last remaining ally, Hungary. But as those forces fell back to make their last stand, their power grew relative to the allies as those overextended attackers came up against a classic "central position" defense.

First the Germans were able to check the Anglo-Americans at Arnhem in September, while advancing Socviet armies in Poland ground to a halt outside Warsaw and along the Vistula. In Hungary, during October, the Axis partners executed a masterful counterstroke against several Soviet tank and cavalry corps, which in effect decapitated the onrushing 2nd Ukrainian Front then surging into that country. But with insufficient infantry on hand to consolidate their gains, the Axis forces were gradually pushed back to the Budapest suburbs by early November. With the momentum of their initial advance into Hungary spent, the Soviets shifted emphasis to clear Slovakia and the remainder of the Balkans.

Budapest had become the heart of the German/Hungarian defense of central Europe, especially after the outer wall of the Carpathian Mountains was breached in September. After it was declared a *Festung* (Fortress) in October, many of Budapest's 1 million inhabitants were put to work building fortifications and entrenchments outside the city. When the Soviets unexpectedly punched through to the eastern suburbs of Pest in November, a brief panic seized the capital city. The fascist Arrow Cross government and about 100,000 citizens were evacuated, while the vast majority put their faith in the reinforcing German units that just managed to parry the Red Army thrust 19 kilometers from the city center. The situation stabilized for a bizarre six weeks while some 900,000 civilians went about their lives under the guns and bombs of Soviet forces a half hour's drive away.

Throughout the late autumn of 1944, all the battlefronts in Europe remained relatively stable. This respite allowed the Germans to partially replenish their forces and rebuild a number of depleted formations. With German and Soviet forces glowering at each other across the Vistula in Poland and from trench lines outside Budapest and along the Danube, Adolf Hitler decided to throw his newly reconstituted panzer reserve into a last gasp offensive against the Americans in the Ardennes.

Three days later, while Bastogne was being encircled by von Manteuffel's *5th Panzer Army* in the so-called "Battle of the Bulge," the Soviets, benefitting from an excellent deception operation, launched a two-pronged offensive north and south of Budapest. By Christmas Day, overall Axis fortunes had nosedived as the hastily erected "Margarethe Line" around the Hungarian capital was breached and Budapest encircled by the 2nd and 3rd Ukrainian Fronts in a classic double envelopment. Within hours of this Axis misfortune, the skies over the Ardennes began to clear and the appearance there of waves of U.S. aircraft signaled the end of German offensive hopes on the western front.

Trapped inside "Fortress Budapest" were approximately 33,000 German and 37,000 Hungarian effectives comprising the *9th SS Mountain Corps*. At least two-thirds of the Germans were first-rate army and SS veterans, while troop quality among the Hungarian soldiers ranged from excellent to worthless. In addition to the hard core of four German and three Hungarian divisions, at least a third of the force was made up of flak, police, and signals units, along with numerous *ad hoc*, recently levied and independent battalion-sized elements. The defenders were reasonably well armed with artillery and armor, but those weapons would be effective only as long as there was ammunition and gasoline for them.

The Soviet 2nd Ukrainian Front had the responsibility of securing the inner ring of encirclement and reducing Budapest. At least 20 Soviet and Romanian divisions, plus numerous independent artillery and engineer formations, totaling around 250,000 soldiers, were slated to take the city. The 3rd Ukrainian Front manned the outer ring of the encirclement after having advanced about 70 kilometers west of the city. Its mission was to block any German relief attempt of the beleaguered garrison. The soldiers of both fronts were mostly seasoned troops, especially after the hard fighting of the past summer and autumn. Both fronts were understrength, with many divisions seriously depleted in manpower and equipment.

At this juncture, Hitler clearly recognized the danger of a rapid Soviet advance from Hungary and the Balkans into the southern portion of the Reich. Such a move would imperil Vienna, outflank German positions in northern Italy, and—worst of all—present a direct threat to Munich and southern Bavaria. Further, the last oil fields still in Axis hands lay in southwest Hungary. "From Budapest we will defend Vienna!" the German propagandist decreed, and the die was cast for a bitter, extended siege of Budapest. in fact, the 51 day siege of Budapest turned into one of the most crucial and ferocious of the final chapters of World War II in Europe.

Joseph Stalin's view of the situation was focused past it toward postwar Europe. The war was presenting the Soviets with a unique chance to extend their sphere of influence into the west; a long term goal that had been stymied since the early 1920s. With the Yalta Conference just months away, the Soviet dictator urged his marshals first to seize Budapest, then Vienna, as quickly as possible. His expectation, then his demand, was that Budapest fall early in November. Failing that, he exhorted his commanders to seize encircled Budapest by the end of December. Heavy political stakes rode on a swift Soviet capture of Budapest and an even swifter resumption of the march on Vienna.

In a fascinating violation of many principles of war, Hitler decided to make a fighting stand in Hungary and Budapest, while the western and eastern borders of the Reich creaked and groaned under the weight of millions of Allied soldiers assembling to make the final drive to the Elbe. In an effort to knock the Allied timetable off balance and divert resources from their main thrusts into Germany's vitals, he deployed significant mechanized formations to Hungary. Their mission was to relieve Budapest and clear the west bank of the Danube of all Soviet forces.

In late December, *Army Group Vistula*'s main reserve, the formidable *4th SS Panzer Corps*, consisting of the elite and refitted *SS Viking* and *Death's Head Divisions*, were moved to Hungary. On New Year's Day, they, along with several veteran army panzer divisions comprising the *3rd Panzer Corps*, launched the first of three successive relief attacks toward Budapest. Attaining tactical surprise each time, these three attacks, code named "Konrad," deeply punctured the 3rd Ukrainian Front's outer encirclement line, pushing to within 20 kilometers of Budapest on each occasion before being stopped or withdrawn. During the final thrust (Konrad III), and after a well executed redeployment to the south, the Germans by 20 January managed to completely split the 3rd Ukrainian Front, pinning several of its corps against the Danube. Caught off balance each time, the Soviets managed to block these final drives on Budapest by skillfully redeploying their forces, coupled with judicious counterattacks into the extended German flanks.

While the Germans continued to throw their last reserves into the Hungarian maelstrom, their weakened front collapsed on the Vistula. Massed Soviet tank armies swept across Poland and East Prussia, reaching the Oder River by 8 February—a position just 50 miles from the Reichstag in Berlin. The Anglo-Americans by that point had mopped up the Ardennes salient and were grinding down the Germans in a war of attrition all along the western and Italian fronts.

Meanwhile the Soviets around the Hungarian capital concentrated on eliminating the defenders in Pest, located on the river's flat eastern bank. Two Soviet and one Romanian corps pushed from the northeast toward the city center. Pest's garrison initially tried to hold along a raised railway embankment that skirted the city, but then fell back to the core area in a series of concentric withdrawals. The fighting became increasingly violent as the defenders' lines contracted into the massive apartment blocks that characterized inner Pest. Ferocious fighting took place at both the eastern and western railway stations. Hungarian troops fought savagely there when faced with direct assaults by their arch national enemies, the Romanians.

A Soviet division also pushed directly from the south, through Budapest's industrial heart, the northern end of Csepel Island. By 17 January, Soviet assault groups stood on Pest's inner ring road, just a kilometer from the vital Danube bridges. Their presence threatened to cut the Pest garrison in half.

With the sounds of the first relief attempt pounding off to the west, the German garrison commander, SS Gen. Karl von Pfeffer Wildenbruch, was finally given permission to evacuate his forces in the eastern bridgehead across the two remaining Danube bridges into Buda. He was not, however, permitted to attempt a breakout west toward the relief forces that were then just 25 kilometers away. By the morning of 18 January, the harrowing withdrawal from Pest was completed and the bridges blown, but not without heavy loss to the garrison.

By that point the garrison was suffering from food and ammunition shortages. Though the *Luftwaffe* mounted a concerted effort to supply Budapest by air, it could only partially meet the defenders' needs. At great cost in airframes and crew, the Germans first landed their transports in a makeshift racetrack airfield in Pest. When that was overrun, they flew gliders and light planes onto a cleared parade ground directly under Castle Hill in Buda. Though the garrison fed heavily off the thousands of horses inside the pocket, those rations did nothing to alleviate the suffering of the hundreds of thousands of civilians huddling in the city shelters.

As the Konrad relief attempts fell away, the Soviets—now dramatically behind their original timetable—concentrated their fury into an assault on Buda's tightly compressed defense. From all sides, and supported by massive quantities of artillery and airpower, they pressed to finish off the garrison.

Fighting with great determination, but with little hope, combined German/Hungarian battlegroups struggled to maintain the high ground girdling Castle Hill, the heart of the defense of Buda. For almost three weeks, strongpoints around Castle Hill kept the Soviets from securing their prize. When the Soviets forced the German defenders off Eagle Hill on 6 February, and captured the southern railway station on the 8th, further defense of Budapest was futile.

On the night of 11 February, over 30,000 German and Hungarian troops, including many walking wounded, massed on and around Castle Hill for a desperate breakout to the west. Alerted by an informer, the Soviets unleashed a massive artillery barrage just as the garrison's assault groups began moving out. The Soviet fire storm fell on the exposed mass of troops, turning the narrow streets and alleys of Castle Hill into a veritable charnel house. Within minutes, all command and control of the breakout was lost and thousands of men fell dead or wounded.

But at least 5,000 soldiers managed to somehow break free from the debacle and filtered into the hills and forests to the west. Reacting quickly, the Soviets mounted a huge manhunt, capturing several thousand unfortunates. After a grueling trek, a mere 785 troops, traveling in small groups, reached German lines about 40 kilometers west of Budapest.

Stalin must have managed a bittersweet smile when he learned of the fall of Budapest while sitting with Churchill and Roosevelt at Yalta. For though he couldn't claim Vienna as a prize, his armies had "liberated" all of Poland and most of the Balkans and now also had Hungary's capital city.

The battle for Hungary continued for another six weeks, fueled by Hitler's desire to retain the oil fields there. Amazingly, with huge Soviet armies almost within earshot of his bunker, *Der Führer* ordered his most capable combat formation, the *6th SS Panzer Army*, to

Hungary. While the Americans were crossing the Rhine at Remagen, and the Soviets were gearing up for their final drive on Berlin, that weakened but still potent army consumed itself in a meaningless death ride into waiting Kursk-style Soviet defenses. Three weeks later, victorious Red Army forces entered Vienna on 8 April, almost two full months after the capture of Budapest and a full five months after Stalin had demanded the Austrian capital's swift capture. Less than a month later the war in Europe was over.

—Peter B. Zwack

Selected Sources

Dept. of the Army. "Art of War Symposium." U.S. Army War College, Carlisle, Pa., 1986.

Duffy, Christopher. *Red Storm on the Reich*. New York: MacMillan, 1991.

Dupuy, Trevor. *Great Battles on the Eastern Front*. New York: Bobbs-Merrill, 1982.

Grechko, A.A. *Liberation Mission*. Moscow: Progress Pubs., 1975.

Strassner, Peter. *European Volunteers: The 5th SS Panzer Division "Viking."* Winnipeg: J.J. Fedorowicz, 1988.

Zhukov, Georgi. *Battles Hitler Lost*. New York: Richardson & Steirman, 1986.

Ziemke, Earl. *Stalingrad to Berlin*. Washington, DC: U.S. Army, 1968.

Personal letters from: Walter Böhm, Friedrich Buck, Fritz Darges, Nordewin von Diest-Koerber, Hartwig Pohlman, Kurt Schulze, and Dr. Peter Szabo.

Chapter XXVIII

Berlin '45
The Potential for World War III
by John Desch

Plenty of time—or so Joseph Stalin thought as he studied the latest situation maps his chief of staff had provided him. On 1 March 1945 his armies were poised along the Oder River, only 40 kilometers from Berlin, in a position to move into central Germany any time he decided. His "allies" in the west had not even closed on the entire left bank of the Rhine, or crossed it anywhere in force (the Battle of Remagen would occur on 7 March).

True, he had stopped the westward advance of Marshal Georgi Zhukov's 1st Belorussian Front (army group) when it seemed to that stocky commander's subordinates Berlin lay within easy reach. But their northern flank had seemed vulnerable. Up there, Marshal Rokossovksy and his 2nd Belorussian Front had greater obstacles to overcome, and the general logistical situation was so dismal along the entire front a halt was prudent in any case.

A pause to clean up the flanks in Pomerania and Silesia would give the Germans time to firm up their defenses in front of the capital city, but their resources were now so slim Stalin remained confident the Nazis' further preparations wouldn't matter. For the time being, he considered the bordering areas more important. Large numbers of Germans had been corralled away from Berlin, and it would take time to clean them out.

The offensive in January had exceeded all expectations by rolling across Poland and crushing the last vestiges of a stable German *Ost Front*. After months of preparation, Zhukov, Koniev and Rokossovsky had smashed through the poorly-manned front and driven hundreds of miles to the Oder River in just two weeks. Many German units had fought desperately, but overwhelming concentrations of Soviet com-

SOVIET ORDER OF BATTLE
16 April, 1945

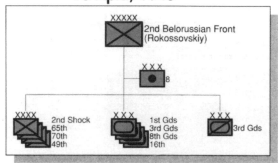

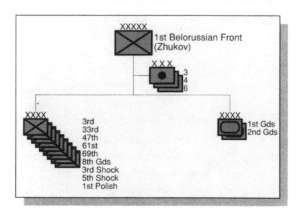

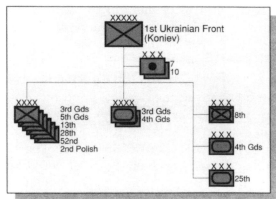

bat power, combined with an unprecedented show of operational finesse, had swept them away.

In the end it had been the lack of supply more than anything else that halted the Soviet offensive. For example, Gen. Chuikov's 8th Guards Army, spearhead of Zhukov's front, had to use captured German shells to help in its siege of Posnan.

The large quantities of loot and alcohol that began falling into the Red Army's hands as it drove west also grew into a problem. The men of one tank brigade had reportedly remained in a state of "total" inebriation for eight days. It got so bad, Stalin issued a short and direct proclamation on the subject, which seemed to halt the worst abuses.

Still, the emerging victory was total. After 1 February the Soviets could do just about whatever they pleased in most of Poland and eastern Germany. The *Wehrmacht* seemed powerless to manage more than delaying actions.

But the Germans had more than once overturned Soviet planning with a well-timed counterattack, often springing from nowhere and containing units previously unknown or thought destroyed. And hadn't they just given the Americans a nasty surprise in the Ardennes? In fact, a counterattack did develop, and just where the STAVKA's (supreme headquarters) collective central nervous system was most exposed—that northern flank where Zhukov's and Rokossovsky's front met.

After some initial success against unprepared and poorly-supplied Soviet convering forces, the attack petered out in the mud—both the seasonal kind on the ground and the bureaucratic kind back in Berlin. But several excellent German divisions had been involved, and until the whole picture had clarified itself it had seemed like a big deal.

It would have pleased the Germans no end to have known the effects their pin-prick attack had on Stalin. He put the operations toward Berlin indefinitely on hold. Pomerania and Silesia were to be cleared first, despite the protestations of the commanders on the spot.

That hero of Stalingrad, Chuikov, felt certain one more push was all that was needed to get into Berlin in February, and there is some merit to his point of view. The Germans to his front were weak, and no extensive fortificaitons had yet been built. Logistics were in bad shape, but the Red Army had done more with less in the past.

The ramifications of a successful capture of Berlin two-three months earlier than happened historically are interesting to consider. Hitler might have fled to Berchtesgaden or some other of his many command posts, but the significance of the capital being in enemy hands would not have been lost on the troops in the field. Certainly the Soviets would have then met the Western Allies farther west—perhaps as far as the Weser River. What effect would that have had on the Yalta settlement? Would the Soviets have relinquished the additional territory? The many possibilities are intriguing.

But none of that was to be. The clearing operations along the flanks were not concluded until late March. By then the Western Allies had hopped the Rhine and were driving for the Elbe River at an amazing pace. Hitler's failure to withdraw behind the Rhine in good order now manifested itself in nothing less than the total collapse of his western front. By 11 April, Gen. Simpson's 9th Army had punched several bridgeheads across the Elbe and was preparing for the next phase—which everyone felt would be the final assault on Berlin.

During early April, then, the Kremlin's recent tendency toward caution changed to an acute desire for haste, the intensity of which bordered on panic. Stalin summoned Zhukov, and his professional rival Koniev from 1st Ukrainian Front, to Moscow for an emergency meeting. It had become an emergency because the current plans called for the final offensive to begin only in mid-May, after winter water levels had receded, the ground had dried for maneuver, and supplies had been brought forward. All that preparation had to be accelerated to completion in only two weeks.

The two field marshals felt a certain degree of trepidation, as they always did when meeting with the Generalissimo. The new task ahead of them, while certainly not unexpected, was going to be more difficult than it would have been, given extra time to prepare. Both men brought plans with them detailing their ideas on how best to capture Berlin, but Zhukov's were the more detailed. His command's relative inactivity in the past few weeks had given him more planning time, and simple geography made it seem Berlin should obviously be his goal.

Stalin, as usual, got directly to the point: "So, who's going to be the first to take Berlin, the Allies or us?"

Koniev, with unrestrained enthusiasm, declared his command would be able to accomplish that task, but he was just as quickly chastened by Stalin for his hastiness in replying. After all, the dictator pointed out, 1st Ukrainian would have to reorient itself from southwest to west—how could that possible be done by 16 April, the new kick-off date?

Stalin had purposely opened the meeting with a question, knowing it would work to ignite competition between the two rival officers. Zhukov, despite the rebuff Koniev had just received, now knew he would be in a race to the great prize—not just with the Western Allies, but also against a Soviet "comrade."

The three men then hammered out a new STAVKA plan for Berlin's seizure. Zhukov's 1st Belorussian Front would indeed launch the main attack from its positions directly east of the city, but Rokossovsky in the north and Koniev in the south would also move forward to guard the flanks. Further, Stalin only drew the boundary between Zhukov's and Koniev's forces as far as Lubben, on the Spree River. From that point it would be a race—he who got to Berlin first would have the glory of being the conqueror of the fascist beast's lair.

The race actually began before the big guns fired the opening barrage. Both marshals hurried to channel as much fuel, ammunition, and general supply to their own front as quickly as possible. To supplement the heavily damaged Polish rail net, both pirated large numbers of trucks from their artillery establishments—a move which worked to increase supply during the offensive, but at the same time rendered much of that vital combat arm nearly immobile.

Rokossovsky, with more to do, had to set back his start date until four days after Zhukov would begin moving. Several reinforcement armies would not arrive from East Prussia until ten days after that. Replacement tanks and their green crews had to be hastily integrated into the veteran, but sadly depleted, first attack echelon. All this meant some of the keen edge the Red Army had shown in January would be dulled. Against a stronger opponent those factors might have been significant.

Nevertheless, and just as during the entire war up until then, the Soviets demonstrated they were capable of prodigious feats when the stakes were high. For example, Zhukov's front alone used 7,772 trucks to haul 7 million artillery shells. When it is recalled that the entire Stalingrad counteroffensive only consumed 1 million artillery rounds, the full magnitude of the Berlin operation is brought into true perspective.

German Preparations

German preparations for the battle fell short of what would have been Eastern Front standards only a few months before; in fact, they fell short of what could have been done even under the existing dire circumstances.

For one, Hitler chose to believe Berlin was not a Soviet objective, and refrained from declaring the city a fortress until mid-March (Such declarations, while purely administrative in themselves, were important in clearing the way for military authority, planning and discipline to take over in cities suddenly near, or an actual part of, the front). Further, *Der Führer* sent his nation's last potent offensive force—*6th SS Panzer Army*, of recent Ardennes fame—to Hungary in a doomed attempt to recover Budapest.

That SS Panzer Army, had it instead been deployed around Berlin, would have had drastic impact on Soviet (and Allied) operations, even though their ultimate outcomes remained a foregone conclusion. The advance to the city itself certainly would have been delayed, and Soviet casualties, heavy as they turned out to be, would have climbed to horrendous levels.

On the slim plus-side of the defenders' ledger, however, several fortified lines were constructed along the Oder-Neisse River lines, incorporating the usual late-war German defensive thoroughness and aumen. Meanwhile a garrison for the capital itself was scraped together from a collection of police, *Volkssturm* (militia), and various SS battalions. Though fuel supply remained the chronic problem it had been for the Germans throughout the second half of the war, ample amounts of food and ammunition were available inside the city, though proper distribution schemes were lacking.

What Hitler had correctly understood was the battle for Berlin would actually be decided along the Oder. He therefore authorized the transfer of hundreds of heavy anti-aircraft guns to the *9th Army* front, thus virtually stripping Berlin of its flak defenses (though its four massive "flak towers" retained their armaments and served as huge pillboxes during the battle).

To man the defensive works themselves, few of the veteran divisions which had served the Reich so well during most of the war were still available. In their place were hodge-podge formations thrown together from a variety of school, auxiliary service, and security units, and given impressive sounding names like the *"Muncheberg"* and *"Kurmark"* divisions. Those outfits for the most part fought desperately to hold back the Soviets, but simply lacked the experience and equipment to do it with any prospect of real success.

28.2

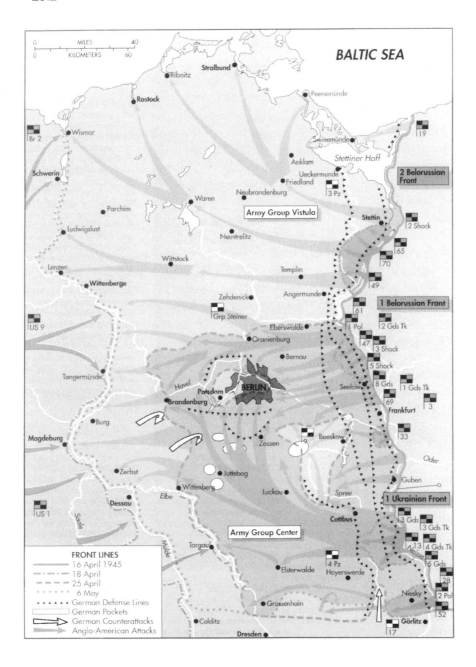

The Offensive Begins

Just as had been planned in Moscow, thousands of Red Army guns opened up to signal the new offensive's start in the early morning hours of 16 April. Over 500,000 shells were fired during the first half-hour along the 1st Belorussian Front alone. The two competing marshals, however, chose different attack techniques, and thereby achieved different results in their opening moves.

Zhukov opted for a short (40 minutes) and intense bombardment to support a night attack made under searchlight illumination—the result was chaos. The dust thrown up by the exploding artillery shells, combined with the disorientation caused by the searchlights trying to pierce through that gloom, plus the marshy terrain in front of the main German positions, all came together to destroy the assault units' cohesion.

Further, the Germans themselves—in a move they had honed into a successful standard practice for use whenever prepared defenders in fixed positions were expecting to meet a massive Soviet attack— had pulled back from their forward trenches at the last minute. Much of Zhukov's bombardment was therefore wasted against empty enemy positions, which the Germans then scampered to reoccupy the instant the shelling stopped.

Then the Soviet tanks, held up by the network of small canals that criss-crossed below Seelow Heights (the main bulwark of the German lines), began to (atypically) be out-paced by their infantry. On top of that confusion, Zhukov, in a miscalculated move to break things open quickly, suddenly threw his two tank armies into the battle (some claim it was done on the direct order of Stalin). The result was only more chaos and congestion.

If the Germans had had more artillery or air resources to commit at that point, 1st Belorussian's drive might have been checked then and there. Even as it was, and despite their inexperience at engaging ground targets, the defending flak gunners inflicted heavy casualties on Zhukov's armored spearheads. In the end, Zhukov's men and machines took four days to achieve the break-through he had planned for noon the first day.

Further south, 1st Ukrainian Front, under Koniev, enjoyed better success. The German fieldworks there were less extensive than those in front of 1st Belorussian, and Koniev went at them after a longer barrage and in daylight. As it turned out, his entire operation ran as if it were a well-rehearsed peacetime exercise. By 0600 hours the first bridgeheads were established across the Neisse; by 0900 light vehicle bridges were in place, and by noon the first all-purpose bridge was completed. By nightfall, the lead elements of 3rd and 4th Guards Tank Armies were racing to bounce across the Spree River on the march.

In both sectors the Germans had committed what reserves they had to try to stem the attacks, and again, the results varied. At Seelow, four mobile divisions contributed mightily to Zhukov's four-day frustration. Along Koniev's front, the German reserves were over-run while still in their assembly areas. A group of hastily assembled panzer divisions moving from the south practically destroyed the new 2nd Polish (Soviet) Army, but the 1st Ukrainian Front enjoyed relatively clear sailing all the way to Berlin.

As Zhukov took out his stress on his subordinates and Stalin considered transferring major elements of his command to Koniev, Rokossovsky's 2nd Belorussian Front completed its preparations in the north. At first several of the 2nd's crossings on the lower Oder were almost crushed, but most of the Germans' mobile forces had already been drawn south to support the battle at Seelow. The scattered Soviet toeholds managed to survive, and soon consolidated themselves into a larger bridgehead that Rokossovsky quickly filled with dozens of fresh assault battalions. When he renewed the pressure on the 25th, many of the defenders simply abandoned their weapons and fled westward, giving the rest of that portion of the campaign more the characteristics of a road march than an exploitation.

Finally, on 20 April, after smashing down the resilient Seelow defenses, Zhukov's front disentangled itself and drove for Berlin. They reached its outskirts two days later. A few burned-out German units had managed to slip through the mass of rampaging Red Army columns, but otherwise there was little in the form of a cohesive defense facing the 1st Belorussian Front.

Battle in the City

Bombed-out Berlin provided ideal defensive cover for even the smallest force, provided only its men were determined to fight. While regular German army units formed a hard core for the defense, numerous SS, Hitler Youth, and *Volkssturm* detachments also fought with tenacity as the tank-heavy Soviet forces bludgeoned their way through the mountains of urban rubble. Many of the buildings still intact were hastily converted into *ad hoc* fortresses, from which hundreds of Panzerfausts (hand-held rocket grenades) were fired at enemy assault groups.

Fortunately for Zhukov, Stalin extended the inter-front boundary to a position just west of the Reichstag—the Berlin landmark most coveted by the communists—and place it within 1st Belorussian's area of operations. It had been a close race with Koniev. His forces were certainly in a position to attack into the city center despite the fact they had had farther to come. But Zhukov had pulled Stalin's military chestnuts out of the Nazi fire more than once during the war, and the dictator reckoned it was a good time for his payback.

The subsequent battle for the inner city was one fought mostly by desperate foreign SS units (soldiers who had real reason to fear capture by the Soviets), augmented by a smattering of remnant regular and *ad hoc* German formations, against the dwindling rifle strength of two Red Army fronts. Intense and dramatic as it was, the fact it lasted only two weeks is testimony to the desperate weakness of the defenders. Had the panzers sent south to fight a fruitless battle for Budapest been kept instead for the defense of Berlin, the fighting—though its final outcome would have been unchanged—could have gone on weeks longer, and even come to rival the Stalingrad meatgrinder in ferocity.

The final German agony was characterized by a house-to-house struggle between skilled Soviet assault groups, backed by all the firepower they could bring to bear (every open space in Berlin was crammed with Red Army guns of all calibers), and desperate and dwindling numbers of defenders. The Soviets used every "trick" in their thick tactical book to smash through or bypass the defense. They tunnelled from basement to basement, floated down canals and streams in rowboats, and drove burning tanks into roadblocks to set them alight.

The Germans, for their part, generally fought well until their ammunition and (seemingly ubiquitous) panzerfausts ran out. Hitler took his own life on 30 April, and what remained of the garrison surrendered two days later. The mop up of pockets of fanatics took two days more.

Over 2,150 tanks and 286,991 men were lost during the battle—and many of the latter were irreplaceable veterans who had fought their way west from Stalingrad. Those figures represent greater losses than the Western Allies suffered from November 1944 to V-E Day throughout the entire European Theater of Operations. No accurate account of the German losses existed—nor are any needed to underscore the tragedy suffered by that people.

The Soviet victory in Berlin had profound and long lasting effects on the postwar Soviet-Allied relationship. With the final and undeniable eradication of Hitlerism in its very capital, Stalin could claim to the Allies—and he took every opportunity to do so—that his country had contributed the lion's share (and an oversized lion at that) of the effort that defeated Germany. The conquest of Berlin provided the political exclamation mark to what otherwise might have seemed an incomplete victory for the Soviets and their system. Berlin itself remained the nexus of East-West tensions and the focal point for several Cold War crises.

Eisenhower's Decision

Before September 1944, relations between the Western Allies and the Soviet Union were civil enough to enable them to cooperate in bringing the Third Reich to its knees. There were squabbles—some petty and some not—covering a wide range of issues, from Lend-Lease to shuttle flights for U.S. bombers. But the disaster of convoy PQ-17 in the Norwegian Sea in May 1943 (which led to a temporary suspension of Lend-Lease shipments via that route) and the destruction of 70 B-17s on the ground near Poltava in early 1944, were really only stress points in what was otherwise a workable relationship.

Then came the Warsaw Uprising in September 1944, which for all its military insignificance laid the foundation for the later breakdown of the Grand Alliance. The unwillingness of Stalin to assist the revolt angered the Allies. They considered the matter of a "Free Poland" to be of the utmost importance—indeed, it was why England had gone to war—and became deeply resentful at seeing its nucleus crushed.

Other pressing events soon overshadowed, but never completely dispelled, the new tension. When the Germans launched their Ardennes offensive, the Allied command asked Stalin if his forces could help by kicking off their own winter drive. They did so on 12 January—two weeks earlier than they had originally planned, but still two weeks after the crisis in the west had passed. But the favor had been asked and the Soviets had responded—another debt Stalin would recall later.

One of the primary purposes of the Yalta Conference was to settle the territorial fate of postwar Germany. It was agreed the Reich would be divided into four roughly equal zones, with one given directly to Poland and the other three occupied by the U.S., Britain, and the U.S.S.R. (France was eventually given a smaller zone carved from the British/U.S. spheres.) Berlin itself, the "seat of German militarism," was deemed important enough to be subdivided into its own areas of occupation.

Several western staff members wanted their forces to be guaranteed unrestricted ground access to Berlin, but negotiations at the conference never progressed far enough for that to be decided. With the two sides of the Grand Alliance still hundreds of miles apart, the chances of an overlap or accidental clash by their forces still seemed remote.

But with the breaking of the Rhine barrier and the Allies' rush to the Elbe River, the increased chances for an uncontrolled collision with the Soviets prompted Gen. Eisenhower to send an unprecedented cable directly to Stalin (with the concurrence of the Combined Chiefs). In that cable he outlined his intention to direct his forces' main thrusts toward Leipzig and the Bavarian Alps. Unmentioned, though, were the reasons that led him to foresake Berlin as a military target.

Put simply, after learning Roosevelt (and reluctantly, Churchill) intended to abide by the Yalta territorial agreements, Eisenhower decided the casualties involved in what would be a purely prestige victory made the operation too costly. That is, he rejected the notion of fighting a bloody battle for a city only to give away it and the territory around it—especially since the Soviets seemed eager to do just that, with the Western Allies in the free-recipient role.

Some have claimed the British prime minister favored a scenario in which the Western Allies' forces captured the city and advanced to the Oder/Neisse; positions from which they would be withdrawn only after a truly "free" Poland had been established. If Eisenhower had launched such a plan, a study of the situation and opposing orders of battle indicate he could have taken Berlin by mid-April, well before the Soviets got there. If Hitler was killed or captured during the fighting (this was an objective of the planned airborne portion of the attack—Operation Eclipse), resistance throughout the remainder of the Reich would have collapsed in direct relation to the quality of the communications available to the various units—with the eastern fighters giving in more slowly than those in the west. In such confusion, with the Allies in Berlin and Soviet spearheads charging desperately and headlong to the west to occupy as much territory as possible, a volatile situation would have been created.

It would have been a situation in which not only an accident might have sparked a new war. As alluded to earlier, Berlin was a tremendously important objective for the Soviets. It was "the lair of the Fascist Beast"—the same beast that had caused so many years of horror and bloodshed in the "Motherland." To have *not* conquered the place would have transformed the entire war into a hollow victory for Moscow. In short, the Soviets would have felt robbed and (especially with the Allies apparently ready to renege on Yalta) abused. Stalin was the kind of man to do something about such feelings if he believed the circumstances were to his advantage.

Just how far the dictator would have gone in such a venture is, of course, a matter of conjecture. Perhaps the recapture of Berlin would have been enough to satisfy Soviet honor. But Allied reactions are equally difficult to gauge. Certainly few in the West wanted a new war, but if one began with another "Pearl Harbor," this time on the ground and much bigger than the original, it is impossible to know the magnitude or direction of the response.

With over 40 years of hindsight perspective, we can see today that Eisenhower's decision then has proved correct. Whatever prestige the Allies would have gained in the conquest of Berlin would have been only temporary, whereas their casualties and damage to the World War II settlement would have been permanent.

Index

Aachen, 311, 312, 318, 320, 326, 333, 335
Alamein, 164
American units
– 1st Army, 309, 311, 321, 323, 327, 334
– 9th Army, 321, 378
– 7th Corps, 311, 313, 315, 316, 318, 319, 320, 321, 330, 331, 334
– 19th Corps, 312, 318, 320, 323, 326, 328, 329, 330, 335, 338, 341
– 1st Infantry Division, 311, 313, 315, 316, 318, 321, 327, 328, 331, 332
– 9th Infantry Division, 311, 314, 317, 318
– 26th Infantry Division, 328
– 29th Infantry Division, 321, 324, 330
– 30th Infantry Divison, 321, 323, 324, 326, 329, 330, 332, 334
– 2nd Armored Division, 321, 324, 326, 327, 330
– 3rd Armored Division, 311, 313, 314, 315, 316, 317, 319
– 7th Armored Division, 321
– 16th Infantry Regiment, 313, 315, 316, 318, 331
– 18th Infantry Regiment, 315, 318, 328, 331
– 26th Infantry Regiment, 315, 331
– 47th Infantry Regiment, 317, 318
– 116th Infantry Regiment, 330
– 117th Infantry Regiment, 323, 324, 327, 328, 329
– 119th Infantry Regiment, 323, 324, 325, 329
– 120th Infantry Regiment, 324, 329
– 1106th Engineer Group, 318
Ardennes (Bulge), 115, 226, 310, 370
Arras, 225, 232, 233
Atrocities, 115, 130
Austria, 165, 176
Axis units
– Armed Forces High Command (OKW), 121, 176
– Army High Command (OKH), 121
– Kriegsmarine, 199, 271
– Army Group Center, 21, 124, 159, 162, 235, 244, 246, 248, 276, 277, 280, 284, 287, 294, 305, 306
– Army Group North, 124, 198, 205, 206, 275, 276, 277, 280, 281, 284, 287, 288, 292, 294, 298, 303, 307
– Army Group South, 147, 151, 199, 209, 210, 212, 213, 215, 253, 280, 287, 345, 352, 359, 363
– Army Group South Ukraine, 343
– Army Group Vistula, 371
– Army Group A, 147
– Army Group B, 147, 327
– Army Group C, 222
– 2nd Army, 183, 243, 248, 352
– 3rd Army, 198, 201, 203, 204, 205-206, 207, 208, 209
– 4th Army, 198, 199, 201, 203, 204, 205-206, 207, 208, 250
– 5th Panzer Army, 370
– 6th Army, 149, 283, 346, 352
– 7th Army, 312
– 8th Army, 199, 208, 210, 212, 213, 214, 215, 217
– 10th Army, 183, 210, 211, 212, 213, 214, 215, 217

Index

THE BATTLE OF THE BULGE
Hitler's Ardennes Offensive 1944-1945
by Danny Parker

In late 1944, Germany was preparing to crush the Allies. Despite the shocking blow Hitler delivered, Allied forces recovered to smash the brutal offensive. When it was over, Hitler had spent the last energies of his crumbling empire.

      Danny S. Parker is a former research consultant to the Joint Chiefs of Staff on the Battle of the Bulge. He is also the author of *To Win the Winter Sky: The Air War over the Ardennes 1944-1945*.

Distinguished Praise for *Battle of the Bulge:*
* "The numerous rare photos and maps, buttressed by valuable new information, make Parker's book a welcome addition to previous histories of one of the most crucial battles ever fought by Americans." —John Toland, author of *Battle: The Story of the Bulge*
* "An epic treatment..." —James Dunnigan, author of *How to Make War*
* **MILITARY BOOK CLUB MAIN SELECTION**

9 X 12, 320 PAGES, 275 ILLUSTRATIONS, 18 MAPS • 0-938289-040-7 • $34.95

TO WIN THE WINTER SKY
Air War over the Ardennes, 1944-1945
by Danny Parker

As Allied and German armies fought on the ground in the Battle of the Bulge, an equally desperate battle raged in the skies overhead. Those who thought they were thoroughly familiar with Hitler's last offensive will find a wealth of new information here, including exclusive interviews with war-time airmen, over 100 rare photos, the unknown story of German MIAs, Luftwaffe jets and other secret weapons, and the innovations in tactics and technology.

Praise for *To Win the Winter Sky:*
* "The story is well told with all the air and ground accounts meshing into a very smooth narrative. The photos, organizational tables, maps, and charts are a veritable gold mine of information, as are the list of references and bibliography." —*Air Power History*
* **MILITARY BOOK CLUB MAIN SELECTION**

6 X 9, 528 PAGES • 153 ILLUSTRATIONS, 8 MAPS • 0-938289-35-7 • $29.95

HITLER'S BLITZKRIEG CAMPAIGNS
The Invasion and Defense of Western Europe, 1939-1940
by J.E. Kaufmann and H.W. Kaufmann

Hitler's Blitzkrieg Campaigns is a unique compilation of narratives, charts, photographs, diagrams, and maps not previously available in the United States. Many years of meticulous research reveals for the first time in English exactly why the Maginot Line and Eben Emael defenses failed, and exactly how the European armies of the first phase of World War II were organized, equipped, and deployed.

    Hitler's Blitzkrieg Campaign represents a major step forward in writing on the battles of 1939 and 1940, with coverage of many aspects of the conflict not generally available to the American reader, and with dozens of maps, diagrams and photographs that even the most die-hard World War II reader has never seen.

• "Fabulous book ... well written and researched." — *The Communiqué*
• **MILITARY BOOK CLUB MAIN SELECTION**

6 X 9, 386 PAGES • 100 PHOTOS, 66 MAPS & CHARTS • 0-938289-20-9 • $29.95

WAR AGAINST HITLER
Military Strategy in the West
edited by Albert A. Nofi

Renowned historian and military commentator Albert A. Nofi brings together for the first time in paperback a series of hard-hitting essays on World War II's most pivotal campaigns. Studies by contributors to the classic military journal *Strategy & Tactics* cover tactics and technology of the battles. Clear, concise and packed with information. Includes maps, charts, and a revised and updated bibliography.

6 X 9, 274 PAGES, 18 MAPS, 34 CHARTS • 0-938289-49-7 • $15.95PB

ROMMEL'S NORTH AFRICA CAMPAIGN
September 1940-November 1942
by Jack Greene and Alessandro Massignani

From 1940 to 1942, some of World War II's greatest legends were born, as Erwin Rommel the "Desert Fox" led his Afrika Korps against the "Desert Rats" of Bernard Montgomery's 8th Army.

Rommel's North Africa Campaign features detailed orders of battle, with German and Italian material available nowhere else. The capabilities of tanks, armor, artillery, aircraft and the vital transport vehicles are covered in depth. The largely unknown story of Rommel's radio-intercept unit is examined, as well as fascinating accounts of Mussolini's Blackshirts, the Young Fascists Division, the Folgore Parachute Division, and the Bersaglieri.

Californian Jack Greene has written *Mare Nostrum: The War in the Mediterranean, War at Sea: Pearl Harbor to Midway.* Bersaglieri veteran Alessandro Massignani has written numerous books and articles on Italy's role in World War II, including *Alpini e Tedeschi sul Don.*

6 X 9, 272 PAGES, 50 ILLUSTRATIONS, 18 MAPS • 0-938289-34-9 • $22.95

MacARTHUR'S NEW GUINEA CAMPAIGN
March-August 1944
by Nathan Prefer

Many World War II scholars consider New Guinea to be the finest example of Douglas MacArthur's operational doctrine, a convincing demonstration of his often-neglected flexibility, and one of the most tactically significant campaigns of the war. This fascinating new book is the only fully up-to-date examination of the ambushes, flank attacks, and combined operations of the New Guinea campaign. Includes specially prepared maps, diagrams of the Japanese bunker system, and complete orders of battle.

6 X 9, 288 PAGES, 6 MAPS, 50 PHOTOGRAPHS • 0-938289-51-9 • $24.95

Call TOLL FREE 1-800-418-6065 to order a catalog or books from Combined Books, Inc., 151 E. 10th Ave., Conshohocken, PA 19428. VISA and MASTERCARD accepted.